Ninth Conference on Lexical and Computational Semantics (*SEM 2020)

Held online due to COVID-19

Barcelona, Spain
12-13 December 2020

ISBN: 978-1-7138-2839-6

COLING 2020

***SEM 2020: The Ninth Conference on Lexical and Computational Semantics**

Proceedings of the Conference

December 12-13, 2020
Barcelona, Spain (Online)

Introduction

Preface by the General Chair and Program Chairs

Welcome to *SEM 2020, the Joint Conference on Lexical and Computational Semantics! *SEM 2020 is sponsored by SIGLEX, the ACL Special Interest Group on the Lexicon. Since its appearance in 2012, *SEM has become a major venue to present recent advances in the area of semantics. Now at its ninth edition, *SEM brings together research on all aspects of lexical and computational semantics, including semantic representations, semantic processing, multilingual semantics, and others.

We are pleased to present this volume containing the papers accepted at *SEM 2020, co-located with COLING 2020. *SEM was held as a virtual conference following COLING, on December 12-13, 2020, due to the exceptional circumstances imposed by the COVID-19 pandemic.

Similar to the previous editions, *SEM 2020 received a high number of submissions, which allowed us to compile a diverse and high-quality program. We received a total of 71 submissions. Out of these, 25 papers were accepted, for an overall acceptance rate of 35.2

Submissions were reviewed in nine different areas:

- Lexical semantics and word representations

- Semantic composition and sentence representations

- Discourse, dialogue and generation

- Multilinguality

- Psycholinguistics and semantic processing

- Resources and evaluation

- Theoretical and formal semantics

- Commonsense reasoning and natural language understanding

- Sentiment analysis and argument mining

The submitted papers were evaluated by a program committee consisting of 18 area chairs, assisted by a panel of 152 reviewers. Each submission was reviewed by three reviewers, who were furthermore encouraged to discuss any divergence in evaluations. The papers in each area were subsequently ranked by the area chairs. The final selection was made by the program co-chairs after an independent check of all the reviews and discussion with the area chairs. Reviewers' recommendations were also used to shortlist a set of papers nominated for the Best Paper Award. The final *SEM 2020 program features 19 presentations. These papers cover different aspects of lexical semantics, cross-lingual representations, natural language inference, sentiment, dialogue, language grounding, and the syntax-semantics interface. We are also very excited to have two excellent keynote speakers: Afra Alishahi (Tilburg University), joint keynote with SemEval 2020, who will talk about "Grounded language learning, from sounds and images to meaning"; and Luke Zettlemoyer (University of Washington, Facebook), who will discuss his work on "De-noising Sequence-to-Sequence Pre-training".

We are deeply thankful to all area chairs and reviewers for their help in the selection of the program, for their readiness in engaging in thoughtful discussions about individual papers, and for providing valuable feedback to the authors. We are grateful to our Publication Chair, Jonathan May, for his help with the compilation of the proceedings. We would also like to thank the COLING workshop organizers for all the valuable help and support with organisational aspects of the conference. Finally, we would like to thank all our authors and presenters for making *SEM 2020 such an exciting event. We hope you will enjoy the conference and draw inspiration from it!

Marianna Apidianaki and Manaal Faruqui, Program Co-Chairs

Iryna Gurevych, General Chair

*SEM 2020 Chairs and Reviewers

General Chair:

Iryna Gurevych, Technische Universität Darmstadt

Program Chairs:

Marianna Apidianaki, University of Helsinki
Manaal Faruqui, Google Assistant

Publications Chair:

Jonathan May, ISI, University of Southern California

Area Chairs:

Lexical semantics and word representations:
Mohammad Taher Pilehvar, Iran University of Science and Technology
Vered Shwartz, Allen Institute for Artificial Intelligence (AI2) and University of Washington

Semantic composition and sentence representations:
Ivan Vulić, University of Cambridge
Germán Kruszewski, Facebook AI Research

Discourse, dialogue, and generation:
Junyi Jessy Li, University of Texas at Austin
Philippe Muller, Université Paul Sabatier, IRIT

Multilinguality:
Alessandro Raganato, University of Helsinki
Shyam Upadhyay, Google Assistant

Psycholinguistics and semantic processing:
Harm Brouwer, Saarland University
Alessandra Zarcone, Fraunhofer IIS

Resources and evaluation:
Darja Fišer, University of Ljubljana
Goran Glavaš, University of Mannheim

Theoretical and formal semantics:
Stergios Chatzikyriakidis, University of Gothenburg
Denis Paperno, Utrecht University

Commonsense reasoning and natural language understanding:
Ellie Pavlick, Brown University
Rachel Rudinger, University of Maryland

Sentiment analysis and argument mining:
Saif Mohammad, National Research Council Canada
Elena Cabrio, Université Côte d'Azur, INRIA, CNRS

Reviewers:

Amjad Abu-Jbara, Lasha Abzianidze, Pooja Aggarwal, Ameeta Agrawal, Laura Aina, Alan Akbik, Md. Shad Akhtar, Firoj Alam, Dimitris Alikaniotis, Laura Alonso Alemany, Ron Artstein, Yoav Artzi, Ehsaneddin Asgari, Giosuè Baggio, Jeremy Barnes, Valentin Barriere, Valerio Basile, Roberto Basili, Jasmijn Bastings, Fernando Batista, Jonathan Berant, Gábor Berend, Jean-Philippe Bernardy, Archna Bhatia, Yonatan Bisk, Eduardo Blanco, Michael Bloodgood, Gemma Boleda, Marianna Bolognesi, Francis Bond, Samuel R. Bowman, Chloé Braud, Ellen Breitholtz, Tomáš Brychcín, Paul Buitelaar, Jose Camacho-Collados, Tommaso Caselli, Hande Celikkanat, Tuhin Chakrabarty, Franklin Chang, Aditi Chaudhary, Muhao Chen, Nancy Chen, Emmanuele Chersoni, Yejin Choi, Christos Christodoulopoulos, Oana Cocarascu, Anne Cocos, Robin Cooper, Bonaventura Coppola, Elena Cotos, Mathias Creutz, Ido Dagan, Joachim Daiber, Debopam Das, Marie-Catherine de Marneffe, Thierry Declerck, Marco Del Tredici, Francesca Delogu, Barry Devereux, Gaël Dias, Brian Dillon, Thi Ngoc Quynh Do, Lucia Donatelli, Jakub Dotlacil, Kevin Duh, Ondřej Dušek, Steffen Eger, Jacob Eisenstein, Katrin Erk, Arash Eshghi, Luis Espinosa Anke, Allyson Ettinger, Stefano Faralli, Mariano Felice, Elisa Ferracane, Karën Fort, Diego Frassinelli, Kevin Gimpel, Jonathan Ginzburg, Voula Giouli, Eleni Gregoromichelaki, Dagmar Gromann, Kristina Gulordava, Ivan Habernal, Shohreh Haddadan, Hannaneh Hajishirzi, Christian Hardmeier, Mareike Hartmann, Dag Haug, Simon Hengchen, Delia Irazú Hernández Farías, Daniel Hershcovich, Ari Holtzman, Pedram Hosseini, Veronique Hoste, Xinyu Hua, Patrick Huber, Julie Hunter, Jena D. Hwang, Ignacio Iacobacci, Nancy Ide, Oana Inel, Lubomir Ivanov, Yangfeng Ji, Zixia Jia, Salud María Jiménez Zafra, Aditya Joshi, Hiroshi Kanayama, Jenna Kanerva, Mladen Karan, Omid Kashefi, Casey Kennington, Roman Klinger, Thomas Kober, Ekaterina Kochmar, Grzegorz Kondrak, Maarit Koponen, Tom Kwiatkowski, Arne Köhn, Alexander König, Caterina Lacerra, Shalom Lappin, Dan Lassiter, Anne Lauscher, John Lawrence, Els Lefever, Alessandro Lenci, Sujian Li, Robert Litschko, Nelson F. Liu, Yang Liu, Nikola Ljubešić, Alessandro Lopopolo, Wei Lu, Christopher D. Manning, Alda Mari, Andrea E. Martin, Eugenio Martínez-Cámara, Aleksandre Maskharashvili, Tobias Mayer, John P. McCrae, Nick McKenna, Ken McRae, Julian Michael, Rada Mihalcea, Tristan Miller, Koji Mineshima, Shachar Mirkin, Amita Misra, Richard Moot, Gaku Morio, Lawrence Moss, Nona Naderi, Nikita Nangia, Huy Nguyen, Vlad Niculae, Debora Nozza, Alexis Palmer, Xiaoman Pan, Viviana Patti, Debjit Paul, Maxime Peyrard, Nghia The Pham, Manfred Pinkal, Yuval Pinter, Adam Poliak, Simone Paolo Ponzetto, Maja Popović, Christopher Potts, Vinodkumar Prabhakaran, Matthew Purver, Anil Ramakrishna, Christian Retoré, German Rigau, Shruti Rijhwani, Ohad Rozen, Alla Rozovskaya, Irene Russo, Mehrnoosh Sadrzadeh, Magnus Sahlgren, Mohammad Salameh, Asad Sayeed, Bianca Scarlini, Christoph Scheepers, Yves Scherrer, David Schlangen, Dominik Schlechtweg, Sabine Schulte im Walde, Esther Seyffarth, Eva Sharma, Weiyan Shi, Ionut-Teodor Sorodoc, Vivek Srikumar, Gabriel Stanovsky, Maria Staudte, Mark Steedman, Egon Stemle, Sara Stymne, Sanjay Subramanian, Elior Sulem, Umut Sulubacak, Aarne Talman, Alexandros Tantos, Andon Tchechmedjiev, Gaurav Singh Tomar, Antonio Toral, Amine Trabelsi, Rocco Tripodi, Chen-Tse Tsai, Alfonso Ureña-López, Tim Van de Cruys, Esther van den Berg, Eva Maria Vecchi, Noortje Venhuizen, Yannick Versley, Serena Villata, Aline Villavicencio, Veronika Vincze, Piek Vossen, Raúl Vázquez, Bonnie Webber, Julie Weeds, Charles Welch, Matthijs Westera, Michael Wiegand, John Wieting, Adina Williams, Genta Indra Winata, Grégoire Winterstein, Shijie Wu, Rong Xiang, Wei Xu, Victoria Yaneva, Yaqin Yang, Hai Ye, Frances Yung, Wajdi Zaghouani, Torsten Zesch, Lei Zhang, Diarmuid Ó Séaghdha, Robert Östling.

Invited Talk: Grounded language learning, from sounds and images to meaning

Afra Alishahi
University of Tilburg

Abstract: Humans learn to understand speech from weak and noisy supervision: they manage to extract structure and meaning from speech by simply being exposed to utterances situated and grounded in their daily sensory experience. Emulating this remarkable skill has been the goal of numerous studies; however researchers have often used severely simplified settings where either the language input or the extralinguistic sensory input, or both, are small-scale and symbolically represented. I present a series of studies on modelling visually grounded language understanding. Using variations of recurrent neural networks to model the temporal nature of spoken language, we examine how form and meaning-based linguistic knowledge emerges from the input signal.

Bio: Afra Alishahi is an Associate Professor of Cognitive Science and Artificial Intelligence at Tilburg University, the Netherlands. Her main research interests are computational modeling of human language acquisition, studying the emergence of linguistic form and function in grounded models of language learning, and developing tools and techniques for analyzing linguistic representations in neural models of language. She has received a number of research grants including an NWO Aspasia, an NWO Natural Artificial Intelligence and an e-Science Center/NWO grant. She has been the recipient of a number of best paper awards at Computational Linguistics and Cognitive Science venues.

Invited Talk: De-noising Sequence-to-Sequence Pre-training

Luke Zettlemoyer

University of Washington

Facebook

Abstract: De-noising auto-encoders can be pre-trained at a very large scale by noising and then reconstructing any input text. Existing methods, based on variations of masked language models, have transformed the field and now provide the de facto initialization to be tuned for nearly every task. In this talk, I will present our work on sequence-to-sequence pre-training that introduces and carefully measures the impact of two new types of noising strategies. I will first describe an approach that allows arbitrary noising, by learning to translate any corrupted text back to the original with standard Transformer-based neural machine translation architectures. I will show that the resulting mono-lingual (BART) and multi-lingual (mBART) models provide effective initialization for learning a wide range of discrimination and generation tasks, including question answering, summarization, and machine translation. I will also present our recently introduced MARGE model, where we self-supervise the reconstruction of target text by retrieving a set of related texts (in many languages) and conditioning on them to maximize the likelihood of generating the original. The objective noisily captures aspects of paraphrase, translation, multi-document summarization, and information retrieval, allowing for strong zero-shot performance with no fine-tuning, as well as consistent performance gain when fine-tuned for individual tasks. Together, these techniques provide the most comprehensive set of pre-training methods to date, as well as the first viable alternative to the dominant masked language modeling pre-training paradigm.

Bio: Luke Zettlemoyer is a Professor in the Paul G. Allen School of Computer Science & Engineering at the University of Washington, and a Research Scientist at Facebook. His research focuses on empirical methods for natural language semantics, and involves designing machine learning algorithms, introducing new tasks and datasets, and, most recently, studying how to best develop self-supervision signals for pre-training. Honors include multiple paper awards, a PECASE award, and an Allen Distinguished Investigator Award. Luke received his PhD from MIT and was a postdoc at the University of Edinburgh.

Table of Contents

Conference Program

Saturday, December 12, 2020

14:00–14:10   *Opening Remarks*

14:10–15:00   **Session 1: Inference**

14:10–14:28   *Improving Medical NLI Using Context-Aware Domain Knowledge*
Shaika Chowdhury, Philip Yu and Yuan Luo

14:28–14:41   *Reading Comprehension as Natural Language Inference:A Semantic Analysis*
Anshuman Mishra, Dhruvesh Patel, Aparna Vijayakumar, Xiang Li, Pavan Kapanipathi and Kartik Talamadupula

14:41–15:00   *Learning as Abduction: Trainable Natural Logic Theorem Prover for Natural Language Inference*
Lasha Abzianidze

15:10–15:54   **Session 2: Cross-lingual Representations and Translation**

15:10–15:23   *Automatic Learning of Modality Exclusivity Norms with Crosslingual Word Embeddings*
Emmanuele Chersoni, Rong Xiang, Qin Lu and Chu-Ren Huang

15:23–15:41   *Joint Training for Learning Cross-lingual Embeddings with Sub-word Information without Parallel Corpora*
Ali Hakimi Parizi and Paul Cook

15:41–15:54   *Semantic Structural Decomposition for Neural Machine Translation*
Elior Sulem, Omri Abend and Ari Rappoport

16:00–17:00   *Keynote: "Grounded language learning, from sounds and images to meaning"*
Afra Alishahi

15:15–16:00 **Session 5: Syntax, Semantics and Grounding**

15:15–15:28 *PISA: A measure of Preference In Selection of Arguments to model verb argument recoverability*
Giulia Cappelli and Alessandro Lenci

15:28–15:41 *Learning Negation Scope from Syntactic Structure*
Nick McKenna and Mark Steedman

15:41–16:00 *A Visuospatial Dataset for Naturalistic Verb Learning*
Dylan Ebert and Ellie Pavlick

16:00–17:00 *Keynote: "De-noising Sequence-to-Sequence Pre-training"*
Luke Zettlemoyer

17:10–18:04 **Session 6: Dialog and Narration**

17:10–17:28 *Find or Classify? Dual Strategy for Slot-Value Predictions on Multi-Domain Dialog State Tracking*
Jianguo Zhang, Kazuma Hashimoto, Chien-Sheng Wu, Yao Wang, Philip Yu, Richard Socher and Caiming Xiong

17:28–17:46 *"where is this relationship going?": Understanding Relationship Trajectories in Narrative Text*
Keen You and Dan Goldwasser

17:46–18:04 *Large Scale Author Obfuscation Using Siamese Variational Auto-Encoder: The SiamAO System*
Chakaveh Saedi and Mark Dras

Improving Medical NLI Using Context-Aware Domain Knowledge

Shaika Chowdhury
Department of Computer Science
University of Illinois at Chicago
schowd21@uic.edu

Philip S. Yu
Department of Computer Science
University of Illinois at Chicago
psyu@uic.edu

Yuan Luo
Department of Preventive Medicine
Northwestern University
yuan.luo@northwestern.edu

Abstract

Domain knowledge is important to understand both the lexical and relational associations of words in natural language text, especially for domain-specific tasks like Natural Language Inference (NLI) in the medical domain, where due to the lack of a large annotated dataset such knowledge cannot be implicitly learned during training. However, because of the linguistic idiosyncrasies of clinical texts (e.g., shorthand jargon), solely relying on domain knowledge from an external knowledge base (e.g., UMLS) can lead to wrong inference predictions as it disregards contextual information and, hence, does not return the most relevant mapping. To remedy this, we devise a **knowledge adaptive** approach for medical NLI that encodes the premise/hypothesis texts by leveraging supplementary external knowledge, alongside the UMLS, based on the word contexts. By incorporating *refined* domain knowledge at both the lexical and relational levels through a **multi-source attention mechanism**, it is able to align the token-level interactions between the premise and hypothesis more effectively. Comprehensive experiments and case study on the recently released MedNLI dataset are conducted to validate the effectiveness of the proposed approach.

1 Introduction

Natural Language Inference is a fundamentally important but challenging task in Natural Language Processing (NLP) as it requires understanding and reasoning over natural language texts (MacCartney and Manning, 2009). As a result, a good performing

NLI system is considered indispensable for downstream NLP applications such as question answering and automatic text summarization (Harabagiu and Hickl, 2006; Lloret et al., 2008). Given a pair of sentences, a premise p and a hypothesis h, the goal of NLI is to determine whether the semantic relationship between p and h is among *entailment*, *contradiction* and *neutral*.

The ability to understand natural language text innately requires to deal with background knowledge [1] (Long et al., 2017; Weissenborn et al., 2017). A robust NLI model usually needs to reason over two types of background knowledge - lexical and relational (Weissenborn et al., 2017). The former pertains to understanding the concepts expressed by the words in the text, while the latter learns the semantic relations between the different concepts. When performing NLI on open domain data, it is assumed that the background knowledge will be implicitly learned from the training corpora. Re-

---

Premise: - DMII complicated by DM neuropathy - PVD s/p L CFA w/balloon angioplasty of SFA and AK [**Doctor Last Name **] artery w/ persistent non-healing ulcer at the lateral and medial malleolus, non-healing L pedalulcer - Hypertension - h/o MDR Pseudomonas and MRSA skin infections - h/o hemorrhagic pancreatitis ([**2857**]) - h/o cholecystitis (still has gallbladder)

Hypothesis: Patient has multiple diabetes related comorbidities.

Label: Entailment

Figure 1: Sample premise-hypothesis pair from MedNLI. The words in red, "DMII" and "DM" in p and "diabetes" in h are semantically similar at the lexical level. The UMLS relation "co-occurs" of the highlighted words in green in p to "diabetes" in h manifests the inferential signal "comorbidities".

---

[1] background/external/domain knowledge are used interchangeably in this paper

*Proceedings of the Ninth Joint Conference on Lexical and Computational Semantics (*SEM)*, pages 1–11
Barcelona, Spain (Online), December 12–13, 2020

lease of large NLI datasets like the Stanford Natural Language Inference (SNLI) (Bowman et al., 2015) and Multi-Genre Natural Language Inference (MultiNLI) (Williams et al., 2017) corpora, with around 570,000 and 433,000 sentence pairs respectively, have made it possible to train deep neural networks, which are capable of encoding this knowledge in their parameters.

For specialized domains (e.g., medical), however, large NLI datasets are extremely scarce and the required implicit knowledge beyond the text surface cannot be extracted from limited data. For example, the recently released MedNLI dataset (Romanov and Shivade, 2018), albeit being the single publicly available NLI dataset in the clinical domain, contains only around 13,000 expert annotated sentence pairs [2]. Therefore, most current literature on medical NLI (Romanov and Shivade, 2018; Jin et al., 2019) have capitalized on the prior semantic knowledge that is encoded in external resources (e.g., UMLS). Nevertheless, a limitation of the existing suite of medical ontologies such as UMLS is that they retrieve mapping (i.e., lexical/relational) irrespective of the textual context, which could mislead the inference model. This is worsened by the distinct linguistic idiosyncrasies present in clinical texts, wherein phrases are compressed with shorthand jargon (i.e., abbreviations) for physicians' convenience. Specifically, this instigates three challenges: 1) some semantically important words do not map to any matching concept in the UMLS [3], 2) a wrong concept mapping is returned that does not reflect the word's actual meaning and 3) the noise introduced by wrong concept mapping could get carried forward when retrieving the relational mapping.

To address the aforementioned issues, we devise an approach for the NLI problem in the medical domain that is equipped with an **adaptive encoding scheme** to integrate context-relevant domain knowledge into the text representation more effectively. In particular, a mixture model is employed to adaptively leverage supplementary external resources, that provide contextual evidence to disambiguate the concept sense for each word, and thus facilitate in learning more semantically refined text embeddings, as well as, account for the missing words. Furthermore, in order to infuse important inferential clues between the premise-hypothesis tokens, context-relevant relational embeddings elicited from knowledge graph is encoded through **multi-source attention mechanism**. We dub the proposed framework as **Multi-Source Knowledge Adaptive Inference Network (MUSKAN)**.

2 Related Works

2.1 Natural Language Inference

Natural Language Inference lies at the core of many NLP problems (Harabagiu and Hickl, 2006; Rush et al., 2015; Pasunuru and Bansal, 2017). Recently, deep learning has achieved great success in NLI. Current neural models for NLI can be categorized into two main groups of frameworks (1) *sentence encoding models* and (2) *sentence pair interaction models*, as discussed below:

In the sentence encoding framework, the sentence pair is modeled by encoding each sentence separately and the semantic relationship computed based on their similarity. InferSent (Conneau et al., 2017) first encodes the sentences using a recurrent model and then performs element-wise product and absolute difference to capture the relations between the sentences. A stacked BiLSTM is used in the Gated BiLSTM model proposed by (Chen et al., 2017b), which first applies intra-sentence gated attention[4] to bring the sentences to fixed length vectors, and then relation information similar to InferSent is computed.

Whereas in the case of sentence pair interaction framework, word-level interactions are captured using some sort of alignment mechanism (e.g., attention), which are then aggregated to a fixed-length vector to make the final decision. ESIM (Chen et al., 2016) first uses BiLSTM to capture sequential context and then models local inference between word pairs using attention; it then enhances them by computing relation information similar to InferSent/Gated BiLSTM but at the word-level, which is then aggregated to fixed length vectors using a second BiLSTM. In addition, it also incorporates syntactic parsing information with a second similar network. Match-LSTM (Wang and Jiang, 2015) first uses LSTMs to encode the sentences, then computes word-by-word matching using an attention scoring function for each time step, where the last

---

[2] compared to open domain NLI datasets
[3] we call such words "missing words" in this paper

[4] note that this attention does not capture cross-features between corresponding words in the two sentences, so not grouped into the second group

hidden state is used to represent the sentence representation.

2.2 NLI and External Knowledge

Utilizing external knowledge has shown improvement in performance for some NLI works (Chen et al., 2017a; Wang et al., 2019; Li et al., 2019). Knowledge from WordNet (Miller, 1995) is leveraged in work by (Chen et al., 2017a) to enhance the different components of the NLI model. (Kang et al., 2018) uses the hypernym/hyponym information from three different external linguistic resources, namely WordNet, PPDB (Ganitkevitch et al., 2013) and SICK (Marelli et al., 2014), to generate adversarial examples which are used to augment and train the text entailment system in order to make it robust. (Wang et al., 2019) uses WordNet, ConceptNet and DBPedia (Auer et al., 2007) to incorporate knowledge graphs into text-based NLI models.

In medical NLI, external knowledge is provided as domain knowledge that exists in the form of medical ontology or knowledge base. Work by (Jin et al., 2019) incorporates relational information from UMLS into pre-trained BioELMO[5] and BioBERT (Lee et al., 2020) embeddings. (Romanov and Shivade, 2018) similarly uses domain-specific knowledge from UMLS, however, they modify the pre-trained embeddings using retrofitting. They also experiment with knowledge-directed attention in ESIM and InferSent models.

The main drawback of the aforementioned approaches is that they rely on the context-independent domain knowledge returned by UMLS, which either returns an inaccurate mapping or no mapping and hence could possibly lead to wrong inference predictions. This work addresses these drawbacks with competitive performance on the MedNLI dataset.

3 Approach Overview

We treat the task of Natural Language Inference (NLI) as a supervised classification task and state it as follows: given a premise sentence $\mathbf{p} = (w_1^p, ..., w_m^p)$ with length m, a hypothesis sentence $\mathbf{h} = (w_1^h, ..., w_n^h)$ with length n and the corresponding lexical (i.e., UMLS concept) and relational (i.e., UMLS relation triples) domain knowledge for the sentences represented as $\mathbf{c^p} = (c_1^p, ..., c_m^p)$, $\mathbf{c^h} = (c_1^h, ..., c_n^h)$ and $\mathbf{r^p} = (r_1^p, ..., r_m^p)$, $\mathbf{r^h} = (r_1^h, ..., r_n^h)$

[5]https://github.com/Andy-jqa/bioelmo

respectively, our goal is to learn a classifier $\mathcal{P}$ (a neural network in our case) which is able to predict the inference relation $y \in Y$ between $\mathbf{p}$ and $\mathbf{h}$ by leveraging the domain knowledge, where $Y = \{entailment, contradiction, neutral\}$. *Entailment* means that when $\mathbf{p}$ is true, then $\mathbf{h}$ must be true; *contradiction* means when $\mathbf{p}$ is true, then $\mathbf{h}$ must be false; *neutral* means neither entailment nor contradiction. More formally,

$$y^* = \arg\max_{y \in Y} \mathcal{P}(y|p, h, c^p, c^h, r^p, r^h) \quad (1)$$

Here, c_i^p and c_j^h are the i-th and j-th concept, and r_i^p and r_j^h are the i-th and j-th relation triple of the premise and hypothesis respectively. Note that a word w_i^p/w_j^h in the premise/hypothesis could also be an abbreviation, which here we collectively call word.

As aforementioned, although incorporating domain knowledge from the UMLS helps to understand medical semantics in the text that go beyond basic linguistic understanding, it could also aggravate the inference process due to the missing words and the inaccurate mappings. To this end, we supplement the UMLS with other external resources in order to soft-align the context-relevant domain information to each word in the text. Figure 2 illustrates a high-level overview of the architecture of our proposed model, **MUSKAN**. It follows the encode-match-classify framework of general text-based NLI models (Chen et al., 2016; Parikh et al., 2016). In the encoder layer, an **adaptive encoding scheme** encodes each word in the premise/hypothesis sentence by integrating *refined* concept embeddings into the text representation, where the refinement is done by leveraging contextual evidence from the supplementary external resources. Then in the matching layer, the adaptive lexical encodings are enhanced with refined relational information codified in knowledge graphs using **multi-source attention**, that facilitates in semantically aligning and aggregating the interactions between the premise-hypothesis words. Finally, the classification layer composes the pair of sentences to a fixed length vector and predicts their relation. More details of each component will be presented in the next sections.

3.1 Adaptive Lexical Encoding

For accurately capturing the relevant lexical semantics of a word in its context, the adaptive encoding

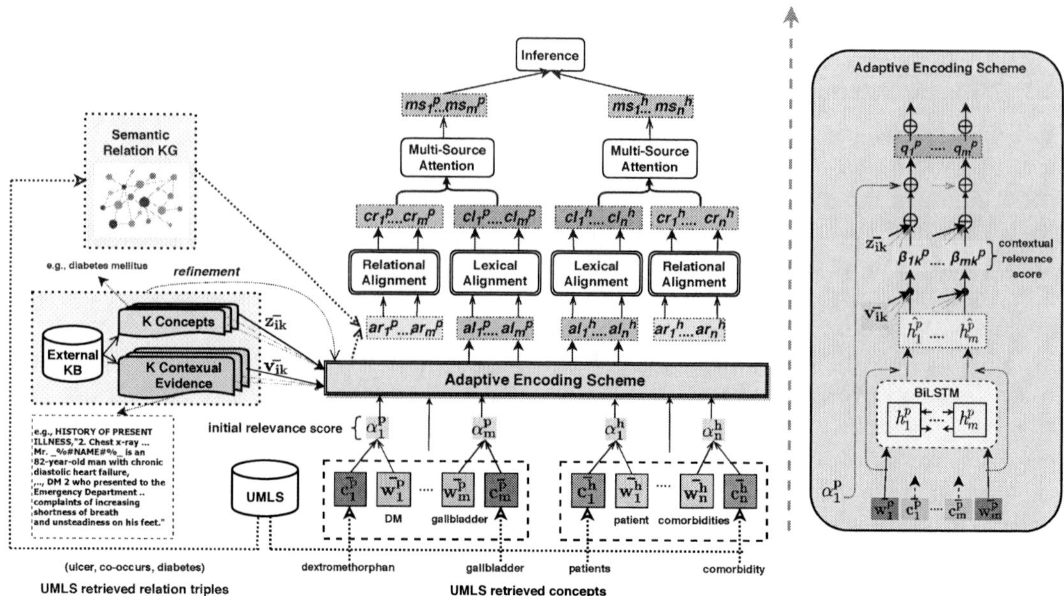

Figure 2: Architecture of our proposed MUSKAN model. The overall framework is shown to the left in a bottom-up fashion, with the sample pair in Figure 1 as the input. The Adaptive Encoding Scheme is illustrated in detail in the figure on the right, taking the premise as an example input.

scheme exploits other external resources alongside the UMLS. A mixture model similar to (Yang and Mitchell, 2019) is employed to refine the initial UMLS concept embedding with a weighted sum of candidate concept vectors, where the weights are adaptively adjusted based on the relevance of the concept's supporting evidence to the word context. The refined concept embeddings are then integrated into the respective text representations to output the final encoded word representation.

To be specific, given the premise $\mathbf{p} = (w_1^p, ..., w_m^p)$ and the corresponding UMLS concepts $\mathbf{c^p} = (c_1^p, ..., c_m^p)$ (the same procedure is utilized for the $\mathbf{h}$ and $\mathbf{c^h}$ hypothesis pair, but for ease of presentation, we only describe the adaptive lexical encoding for the premise; subsequently, we drop the superscript p), each word is first converted to a d-dimensional vector using a pre-trained word embedding method to yield the embedded representations $\bar{\mathbf{p}} = (\bar{w}_1, ..., \bar{w}_m)$ and $\bar{\mathbf{c}} = (\bar{c}_1, ..., \bar{c}_m)$ respectively [6]. We then compute the initial relevance score, α_i, between the i-th word and its concept to get an idea of the degree to which the UMLS-retrieved lexical knowledge is useful in distilling the semantic

meaning of the current word. It is computed as,

$$\alpha_i = \bar{w}_i^\top W_a \bar{c}_i \tag{2}$$

where W_a is a trainable weight matrix. However, as the UMLS returns mappings without considering the context in which the word occurs, it is possible that the retrieved concept expresses rather a wrong meaning, which could mislead the inference process. For example, consider the term "DM" in Figure 1; "dextromethorphan" is returned as the matching concept by the UMLS [7], but "diabetes mellitus" is actually the correct concept in that specific context. Evidently, this wrong domain knowledge can avert the model from establishing important inferential clues like the semantic similarity between "diabetes mellitus" in the premise and "diabetes" in the hypothesis, which would otherwise help it to conclude in a conclusive manner that the semantic relationship is entailment. Besides, the UMLS does not offer total coverage of concepts across the whole natural language, which means that for some medical domain-specific jargon, such as the abbreviations "SFA" and "MDR", there exists no corresponding concepts.

To tackle these issues, we resort to external resources that can provide supporting evidence to val-

---

[6] note that in the case of missing words without any concept/relation mapping, we provide a synthetic placeholder and set its embedding to zero

[7] based on the highest MetaMap Indexing (MMI) score

idate the relevant domain knowledge in the right textual context. Concretely, for the i-th word in $\mathbf{p}$, a set of K candidate concepts, $z_{i1}, ..z_{iK}$, related to it and their corresponding supporting evidences, $v_{i1}, ..v_{iK}$, are first retrieved (discussed in Sections 3.1.1 and 3.1.2). The candidate concepts and their supporting evidences are then embedded as d-dimensional vectors, $\bar{\mathbf{z}}_{\mathbf{i}} = (\bar{z}_{i1}, ..., \bar{z}_{iK})$ and $\bar{\mathbf{v}}_{\mathbf{i}} = (\bar{v}_{i1}, ..., \bar{v}_{iK})$ respectively, using the same pre-trained embedding method as discussed before. LSTM (Hochreiter and Schmidhuber, 1997) is a special variant of Recurrent Neural Networks (Williams and Zipser, 1989) and has shown to capture long-range dependencies and nonlinear dynamics between words. In order to model the contextual information of each word that is indicative of its semantic meaning, we use a BiLSTM that processes the premise $\mathbf{p}$ in both forward and backward directions and produces the hidden states $\hbar = \{\hbar_1, ..., \hbar_m\}$. Subsequently, for the i-th word, its context vector $\hat{\hbar}_i \in \mathbb{R}^{2h}$ is computed as:

$$\hat{\hbar}_i = \sigma(W_b \hbar_i + W_c \bar{w}_i) \qquad (3)$$

where W_b and W_c are weight matrices to be learned, h is the number of hidden units and σ indicates the sigmoid function. In order to gauge the suitability of each candidate concept, z_{ik} where $k \in [1, K]$, as a more semantically similar concept to the word compared to the initially retrieved context-independent UMLS concept c_i, we compute the relevance of its embedded supporting evidence to the current word context as:

$$\beta_{ik} = \hat{\hbar}_i^{\mathsf{T}} W_d \bar{v}_{ik} \qquad (4)$$

where W_d is a trainable weight matrix. The initial concept embedding is, henceforth, refined with a mixture model that is formulated as a weighted sum of the candidate concept vectors, where the weights are the relevance scores. The *refined lexical knowledge vector*, $q_i \in \mathbb{R}^d$, is defined as:

$$q_i = \alpha_i \bar{c}_i + \sum_{k=1}^{K} \beta_{ik} \bar{z}_{ik} \qquad (5)$$

Here, $\alpha_i + \sum_{k=1}^{K} \beta_{ik} = 1$ to ensure that the weights are adaptively adjusted according to the concepts' relevance to the word context, and apparently the contribution from the most relevant concept will be properly emphasized with a higher relevance score. In the case of missing words which have no corresponding UMLS concepts and hence make the first term in equation 5 zero, the candidate concept vectors retrieved from external resource will compensate for that through the second term.

Finally, the refined knowledge vector is integrated into its original contextual representation to get the *adaptive lexical embedding*:

$$al_i = \hbar_i + q_i \qquad (6)$$

We consider al_i as the final representation of the i-th word that results in the encoded premise $\mathbf{al^p} = (al_1^p, ..., al_m^p)$ (similarly for the encoded hypothesis $\mathbf{al^h} = (al_1^h, ..., al_n^h)$), which are passed as inputs into the next component.

3.1.1 Candidate Concepts

To select K candidate concepts for each concept, we measure the relevance between the respective contextual evidence (collected as described in Section 3.1.2) by performing dot product between their embeddings. For each abbreviation, its possible expansions in the Abbreviation Sense Inventory dataset are considered as the candidate concepts. While for each word (non-abbreviation), the candidates are selected from the total concept space ($\sim$5300 medical concepts). We set K to 5 based on hyperparameter analysis on the validation set.

3.1.2 Contextual Evidence

The contextual evidence for each word/abbreviation in the medical text is collected as snippet of clinical note from two different external resources respectively. For each word (non-abbreviation) in the text, we leverage the clinical notes in the MIMIC-III critical care dataset (Johnson et al., 2016) to extract the relevant snippet in which the word appears. While for abbreviations, we first check against the more specialized Clinical Abbreviation Sense Inventory dataset (Moon et al., 2012). It contains 440 most frequently used abbreviations selected from 352,267 dictated clinical notes. Each abbreviation instance is annotated with its long form, the source sentence where the abbreviation appears, along with other information. The source sentence is fed as the contextual evidence for the abbreviation. If it happens that the abbreviation is not found in the specialized dataset, then we resort to the MIMIC-III critical care dataset.

3.2 Matching with Multi-Source Attention

In order to capture fine-grained word-level information for semantic comparisons that lead to improved

5

local inferential decisions, our proposed model attends over the word pair interactions between the encoded premise $\mathbf{al^p}$ and the encoded hypothesis $\mathbf{al^h}$ at both the lexical and relational levels using **multi-source attention mechanism**. Figure 1 depicts the motivations for introducing this scheme. At the lexical level words are aligned to model their semantic similarity (i.e., in red), while the relational alignment reveals the innate semantic relations existing between medical entities (i.e., in green). This fine-grained alignment simulated by the multi-source attention is important for medical NLI as the semantic relation between the premise-hypothesis depends largely on the relations of aligned semantic units, which in turn require reasoning over a range of domain-specific knowledge phenomena.

The adaptive encodings outputted from the previous component already capture the lexical semantics appropriately, so *lexical alignment* soft-aligns the adaptive representations of the i-th word in the encoded premise $\mathbf{al^p}$ and the j-th word in the encoded hypothesis $\mathbf{al^h}$ into an alignment matrix L $\in \mathbb{R}^{m \times n}$. It is calculated as:

$$l_{ij} = al_i^{pT} \cdot al_j^h \qquad (7)$$

Using these cross-sentence word attention weights, the *lexical context vector*, $\mathbf{cl_i^p}$, of the i-th word in the encoded premise is computed to characterize the most semantically similar parts in the encoded hypothesis and vice versa:

$$\gamma_{ij} = \frac{exp(l_{ij})}{\sum\limits_{k=1}^{n} exp(l_{ik})}, \quad cl_i^p = \sum\limits_{j=1}^{n} \gamma_{ij} al_i^p \qquad (8)$$

$$\delta_{ij} = \frac{exp(l_{ij})}{\sum\limits_{k=1}^{m} exp(l_{kj})}, \quad cl_j^h = \sum\limits_{i=1}^{m} \delta_{ij} al_i^h \qquad (9)$$

As for *relational alignment*, first the knowledge graph for each word - summarizing its relationships with other concepts in the medical domain - is retrieved from the UMLS (next sub-section). It then converts them to adaptive relational embeddings ar^p/ar^h with a graph representation technique, which are attended over the same way as the lexical alignment (al^p/al^h in equations 7, 8, 9 replaced with ar^p/ar^h), but for modeling the explicit dependency relationship between the word graph representations to produce the *relational context vectors*,

$\mathbf{cr^p}$ and $\mathbf{cr^h}$, for the premise and hypothesis respectively.

The interactive features in the lexical context vector and the relational context vector are then merged as the *multi-source context vector*:

$$ms_i^p = W_{m1}([cl_i^p; cr_i^p]) + b_{m1} \qquad (10)$$

$$ms_j^h = W_{m2}([cl_j^h; cr_j^h]) + b_{m2} \qquad (11)$$

where W_{m1} and W_{m2} are trainable weight matrices and [;] indicates concatenation.

3.2.1 Adaptive Embedding of Relational Knowledge

The relational information between medical concepts can provide invaluable inferential clues to enhance the interactive features between the word pairs in the sentences. In order to create the relational knowledge graph, we resort to the Semantic Network within the UMLS. We first use MetaMap to map the words/phrases of the premise-hypothesis pairs in the MedNLI dataset to their corresponding UMLS concepts. This gives us a total of ~ 5300 unique medical concepts, which form the nodes of the knowledge graph. Two medical concepts form an edge if there exists a relationship between their respective semantic types in the Semantic Network and we get a total of $\sim 15,000,000$ edges.

We employ graph attention (Veličković et al., 2017; Guan et al., 2019) to represent the knowledge graph as low-dimensional vector(s) for each medical concept(s). In order to propagate the *refined* lexical knowledge into the relational embeddings, we compute a mixture of the graph embeddings between the UMLS retrieved concept and its K candidate concepts, where the same α and β weights from adaptive lexical encoding are used. This way, the graph embedded relational knowledge will align appropriately with the context-aware medical concept. First, for each concept and its candidates, their respective one-hop graph is retrieved from the aforementioned relational knowledge graph. That is, say for the i-th medical concept (similarly for its candidate concepts z_{ik}, where $k \in [1, K]$), its one-hop graph $G(i)$ is represented using its relation triples as $G(i) = \{r_1, ... r_{N_{deg_i}}\}$. Here, the n-th triple indicates semantic relationship of the i-th concept with a neighboring concept and can be written as $(head_n, r_n, tail_n)$, where the i-th concept is the head concept in each. Note that we use the concept's preferred name for each concept, and hence represent

Table 1: Accuracy performance of different models on the development and test sets of MedNLI. We use 768-d BioBERT embeddings in all. g/l indicates the percentage gain(+)/loss(-) compared to ESIM w/K.

	GBLM	IS	IS w/K	MLM	ESIM	ESIM w/K	MUSKAN	Ab$_1$	Ab$_2$
Dev	73.11	74.02	74.79	74.98	76.37	78.88	**80.09**	76.99	78.13
Dev g/l	-7.31	-6.16	-5.19	-4.94	-3.18	N/A	+1.53	-2.39	-0.95
Test	72.15	73.82	74.14	74.03	75.19	77.26	**79.42**	76.02	77.55
Test g/l	-6.61	-4.45	-4.04	-4.18	-2.68	N/A	+2.79	-1.60	+0.37

all head and tail concepts using the previous pre-trained embedding. Graph attention uses attention mechanism to learn the relative weight between two connected concepts (Wu et al., 2020), that is used to obtain the graph vector, $\hat{g}_i$, as:

$$\hat{g}_i = \sum_{n=1}^{N_{deg_i}} \mu_n [head_n; tail_n] \tag{12}$$

$$\mu_n = \frac{exp(\hat{\mu}_n)}{\sum_{n'=1}^{N_{deg_i}} \hat{\mu}_{n'}} \tag{13}$$

$$\hat{\mu}_n = (W_{r1} rel_n) tanh(W_{r2} head_n + W_{r3} tail_n) \tag{14}$$

where N_{deg_i} is the degree of concept i, and rel_n is a trainable relation vector for relation r_n and is randomly initialized.

The *adaptive relational embedding* is then computed as a mixture model using the graph vectors for the concept and its candidates, as shown below:

$$g_i = \alpha_i \hat{g}_i + \sum_{k=1}^{K} \beta_{ik} \hat{g}_{ik} \tag{15}$$

For notation consistency, we instead use the notations ar_i^p and ar_j^h to denote the adaptive relational embedding of the i-th/j-th concept in the premise and hypothesis respectively.

3.3 Inference

In order to aggregate the inferential semantics at the word level to a sentence representation, we first enrich the context vectors with similarity and closeness information (Chen et al., 2016; Kumar et al., 2016):

$$s_i^p = F([al_i^p; ar_i^p; ms_i^p; al_i^p - ms_i^p; ar_i^p - ms_i^p;$$
$$al_i^p \odot ms_i^p; ar_i^p \odot ms_i^p]) \tag{16}$$

$$s_j^h = F([al_j^h; ar_j^h; ms_j^h; al_j^h - ms_j^h; ar_j^h - ms_j^h;$$
$$al_j^h \odot ms_j^h; ar_j^h \odot ms_j^h]) \tag{17}$$

where $F(.)$ is a standard projection layer with ReLU activation function followed by a BiLSTM.

Finally, a pooling layer, comprising max and mean pooling, is used to convert the vectors into a fixed-length vector and then fed into a 2-layer multi-layer perception (MLP) classifier to make the final inference prediction. The entire model is trained end-to-end, through minimizing the cross-entropy loss.

4 Experiments and Results

4.1 Data

We evaluate performance of our model on the only publicly available dataset for this task, namely MedNLI (Romanov and Shivade, 2018). Each instance in this expert-annotated dataset is a premise-hypothesis pair, along with a gold label indicating their inferential relationship. The training, development and test sets consist of 11,232, 1395 and 1422 sentence pairs respectively.

4.2 Baselines

We compare our model against both sentence encoding-based (InferSent (IS) and Gated BiL-STM (GBLM)) and sentence pair interaction-based (ESIM and Match-LSTM (MLM)) baselines. Furthermore, we incorporate domain knowledge in the form of UMLS medical concepts and relation information into the best performing model from each group (i.e., InferSent and ESIM). In the case of InferSent, the knowledge features are fed during encoding into the text representation; for ESIM, we also incorporate it into the attention. We refer to these knowledge-enhanced versions of the baselines with the "w/K" suffix.

4.3 Implementation Details

We use pre-trained 768-d BioBERT (Lee et al., 2020) vectors to initialize all word and concept embeddings in the adaptive lexical encoding step, with update during training. The hidden states of both the BiLSTMs during encoding and inference are set to 384. An Adam optimizer (Kingma and Ba, 2014) with an initial learning rate of 0.0005 is used to optimize all the trainable weights. The mini-batch size is set to 64.

4.4 Results

Table 1 reports the accuracy of the models on the development and test sets of the MedNLI dataset. MUSKAN outperforms all the baselines by a significant margin with a test accuracy of 79.42%. Specifically, there is a 2.79% performance improvement in comparison to the best performing baseline, ESIM w/K. Although ESIM w/K exploits the semantic knowledge in UMLS, we can assert that refining this knowledge using an adaptive encoding scheme based on contextual evidence is able to alleviate the noise introduced by the domain knowledge, and hence leads to a major boost in performance.

A general observation is that the sentence encoding baselines perform poorly compared to the counterpart sentence interaction ones. The main limitation of the encoding approaches is that they fail to capture the interactions between the premise-hypothesis words, that could otherwise provide important alignment information for inference.

To further ascertain the effectiveness of our model, we evaluate the contributions of key factors in our method by performing an ablation study. The ablated versions of our model are shown on the far right of Table 1 as Ab_1 and Ab_2. Since our proposed method encodes the premise-hypothesis sentences by integrating the *refined* domain knowledge into the text representation, we wonder how the model would perform without this adaptive encoding. So in the encoding step of Ab_1, we concatenate the initial UMLS retrieved concept embedding to the corresponding text representation, which is then passed as input to the subsequent component. We observe that this leads to a drop in performance by 4.28% compared to the whole model. This verifies our intuition that embedding the context-relevant domain knowledge can indeed improve understanding the semantics of the text. In the case of Ab_2, we use just the adaptive lexical encoding to compute the attention matrix, and can see that this declines the performance by 2.35%. This shows that our proposed model works more effectively by capturing the cross-features from both adaptive lexical and adaptive relational representations at the same time using multi-source attention.

4.5 Case Study

There are two different visualizations to demonstrate our model's interpretability. First, the visualization of *lexical alignment* shows how adaptive lexical encoding helps to align the semantically similar words in the premise-hypothesis sentence pair. Next, the *multi-source attention* visualization enhances the lexical alignment by highlighting the salient words that well represent the semantic relation between them.

The sub-figures in Figure 3 depict the attention heatmaps yielded by the best performing baseline, ESIM w/K, and our proposed MUSKAN. The darker shade indicates higher importance in classification. The alignment of the words "feeling", "fatigued", "light", and "headed" in p to "weakness" in h is critical in deciding if the former entails the latter. From the highlighted words in the middle sub-figure in Figure 3 for lexical alignment matrix of our proposed model, it can be seen that integrating context-aware medical concepts into the text representation is in fact able to capture this semantics. The abbreviation "USOH" stands for "usual state of health" and expresses a transition from normal to a deterioration of patient's health in this context. In the right sub-figure for multi-source attention matrix, the higher attention put on the words "onset", "prior", "to", "admission", "started" and PCP", and their alignment with "new" are able to capture this nuance. We hypothesize that this is facilitated by the semantic relation information between the medical concepts incorporated through the multi-source attention. On the other hand, from the left sub-figure, it can be seen that ESIM w/K fails to model these context-aware lexical and relational associations due to missing words (e.g., USOH) and inaccurate mappings (e.g., PCP), which result in a wrong prediction.

4.6 Error Analysis

We perform error analysis on the result of MUSKAN which divulges open challenges and directions towards pending future research in medical NLI. Typical errors made by our approach include:

Numeric values: For some premises, the text can describe clinical measurements as numeric val-

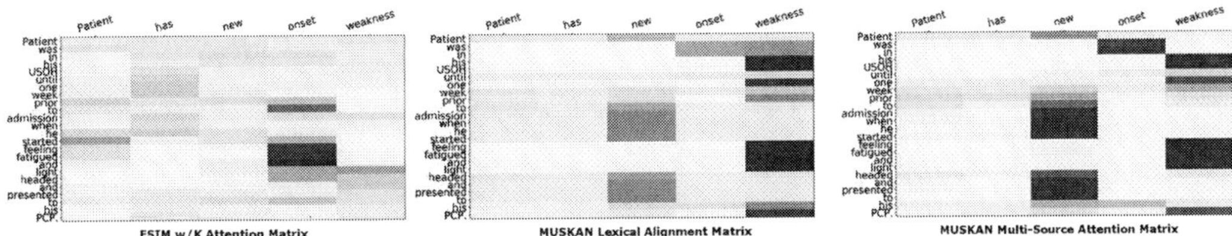

Figure 3: Visualizations of the attention heatmaps for the following instance from the test set of the MedNLI dataset: {*p*: Patient was in his USOH until one week prior to admission when he started feeling fatigued and light headed and presented to his PCP. *h*: Patient has new onset weakness. *y*: Entailment}.

ues, which make it difficult for the model to semantically relate these to the condition conveyed in the hypothesis. For example, looking at the premise in Figure 4a, we can see that the different vital signs, represented with the abbreviation "VS", are expressed in terms of numeric values (e.g., T 98.9, HR 73, BP 121/90). However, for the model to infer that these values indicate that the patient is "hemodynamically stable" is challenging. Hypothesizing, we attribute this fail to the fact that medical notes lack in covering such knowledge and, perhaps, leveraging other external resources such as the Wikipedia or the laboratory test results available in electronic health records (EHR) might help to mitigate this drawback.

Ambiguity: Some instances in the dataset contain words/phrases used in everyday conversation, which could appear as vague terms with respect to medical perspective and result in misclassification. As an example, "handfuls" in the premise in Figure 4b is actually referring to "more medications than directed" in the hypothesis and is an "entailment". However, the ambiguity here lies in that "overdose of Dilaudid" (which has label "neutral") possibly expresses similar concept, and hence leads to a false positive.

5 Conclusion and Future Work

This work discloses the effectiveness of context-aware domain knowledge in medical NLI and proposes a systematic approach to infuse such knowledge using an adaptive encoding scheme. By employing a multi-source attention mechanism that is able to model both the lexical and relational semantics, it is able to mitigate the noise introduced by the abbreviation-like jargon prevalent in medical text. Through both qualitative and quantitative analysis, our proposed framework advances the limited work so far done on medical NLI.

There are several possible directions that could

> **Premise**: *In the ED, initial VS revealed T 98.9, HR 73, BP 121/90, RR 15, O2 sat 98% on RA.*
>
> **Hypothesis**: *The patient is hemodynamically stable*
>
> **Label**: *Entailment*

(a)

> **Premise**: *Today she got into an argument with her husband and felt that she \"wanted to sleep\" and therefore took \"handfuls\" of dilaudid.*
>
> **Hypothesis**: *She took more medication than directed*
>
> **Label**: *Entailment*

(b)

Figure 4: Samples from MedNLI dataset to demonstrate error analysis for (a) Numeric values and (b) Ambiguity

be explored as future work. Firstly, it would be interesting to investigate if enriching the refined domain knowledge with explicit syntactic information (e.g., parse tree) of the premise-hypothesis is helpful. Secondly, we could extract knowledge from other relevant medical knowledge bases and incorporate deeper subgraph information (e.g., two hops). Furthermore, we could test the utility of the proposed framework on downstream NLP applications that similarly suffer from small data size.

6 Acknowledgments

We would like to thank the anonymous reviewers for their careful reading of our manuscript and providing helpful comments and suggestions. This work is supported in part by NSF under grants III-1763325, III-1909323, and SaTC-1930941.

References

Auer, S., Bizer, C., Kobilarov, G., Lehmann, J., Cyganiak, R., and Ives, Z. (2007). Dbpedia: A nucleus for a web of open data. In *The semantic web*, pages 722–735. Springer.

Bowman, S. R., Angeli, G., Potts, C., and Manning, C. D. (2015). A large annotated corpus for learning natural language inference. *arXiv preprint arXiv:1508.05326*.

Chen, Q., Zhu, X., Ling, Z., Wei, S., Jiang, H., and Inkpen, D. (2016). Enhanced lstm for natural language inference. *arXiv preprint arXiv:1609.06038*.

Chen, Q., Zhu, X., Ling, Z.-H., Inkpen, D., and Wei, S. (2017a). Neural natural language inference models enhanced with external knowledge. *arXiv preprint arXiv:1711.04289*.

Chen, Q., Zhu, X., Ling, Z.-H., Wei, S., Jiang, H., and Inkpen, D. (2017b). Recurrent neural network-based sentence encoder with gated attention for natural language inference. *arXiv preprint arXiv:1708.01353*.

Conneau, A., Kiela, D., Schwenk, H., Barrault, L., and Bordes, A. (2017). Supervised learning of universal sentence representations from natural language inference data. *arXiv preprint arXiv:1705.02364*.

Ganitkevitch, J., Van Durme, B., and Callison-Burch, C. (2013). Ppdb: The paraphrase database. In *Proceedings of the 2013 Conference of the North American Chapter of the Association for Computational Linguistics: Human Language Technologies*, pages 758–764.

Guan, J., Wang, Y., and Huang, M. (2019). Story ending generation with incremental encoding and commonsense knowledge. In *Proceedings of the AAAI Conference on Artificial Intelligence*, volume 33, pages 6473–6480.

Harabagiu, S. and Hickl, A. (2006). Methods for using textual entailment in open-domain question answering. In *Proceedings of the 21st International Conference on Computational Linguistics and the 44th annual meeting of the Association for Computational Linguistics*, pages 905–912. Association for Computational Linguistics.

Hochreiter, S. and Schmidhuber, J. (1997). Long short-term memory. *Neural computation*, 9(8):1735–1780.

Jin, Q., Dhingra, B., Cohen, W. W., and Lu, X. (2019). Probing biomedical embeddings from language models. *arXiv preprint arXiv:1904.02181*.

Johnson, A. E., Pollard, T. J., Shen, L., Li-wei, H. L., Feng, M., Ghassemi, M., Moody, B., Szolovits, P., Celi, L. A., and Mark, R. G. (2016). Mimic-iii, a freely accessible critical care database. *Scientific data*, 3:160035.

Kang, D., Khot, T., Sabharwal, A., and Hovy, E. (2018). Adventure: Adversarial training for textual entailment with knowledge-guided examples. *arXiv preprint arXiv:1805.04680*.

Kingma, D. P. and Ba, J. (2014). Adam: A method for stochastic optimization. *arXiv preprint arXiv:1412.6980*.

Kumar, A., Irsoy, O., Ondruska, P., Iyyer, M., Bradbury, J., Gulrajani, I., Zhong, V., Paulus, R., and Socher, R. (2016). Ask me anything: Dynamic memory networks for natural language processing. In *International conference on machine learning*, pages 1378–1387.

Lee, J., Yoon, W., Kim, S., Kim, D., Kim, S., So, C. H., and Kang, J. (2020). Biobert: a pre-trained biomedical language representation model for biomedical text mining. *Bioinformatics*, 36(4):1234–1240.

Li, T., Zhu, X., Liu, Q., Chen, Q., Chen, Z., and Wei, S. (2019). Several experiments on investigating pretraining and knowledge-enhanced models for natural language inference. *arXiv preprint arXiv:1904.12104*.

Lloret, E., Ferrández, O., Munoz, R., and Palomar, M. (2008). A text summarization approach under the influence of textual entailment. In *NLPCS*, pages 22–31.

Long, T., Bengio, E., Lowe, R., Cheung, J. C. K., and Precup, D. (2017). World knowledge for reading comprehension: Rare entity prediction with hierarchical lstms using external descriptions. In *Proceedings of the 2017 Conference on Empirical Methods in Natural Language Processing*, pages 825–834.

MacCartney, B. and Manning, C. D. (2009). *Natural language inference*. Citeseer.

Marelli, M., Menini, S., Baroni, M., Bentivogli, L., Bernardi, R., Zamparelli, R., et al. (2014). A sick cure for the evaluation of compositional distributional semantic models. In *LREC*, pages 216–223.

Miller, G. A. (1995). Wordnet: a lexical database for english. *Communications of the ACM*, 38(11):39–41.

Moon, S., Pakhomov, S., and Melton, G. (2012). Clinical abbreviation sense inventory.

Parikh, A. P., Täckström, O., Das, D., and Uszkoreit, J. (2016). A decomposable attention model for natural language inference. *arXiv preprint arXiv:1606.01933*.

Pasunuru, R. and Bansal, M. (2017). Multi-task video captioning with video and entailment generation. *arXiv preprint arXiv:1704.07489*.

Romanov, A. and Shivade, C. (2018). Lessons from natural language inference in the clinical domain. *arXiv preprint arXiv:1808.06752*.

Rush, A. M., Chopra, S., and Weston, J. (2015). A neural attention model for abstractive sentence summarization. *arXiv preprint arXiv:1509.00685*.

Veličković, P., Cucurull, G., Casanova, A., Romero, A., Lio, P., and Bengio, Y. (2017). Graph attention networks. *arXiv preprint arXiv:1710.10903*.

Wang, S. and Jiang, J. (2015). Learning natural language inference with lstm. *arXiv preprint arXiv:1512.08849*.

Wang, X., Kapanipathi, P., Musa, R., Yu, M., Talamadupula, K., Abdelaziz, I., Chang, M., Fokoue, A., Makni, B., Mattei, N., et al. (2019). Improving natural language inference using external knowledge in the science questions domain. In *Proceedings of the AAAI Conference on Artificial Intelligence*, volume 33, pages 7208–7215.

Weissenborn, D., Kočiskỳ, T., and Dyer, C. (2017). Dynamic integration of background knowledge in neural nlu systems. *arXiv preprint arXiv:1706.02596*.

Williams, A., Nangia, N., and Bowman, S. R. (2017). A broad-coverage challenge corpus for sentence understanding through inference. *arXiv preprint arXiv:1704.05426*.

Williams, R. J. and Zipser, D. (1989). A learning algorithm for continually running fully recurrent neural networks. *Neural computation*, 1(2):270–280.

Wu, Z., Pan, S., Chen, F., Long, G., Zhang, C., and Philip, S. Y. (2020). A comprehensive survey on graph neural networks. *IEEE Transactions on Neural Networks and Learning Systems*.

Yang, B. and Mitchell, T. (2019). Leveraging knowledge bases in lstms for improving machine reading. *arXiv preprint arXiv:1902.09091*.

Reading Comprehension as Natural Language Inference:
A Semantic Analysis

Anshuman Mishra [*1], Dhruvesh Patel[*1], Aparna Vijayakumar[*1],
Xiang Lorraine Li[1], Pavan Kapanipathi[2], and Kartik Talamadupula[2]

[1] College of Information and Computer Sciences, University of Massachusetts Amherst
[2]IBM Research

Abstract

In the recent past, Natural language Inference (NLI) has gained significant attention, particularly given its promise for downstream NLP tasks. However, its true impact is limited and has not been well studied. Therefore, in this paper, we explore the utility of NLI for one of the most prominent downstream tasks, viz. Question Answering (QA). We transform one of the largest available MRC dataset (RACE) to an NLI form, and compare the performances of a state-of-the-art model (RoBERTa) on both these forms. We propose new characterizations of questions, and evaluate the performance of QA and NLI models on these categories. We highlight clear categories for which the model is able to perform better when the data is presented in a coherent entailment form, and a structured question-answer concatenation form, respectively.

1 Introduction

Given two sentences, a premise and a hypothesis, the task of Natural Language Inference (NLI) is to determine whether the premise entails the hypothesis or not. [†] The concept of semantic entailment is central to natural language understanding (Van Benthem et al., 2008; MacCartney and Manning, 2009) and therefore, NLI models have been used to help with various downstream tasks like reading comprehension (Trivedi et al., 2019), summarization (Falke et al., 2019; Kryściński et al., 2019), and dialog systems (Welleck et al., 2019). However, the performance of an NLI system on these down-

---

[†]The "not entailment" can further be subdivided into "neutral" and "contradiction". However, we only use the two-class version of the problem in this work.

stream tasks has not been studied with respect to semantic or reasoning categories.

In this work, we use NLI to perform the task of multiple choice reading comprehension (MRC, or RC). We analyse the performance of an NLI model on this task through the lens of semantics by identifying the reasoning categories (type of questions) where it is beneficial to use an NLI model.

Drawing inspiration from the prior work in the area (Clark et al., 2018; Demszky et al., 2018; Trivedi et al., 2019), we use rule-based conversion to create an NLI version of the largest available RC dataset - RACE (Lai et al., 2017). We train a RoBERTa based RC model on the original dataset, and a similar RoBERTa based NLI model on the NLI version of the dataset. We evaluate and analyse the performance of both these models by characterizing the question types that are better suited for an NLI model and a QA model.

2 Related Work

Reading comprehension (RC) is one of many potential downstream tasks that can benefit from NLI (MacCartney and Manning, 2009). It is easy to see that RC naturally reduces to a two-class NLI problem; specifically, it can be cast as the task of identifying if a given piece of text entails the statement formed by converting a question and a potential answer to an assertive statement (hypothesis).

Given the intuitive conversion between RC and NLI, Demszky et al. (2018) designed both a rule-based conversion system as well as a trained neural model to convert question-answering datasets such as SQuAD (Rajpurkar et al., 2016) and RACE (Lai et al., 2017) to an NLI form. However, it is unclear what these converted NLI datasets offer compared to the original question-answering datasets w.r.t semantics. We show that converting a RC task to an NLI task helps in answering certain types of

*Proceedings of the Ninth Joint Conference on Lexical and Computational Semantics (*SEM)*, pages 12–19
Barcelona, Spain (Online), December 12–13, 2020

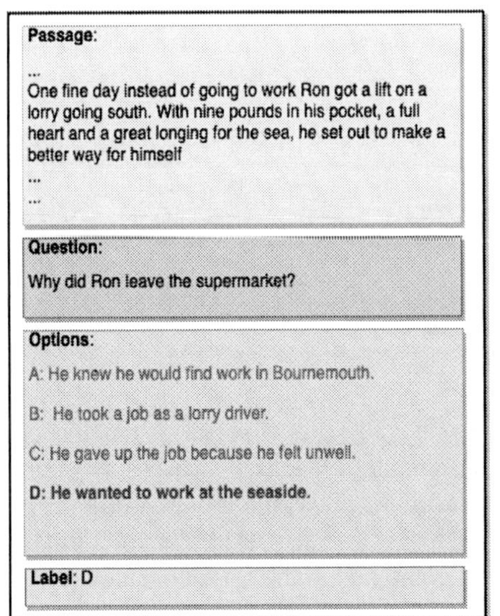

(a) QA sample   (b) Converted NLI sample

Figure 1: A RC sample with multiple answer choices converted to an NLI sample.

questions. This establishes the usefulness of the converted datasets.

Jin et al. (2019) show that despite the different form of NLI and QA tasks, performing coarse pretraining of models on NLI datasets like SNLI (Bowman et al., 2015) and MultiNLI (Williams et al., 2018) not only improves the performance of these models on downstream reading comprehension tasks, but also helps with faster convergence. We show that – for certain types of questions in reading comprehension datasets – simply transforming the task to NLI can show improvement in performance, even without pretraining on any NLI dataset.

Trivedi et al. (2019) introduced a learnt weight-and-combine architecture to effectively re-purpose pretrained entailment models (trained on SNLI and MultiNLI) to solve the task of multi-hop reading comprehension. They show that for certain datasets, this strategy can produce good results. However, their study focuses mainly on improving model performance using a pre-trained NLI model, and lacks an analysis of the reasoning differences arising due to the different form of the NLI and QA tasks. We focus our analysis on this aspect.

3 NLI for Reading Comprehension

This section describes our experimental setup for comparing a QA based approach and an NLI based approach for the task of reading comprehension. We first obtain a parallel NLI and QA dataset by converting existing RC dataset into an NLI dataset. We then train two models, one on each form of the data, and analyse their performance.

3.1 Converting RC to NLI

We use the RACE dataset (Lai et al., 2017) for our experiments. It is a large-scale reading comprehension dataset comprising of questions collected from the English exams for junior Chinese students. We pick RACE because it is in a general domain and large enough to perform conclusive analysis. Each question in the dataset contains four answer options, out of which only one is correct. However, about 44% of the RACE dataset consists of cloze style (fill-in-the-blank) questions which are already in NLI form. Hence, in order to have a fair comparison, we only use the subset of RACE dataset which does not contain cloze style questions. This subset consists of 48890 train, 2496 validation and 2571 test examples.

We convert a RC example into an NLI example by reusing the passage as premise and paraphrasing the question along with each answer option as individual hypotheses as shown in Figure 1. Specifically, we generate the dependency parse of both the question and the answer option by using Stanford NLP package (Qi et al., 2018), then we follow the conversion rules proposed in Demszky et al. (2018) to generate a hypothesis sentence[*]. We make a few

---

[*] Appendix C presents example conversions generated us-

Figure 2: For the QA model, the input corresponding to each option contains question+option concatenation as the second sequence.

Figure 3: For the NLI model, the input corresponding to each option contains *hypothesis* generated using the question and option as the second sequence.

Dataset	Dataset Format	
	QA	NLI
RACE	**85.78**	-
RACE-subset	79.84	**82.09**

Table 1: Accuracy on the test set obtained by using different formats of the data.

additions to these rules to handle a some peculiar question categories in the RACE dataset. The most prominent of the added rules is the one for questions containing *"which of the following are (not) true"*. Such questions are very frequent (about 6% of all questions) and are not handled correctly by the rules in Demszky et al. (2018).

3.2 Model

In order to perform apple-to-apple comparison we use the same model architecture for both QA and NLI. Specifically, we use the state-of-the-art reading comprehension model – consisting of a RoBERTa model (pretrained on the masked language modeling objective) as the encoder and a two layer feed-forward network on its [CLS] token as the classification head – as described in Liu et al. (2019). The input sentence is the combination of the passage and its hypothesis. The hypothesis are created using the rule-based conversion method mentioned in Section 3.1 (NLI setup) or by concatenation of question and answer option (QA setup). The input to the QA setup and the NLI setup, corresponding to the first option in Figure 1, is shown in Figure 2 and 3.

4 Analysis

Table 1 shows the accuracy achieved by the RoBERTa model on the RACE dataset and its subset when presented in different forms. As we can

see, the NLI model performs much better than the QA model on RACE subset. We think that the reason for this is the more natural form of the hypothesis statement used by the NLI model (Figure 3) compared to the Q+A concatenation form used by the QA model (Figure 2). Moreover, while the RACE-subset consists of only those questions which have question-words such as {*who, what, when...*}, about 95% of the rest of the dataset, i.e. RACE \ RACE-subset, consists of only fill-in-the-blank (FITB) type questions. These FITB questions are largely with the blank at the end of the question and a naive question-answer concatenation is very similar to a NLI form hypothesis. We believe that helps the QA model to perform better on the full RACE dataset compared to the RACE-subset, where NLI model is able to outperform the QA model showing the clear benefits of coherent conversion on complex question formulations (such as W word questions).

In order to analyse the performance difference from a semantic perspective, we characterize question into 7 semantic categories by identifying the kind of reasoning required to answer the question. Table 2 succinctly describes the reasoning categories.

4.1 Categories based on manual analysis

In order to perform manual analysis, we construct a *delta subset* consisting the 328 dev set examples on which the predictions of the QA and NLI models differ. We further divide the *delta subset* into *gain* and *loss* subsets. The *gain subset* consists of questions which the NLI model gets right, but the QA model gets wrong, and the *loss subset* is its complement in the *delta*.

We manually annotate these 328 (192 in *gain* and 136 in *loss*) examples into one of the 7 categories. However, about half the examples in the *delta subset* were not properly converted by the rules leading to unnatural or incoherent hypothesis

---

ing these rules.

Category	Description	Example
Linguistic Matching	Matching words between the question and a sentence in the passage	**Passage** : Food cooks quickly in parabolic cookers **Question**: If you want to cook food quickly, which kind of sun-cooker is your best choice?
Main Idea	Require topicality judgements	What's the best title for this passage?
Negation	Picking the incorrect statement	Which of the following statements is NOT true?
Dialogue	Can be inferred from a dialogue or direct speech in the passage	By saying "her pen dared travel where her eyes would not", the writer means
Math	Mathematically combining facts	How many functions of snow are discussed in the text?
Deductive	None of the above but can be answered precisely from the text	Which of the following statements is TRUE?
Inductive	None of the above and cannot be answered precisely from the text	How old is most likely the writer's father?

Table 2: Reasoning Categories (exclusive)

Type	Heuristics
Main Idea	Questions containing the words 'mainly', 'title', 'purpose' or 'topic'
Negation	Questions containing the 'not', 'except' or 'which of the following is wrong'
Dialogue	Passages containing more than 10 quotation marks (")
Math	Questions containing the words 'how many', 'how old' or 'how much'
Deductive	Questions containing the word 'true'

Table 3: Heuristically Determined Question Types in RACE-subset (non-exclusive).

sentences. Hence, for the purpose of illustration, we removed these examples leaving a total of 175 examples (109 in *gain* and 66 in *loss*) to do further analysis. Figures 4 and 5 show the distribution of labels over the Gain and Loss regions respectively. The distribution reflects that the QA models clearly outperforms the NLI model in negation questions whereas the NLI model outperforms the QA model in dialogue and deductive reasoning categories.

4.2 Categories based on heuristics

We also define another set of non-exclusive categories using heuristics, as described in Table 3. As shown in Table 4, the NLI model outperforms the QA model significantly in the dialogue, math and deductive reasoning categories. This overall trend further emphasizes the benefits of proper hypothesis generation as opposed to question and answer concatenation for the reading comprehension task.

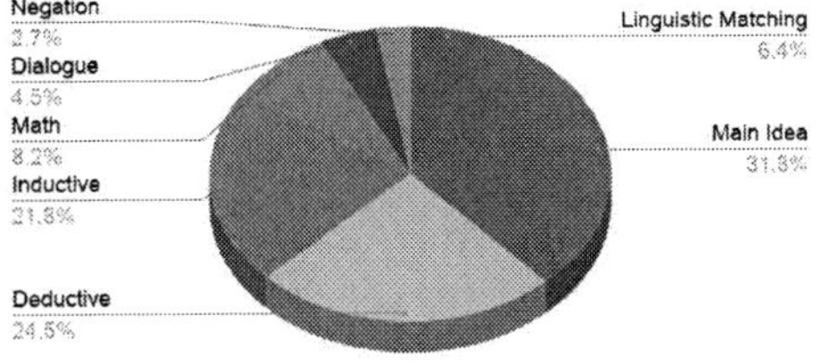

Figure 4: Reasoning categories of the gain region

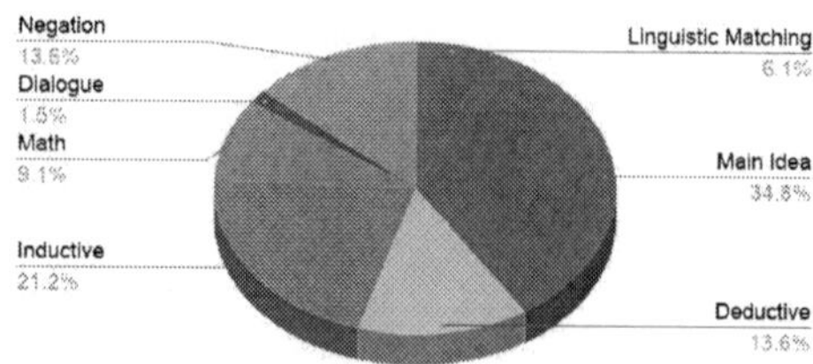

Figure 5: Reasoning categories of the loss region

Type	Fraction	QA	NLI
Main Idea	0.12	84.19	**84.83**
Negation	0.06	**80.86**	77.77
Dialogue	0.12	80.65	**83.60**
Math	0.03	45.00	**55.00**
Deductive	0.04	81.91	**88.29**

Table 4: Model performances on heuristically determined question types for RACE-Subset.

5 Conclusion

There is limited work providing a comprehensive analysis of how NLI can be used for QA. In our work, we show that NLI can be used for the task of reading comprehension simply by converting the data into NLI form. We convert a large RC dataset into NLI form and perform a comparative study of the performance of the RoBERTa model trained on QA and NLI settings. We propose a categorization of questions that allows for effective comparison of models trained on NLI and QA forms of data. Our analysis clearly shows that using the NLI-based approach is at par with a QA-based approach for most reasoning categories, and it is even better for some. Specifically, we find that questions involving deductive reasoning, dialogue interpretation and math are better handled by a model trained on the NLI form of data than the QA form. However, questions involving negation favor the QA form. Our work allows for careful selection of modeling strategy based on the type of data at hand.

References

Samuel R. Bowman, Gabor Angeli, Christopher Potts, and Christopher D. Manning. 2015. A large annotated corpus for learning natural language inference. *Conference Proceedings - EMNLP 2015: Conference on Empirical Methods in Natural Language Processing*, pages 632–642.

Peter Clark, Isaac Cowhey, Oren Etzioni, Tushar Khot, Ashish Sabharwal, Carissa Schoenick, and Oyvind Tafjord. 2018. Think you have solved question answering? try arc, the ai2 reasoning challenge. *arXiv preprint arXiv:1803.05457*.

Dorottya Demszky, Kelvin Guu, and Percy Liang. 2018. Transforming question answering datasets into natural language inference datasets. *ArXiv*, abs/1809.02922.

Tobias Falke, Leonardo FR Ribeiro, Prasetya Ajie Utama, Ido Dagan, and Iryna Gurevych. 2019. Ranking generated summaries by correctness: An interesting but challenging application for natural language inference. In *Proceedings of the 57th Annual Meeting of the Association for Computational Linguistics*, pages 2214–2220.

Di Jin, Shuyang Gao, Jiun-Yu Kao, Tagyoung Chung, and Dilek Hakkani-tur. 2019. Mmm: Multi-stage multi-task learning for multi-choice reading comprehension. *arXiv preprint arXiv:1910.00458*.

Wojciech Kryściński, Bryan McCann, Caiming Xiong, and Richard Socher. 2019. Evaluating the factual consistency of abstractive text summarization. *arXiv preprint arXiv:1910.12840*.

Guokun Lai, Qizhe Xie, Hanxiao Liu, Yiming Yang, and Eduard H. Hovy. 2017. Race: Large-scale reading comprehension dataset from examinations. In *EMNLP*.

Yinhan Liu, Myle Ott, Naman Goyal, Jingfei Du, Mandar Joshi, Danqi Chen, Omer Levy, Mike Lewis, Luke Zettlemoyer, and Veselin Stoyanov. 2019. Roberta: A robustly optimized bert pretraining approach. *arXiv preprint arXiv:1907.11692*.

Bill MacCartney and Christopher D Manning. 2009. *Natural language inference*. Citeseer.

Peng Qi, Timothy Dozat, Yuhao Zhang, and Christopher D. Manning. 2018. Universal dependency parsing from scratch. In *Proceedings of the CoNLL 2018 Shared Task: Multilingual Parsing from Raw Text to Universal Dependencies*, pages 160–170, Brussels, Belgium. Association for Computational Linguistics.

Pranav Rajpurkar, Jian Zhang, Konstantin Lopyrev, and Percy Liang. 2016. Squad: 100, 000+ questions for machine comprehension of text. In *EMNLP*.

Harsh Trivedi, Heeyoung Kwon, Tushar Khot, Ashish Sabharwal, and Niranjan Balasubramanian. 2019. Repurposing entailment for multi-hop question answering tasks. In *Proceedings of the 2019 Conference of the North American Chapter of the Association for Computational Linguistics: Human Language Technologies, Volume 1 (Long and Short Papers)*, pages 2948–2958.

Johan Van Benthem et al. 2008. *A brief history of natural logic*. LondonCollege Publications.

Sean Welleck, Jason Weston, Arthur Szlam, and Kyunghyun Cho. 2019. Dialogue natural language inference. In *ACL*.

Adina Williams, Nikita Nangia, and Samuel Bowman. 2018. A broad-coverage challenge corpus for sentence understanding through inference. In *Proceedings of the 2018 Conference of the North American Chapter of the Association for Computational Linguistics: Human Language Technologies, Volume 1 (Long Papers)*, pages 1112–1122. Association for Computational Linguistics.

A Model Architecture

Figures 6 and 7 show the model architecture for the QA and NLI models, respectively. As seen the architecture of the model is the same, the only difference is in the input form.

B Hyperparameter Settings

Hyperparam	RACE-subset	
	NLI-form	QA-form
learning rate	1e-5	1e-5
weight decay	0.01	0.01
warmup steps	1300	1300
batch size	16	16
max epochs	4	4

Table 5: Hyperparamter Setting

Table 5 lists the hyperparameter settings for both versions of the dataset.

C Conversion examples

Table 6 shows examples of NLI-form obtained applying rule-based conversion on QA examples from the RACE-subset.

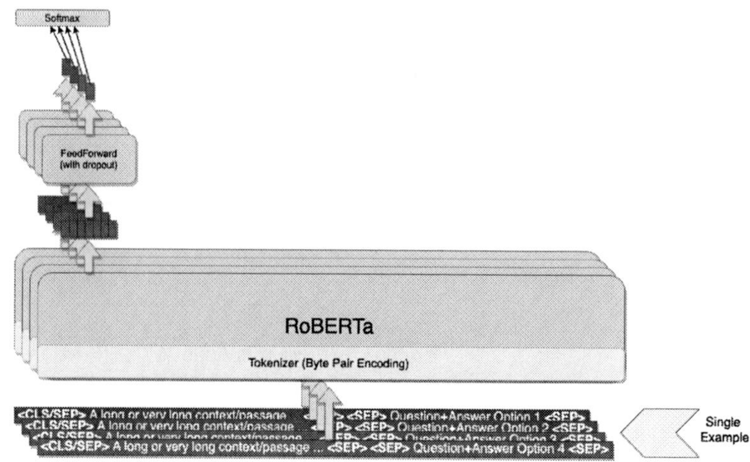

Figure 6: QA model

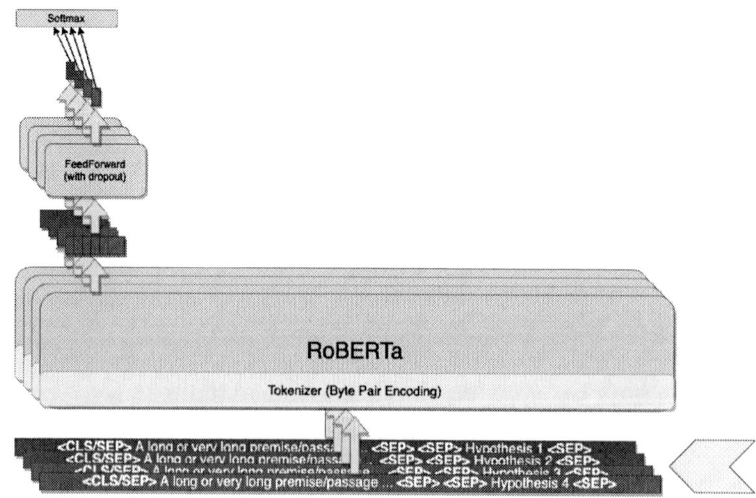

Figure 7: NLI model

QA example	NLI-form
Q: How do suburban commuters travel to and from the city in Copenhagen at present? **A:** About one third of the suburban commuters travel by bike.	Suburban commuters travel to about one third of the suburban commuters travel by bike and from the city in Copenhagen at present.
Q: What's the best title of the passage? **A:** Blame! Blame! Blame!	The best title of the passage's blame.
Q: What influence did the experiment have on Alexander ? **A:** He realized that slowing down his life speed could bring him more content.	The experiment had he realized that slowing down his life speed could bring him more content on Alexander.
Q: Which of the following is TRUE about the report findings? **A:** The reading scores among older children have improved.	The reading scores among older children have improved is TRUE.

Table 6: Examples of Rule-based conversion applied to samples from the RACE-subset.

Learning as Abduction:
Trainable Natural Logic Theorem Prover for Natural Language Inference

Lasha Abzianidze
UiL OTS, Utrecht University
`l.abzianidze@uu.nl`

Abstract

Tackling Natural Language Inference with a logic-based method is becoming less and less common. While this might have been counterintuitive several decades ago, nowadays it seems pretty obvious. The main reasons for such a conception are that (a) logic-based methods are usually brittle when it comes to processing wide-coverage texts, and (b) instead of automatically learning from data, they require much of manual effort for development. We make a step towards to overcome such shortcomings by modeling learning from data as abduction: reversing a theorem-proving procedure to abduce semantic relations that serve as the *best* explanation for the gold label of an inference problem. In other words, instead of proving sentence-level inference relations with the help of lexical relations, the lexical relations are *proved* taking into account the sentence-level inference relations. We implement the learning method in a tableau theorem prover for natural language and show that it improves the performance of the theorem prover on the SICK dataset by 1.4% while still maintaining high precision ($> 94\%$). The obtained results are competitive with the state of the art among logic-based systems.

1 Introduction

Natural language inference (NLI) is a well-established task for measuring intelligent systems' capacity of natural language understanding (Cooper et al., 1996; Dagan et al., 2005). To improve and better evaluate the systems on the NLI task, many annotated NLI datasets are prepared and used for training and evaluating NLP models. Generally speaking, an NLI dataset is a set of natural language sentence pairs, called premise-hypothesis

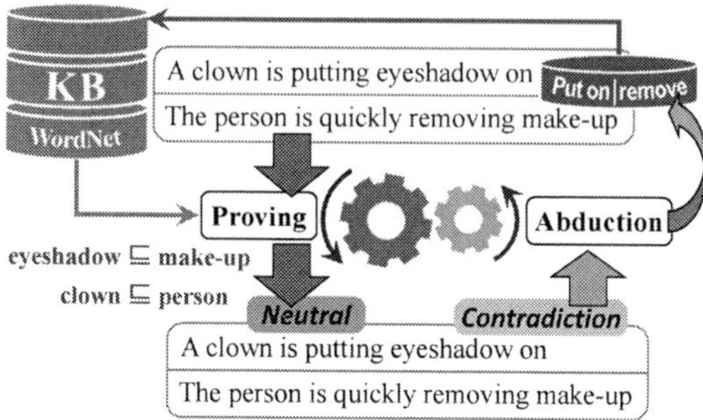

Figure 1: Theorem proving retrieves necessary semantic relations from KB, e.g., *eyeshadow* is make-up. To learn domain-specific relations, e.g., *put on* is incompatible with remove (not found in KB), abduction reverse proves semantic relations from training samples.

pairs, that are annotated by crowd workers with one of three inference labels (*entailment*, *contradiction*, and *neutral*), representing a semantic relation from a premise to a hypothesis.

Currently, the state-of-the-art systems in NLI are exclusively based on Deep Learning (DL). One of the reasons for this is that DL-based systems can eagerly learn from task-related data and also take an advantage form high-quality pre-trained word embeddings. The training phase helps them to obtain competitive scores on the in-domain test part. On the other hand, logic-based systems are becoming less favored for NLI since it is hard to scale them up for reasoning with wide-coverage sentences. Despite some rare exceptions (Martínez-Gómez et al., 2017; Yanaka et al., 2018), it is notoriously hard to effectively and efficiently train logic-based systems on NLI datasets.

Although DL-based systems are more robust than logic-based ones, the latter systems offer unique virtues such as a transparent reasoning procedure and reasoning with multiple premises. An opaque decision procedure of DL-based systems makes it difficult to estimate a share of knowledge from what was learned by the systems, because

*Proceedings of the Ninth Joint Conference on Lexical and Computational Semantics (*SEM)*, pages 20–31
Barcelona, Spain (Online), December 12–13, 2020

not all what is learned is knowledge. Behind high performance of DL-based systems on particular NLI datasets, one might miss the systems' inability of generalization (Glockner et al., 2018) or the exploitation of annotation artefacts (Poliak et al., 2018; Gururangan et al., 2018).

In this paper, we are not comparing logic- and DL-based approaches with respect to the NLI task. Rather, we are proposing a learning method which demonstrates how a logic-based NLI system can be trained on NLI dataset, the aspect in which DL approaches to NLI significantly outperform symbolic approaches. The proposed learning algorithm is inspired by abductive reasoning, which is often referred to as *inference to the best explanation*. Following the abduction, the algorithm allows learning those semantic relations over words and short phrases that *best* explain gold inference labels of NLI problems (see Figure 1). In this way, the current work contributes to automated knowledge acquisition from data, which is considered as a major issue in NLI (Dagan et al., 2013, p. 7).

The paper makes contributions along two lines: (a) describing how learning as abduction enables a trainable theorem prover for NLI, and (b) implementing the algorithm and evaluating its effectiveness. The original aspect of the research is the conceptual simplicity of the learning algorithm. In particular, the standard workflow of the logic-based theorem prover is *reversed*: instead of proving sentence-level inference relations with the help of lexical relations, the lexical relations are *proved* taking into account the sentence-level inference relations. Throughout the paper we answer the following research questions:

Q1 What is a computationally feasible learning method that allows training the natural language theorem prover on NLI problems?

Q2 How can learning pseudo-knowledge be avoided?

Q3 Can the learned knowledge replace the lexical knowledge database like WordNet?

Q4 To what extent the learned knowledge boosts the performance of the prover?

The rest of the paper briefly introduces the natural language theorem prover (Section 2), describes the new learning algorithm motivated by abduction (Section 3), outlines settings of experiments (Section 4), reports and analyzes results of the experiments (Section 5 and Section 6), overviews related work and compares it with the current one (Section 7), and finally, concludes the paper by answering the research questions (Section 8).

2 Natural Language Theorem Prover

For our experiments, we employ a natural language theorem prover, called LangPro (Abzianidze, 2017a), which is an implementation of Natural Tableau—an analytic tableau system for natural logic (Muskens, 2010; Abzianidze, 2017b). An inference procedure is more central to Natural Tableau and its prover than it is usually for other logic-based NLI systems (Bos and Markert, 2005; Mineshima et al., 2015), which first derives meaning representations and then uses a proof engine for inference. The inference in Natural Tableau not only helps to prove semantic relations but also further expands semantics of logical forms (e.g., shifting from higher to lower-order terms). This makes it difficult to separate inference and semantic representations in Natural Tableau. Its central role of inference makes LangPro a suitable candidate for the data-driven learning experiment based on automated theorem proving.

The logic behind Natural Tableau and the prover is a *higher-order logic* (aka *simple type theory*) which also acts as a version of *natural logic* (van Benthem, 2008; Moss, 2010). The λ-terms, given below with their corresponding sentences, represent logical forms of the natural logic.

A hedgehog is cradled by a boy $\qquad$ (1)

a hedgehog $\left(\mathbf{be}\left(\lambda x.\,\mathbf{a\ boy}\left(\lambda y.\,\mathbf{by}\ y\,\mathbf{cradle}\ x\right)\right)\right)$ (1a)

A person holds an animal $\qquad$ (2)

a person $\left(\lambda x.\,\mathbf{an\ animal}\left(\lambda y.\,\mathbf{hold}\ y\ x\right)\right)$ (2a)

Most dogs which jumped also barked loud (3)

most $\left(\mathbf{which\ jump\ dog}\right)\left(\mathbf{also}\left(\mathbf{loud\ bark}\right)\right)$ (3a)

In addition to the lexical terms, the terms employ only variables and constants. Therefore, common logical connectives (e.g., $\wedge$, $\neg$) and quantifiers (e.g., $\exists$, $\forall$) are not part of the formal language. The terms are built using the λ abstraction and function application.[1] The role of variables and λ is to access and fill certain argument positions and control scope. Variables and λ are mainly used for terms with arity two or more, like **cradle** and **hold**. Abzianidze (2015) showed that the terms can be automatically obtained from the derivations of Combinatory Cat-

---

[1] In formal semantics literature, the function application is often denoted as @, but for better readability, we omit it. The function application is left-associative, e.g., $ABC = (AB)C$. To keep the terms leaner, we hide typing information of lexical terms, like **which** being of type $\left((\mathbf{np}\rightarrow\mathbf{s})\rightarrow\mathbf{n}\right)\rightarrow\mathbf{n}$.

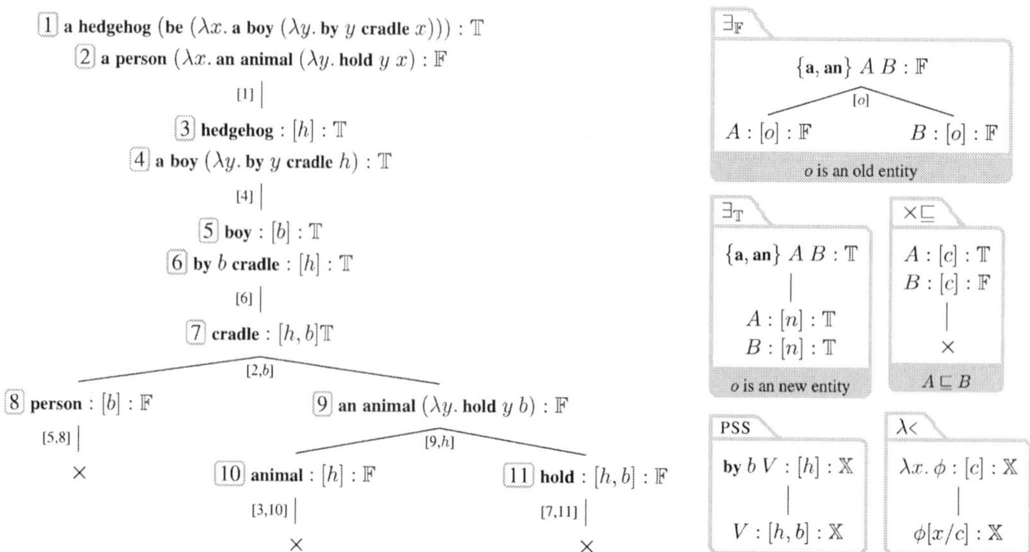

Figure 2: On the left, a closed tableau which proves the entailment relation by failing to refute it. On the right, a set of inference rules that help to unfold semantics of larger terms.

egorial Grammar (CCG, Steedman, 2000). Since the workflow for the theorem proving is important to understand the proposed learning algorithm, we demonstrate on the example how inference problems are solved by the prover.

After the sentences of an NLI problem are parsed with a parser and converted into λ-terms, the *natural tableau prover* verifies the problem on entailment and contradiction relations. For example, to prove that (1) entails (2), the tableau prover searches for a situation that makes (1a) true and (2a) false. In other words, it attempts to build a counterexample model that refutes the entailment relation. In Figure 2, the proof tree, so-called tableau, depicts the search for the counterexample.

The tableau starts with (1a) being true and (2a) false, expressed by the entries 1 and 2. But what are the meanings of 1 and 2? To flesh out their meanings, inference rules are applied to the entries. In particular, 1 produces 3 and 4 with the help of the rule ($\exists_\mathbb{T}$), which says: if *an A does B* is true, then *there is some entity, let's name it n, which is A and does B*.[2] Further applying ($\exists_\mathbb{T}$) to 4 introduces 5 and 6. 7 is obtained from 6 with the help of (PSS), which paraphrases passive constructions with any truth sign ($\mathbb{X}$) as active constructions. So far, the prover managed to fold out semantics of 1: there are b and h who are a boy 5 and a hedgehog

3, respectively, and b cradles h 7.

Now it is a proper time to note that a branch in a proof tree represents a set of situations/models, and entries sitting on the branch describe corresponding situations. Therefore, for now, a single set of situations is built such that in all the situations a boy cradles a hedgehog, and 2 is false. To decompose the meaning of 2, ($\exists_\mathbb{F}$) is applied to it. This splits the set of situations into two parts, the situations where b is not a person and the situations where 9 holds.[3] The situations of the left branch don't make sense as ($\times\sqsubseteq$) detects that in those situations b is a boy 5 but not a person 8. The situations of the right branch are further categorized when applying ($\exists_\mathbb{F}$) to 9. As a result, both groups of situations are inconsistent as in one group h is a hedgehog but not an animal, and in another group, *cradle* relation is not *hold* relation. In the end, all the branches are closed, i.e., the tableau is closed, as they model inconsistent situations. This means that the refutation attempt has failed, and there is no counterexample for the entailment relation. Hence, it is proved that (1a) entails (2a), and accordingly (1) entails (2).

In principle, it is also necessary to verify the NLI problem for contradiction. In that case, the tableau proof starts with 1 and 2 being true. If neither entailment nor contradiction is proved, the problem is classified as neutral.

---

[2]Obtaining 4 from 1 additionally requires application of ($\lambda_<$) and the rule for auxiliaries that will treat **be** as an identity function and discard it.

[3]In the latter set of situations b is also a person. This is not explicitly asserted in the tableau because it is redundant due to the completeness of the set of first-order logic tableau rules.

3 Learning as Abduction

3.1 What to learn?

The tableau proof in Figure 2 illustrated how inference over sentences is reduced to the semantic relations over lexical items. Namely, to prove that (1) entails (2), the prover needs to know: **boy** $\sqsubseteq$ **person**, **hedgehog** $\sqsubseteq$ **animal**, and **cradle** $\sqsubseteq$ **hold**. One could employ existing (lexical) knowledge resources as a reply to the need for lexical relations, but it is well known that such resources are never enough. Compared to NLI systems with learning algorithms, logic-based NLI systems are much more vulnerable when it comes to the knowledge sparsity because a small, missing piece of knowledge can corrupt the entire reasoning process and the judgment.

While knowledge resources are still valuable for reasoning, learning from data is a crucial component of success when it comes to evaluation against large datasets. In the tableau prover, two components directly contribute to the proof procedure: an inventory of rules (IR) and a set of relations (aka facts), called knowledge base (KB). In principle, the distinction between inference rules and relations is not straightforward. That's why we hereafter adopt the distinction between the inference rules and the facts of the KB as it is done in the tableau prover. Some approaches might consider **boy** $\sqsubseteq$ **person** relation as an inference rule like $\forall x.\mathbf{boy}(x) \to \mathbf{person}(x)$, but following Natural Tableau, hereafter they will be considered as facts of KB. In general, a rule is schematic and can rewrite entries that match its antecedent entries (and even allow branching that acts as disjunction, see Figure 2). On the other hand, relations in KB are fully lexicalized and have the form of $A \sqsubseteq B$ or $A \,|\, B$, where A and B are atomic or compound terms. In this way, apart from **clean** $|$ **dirty** and **chop** $\sqsubseteq$ **cut**, the relations like **webcam** $\sqsubseteq$ **digital camera** and **lie down** $|$ **run away** are also considered as facts despite corresponding to relations over short phrases.

Both IR and KB would benefit from data-driven learning. Learning new rules can be as important as learning new relations. However, as an initial step, we find learning relations more feasible and effective than learning rules for two reasons: (a) relations are fully-specified unlike the rules, and (b) given that relations include phrases too, learning relations could compensate rules to a large extent. Moreover, results from the relation learning can provide further insight into learning rules. For instance, many relations with the terms of similar structure can provide evidence for creating a rule.

3.2 Abductive Reasoning and Learning

After deciding to learn relations for KB, the next step is to design a learning algorithm that takes a set of labeled NLI problems and produces a set of relations that boost the performance of the prover. From a perspective of the tableau method, such relations should help to close corresponding tableau trees for the problems with entailment and contradiction labels. Put differently, we search for relations explaining gold labels of NLI problems.

We formally define tableau-based abductive reasoning for NLI as a search problem: given a labeled NLI problem $\mathcal{L}(P, H)$ and an optional KB denoted as K, find an explanation set of relations E such that $\mathcal{L}(K \wedge E \wedge P, H)$ is provable. Additionally, E has to satisfy at least the following conditions:

A1 E is consistent with K;

A2 E is minimal in the sense that $E \subseteq E'$ if $\mathcal{L}(K \wedge E' \wedge P, H)$ is provable;

A3 Relations in E have some restricted form.

These conditions serve as minimal criteria for the concept of *best* when assessing the explanations (Mayer and Pirri, 1993).

To illustrate abductive reasoning, let's consider an altered version of the example from Section 2 where *person* and *animal* are modified. The alternation is such that it prevents the prover from finding a proof for the entailment relation. The corresponding open tableau is given in Figure 3. The tableau is saturated, meaning that all possible rule applications were made while growing the tree. Given that entailment is the gold label for the NLI problem, we need additional relations to close all the branches since **hedgehog** $\sqsubseteq$ **animal**, **boy** $\sqsubseteq$ **person**, and **cradle** $\sqsubseteq$ **hold** are not sufficient anymore.

The search for a set of relations that closes all open branches can be seen as searching for antecedent nodes of the closure rules, e.g., $(\times \sqsubseteq)$ and $(\times \,|\,)$, and learning the constraint relations of the rules, e.g., $A \sqsubseteq B$ and $A \,|\, B$, respectively. Learning the relations enabling certain nodes to close a branch represents backwards application of closure rules. This way of extracting relations suits well to LangPro as it is implemented in Prolog, which can be run forwards and backwards. While for rule application, a set of relations `Rels` is specified in `cl_rule/3` (see Figure 3), during abductive learning `Rels` is initially unspecified and later specified

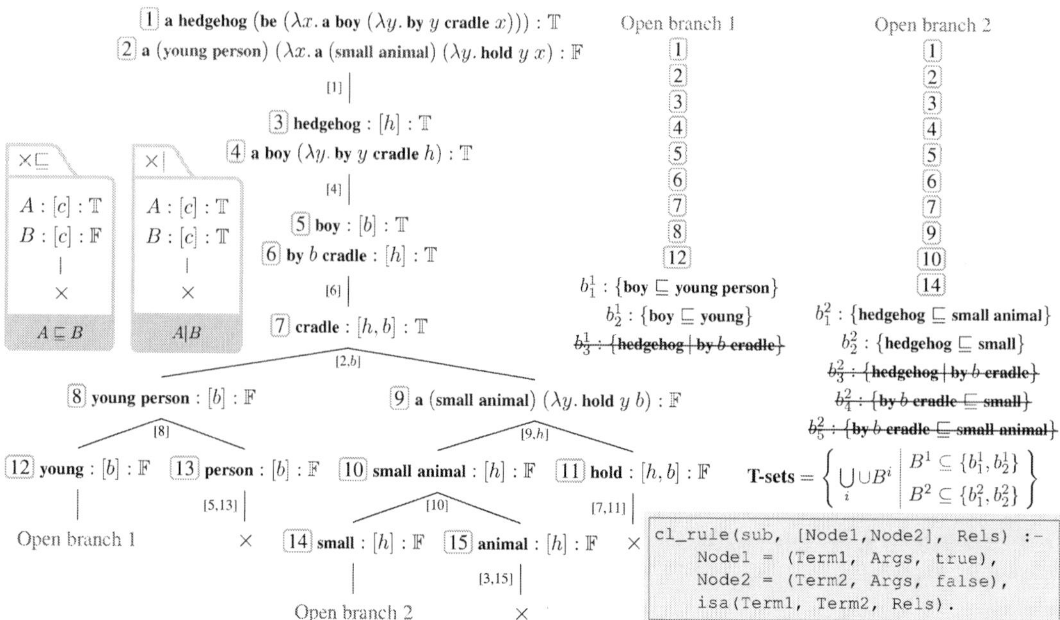

Figure 3: An open tableau represents a failed attempt to prove the entailment. Each open branch can be closed by three B-sets using ($\times\sqsubseteq$) and ($\times|$) rules. B-sets for kth open branch are generated by uniting basis sets $b_{i\ldots j}^{k}$ of the branch. Basis sets are obtained by applying closure rules backwards. A union of B-sets of all open branches forms a T-set which is sufficient knowledge to close the tableau and solve the NLI problem.

by `isa/3`. For example, when $\text{Node1} = \boxed{3}$ and $\text{Node2} = \boxed{10}$, `cl_rule/3` fails if `Rels` is specified and doesn't contain **hedgehog** $\sqsubseteq$ **small animal**, but if `Rels` is unspecified, `cl_rule/3` succeeds and `Rels` becomes a list containing **hedgehog** $\sqsubseteq$ **small animal**.

In the running example (Figure 3), when considering only two closure rules ($\times\sqsubseteq$) and ($\times|$), there are several sets of relations that close an open branch. Let's call such a set of relations a **B-set**. So, a B-set is specific to an open branch and closes it. For example, a union of any non-empty subset of $\{b_1^1, b_2^1\}$ is a B-set for the first open branch. The sets b_1^1 and b_2^1 are a **basis** of the B-sets of the first open branch, i.e., minimal sets that generate all B-sets of the branch. The same applies to b_1^2 and b_2^2 for the second open branch. Note that basis sets are automatically B-sets. b_3^1 and $b_{3,4,5}^2$ sets are not B-sets as some of the terms in the relations are not fully lexicalized. Let's call a set of relations a **T-set** if they help to close an entire tableau, i.e., close all open branches. Therefore T-sets are potential explanations for the NLI problem. For instance, $\{\textbf{boy} \sqsubseteq \textbf{young}, \textbf{hedgehog} \sqsubseteq \textbf{small}\}$ is one of the nine T-sets for the tableau. The largest T-set is a union of all the basis B-sets. To learn the *best* T-set from the possible options, the next section presents criteria used to define the notion of *the best*.

3.3 Searching for *the best*

The tableau proof presented in Section 2 is a toy example compared to the actual proof tree produced by the theorem prover which consists of 53 entries distributed over 8 branches.[4] This means that during the abduction, there will be more branches and more nodes per branch than in Figure 2. Also, taking into account all 16 closure rules of the prover, this amounts to a large number of B-sets and T-sets. A set of all T-sets will serve as a search space for explanations in abductive reasoning. To make the reasoning efficient, we filter out certain T-sets following (A1-A3) conditions.

First, according to (A3), we decrease the number of possible T-sets by allowing only relations with **term shapes** of $A, AB, (AB)C, A(BC)$, where each meta-variable is a lexical term. In this way, T-sets with relations over terms of size four, like (**and big brown**) **dog**, will be ignored.

To further narrow down types of learned relations along the lines of (A3), we consider relations over **syntactically comparable terms**, where possible categories for open class words are noun,

---

[4]The reason for the increase is that not all rule applications are relevant for the final proof, but this is impossible to anticipate beforehand.

verb or adjective/adverb.[5] This means that relations like **boy** | **run** and **boy** $\sqsubseteq$ **young** will be ignored while keeping relations like **boy** | **hedgehog** and **boy** $\sqsubseteq$ **young person**. We opt for this restriction because in-category semantic relations tend to be more genuine than cross-category relations. So, we expect learned in-category relations to generalize better in different contexts.

One of the criteria for the best explanation is minimality (A2). We interpret this as an ***amount of information*** and prefer minimal T-sets in terms of set inclusion to larger ones. Therefore, the amount of information induces a partial ordering over T-sets. Candidates for minimal T-sets can be formed by uniting minimal B-sets per open branch, where basis sets, e.g., b_i^j, are minimal B-sets. For example, minimal T-sets for the tableau in Figure 3 are $b_1^1 \cup b_1^2$, $b_1^1 \cup b_2^2$, $b_2^1 \cup b_1^2$, and $b_2^1 \cup b_2^2$. The intuition behind the information criterion is to learn as few relations as possible sufficient for proving an NLI problem and, hopefully, to prevent overfitting during the training.

Following (A1), a relation has to be ***semantically consistent with existing KB***. In this way, relations like **hedgehog** | **animal** or **big** $\sqsubseteq$ **small** will be dubbed inconsistent with KB which includes **hedgehog** $\sqsubseteq$ **animal** and **big** | **small**. In experiments, instead of doing a complete consistency checking of the entire KB every time a new relation is considered, we perform a lazy check by verifying whether $A \mid B$ and one of $A \sqsubseteq B$ and $B \sqsubseteq A$ together occur in KB. We go further and ignore relations of form $B \mid AB$ taking into account that subsective lexical modifiers are prevalent. Hence, relations like **small animal** | **animal** will be dropped.

Additionally, we consider only such T-sets that are ***semantically consistent with sentences*** of the corresponding NLI problem. This can be seen as further elaboration on (A2) since the sentences are usually consistent with background knowledge. The example of a bad T-set, inconsistent with the sentence, is the one containing **baby** | **panda** when one of the sentences of the NLI problem asserts the existence of a baby panda: *Two baby pandas are playing* (SK-5435).[6] Both filters concerning semantic consistency with KB or sentences are used to weed out pseudo-knowledge.

Another adopted criterion for the best T-sets is an ***impact on accuracy*** on the training data, which is calculated as a difference between the number of solved and unsolved problems in the training data when a T-set is adopted. T-sets with no positive impact on accuracy will be ignored as it doesn't contribute to the performance. This criterion can be broadly related to (A1), where a T-set is supposed to conform to the gold labels. For example, if a T-set {**boy** $\sqsubseteq$ **young**, **hedgehog** $\sqsubseteq$ **small**} helps to solve two new problems but unsolves at least two previously solved ones, then it won't be learned. For the same NLI problem, a T-set with the highest impact will be preferred over others. The motivation behind this criterion is to favor the relations that boost accuracy on the training data.

Despite introduced filters and comparison orders for T-sets, some problems can still have more than one best T-sets. In such cases, we take into account the ***number of terms*** in T-sets (by counting occurrences of atomic terms). At the end we opt for the T-set with the smallest number of terms. This decision somewhat complies with (A2).

4 Experiments

We design experiments to evaluate learning as abduction for NLI. First, we implement the abductive learning for LangPro (Abzianidze, 2017a). The implementation takes advantage of Prolog's virtue of satisfying goals in the forward and backward fashion and uses it to apply closure rules in backwards during the search for B-sets. This leaves the inventory of tableau rules intact.[7] The workflow of the abductive learning is depicted in Figure 4.

Searching for the best T-set is an NP-hard problem.[8] To make the implementation efficient (Q1), we significantly reduce a space of T-sets by considering only those T-sets that coincide with B-sets. In other words, we require existence of the shared B-sets across all open branches. The example in Figure 3 doesn't have such T-set as different B-sets close the open branches. If a tableau has a single open branch, its B-sets are automatically T-sets.

To test the learning algorithm, we use the SICK dataset (Marelli et al., 2014b) for three reasons. First, compositional lexical knowledge involved in the dataset is suitable for the abductive learning. Second, it is large enough (up to 10K problems) to support learning from a training part and eval-

---

[5]For each term, a head and a syntactic category can be detected using POS tags and CCG categories, which are assigned by a CCG parser and kept in the term representation.

[6]The sentences or problems drawn from the SICK dataset (Marelli et al., 2014b) are supplemented with the problem IDs.

[7]The code is available at `https://github.com/kovvalsky/LangPro`

[8]The NP-complete set cover problem can be reduced to it.

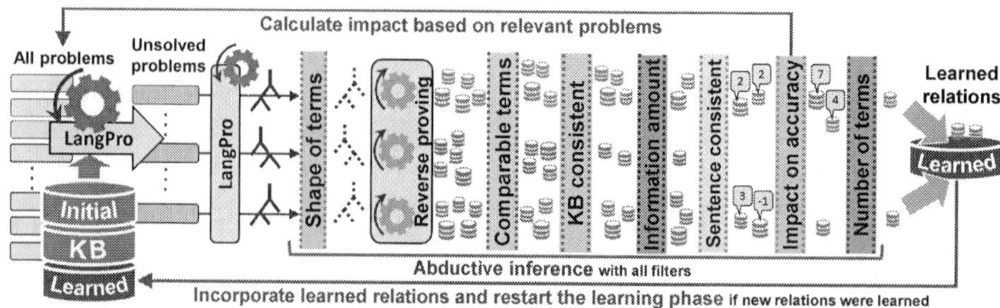

Figure 4: Learning starts with an initial KB. Abduction is carried out on unsolved entailment and contradiction problems. Inferred knowledge, i.e., T-sets, pass several filters to select the *best* knowledge. The learned knowledge is added to the initial KB, and the learning phase repeats until no new knowledge is learned.

uation on an unseen part. Third, SICK has been used for evaluating logic-based NLI systems, including LangPro, and this allows comparison to the existing results. Our data partition follows the SemEval-14 task-1 (Marelli et al., 2014a): SICK-train&trial (4500 + 500 problems) is a training data and SICK-test (4927 problems) a hidden test data. The error analysis is conducted only on the training data. To choose optimal learning parameters (see Subsection 3.3) and measure impact of the filters and knowledge resources, we run the learning algorithm with stratified three-fold cross-validation (CV) on the training data. The stratified version is due to a skewed distribution of gold labels in SICK. We opt for three-fold CV as it better reflects 1:1 ratio between SICK-train&trial and -test sizes.

Logic-based NLI systems using logical forms from syntactic trees often employ output of several parsers to increase the quality of logical forms (Abzianidze, 2015; Beltagy et al., 2016; Martínez-Gómez et al., 2017; Yanaka et al., 2018). In our CV experiments, we use the re-banked C&C CCG parser (Clark and Curran, 2007; Honnibal et al., 2010). The ensemble of parsers, used for evaluation on SICK-test, additionally includes Easy-CCG (Lewis and Steedman, 2014) and DepCCG (Yoshikawa et al., 2017) with standard models.

5 Results

Initially we run LangPro with WordNet (Miller, 1995) relations and all filters enabled (see Subsection 3.3). The results in Table 1 lead to several findings. The abductive learning does help to improve accuracy. LangPro without abduction (with 800 rule applications) gets 81.7% accuracy on SICK-train&test while with abduction it obtains 82.9% on average over unseen parts of CV on SICK-train&test. Differences between average accuracies on training and test parts show that overfit-

ting during training is moderate. When the prover is limited to 50 rule app., accuracy drops only to 82.64%. However, the entire CV takes almost 10 times less CPU time for 50 rule app. compared to 800. These results answer (Q1) by rendering the abductive learning as a computationally feasible learning method.

We conduct ablation experiments to verify the contributions of the filters. Table 1 shows that filters concerning semantic consistency and syntactic comparability together have little impact on accuracy (.32%), but they contribute to efficiency by halving CPU time. This means that other filters like impact on accuracy and term size greatly contribute to preventing pseudo-knowledge. When relations in T-sets are restricted to atomic terms (i.e., terms of length 1), accuracy is almost unchanged (-0.16%) while efficiency slightly increases. The increase in efficiency is clear as fewer T-sets will be considered during learning. Little change in accuracy means that mostly relations over atomic terms generalize well over the unseen part.

We also tested whether the learned relations can compensate for the WordNet relations (Q3). The results show that WordNet relations still contribute to high accuracy as their exclusion drops accuracy by 2.44%. Abzianidze (2015) uses hand-crafted KB of ~30 lexical relations collected from SICK-train&trial. When this KB is add, only six more problems on average (0.36%) is classified correctly.

To answer (Q4), we compare LangPro with and without abduction on unseen SICK-test. The results in Table 3 show that the abductive learning consistently increases accuracy regardless of the used CCG parser. This also means that the abductive learning generalizes across CCG parsers. When predictions of three LangPro versions with C&C, EasyCCG and DepCCG parsers are aggregated, accuracy gain from abduction still remains (+1.36%,

LangPro + Abductive learning:	Train	Test	CPU
All filters + WordNet	av. acc%	av. acc%	time
max 800 rule applications	89.02	82.90	2041
max 50 rule applications	88.57	82.64	220
Ablation with max 50 rule app.	Δ	Δ	Δ
− CT, CwS, CwKB	+1.39	-0.32	+115%
− terms of length 2 & 3	-2.68	-0.16	-17%
− WN rels: ant,hyp,der,sim	-0.98	-2.44	-11%
+ Hand-crafted ✍ KB	+0.04	+0.36	+1%

Table 1: Results of the CV on SICK-train&trial (majority baseline = 56.4%). Ablation experiments disable filters for comparable terms (CT) and consistencies with sentences (CwS) and KB (CwKB). CPU time (for 2.5 GHz) is measured in minutes for the entire CV.

Correct (26.6%)	Wrong (28.8%)
add X *to* Y | **remove** X *from* Y	*the* **blonde** *girl* | *a* **little** *girl*
a X **lie down** | *a* X **run around**	**aim** *a gun* $\sqsubseteq$ **draw** *a gun*
perform **acrobatics** $\sqsubseteq$ *perform a* **trick**	**ride** *in* X | **get** *out of* X

Reversed (28.9%)	Contextual (15.7%)
have *lunch* $\sqsubseteq$ **eat**	*hang on a* **cord** $\sqsubseteq$ *hang on a* **rope**
look *at* X $\sqsubseteq$ **stare** *at* X	*man in a* **cap** $\sqsubseteq$ *man in a* **hat**
prepare some **food** $\sqsubseteq$ *prepare a* **meal**	**in** *the dark* $\sqsubseteq$ **at** *night*

Table 2: Examples of learned lexical relations. The terms of the relations are in boldface while padded gray contexts come from the source SICK problems. The relations are manually assessed by the author outside context of SICK problems.

drilling a hole in a piece of wood.

7 Related Work & Comparison

The closest work to ours, to the best of our knowledge, represents Yanaka et al. (2018). They use abduction for a logic-based NLI system to automatically acquire phrase correspondences from labeled NLI problems. Their method, called P2P, converts logical formulas into graphs and carries out subgraph matching with variable unification. Our work differs from theirs in four aspects: (i) employed formal logics and proof procedures essentially differ from each other.[9] (ii) Converting formulas into graphs and matching subgraphs is external to their theorem proving while in our approach the abductive learning is the theorem proving run backwards. (iii) P2P abstracts from term comparability constraint and learns relations across word classes. It also reduces lexical relations to smaller axioms.[10] In total P2P extracts 9445 axioms from SICK-train&trial compared to 312 relations by our abductive learning. (iv) P2P scarifies a substantial amount of precision (12.9%) to gain 1.2% of accuracy while our abductive learning achieves more gain in accuracy with much less drop in precision.

There have been several logic-based NLI systems evaluated on SICK. We believe Table 3 lists all (but not only) of those systems along with their scores. The research line by Mineshima et al. (2015); Martínez-Gómez et al. (2017); Yanaka et al. (2018) was already described while compar-

additional 67 problems solved). It is worth noting that while abduction increases the overall accuracy, almost perfect precision (>97.6%) of LangPro decreases only to 94.3%. We argue that this is an important virtue of the abductive learning from a logic perspective since logic-based NLI systems are expected to have highly reliable proofs.

6 Error Analysis

In total 312 relations were learned with abduction from SICK-train&trial based on a single parser. Table 2 lists some of the learned relations. We classify relations into four groups based on whether they are mostly *correct, wrong, reversed* version of a correct relation, and highly *context-dependent*.

Despite having a sequence of filters, substantial pseudo-knowledge (29%) still leaked during the learning. One of the main reasons for this is a strong learning bias towards minimal explanations which often leads to ignoring context. This way, from SK-9624 *...is looking toward the stars...* entailing *...is looking toward the sky...*, star $\sqsubseteq$ sky relation was wrongly learned. Additionally, learning **in the dark** $\sqsubseteq$ **at night** is preferred to currently learned **in** $\sqsubseteq$ **at**. This is a common drawback of pure logic-based approaches which is induced by a general principle, called a *rule of replacement*, which licenses replacement of equivalent terms.

A number of incorrect learned relations are conditioned by noisy gold labels of SICK (Kalouli et al., 2017). **dog** $\sqsubseteq$ **bull dog** was learned due to SK-2608, *A monkey is brushing the dog* contradicting *The monkey is not brushing a bull dog*; **person** $\sqsubseteq$ **man** is due to SK-4680, *Someone is drilling a hole in a strip of wood with a power drill* entailing *A man is*

---

[9] Yanaka et al. (2018) employs higher-order logic most fragment of which is first-order while most of the logical forms used by Natural Tableau are higher-order. Their system is based on natural deduction while ours on semantic tableau.

[10] For example, P2P captures *cut* entails *chop down* by learning $\forall x(\text{cut}(x) \rightarrow \text{chop}(x))$ and $\forall x(\text{cut}(x) \rightarrow \text{down}(x))$.

System	Parsers	Learn	MLc	KB&Res.	P%	R%	A%
➥LangPro	C	–	–	WN	97.8	58.0	81.3
➥LangPro	C	Abd	–	WN	94.9	63.4	82.7
➥LangPro	E	–	–	WN	97.7	57.7	81.1
➥LangPro	E	Abd	–	WN	94.9	63.0	82.5
➥LangPro	D	–	–	WN	97.8	59.2	81.8
➥LangPro	D	Abd	–	WN	94.8	64.3	83.0
➥LangPro	CDE	–	–	WN	97.6	62.2	83.0
➥**LangPro**	CDE	Abd	–	WN	94.3	**67.9**	**84.4**
LangPro 2015	CE	–	–	WN,⊿KB	**98.0**	58.1	81.4
MG et al. 2017	CE	W2W	–	WN,VO	**97.1**	63.6	83.1
Yanaka et al.	CDE	W2W,P2P–	–	WN,VO	84.2	**77.3**	**84.3**
★Bjerva et al.	C	–	SVM	WN,PP	93.6	60.6	**81.6**
Pavlick et al.	C	–	–	WN,PP$^+$			78.4
★Beltagy et al.	C	–	SVM	WN	97.9	38.7	73.2
Beltagy and Erk	C	–	SVM	WN			76.5
Beltagy et al.	CE	Rob.Res.	SVM	WN,PP,Dist,⊿Rules			**85.1**
Hu et al. (2020)	CE	–	–	WN	83.8	70.7	77.2
+ BERT (Devlin et al., 2019)							**85.4**
★Lai and Hockenmaier (winner of the SemEval task)							**84.6**
Yin and Schütze DL with GRU & Attentive Pooling							**87.1**

Table 3: Comparison of LangPro$_{800}$+Abduction and other logic-based systems on SICK-test. Some results are not directly comparable as the systems use different KB, resources, CCG parsers, or even employ a machine learning classifier (MLc). Systems are grouped based on their characteristic approaches to NLI. The last two systems are not based on logic. A list of abbreviations: current work (➥), SemEval-14 task-1 participants (★), C&C parser (C), EasyCCG (E), DepCCG (D), PPDB (PP, Ganitkevitch et al., 2013), and VerbOcean (VO, Chklovski and Pantel, 2004).

ing their approach to ours. The work by Bjerva et al. (2014); Pavlick et al. (2015) employ Boxer (Bos, 2008) to obtain first-order logic formulas from sentences and use an SVM classifier on top of Nutcracker (Bos and Markert, 2005), which reasons using off-the-shelf theorem prover and model builder. Beltagy et al. (2014, 2016) also uses Boxer to get first-order logic formulas but employs probabilistic logic inference in Markov Logic Networks. To hit the high score on SICK, they combine multiple components including distributional semantics, a set of hand-crafted rules, resolution-based on-fly generation of inference rules, and an SVM classifier as the final predictor. Hu et al. (2019) use a lightweight system, called MonaLog, based on monotonicity reasoning. It is further combined with BERT (Devlin et al., 2019) to reclassify problems that were predicted by MonaLog as neutral.

Abductive reasoning was already employed by Raina et al. (2005) at the first Recognizing Textual Entailment challenge (Dagan et al., 2005). They used resolution method and a learned cost model to select the cheapest set of assumptions supporting the entailment. Hobbs et al. (1993) uses weighted abduction to model text interpretation as the minimal explanation of why text would be true. The title of the current paper is inspired by this work.

8 Conclusion

Table 3 shows that the abductive learning component is crucial for logic-based reasoning systems to achieve competitive results. We have implemented and showed that learning as abduction works successfully for tableau theorem prover the theorem prover to learn lexical relations from data. Our findings answer the predefined research question as follows. (Q1) Implementing abduction as backwards theorem proving represents a computationally feasible approach for data-driven learning. This was achieved by reducing the explanation space: considering only those T-sets that are shared by all open branches and applying several filters to them. (Q2) Pseudo-knowledge is partially prevented with a sequence of filters and comparison criteria. Abductive bias towards minimality often leads to relations that require additional context. Overall, pseudo-knowledge doesn't harm high precision of the theorem proving. (Q3) Despite knowledge learned from data, the lexical relations extracted from WordNet are crucial to reach the state-of-the-art results. (Q4) Abductive learning consistently increases the accuracy score of the prover regardless of using different parsers individually or in ensemble.

For future work it is interesting to explore the ways that consider larger explanation space and are not strictly preferring short phrases to longer ones. The latter will allow relations with more context.

Acknowledgments

I would like to thank three anonymous reviewers for their valuable comments and the CIT of the University of Groningen for providing access to the Peregrine HPC cluster. This work was supported by the NWO-VICI grant (288-89-003) while I was at the University of Groningen and by the European Research Council (ERC) under the European Unions Horizon 2020 research and innovation programme (grant agreement No. 742204) since I joined Utrecht University.

References

Lasha Abzianidze. 2015. A tableau prover for natural logic and language. In *Proceedings of the 2015 Conference on Empirical Methods in Natural Language Processing*, pages 2492–2502, Lisbon, Portugal. Association for Computational Linguistics.

Lasha Abzianidze. 2017a. LangPro: Natural language theorem prover. In *Proceedings of the 2017 Conference on Empirical Methods in Natural Language Processing: System Demonstrations*, pages 115–120, Copenhagen, Denmark. Association for Computational Linguistics.

Lasha Abzianidze. 2017b. *A natural proof system for natural language*. Ph.D. thesis, Tilburg University.

I. Beltagy, Stephen Roller, Pengxiang Cheng, Katrin Erk, and Raymond J. Mooney. 2016. Representing meaning with a combination of logical and distributional models. *Computational Linguistics*, 42(4):763–808.

Islam Beltagy and Katrin Erk. 2015. On the proper treatment of quantifiers in probabilistic logic semantics. In *Proceedings of the 11th International Conference on Computational Semantics*, pages 140–150, London, UK. Association for Computational Linguistics.

Islam Beltagy, Stephen Roller, Gemma Boleda, Katrin Erk, and Raymond Mooney. 2014. UTexas: Natural language semantics using distributional semantics and probabilistic logic. In *Proceedings of the 8th International Workshop on Semantic Evaluation (SemEval 2014)*, pages 796–801, Dublin, Ireland. Association for Computational Linguistics.

Johan van Benthem. 2008. A brief history of natural logic. In *Technical Report PP-2008-05*. Institute for Logic, Language & Computation.

Johannes Bjerva, Johan Bos, Rob van der Goot, and Malvina Nissim. 2014. The meaning factory: Formal semantics for recognizing textual entailment and determining semantic similarity. In *Proceedings of the 8th International Workshop on Semantic Evaluation (SemEval 2014)*, pages 642–646, Dublin, Ireland. Association for Computational Linguistics.

Johan Bos. 2008. Wide-coverage semantic analysis with boxer. In *Semantics in Text Processing. STEP 2008 Conference Proceedings*, Research in Computational Semantics, pages 277–286. College Publications.

Johan Bos and Katja Markert. 2005. Recognising textual entailment with logical inference. In *Proceedings of the 2005 Conference on Empirical Methods in Natural Language Processing (EMNLP 2005)*, pages 628–635.

Timothy Chklovski and Patrick Pantel. 2004. VerbOcean: Mining the web for fine-grained semantic verb relations. In *Proceedings of the 2004 Conference on Empirical Methods in Natural Language Processing*, pages 33–40, Barcelona, Spain. Association for Computational Linguistics.

Stephen Clark and James R. Curran. 2007. Wide-coverage efficient statistical parsing with CCG and log-linear models. *Computational Linguistics*, 33(4):493–552.

Robin Cooper, Dick Crouch, Jan Van Eijck, Chris Fox, Josef Van Genabith, Jan Jaspars, Hans Kamp, David Milward, Manfred Pinkal, Massimo Poesio, Steve Pulman, Ted Briscoe, Holger Maier, and Karsten Konrad. 1996. *FraCaS: A Framework for Computational Semantics*. Deliverable D16.

Ido Dagan, Oren Glickman, and Bernardo Magnini. 2005. The pascal recognising textual entailment challenge. In *Proceedings of the PASCAL Challenges Workshop on Recognising Textual Entailment*.

Ido Dagan, Dan Roth, Mark Sammons, and Fabio Massimo Zanzotto. 2013. *Recognizing Textual Entailment: Models and Applications*. Synthesis Lectures on Human Language Technologies. Morgan & Claypool Publishers.

Jacob Devlin, Ming-Wei Chang, Kenton Lee, and Kristina Toutanova. 2019. BERT: Pre-training of deep bidirectional transformers for language understanding. In *Proceedings of the 2019 Conference of the North American Chapter of the Association for Computational Linguistics: Human Language Technologies, Volume 1 (Long and Short Papers)*, pages 4171–4186, Minneapolis, Minnesota. Association for Computational Linguistics.

Juri Ganitkevitch, Benjamin Van Durme, and Chris Callison-Burch. 2013. PPDB: The paraphrase database. In *Proceedings of NAACL-HLT*, pages 758–764, Atlanta, Georgia. Association for Computational Linguistics.

Max Glockner, Vered Shwartz, and Yoav Goldberg. 2018. Breaking NLI systems with sentences that require simple lexical inferences. In *Proceedings of the 56th Annual Meeting of the Association for Computational Linguistics (Volume 2: Short Papers)*, pages 650–655, Melbourne, Australia. Association for Computational Linguistics.

Suchin Gururangan, Swabha Swayamdipta, Omer Levy, Roy Schwartz, Samuel Bowman, and Noah A. Smith. 2018. Annotation artifacts in natural language inference data. In *Proceedings of the 2018 Conference of the North American Chapter of the Association for Computational Linguistics: Human Language Technologies, Volume 2 (Short Papers)*, pages 107–112, New Orleans, Louisiana. Association for Computational Linguistics.

Jerry R. Hobbs, Mark Stickel, and Paul Martin. 1993. Interpretation as abduction. *Artificial Intelligence*, 63:69–142.

Matthew Honnibal, James R. Curran, and Johan Bos. 2010. Rebanking CCGbank for improved NP interpretation. In *Proceedings of the 48th Annual Meeting of the Association for Computational Linguistics*, pages 207–215, Uppsala, Sweden. Association for Computational Linguistics.

Hai Hu, Qi Chen, and Larry Moss. 2019. Natural language inference with monotonicity. In *Proceedings of the 13th International Conference on Computational Semantics - Short Papers*, pages 8–15, Gothenburg, Sweden. Association for Computational Linguistics.

Hai Hu, Qi Chen, Kyle Richardson, Atreyee Mukherjee, Lawrence S Moss, and Sandra Kübler. 2020. Monalog: a lightweight system for natural language inference based on monotonicity. *Proceedings of the Society for Computation in Linguistics*, 3(1):319–329.

Aikaterini-Lida Kalouli, Valeria de Paiva, and Livy Real. 2017. Correcting contradictions. In *Proceedings of the Computing Natural Language Inference Workshop*.

Alice Lai and Julia Hockenmaier. 2014. Illinois-LH: A denotational and distributional approach to semantics. In *Proceedings of the 8th International Workshop on Semantic Evaluation (SemEval 2014)*, pages 329–334, Dublin, Ireland. Association for Computational Linguistics.

Mike Lewis and Mark Steedman. 2014. A* CCG parsing with a supertag-factored model. In *Proceedings of the 2014 Conference on Empirical Methods in Natural Language Processing (EMNLP)*, pages 990–1000, Doha, Qatar. Association for Computational Linguistics.

Marco Marelli, Luisa Bentivogli, Marco Baroni, Raffaella Bernardi, Stefano Menini, and Roberto Zamparelli. 2014a. SemEval-2014 task 1: Evaluation of compositional distributional semantic models on full sentences through semantic relatedness and textual entailment. In *Proceedings of the 8th International Workshop on Semantic Evaluation (SemEval 2014)*, pages 1–8, Dublin, Ireland. Association for Computational Linguistics.

Marco Marelli, Stefano Menini, Marco Baroni, Luisa Bentivogli, Raffaella Bernardi, and Roberto Zamparelli. 2014b. A SICK cure for the evaluation of compositional distributional semantic models. In *Proceedings of the Ninth International Conference on Language Resources and Evaluation (LREC-2014)*, pages 216–223, Reykjavik, Iceland. European Languages Resources Association (ELRA).

Pascual Martínez-Gómez, Koji Mineshima, Yusuke Miyao, and Daisuke Bekki. 2017. On-demand injection of lexical knowledge for recognising textual entailment. In *Proceedings of the 15th Conference of the European Chapter of the Association for Computational Linguistics: Volume 1, Long Papers*, pages

710–720, Valencia, Spain. Association for Computational Linguistics.

Marta Cialdea Mayer and Fiora Pirri. 1993. First order abduction via tableau and sequent calculi. *Logic Journal of the IGPL*, 1(1):99–117.

George A. Miller. 1995. Wordnet: A lexical database for english. *Communications of the ACM*, 38(11):39–41.

Koji Mineshima, Pascual Martínez-Gómez, Yusuke Miyao, and Daisuke Bekki. 2015. Higher-order logical inference with compositional semantics. In *Proceedings of the 2015 Conference on Empirical Methods in Natural Language Processing*, pages 2055–2061, Lisbon, Portugal. Association for Computational Linguistics.

Lawrence S. Moss. 2010. Natural logic and semantics. In Maria Aloni, Harald Bastiaanse, Tikitu de Jager, and Katrin Schulz, editors, *Logic, Language and Meaning: 17th Amsterdam Colloquium, Amsterdam, The Netherlands, December 16-18, 2009, Revised Selected Papers*, pages 84–93. Springer Berlin Heidelberg, Berlin, Heidelberg.

Reinhard Muskens. 2010. An analytic tableau system for natural logic. In Maria Aloni, Harald Bastiaanse, Tikitu de Jager, and Katrin Schulz, editors, *Logic, Language and Meaning*, volume 6042 of *Lecture Notes in Computer Science*, pages 104–113. Springer Berlin Heidelberg.

Ellie Pavlick, Johan Bos, Malvina Nissim, Charley Beller, Benjamin Van Durme, and Chris Callison-Burch. 2015. Adding semantics to data-driven paraphrasing. In *Proceedings of the 53rd Annual Meeting of the Association for Computational Linguistics and the 7th International Joint Conference on Natural Language Processing (Volume 1: Long Papers)*, pages 1512–1522, Beijing, China. Association for Computational Linguistics.

Adam Poliak, Jason Naradowsky, Aparajita Haldar, Rachel Rudinger, and Benjamin Van Durme. 2018. Hypothesis only baselines in natural language inference. In *Proceedings of the Seventh Joint Conference on Lexical and Computational Semantics*, pages 180–191, New Orleans, Louisiana. Association for Computational Linguistics.

Rajat Raina, Andrew Y. Ng, and Christopher D. Manning. 2005. Robust textual inference via learning and abductive reasoning. In *Proceedings of AAAI 2005*. AAAI Press.

Mark Steedman. 2000. *The Syntactic Process*. MIT Press, Cambridge, MA, USA.

Hitomi Yanaka, Koji Mineshima, Pascual Martínez-Gómez, and Daisuke Bekki. 2018. Acquisition of phrase correspondences using natural deduction proofs. In *Proceedings of the 2018 Conference of the North American Chapter of the Association for*

Computational Linguistics: Human Language Technologies, Volume 1 (Long Papers), pages 756–766, New Orleans, Louisiana. Association for Computational Linguistics.

Wenpeng Yin and Hinrich Schütze. 2017. Task-specific attentive pooling of phrase alignments contributes to sentence matching. In *Proceedings of the 15th Conference of the European Chapter of the Association for Computational Linguistics: Volume 1, Long Papers*, pages 699–709, Valencia, Spain. Association for Computational Linguistics.

Masashi Yoshikawa, Hiroshi Noji, and Yuji Matsumoto. 2017. A* CCG parsing with a supertag and dependency factored model. In *Proceedings of the 55th Annual Meeting of the Association for Computational Linguistics (Volume 1: Long Papers)*, pages 277–287, Vancouver, Canada. Association for Computational Linguistics.

Automatic Learning of Modality Exclusivity Norms
with Crosslingual Word Embeddings

Emmanuele Chersoni, Rong Xiang, Qin Lu, Chu-Ren Huang
The Hong Kong Polytechnic University, 11 Yuk Choi Road, Hong Kong (China)
{emmanuelechersoni, xiangrong0302}@gmail.com,
csluqin@comp.polyu.edu.hk, churen.huang@polyu.edu.hk

Abstract

Collecting modality exclusivity norms for lexical items has recently become a common practice in psycholinguistics and cognitive research. However, these norms are available only for a relatively small number of languages and often involve a costly and time-consuming collection of ratings.

In this work, we aim at learning a mapping between word embeddings and modality norms. Our experiments focused on *crosslingual word embeddings*, in order to predict modality association scores by training on a high-resource language and testing on a low-resource one. We ran two experiments, one in a monolingual and the other one in a crosslingual setting. Results show that modality prediction using off-the-shelf crosslingual embeddings indeed has moderate-to-high correlations with human ratings even when regression algorithms are trained on an English resource and tested on a completely unseen language.

1 Introduction

The expression *modality exclusivity norms* refers to a collection of words and their association scores with sensory modalities. The use of modality norms has been a recent trend in psycholinguistic and cognitive science, based on the observation that words with sensory meanings are associated with certain perceptual regions of the brain (Barsalou, 1999; Goldberg et al., 2006; Barros-Loscertales et al., 2012). Words are typically associated with multiple modalities: for example, the word *sweet* can be used to describe sounds, flavours, looks etc. (Connell, 2007; Lynott and Connell, 2009, 2013). Psycholinguistic studies use modality exclusivity norms to control for

the perceptual strength of lexical items used in their experiments, motivating the publication of datasets in which words are rated according to their association with each of the five senses (see the example in Table 1). Moreover, such norms have also been shown to be useful for other NLP tasks, such as metaphor detection (Wan et al., 2020a,b). Normative studies on modality for English words are relatively common (Lynott and Connell, 2009; Juhasz et al., 2011; Lynott and Connell, 2013; Lynott et al., 2019), and similar norms have also been made available for other languages such as French (Bonin et al., 2015), Serbian (Đurđević et al., 2016), Dutch (Speed and Majid, 2017), Russian (Miklashevsky, 2018), Chinese (Chen et al., 2019) and Italian (Vergallito et al., 2020). But in general, the number of languages for which they are available is still limited, and collecting modality norms is a time-consuming process, especially for low-resource languages.

word	Taste	Sight	Sound	Smell	Touch
dress	0.02	4.86	0.4	0.86	4.37

Table 1: Modality norms for the word *dress*.

Our working hypothesis for this study is that the commonalities in human perceptual cognition would lead to reliable automatic induction of modality exclusivity norms for unseen words (i.e. words without experimental data) in the same language. In addition, the five primary sensory modalities are assumed to be universal, and consequently, the prediction of norms in a new language can be carried out with the same procedure. *Crosslingual word embeddings* provide an ideal model for the prediction of modality exclusivity norms in low-resource languages, as they represent words of multiple languages in a shared feature space. It is thus

*Proceedings of the Ninth Joint Conference on Lexical and Computational Semantics (*SEM)*, pages 32–38
Barcelona, Spain (Online), December 12–13, 2020

possible to train a regressor on a resource-rich language, e.g English, and predict modality ratings for words in an unseen language. We experimented with this crosslingual transfer method on Italian, Dutch and Chinese norms. Results show that a) crosslingual embeddings perform similarly to or slightly better than monolingual embeddings in a monolingual setting; b) even after training only on English data, the regressor can predict norms in a totally unseen language with moderate-to-high correlations with human judgements.

2 Related Work

Although word vectors have been a standard for word representations for almost two decades (Lenci, 2018), they became an essential ingredient for most NLP applications only after the introduction of *word embeddings* (Mikolov et al., 2013a; Pennington et al., 2014; Bojanowski et al., 2017). Differently from the first generation models using co-occurrence counting and weighting, word embeddings are estimated via neural network training with the objective of maximizing the probability of the contexts of a target word, and they gained popularity due to the availability of efficient and easy-to-use tools (Mikolov et al., 2013a). The development of research on crosslingual transfer and the availability of new benchmarks for multilingual NLP has recently led to the introduction of the so-called *crosslingual embeddings*, vector space models that represent words from multiple languages through some form of mapping from a monolingual to a multilingual space (Conneau et al., 2018; Ruder et al., 2019). A classical study by Mikolov et al. (2013b) learnt a linear projection to transform the space of a source language to the space of a target language by maximizing the similarity between the two spaces. Other approaches apply Canonical Correlation Analysis to simultaneously project words from two languages into a shared embedding space where the correlation between projected vectors are maximized (Faruqui and Dyer, 2014). Other works make use of the max-margin method such that, for embeddings projected from a source language, they maximize the margin between the correct translations and other candidates (Lazaridou et al., 2015; Joulin et al., 2018). For this study, we use the off-the-shelf crosslingual embeddings by Joulin et al. (2018) based on FastText (Bojanowski et al., 2017)

and trained on Wikipedia. [1]

Despite the success of word embeddings, a common criticism is that they are not grounded in perception, as words are only defined in relation to each other and not to entities and actions in the physical world (Glenberg and Robertson, 2000; Fagarasan et al., 2015; Li and Gauthier, 2017). To address this issue, Fagarasan et al. (2015) used a regression method to map embeddings onto the conceptual properties of the McRae norms (McRae et al., 2005). A similar approach, using feedforward neural networks for predicting properties, was recently described by Li and Summers-Stay (2019). The work by Derby et al. (2019) goes in the opposite direction: instead of predicting norms from embeddings, they combined pretrained vectors and property vectors to inject conceptual knowledge into a new type of word representations. Their *Feature2Vec* system showed a strong performance in the predicting norms of unseen words, compared to previous proposals. Finally, Utsumi (2018, 2020) proposed a similar mapping technique to exploit semantic feature norms by Binder et al. (2016) to analyze the semantic content of word embeddings in terms of neurobiologically-motivated features. Turton et al. (2020) also experimented with embeddings based on Binder features, showing that they can achieve performances comparable to Word2Vec (Mikolov et al., 2013a) and GloVe (Pennington et al., 2014) on similarity datasets.

3 Our Proposed Approach

In this work, we used regressors trained on crosslingual word embeddings to predict modality ratings in two different scenarios. In the *monolingual* scenario, we adopt a 5-fold cross-validation to predict the modality norms of an English dataset (Lynott and Connell, 2009, 2013). In the *crosslingual* scenario, a regressor is trained on a high-resource language, e.g. English, to predict the modality norms of an unseen language.

3.1 Datasets

Four modality norms datasets are used in this work: the English norms by Lynott and Connell (2009,

---

[1]We ran experiments also with the Numberbatch embeddings by Speer and Lowry-Duda (2017), which are obtained by retrofitting different types of word embeddings with a subgraph of ConceptNet (Speer et al., 2017). However, while these vectors showed a strong performance in predicting the norms in the monolingual setting, they never achieved significant correlations with human judgements in the crosslingual prediction, and thus we omitted them from the Results section.

2013) (1002 words); the Italian norms by Vergallito et al. (2020) (1121 words); the Dutch norms by Speed and Majid (2017) (485 words); the Chinese norms by Chen et al. (2019) (291 words). The latter three datasets were collected using a similar methodology, inherited by the original study on English. The questions used for data collection are typically in the following form: "To what extent you experience a (target word) by (sensory modality)". Human participants had to provide a rating from 1 to 7 for each of the five sensory modalities, *taste, sight, sound, smell* and *touch*. All the datasets contain the mean ratings (thus, five modality scores for each word), which are the target variables to be predicted by our embedding-based regressors. The proportion of the dominant modality (i.e. the modality with the highest rating score per word) for each language is depicted in Figure 1. Generally, *sight* is the most represented modality while *smell* is relatively scarce.

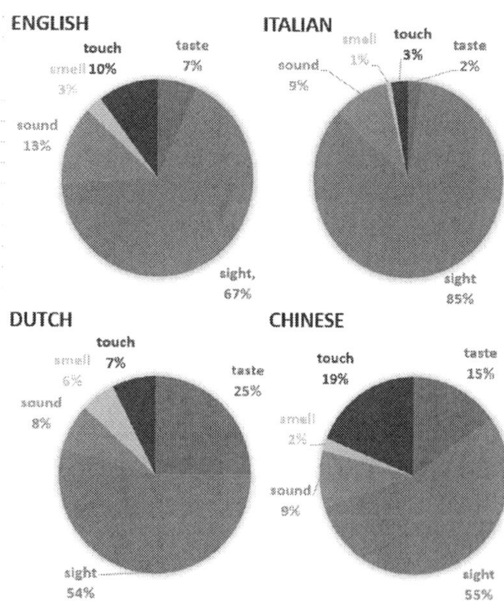

Figure 1: Percentages of dominant modality.

3.2 Models

Using the scikit-learn package (Pedregosa et al., 2011), we tested several regressors on this task. We show the results for the two top-performing ones: Multilayer Perceptron (MLP) and Ridge Regression (RR). As a result of parameter tuning, we adopt the following settings for MLP: 2 hidden layers, respectively of 50 and 10 hidden units , and the identity activation function. All the other hyperparameters correspond to the default settings of the scikit-learn library.

In all settings, regressors are trained on the embeddings of the words to predict the modality ratings in the original norms. For the *monolingual* scenario, both monolingual and crosslingual embeddings are trained on Wikipedia with the FastText library (Joulin et al., 2018). [2] As a baseline for the monolingual scenario, we also include models trained on random embeddings ($RANDOM$).

3.3 Experiment 1

In the monolingual scenario, we test whether word embeddings are capable to predict modality ratings of English. Although there were previous studies on mapping word embeddings on conceptual properties (Louwerse and Connell, 2011), the prediction on modality norms is not obvious. Firstly, most of those studies predict discrete properties (e.g. whether one concept is primarily experienced through a given sensory modality or not), and not continuous values. Secondly, modality norms represent semantic features that are learned through bodily experience, and it has yet to be tested whether they can be predicted by text-based vectors, to the best of our knowledge.

We used 5-fold cross-validation, by splitting the complete dataset into five sets. In each iteration, we leave one group out and use it as a test set, while training on the instances of all the other groups. Table 2 shows the results for Random, Monolingual and Crosslingual Embeddings, reporting the Spearman correlations, respectively, per modality and per word. [3] Concerning the differences between modalities, it can be observed that both embedding types achieve a correlation above 0.5 on all senses and are well above the random baseline, which never manages to achieve a significant correlation per modality. Smell, the least represented modality in the data, is also the least correlated while Sound and Touch are the easiest to predict. Surprisingly, we can observe that Crosslingual Embeddings perform similarly, and even slightly better than the Monolingual vectors for all modalities.

Figure 2 shows the scores for two best performing regressors, and we can observe that the Multi-

---

[2]The crosslingual embeddings can be found at https://fasttext.cc/docs/en/aligned-vectors.html and the monolingual vectors at https://fasttext.cc/docs/en/pretrained-vectors.html.

[3]Word correlations are computed between vectors of just five values, which is not ideal. Also for this reason, Random embeddings achieve relatively high values for this metric.

Embedding	taste	sight	sound	smell	touch	word
random	-0.084	-0.002	-0.003	-0.032	0.017	0.566
monolingual	0.502	0.543	0.652	0.464	0.641	0.781
crosslingual	**0.529**	**0.595**	**0.699**	**0.486**	**0.674**	**0.808**

Table 2: Spearman correlations per modality and per word (average across two best regressors).

layer Perceptron and the Ridge Regression perform similarly, with no significant differences. [4]

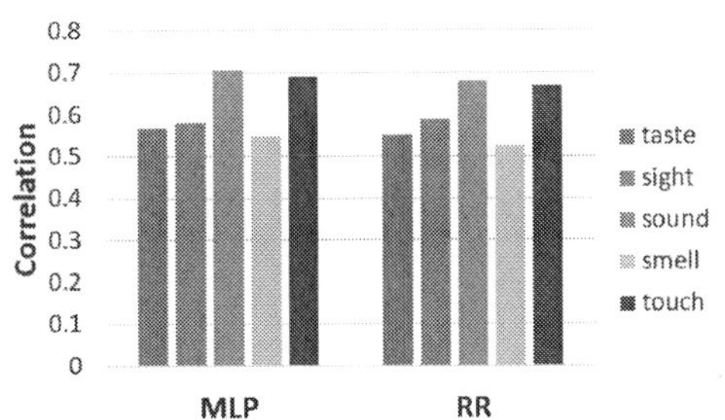

Figure 2: Monolingual Performance with Crosslingual Embeddings (Spearman correlation per modality).

Language	Avg Score
Italian	0.668
Dutch	0.663
Chinese	0.546

Table 3: Spearman correlations score per word in the crosslingual setting (scores of the two top regressors have been averaged).

3.4 Experiment 2

In the second experiment, we tested the Crosslingual Embeddings on the prediction of modality norms of Italian, Dutch and Chinese after training only on English data. The summary of the performance per sense modality is given in Figure 3 and per word in Table 3. For the error analysis, we extracted the least correlated words and reported the bottom five for each language in Table 4.

The global performance of the mappers with the Crosslingual Embeddings is not too distant from the monolingual setting. The correlations-by-modality are generally around 0.5, but there are also some notable exceptions. For example, the sound modality for Chinese seems to be particularly difficult to predict. This could be due to differences in the sensory lexicon: European languages like English and Italian have quite a lot of words where the sound is the dominant component (it is

---

the second most common dominant modality after sight), while those are rarer in Chinese (the second rarest modality after smell: see also the percentages in Figure 1). It is also noticeable that, despite being the most frequent dominant modality, sight is never the best predicted one. Actually, sight is the most internally complex modality, and recent proposals for categorizing sensory-related semantics have further divided this sense in several sub-modalities. [5] For this reason, future studies aiming at modeling this modality should probably try to adopt a more fine-grained annotation scheme.

Looking at the correlations-by-word, the values for Chinese are much lower than for the other languages. This was expected: compared to Dutch and Italian, which are both Indo-European languages, Chinese is way more distant from English.

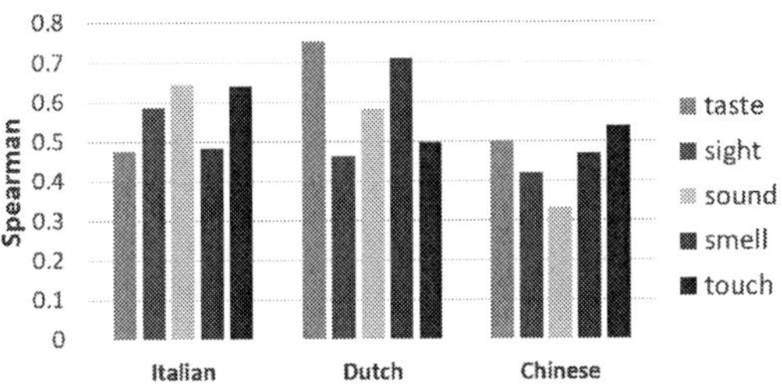

Figure 3: Spearman correlation scores per modality in the crosslingual setting (scores of the two top regressors have been averaged).

In Table 4, we can observe that many of the worst predictions are either words with a taste dominant, which are relatively rare in the English data but more common in the other languages (Dutch and Chinese), or polysemic words with strong associations with multiple senses (e.g. 'good' in Italian and 'sweet' in Chinese). Concerning this last point, we decided to test whether there is a relationship between prediction accuracy and modality exclusivity. Modality Exclusivity (ME) scores are included in the original datasets and are defined as follows:

$$ME(w) = \frac{max(w) - min(w)}{\sum(w)} \qquad (1)$$

where $max(w)$ and $min(w)$ are, respectively, the mean ratings of the strongest and of the weakest sense modality for the word w. Scores close to 1 indicate that the concept described by the word is experienced only through one sensory modality,

---

[4] p-values computed with Fisher's r-to-z transformation.

[5] E.g. Binder et al. (2016) identifies 15 different vision-related meaning components, each one associated with a distinct neural processing system

Dataset	Error Cases
Italian	buono ('good', taste), pizza ('pizza', taste), affogare ('to drown', sight), buono ('good', smell), puzza ('stink', smell)
Dutch	parmezaan ('parmesan', taste), openhaard ('fireplace', sight), dragon ('dragon', taste), zalm ('salmon', taste), roosmarijn ('rose marin', smell)
Chinese	雜 ('mixed taste', sound), 口氣 ('tone', smell) 火鍋 ('hotpot', smell), 甘 ('sweet', taste), 苦 ('bitter', taste)

Table 4: Words with lowest correlations (English translation and worst predicted modality in brackets).

Language	Translated Words
Italian	148/1121 (13.2%)
Dutch	46/485 (9.48%)
Chinese	108/291 (37.1%)

Table 5: Number and percentage of words that are translations of English items for each dataset.

while multimodal concepts are typically associated with lower scores. Strongly multimodal concepts might be more difficult to predict, as their scores for the five modalities are generally closer than in the unimodal concepts. We tested this hypothesis by measuring the Spearman correlation between the word correlations and the modality exclusivity scores from the original dataset, but no strong evidence was found: the models showed no significant correlation for the Italian data, while finding positive weak correlations (between 0.2 and 0.3) on the Dutch and on the Chinese data.

We also needed to check whether words that are direct translations of words in the English data are predicted better than the others. The number of words translated from English and the percentages can be seen in Table 5, and in the Chinese dataset they represent more than 37% of the dataset items. A high number of these words might inflate the evaluation scores, as the models could be just memorizing the English representations, and the crosslingual transfer would be working just because the vectors are well-aligned in the target language. However, in our analysis we did not find evidence for this: we compared the word correlation scores of translations with the other items by means of a Mann-Whitney U test, without finding any significant difference for any of the datasets, with just a single exception (the Ridge Regression model on Dutch data, where translations have significantly higher scores at $p < 0.05$). In conclusion, neither modality exclusivity nor the number of translations had a big impact on our results.

4 Conclusions

In this paper, we have proposed the first study dedicated to the prediction of modality norms via word embeddings mapping. We experimented with crosslingual embeddings in order to assess the potential for crosslingual transfer.

Our results first showed that modality norms can be reliably predicted even by purely text-based vectors. This is in accordance with cognitive hypotheses claiming that various aspects of experiential information are redundantly encoded in linguistic expressions (e.g. the Symbol Interdependency Hypothesis) (Louwerse, 2008; Riordan and Jones, 2011). Moreover, crosslingual vectors turned out to be better performing than their monolingual counterparts. This result is certainly surprising, although it is unclear whether it is due to differences in the training data, or the mapping itself benefits performance by abstracting away from language-specific patterns to a more 'conceptual' space.

Even more importantly, given the availability of crosslingual embeddings for a low-resource language, it is possible to train a regressor on a high-resource language (e.g. English) and to predict the norms for the low-resource one. In our experiments, we obtained moderate-to-high correlations even in the crosslingual setting. We think this is potentially a very useful application for the research on modality norms.

In this first study we used a relatively simple methodology, but several refinements are possible for improving the prediction quality. Two possible directions would be, firstly, to exploit the presence of words that are direct translations from English to the other languages to apply retrofitting techniques (Faruqui et al., 2015; Mrkšić et al., 2016, 2017; Vulić et al., 2018) to the crosslingual space, and secondly, to tackle the task by introducing more advanced neural architectures for the representation of words in context, e.g. multilingual transformers (Devlin et al., 2019; Pires et al., 2019).

References

Alfonso Barros-Loscertales, Julio González, Friedemann Pulvermüller, Noelia Ventura-Campos, Juan Carlos Bustamante, Víctor Costumero, María Antonia Parcet, and César Ávila. 2012. Reading Salt Activates Gustatory Brain Regions: fMRI Evidence for Semantic Grounding in a Novel Sensory Modality. *Cerebral Cortex*, 22(11):2554–2563.

Lawrence W Barsalou. 1999. Perceptual Symbol Systems. *Behavioral and Brain Sciences*, 22(4):577–660.

Jeffrey R Binder, Lisa L Conant, Colin J Humphries, Leonardo Fernandino, Stephen B Simons, Mario Aguilar, and Rutvik H Desai. 2016. Toward a Brain-Based Componential Semantic Representation. *Cognitive Neuropsychology*, 33(3-4):130–174.

Piotr Bojanowski, Edouard Grave, Armand Joulin, and Tomas Mikolov. 2017. Enriching Word Vectors with Subword Information. *Transactions of the Association for Computational Linguistics*, 5:135–146.

Patrick Bonin, Alain Méot, Ludovic Ferrand, and Aurélia Bugaïska. 2015. Sensory Experience Ratings (SERs) for 1,659 French Words: Relationships with Other Psycholinguistic Variables and Visual Word Recognition. *Behavior Research Methods*, 47(3):813–825.

I-Hsuan Chen, Qingqing Zhao, Yunfei Long, Qin Lu, and Chu-Ren Huang. 2019. Mandarin Chinese Modality Exclusivity Norms. *PloS One*, 14(2).

Alexis Conneau, Guillaume Lample, Marc'Aurelio Ranzato, Ludovic Denoyer, and Hervé Jégou. 2018. Word Translation Without Parallel Data. In *Proceedings of ICLR*.

Louise Connell. 2007. Representing Object Colour in Language Comprehension. *Cognition*, 102(3):476–485.

Steven Derby, Paul Miller, and Barry Devereux. 2019. Feature2Vec: Distributional Semantic Modelling of Human Property Knowledge. In *Proceedings of EMNLP*.

Jacob Devlin, Ming-Wei Chang, Kenton Lee, and Kristina Toutanova. 2019. BERT: Pre-training of Deep Bidirectional Transformers for Language Understanding. In *Proceedings of NAACL 2019*.

Luana Fagarasan, Eva Maria Vecchi, and Stephen Clark. 2015. From Distributional Semantics to Feature Norms: Grounding Semantic Models in Human Perceptual Data. In *Proceedings of IWCS*.

Manaal Faruqui, Jesse Dodge, Sujay K Jauhar, Chris Dyer, Eduard Hovy, and Noah A Smith. 2015. Retrofitting Word Vectors to Semantic Lexicons. In *Proceedings of NAACL*.

Manaal Faruqui and Chris Dyer. 2014. Improving Vector Space Word Representations Using Multilingual Correlation. In *Proceedings of EACL*.

Arthur M Glenberg and David A Robertson. 2000. Symbol Grounding and Meaning: A Comparison of High-Dimensional and Embodied Theories of Meaning. *Journal of Memory and Language*, 43(3):379–401.

Robert F Goldberg, Charles A Perfetti, and Walter Schneider. 2006. Perceptual Knowledge Retrieval Activates Sensory Brain Regions. *Journal of Neuroscience*, 26(18):4917–4921.

Armand Joulin, Piotr Bojanowski, Tomas Mikolov, Hervé Jégou, and Edouard Grave. 2018. Loss in Translation: Learning Bilingual Word Mapping with a Retrieval Criterion. In *Proceedings of EMNLP*.

Barbara J Juhasz, Melvin J Yap, Joanna Dicke, Sarah C Taylor, and Margaret M Gullick. 2011. Tangible Words Are Recognized Faster: The Grounding of Meaning in Sensory and Perceptual Systems. *Quarterly Journal of Experimental Psychology*, 64(9):1683–1691.

Angeliki Lazaridou, Georgiana Dinu, and Marco Baroni. 2015. Hubness and Pollution: Delving into Cross-Space Mapping for Zero-Shot Learning. In *Proceedings of ACL*.

Alessandro Lenci. 2018. Distributional Models of Word Meaning. *Annual Review of Linguistics*, 4:151–171.

Dandan Li and Douglas Summers-Stay. 2019. Mapping Distributional Semantics to Property Norms with Deep Neural Networks. *Big Data and Cognitive Computing*, 3(2):30.

Lucy Li and Jon Gauthier. 2017. Are Distributional Representations Ready for the Real World? Evaluating Word Vectors for Grounded Perceptual Meaning. In *Proceedings of the ACL Workshop on Language Grounding for Robotics*.

Max Louwerse. 2008. Embodied Relations Are Encoded in Language. *Psychonomic Bulletin & Review*, 15(4):838–844.

Max Louwerse and Louise Connell. 2011. A Taste of Words: Linguistic Context and Perceptual Simulation Predict the Modality of Words. *Cognitive science*, 35(2):381–398.

Dermot Lynott and Louise Connell. 2009. Modality Exclusivity Norms for 423 Object Properties. *Behavior Research Methods*, 41(2):558–564.

Dermot Lynott and Louise Connell. 2013. Modality Exclusivity Norms for 400 Nouns: The Relationship between Perceptual Experience and Surface Word Form. *Behavior Research Methods*, 45(2):516–526.

Dermot Lynott, Louise Connell, Marc Brysbaert, James Brand, and James Carney. 2019. The Lancaster Sensorimotor Norms: Multidimensional Measures of Perceptual and Action Strength for 40,000 English Words. *Behavior Research Methods*, pages 1–21.

Ken McRae, George S. Cree, Mark S. Seidenberg, and Chris McNorgan. 2005. Semantic Feature Production Norms for a Large Set of Living and Nonliving Things. *Behavior Research Methods*, 37(4):547–559.

Alex Miklashevsky. 2018. Perceptual Experience Norms for 506 Russian Nouns: Modality Rating, Spatial Localization, Manipulability, Imageability and Other Variables. *Journal of Psycholinguistic Research*, 47(3):641–661.

Tomas Mikolov, Kai Chen, Greg Corrado, and Jeffrey Dean. 2013a. Efficient Estimation of Word Representations in Vector Space. *arXiv preprint arXiv:1301.3781*.

Tomas Mikolov, Quoc V Le, and Ilya Sutskever. 2013b. Exploiting Similarities Among Languages for Machine Translation. *arXiv preprint arXiv:1309.4168*.

Nikola Mrkšić, Diarmuid O Séaghdha, Blaise Thomson, Milica Gašić, Lina Rojas-Barahona, Pei-Hao Su, David Vandyke, Tsung-Hsien Wen, and Steve Young. 2016. Counter-fitting Word Vectors to Linguistic Constraints. In *Proceedings of NAACL*.

Nikola Mrkšić, Ivan Vulić, Diarmuid Ó Séaghdha, Ira Leviant, Roi Reichart, Milica Gašić, Anna Korhonen, and Steve Young. 2017. Semantic Specialization of Distributional Word Vector Spaces Using Monolingual and Cross-lingual Constraints. *Transactions of the Association for Computational Linguistics*, 5:309–324.

Fabian Pedregosa, Gaël Varoquaux, Alexandre Gramfort, Vincent Michel, Bertrand Thirion, Olivier Grisel, Mathieu Blondel, Peter Prettenhofer, Ron Weiss, Vincent Dubourg, et al. 2011. Scikit-learn: Machine Learning in Python. *Journal of Machine Learning Research*, 12:2825–2830.

Jeffrey Pennington, Richard Socher, and Christopher Manning. 2014. Glove: Global Vectors for Word Representation. In *Proceedings of EMNLP*.

Telmo Pires, Eva Schlinger, and Dan Garrette. 2019. How Multilingual is Multilingual BERT? In *Proceedings of ACL*.

Brian Riordan and Michael N. Jones. 2011. Redundancy in Perceptual and Linguistic Experience: Comparing Feature-Based and Distributional Models of Semantic Representation. *Topics in Cognitive Science*, 3(2):303–345.

Sebastian Ruder, Ivan Vulić, and Anders Søgaard. 2019. A Survey of Cross-lingual Word Embedding Models. *Journal of Artificial Intelligence Research*, 65:569–631.

Laura J Speed and Asifa Majid. 2017. Dutch Modality Exclusivity Norms: Simulating perceptual Modality in Space. *Behavior Research Methods*, 49(6):2204–2218.

Robyn Speer, Joshua Chin, and Catherine Havasi. 2017. Conceptnet 5.5: An Open Multilingual Graph of General Knowledge. In *Proceedings of AAAI*.

Robyn Speer and Joanna Lowry-Duda. 2017. Conceptnet at Semeval-2017 task 2: Extending Word Embeddings with Multilingual Relational Knowledge. In *Proceedings of SemEval*.

Jacob Turton, David Vinson, and Robert Elliott Smith. 2020. Extrapolating Binder Style Word Embeddings to New Words. In *Proceedings of the LREC Workshop on Linguistic and Neurocognitive Resources*.

DF Đurđević, M Popović Stijačić, and J Karapandžić. 2016. A Quest for Sources of Perceptual Richness: Several Candidates. *Studies in Language and Mind*, pages 187–238.

Akira Utsumi. 2018. A Neurobiologically Motivated Analysis of Distributional Semantic Models. In *Proceedings of CogSci*.

Akira Utsumi. 2020. Exploring What Is Encoded in Distributional Word Vectors: A Neurobiologically Motivated Analysis. *Cognitive Science*, 44(6):e12844.

Alessandra Vergallito, Marco Alessandro Petilli, and Marco Marelli. 2020. Perceptual Modality Norms for 1,121 Italian Words: A Comparison with Concreteness and Imageability Scores and an Analysis of their Impact in Word Processing Tasks. *Behavior Research Methods*, pages 1–18.

Ivan Vulić, Goran Glavaš, Nikola Mrkšić, and Anna Korhonen. 2018. Post-specialisation: Retrofitting Vectors of Words Unseen in Lexical Resources. In *Proceedings of NAACL*.

Mingyu Wan, Kathleen Ahrens, Emmanuele Chersoni, Menghan Jiang, Qi Su, Rong Xiang, and Chu-Ren Huang. 2020a. Using Conceptual Norms for Metaphor Detection. In *Proceedings of the ACL Workshop on Figurative Language Processing*.

Mingyu Wan, Baixi Xing, Pengyuan Liu, Qi Su, and Chu-Ren Huang. 2020b. Enhancing Metaphor Detection with Sensorimotor Scores. In *Proceedings of COLING*.

Joint Training for Learning Cross-lingual Embeddings with Sub-word Information without Parallel Corpora

Ali Hakimi Parizi
Faculty of Computer Science
University of New Brunswick
ahakimi@unb.ca

Paul Cook
Faculty of Computer Science
University of New Brunswick
paul.cook@unb.ca

Abstract

In this paper, we propose a novel method for learning cross-lingual word embeddings, that incorporates sub-word information during training, and is able to learn high-quality embeddings from modest amounts of monolingual data and a bilingual lexicon. This method could be particularly well-suited to learning cross-lingual embeddings for lower-resource, morphologically-rich languages, enabling knowledge to be transferred from rich- to lower-resource languages. We evaluate our proposed approach simulating lower-resource languages for bilingual lexicon induction, monolingual word similarity, and document classification. Our results indicate that incorporating sub-word information indeed leads to improvements, and in the case of document classification, performance better than, or on par with, strong benchmark approaches.

1 Introduction

State-of-the-art approaches in natural language processing (NLP) typically require a substantial amount of human-annotated data (i.e, for supervised approaches to tasks such as part-of-speech tagging or dependency parsing) or they need a very large amount of unannotated text for training (e.g., methods for learning word embeddings). This poses a particular problem for building NLP systems for low-resource languages. There are thousands of human languages, and creating annotated datasets for all of them would be very expensive. Furthermore, many languages have a relatively small number of speakers, and in many cases large amounts of text are not readily-available for building corpora for these languages. A further related challenge is posed by morphologically-rich

languages, because many word-forms would not be expected to be observed in a training corpus. One way to address these problems is to transfer knowledge from a rich-resource language to a lower-resource language.

Word Embeddings are a key feature in approaches for a wide range of NLP tasks, such as part-of-speech tagging (Al-Rfou' et al., 2013), dependency parsing (Chen and Manning, 2014), and named entity recognition (Pennington et al., 2014). If we are able to transfer the knowledge captured in word embeddings for a rich-resource language to another low-resource language, then developing NLP tools could become more feasible for the low-resource language. There has therefore been a wealth of research on cross-lingual word embeddings (e.g., Mikolov et al., 2013b; Vulić and Moens, 2016; Lample et al., 2018), in which embeddings for multiple languages are learned in a shared space, and which can be used to transfer knowledge between languages, such as from a rich-resource language to a low-resource one (Ruder et al., 2019).

Despite the wide range of research on learning cross-lingual embeddings, there are some limitations of these methods that have not been addressed. In the case of a low-resource language, due to the relatively small size of available corpora, a relatively small number of embeddings would be learned. Moreover, in the case of a morphologically-rich language, many wordforms would not be observed in the corpus on which embeddings are trained. As a result, given a subsequent text to process, many words would be expected to be out-of-vocabulary (OOV) with respect to the embedding model. This is a very important issue, because in the case of OOVs, we do not have an embedding for these words, and models for downstream NLP tasks that use embeddings would therefore lack information for these words. Where

*Proceedings of the Ninth Joint Conference on Lexical and Computational Semantics (*SEM)*, pages 39–49
Barcelona, Spain (Online), December 12–13, 2020

the number of OOVs is relatively high, such as for low-resource and morphologically-rich languages, this could lead to particularly poor performance in down-stream tasks. This problem has been addressed in monolingual settings by learning embeddings for sub-word units, and then composing representations for OOVs based on their sub-words (Bojanowski et al., 2017; Zhu et al., 2019).

Recently, with advances in language modelling (Artetxe and Schwenk, 2019) and contextualized language models (Devlin et al., 2019; Conneau and Lample, 2019), transfer learning has become feasible between languages by using a byte pair encoding (BPE, Sennrich et al., 2016) shared vocabulary, and fine-tuning the models for specific tasks (Wu and Dredze, 2019). Nevertheless, these models require a substantial amount of training data (Conneau and Lample, 2019), and in some cases parallel corpora (Artetxe and Schwenk, 2019; Conneau and Lample, 2019), and are very computationally expensive to train. There is therefore a need for methods that can be trained from a more-limited amount of data and require less computational resources for training, but that nevertheless show comparable performance.

In this paper, we propose a model that can learn cross-lingual word embeddings from a modest amount of monolingual data and a bilingual dictionary. We rely on bilingual dictionaries because they are relatively-widely available. For example, Panlex (Baldwin et al., 2010) is a translation resource that combines many bilingual dictionaries and provides translations for 5700 languages. Our proposed model is an extension of the method proposed by Duong et al. (2016). In their work, they only considered word embeddings, and so their method is unable to form representations for OOVs, and therefore is not expected to perform well for low-resource or morphologically-rich target languages. We extend the method of Duong et al. (2016) by incorporating sub-word information in the process of training cross-lingual word embeddings. In this way, we form a shared embedding space that not only contains embeddings for both source and target language words, but that has also been enriched with sub-word embeddings enabling representations to be formed for OOVs.

To evaluate our proposed model, we use modest amounts of data for relatively well-resourced languages. We first consider two intrinsic evaluations: (1) the widely-considered task of bilingual lexi-

con induction (BLI), and (2) a monolingual word similarity task to show the effectiveness of our proposed approach when the embeddings are used in a monolingual setting. Our results on these tasks demonstrate that incorporating sub-word information leads to improvements for both cross-lingual and monolingual representations. For extrinsic evaluation, to show the impact of having sub-word knowledge in a down-stream NLP task, we consider cross-lingual document classification. Again our results indicate that incorporating sub-word information leads to improvements, and furthermore we find our proposed model to perform on par with, or better than, strong benchmark approaches.

2 Related Work

A variety of methods have been proposed for learning cross-lingual word embeddings. These methods vary with respect to the level of supervision, and the cross-lingual signals used, such as parallel corpora and bilingual dictionaries.

Klementiev et al. (2012) propose a method to learn cross-lingual representations by training a language model on the source and target language and optimizing their objective function jointly. This method, however, requires a parallel corpus, which is not available for many languages, especially low-resource ones. More recently, Artetxe and Schwenk (2019) propose a bi-directional LSTM language model that is trained on a very large parallel corpus, containing 223 million parallel sentences, and jointly learns representations for 93 languages. Aside from requiring a parallel corpus, it is also computationally expensive to train.

Mikolov et al. (2013b) argue that the geometric arrangement of word embeddings in two different languages is the same. They therefore propose a method to learn a linear transformation to align the vector spaces of two languages by using a seed lexicon of known translation pairs. Xing et al. (2015) show that normalizing all word vectors to be unit length, and applying an orthogonality constraint on the transformation matrix, improves the approach of Mikolov et al. Artetxe et al. (2017) introduce an alignment-based method which relaxes the requirement of having a bilingual seed lexicon. Their approach begins with a very small seed lexicon — as few as 25 pairs — and in a process of self-learning and through several rounds of bootstrapping, increases the size of the bilingual dictionary. Artetxe et al. (2018b) further relax the need for a bilingual dictionary, and propose a fully unsupervised approach. Their method solves the same mapping problem as Artetxe et al. (2017), but creates the initial seed lexicon in an unsupervised manner by exploiting the similarity distribution of words in the source and target language.

All of these mapping-based methods require pre-trained monolingual word embeddings, the quality of which the final cross-lingual word embeddings are greatly dependent upon. This is problematic in the case that we do not have access to enough training data to learn high quality monolingual embeddings, as would be the case for many low-resource languages. Moreover, it has been shown that fully unsupervised methods do not perform well across all languages, especially in the case of morphologically rich languages, and when the monolingual embeddings do not come from the same domain (Søgaard et al., 2018; Vulić et al., 2019). Furthermore, Ormazabal et al. (2019) show that the isomorphism assumption — i.e., that embeddings for different languages have a similar geometric arrangement, which is key to the success of mapping-based models — does not always hold. They show that methods which jointly learn the embedding space for the source and target language from a parallel corpus are superior to mapping-based methods. However, parallel corpora are a very expensive cross-lingual signal.

In an alternative approach to learning cross-lingual word embeddings, a pesudo-bilingual corpus is first constructed using a bilingual dictionary, and embeddings for the source and target language are then learned from this corpus. Gouws and Søgaard (2015) concatenate and shuffle the source and target language corpora, and then randomly replace words in this corpus using a bilingual dictionary. They then run CBOW on the constructed corpus to learn word embeddings for both the source and target language. Similarly, Duong et al. (2016) also propose a method that replaces words in a pseudo-bilingual corpus with their translation during training. However, they further propose a way to handle polysemy by choosing the best translation for a word by considering its context using the expectation-maximization algorithm. Compared to mapping-based methods, this approach does not require as large of a corpus for training, because for each word, the context in not only the source language, but also the target language, is used. However, these pseudo-bilingual corpus methods are more expensive to train than mapping-based methods, because the embeddings are learned from scratch, in contrast to mapping-based methods which use pre-trained embeddings and only need to learn the mapping function.

Recent approaches to learning cross-lingual embeddings have been trained on concatenated monolingual corpora. Multilingual BERT (mBERT) is a BERT model (Devlin et al., 2019) trained on concatenated Wikipedia corpora for 105 languages. Wu and Dredze (2019) show that since mBERT uses a shared vocabulary for all languages, it can represent embeddings for all languages in a shared space, rather than representing each language in a separate space. This model is therefore able to learn deep contextualized cross-lingual word embeddings without any cross-lingual signal, but is computationally expensive to train. Chaudhary et al. (2018) present a method that uses sub-word information, such as lemmas, morpheme tags, and phoneme n-grams, to transfer knowledge from rich-resource languages to low-resource ones. They train skip-gram on concatenated monolingual corpora of two related languages and learn representations in a shared space by relying on similar subwords to map related words close to each other in the shared space. They also consider an approach which first trains a model on the rich-resource language and then uses the trained sub-word embeddings to initialize the model for the low-resource language.

The approach for learning cross-lingual embeddings proposed in this paper incorporates sub-word information — similar to Chaudhary et al. (2018) and mBert — but in contrast to Chaudhary et al. does not require language-specific tools such as morphological analyzers which might not be available for low-resource languages, and in contrast to mBert is less computationally-expensive to train. The proposed approach is an extension of Duong et al. (2016) that incorporates sub-word information, and requires only modest size monolingual corpora and a bilingual lexicon for training.

3   Methodology

In this section we first describe the approach of Duong et al. (2016) to learning cross-lingual word embeddings, and then present our proposed model, which is an extension of this approach.

3.1 Learning Cross-lingual Word Embeddings with Pseudo-bilingual Corpora

Duong et al. (2016) introduce an approach to learning cross-lingual word representations that can jointly learn representations for words in two languages — referred to as the source and target language — without requiring a parallel corpus. This method is an extension of CBOW (Mikolov et al., 2013a) that uses two monolingual corpora and a bilingual dictionary. A prefix is added to each word in each monolingual corpus indicating its language. Then, the monolingual corpora are concatenated and the sentences are shuffled. The CBOW objective function, shown below, is only capable of capturing monolingual similarities:

$$O = \sum_{i \in D} (\log \sigma(u_{w_i}^T h_i) + \sum_{j=1}^{p} \mathbb{E}_{w_j \sim P_n(w)} \log \sigma(-u_{w_j}^T h_i)) \quad (1)$$

Equation 2 is therefore proposed to adapt it to cross-lingual settings:

$$O = \sum_{i \in D_s \cup D_t} (\alpha \log \sigma(u_{w_i}^T h_i) + (1 - \alpha) \log \sigma(u_{\bar{w}_i}^T h_i) + \sum_{j=1}^{p} \mathbb{E}_{w_j \sim P_n(w)} \log \sigma(-u_{w_j}^T h_i)) \quad (2)$$

where h_i encodes the context vector, $\bar{w}_i$ is the translation of w_i, α is a weight parameter, and D_s and D_t are the source and target language vocabularies, respectively.

Duong et al. (2016) also propose an approach to find the best translation for polysemous words using the expectation maximization algorithm and cosine similarity between the context vector — the average of the embeddings for the words in the context — and possible translations. Thus the translation for a word is selected based on its context.

Duong et al. (2016) further argue that each of the matrices V and U in word2vec encode different information: V is better for capturing monolingual characteristics, whereas U preserves cross-lingual information. In each update, the context words are pushed closer together in V space, while the target word and its translation become closer in U space and further away from the negative samples. Duong et al. achieve their best results in both monolingual and cross-lingual evaluations by combining V and U during the training phase using a regularization term, δ, in the objective function as shown in Equation 3.

$$O' = O + \delta \sum_{w \in V_s \cup V_t} \| u_w - v_w \|_2^2 \quad (3)$$

For the remainder of the paper we refer to this approach as DUONG2016.

3.2 Joint Training Incorporating Sub-word Information

Incorporating sub-word information in training word embeddings enhances the quality of the learned embeddings (Bojanowski et al., 2017). Moreover, because sub-word embeddings can be used to construct representations for OOVs, approaches that incorporate sub-word embeddings are better-suited for low-resource and morphologically-rich languages which are expected to have relatively high rates of OOVs. In this paper, we extend DUONG2016 by incorporating sub-word information during training.

To incorporate sub-word information, we follow a similar approach to Bojanowski et al. (2017). Each word in the training corpus is augmented with special beginning and end of word markers. Each word is then represented as a bag of character sequences (i.e., sub-words); in our experiments we consider sequences of length 3–6 characters. We additionally include the entire word itself (with beginning and end of word markers) among the sub-words. The embedding for a word is formed by averaging its sub-word embeddings. This gives the following objective function:

$$O = \sum_{i \in D_s \cup D_t} (\alpha \log S(w_i, c) + (1 - \alpha) \log S(\bar{w}_i, c) + \sum_{j=1}^{p} \mathbb{E}_{w_j \sim P_n(w)} \log -S(w_j, c)) \quad (4)$$

where c is the context. S, shown in Equation 5, measures the similarity between a word and context, taking into account sub-words:

$$S(w, c) = \frac{1}{|G_w|} \sum_{g \in G_w} z_g^T v_c \quad (5)$$

Language	Family	# Tokens	# Types	# Embeddings	# Dict. entries
Chinese	Sino-Tibetan	30M (64%)	0.2M (20%)	86K (43%)	1983K
Dutch	Germanic	84M (64%)	1.3M (8%)	303K (28%)	406K
English	Germanic	121M	1.1M	240K	-
French	Romance	135M (80%)	1.1M (9%)	288K (30%)	1068K
German	Germanic	92M (68%)	1.8M (8%)	411K (25%)	964K
Italian	Romance	119M (68%)	1.2M (7%)	304K (22%)	560K
Japanese	Japanese	22M (76%)	0.3M (21%)	107K (47%)	736K
Russian	Slavic	84M (56%)	1.7M (7%)	445K (68%)	1594K
Spanish	Romance	130M (75%)	1.1M (7%)	279K (22%)	712K

Table 1: The size of the corpus for each language, in terms of the number of tokens and types. The language family, number of embeddings learned from each corpus, and number of entries in the bilingual dictionary, is also shown for each language. The parenthetical numbers indicate coverage in the dictionary.

where G_w is the set of sub-words appearing in w, and z_g is the sub-word embedding for g. To calculate v_c, we average representations for each word appearing in c, where each word is represented by the average of its sub-word embeddings.[1]

4 Resources

For evaluation, we simulate lower-resource languages using 9 well-resourced languages: Chinese, Dutch, English, French, German, Italian, Japanese, Russian, and Spanish. These languages include those considered by Duong et al. (2016), as well as those in the MLDoc dataset (Schwenk and Li, 2018, which we use for evaluation in Section 5.3). Following previous work (e.g., Duong et al., 2016; Lample et al., 2018), we only consider pairs of languages with English as either the source or target language, and one of the remaining 8 languages as the other language.

To train word embeddings for each language, we use pre-processed Wikipedia dumps (Al-Rfou' et al., 2013), which are already tokenized and cleaned. To simulate the case of lower-resource languages, following Duong et al. (2016), we randomly select 5 million sentences for each language from their Wikipedia dump. Table 1 shows the number of tokens and types in each corpus.

We use a bilingual dictionary as the cross-lingual signal in our proposed approach. Our study builds on the work of Duong et al. (2016), and so for languages that they consider — Dutch, German, Italian, Japanese, and Spanish — we use the same dictionaries that they did, which were extracted

from Panlex.[2] For Chinese, French, and Russian we extract dictionaries from Panlex using a similar approach to Duong et al.

Table 1 also shows the size of each dictionary, with English as the source language, and the other language as the target language.[3] The coverage of the dictionary with respect to the number of tokens, types, and embeddings learned is also shown. For example, 68% coverage for Italian tokens means that 68% of tokens in the Italian corpus occur in the bilingual dictionary.

5 Experimental Results

We present experimental results for two intrinsic evaluations, bilingual lexicon induction and monolingual word similarity, and an extrinsic evaluation on cross-lingual document classification.

5.1 Bilingual Lexicon Induction

Bilingual lexicon induction (BLI) is a standard task to evaluate the quality of cross-lingual word embeddings (Vulić and Moens, 2013; Artetxe et al., 2017; Ruder et al., 2019). In this task, we try to find the translation of a source language word in the target language by looking at its nearest neighbours. Ideally, a word and its translation would be located close to each other in the shared cross-lingual word embedding space. Here we focus on comparing our proposed method with DUONG2016 and so consider the same four languages as Duong et al. (2016): English, Dutch, Italian, and Spanish. In all cases, English is the target language and the other languages are treated as the source language.

---

[1] This differs from fastText which sums the sub-word embeddings.

[2] https://github.com/longdt219/XlingualEmb

[3] The dictionary size for English is therefore not shown.

Model	es–en			it–en			nl–en		
	@1	@5	@10	@1	@5	@10	@1	@5	@10
DUONG2016 ($c = 48, d = 200$)	54.59	83.12	86.87	45.98	77.11	81.79	40.73	71.72	77.06
DUONG2016 ($c = 5, \; d = 200$)	28.20	70.26	76.36	21.08	60.78	67.47	24.36	55.07	62.65
DUONG2016 ($c = 20, d = 200$)	50.50	82.92	87.07	41.83	77.11	81.53	41.41	72.19	77.88
DUONG2016 ($c = 48, d = 300$)	50.90	83.86	87.54	44.24	77.44	82.33	38.16	71.31	77.67
Our Model ($c = 48, d = 200$)	60.15	79.84	84.26	54.62	73.83	78.92	42.25	67.39	72.80
Our Model ($c = 5, \; d = 200$)	41.39	78.63	85.06	36.21	72.42	79.45	36.54	69.15	76.25
Our Model ($c = 20, d = 200$)	59.14	83.12	87.27	54.02	77.64	82.00	47.56	73.00	78.69
Our Model ($c = 20, d = 300$)	60.21	84.53	89.28	55.15	80.12	84.94	46.21	74.83	80.11
VecMap	**81.27**	**91.07**	**93.27**	**76.13**	**86.87**	**89.47**	**71.53**	**83.93**	**86.53**

Table 2: Precision@N for bilingual lexicon induction. The best performance, for each dataset and evaluation measure, is shown in boldface.

Following previous work (e.g. Lample et al., 2018; Joulin et al., 2018; Jawanpuria et al., 2019), we consider MUSE test sets for evaluation. Word pairs occurring in both the MUSE test sets and our training dictionaries are removed from the training data before training the embeddings. We report precision@N — for $N = 1$, 5, and 10 — where the system is scored as correct if the gold-standard target word is amongst the top-N most similar target language words (Ruder et al., 2019). We use cosine as the similarity measure.

Results are shown in Table 2. We begin by considering DUONG2016 and our model using the best parameter settings from Duong et al. (2016), i.e., a learning rate of 0.025, 25 negative samples, a window size (c) of 48, an embedding size (d) of 200, sub-sampling of $1e^{-4}$, α of 0.5, and δ set to 0.01.[4] In terms of precision@1, our model outperforms DUONG2016 for each language, but for precision@5 and precision@10, DUONG2016 performs better.

A window size of 48 takes into account a relatively large amount of context for the target word; however, when incorporating sub-words, as for our proposed model, this wide context could also add noise because of the large number of sub-words in the context, and the wide range of contexts in which sub-words occur. We therefore consider a window size of 5, the fastText default, and 20, which balances having a larger window size against introducing too much noise. Results are shown for this setup for both DUONG2016 and our model For both models, a window size of 5 performs relatively poorly. For DUONG2016, the original window size of 48 performs best in terms of preci-

sion@1 for Spanish and Italian, but not Dutch. For our model, the intermediate window size of 20 performs best, except for precision@1 for Spanish and Italian. These results suggest that a model including sub-word information might not be able to use information from a very wide context as effectively as a word-only model.

Next we consider increasing the embedding size to 300, which is commonly used for fastText (Bojanowski et al., 2017). We consider this for the best window size for each model, i.e., 48 for DUONG2016 and 20 for our model.[5] Our model with a window size of 20 and embedding size of 300 outperforms DUONG2016 for all parameter settings considered, for all languages and evaluation measures. The difference between our model in this configuration, and DUONG2016 using its original parameter settings, is significant ($p < 4.31e^{-6}$) using a one-sided McNemar's test with continuity correction. This demonstrates that incorporating sub-word knowledge during training of cross-lingual word embeddings enhances the quality of the resulting word representations.

These are not state-of-the-art results, where prior work has obtained higher precision. As a point of comparison, we also present results for VecMap (Artetxe et al., 2018a) a supervised mapping-based approach. These results for VecMap are achieved using fastText embeddings trained on full Wikipedia corpora for each language. Our model, on the other hand, is trained on substantially smaller corpora because we focus on approaches that could be applied to lower-resource languages. mBERT and Chaudhary et al. (2018) are further points of comparison that we do not include because of the resource requirements, and reliance

---

[4]The differences between the results for DUONG2016 here and the numbers reported in Duong et al. (2016) are due to differences in the test set. We use the MUSE test set, which was not available in 2016, but is more widely used now.

[5]We also considered a window size of 20 and embedding size of 300 for DUONG2016, but this did not give improvements.

Model	WS-en	WS-de	RW-en	RW-en+OOV
DUONG2016	74.46	69.72	44.06	37.68
Our Model	**75.67**	**70.49**	**51.57**	**49.51**
trained on 5 million sentences				
fastText (CBOW, $c = 48, d = 200$)	55.40	46.91	40.56	39.77
fastText (CBOW, $c = 20, d = 300$)	53.66	43.73	37.92	37.35
fastText (skipgram, $c = 5, d = 300$)	69.02	63.79	49.50	47.94
trained on 10 million sentences				
fastText (CBOW, $c = 48, d = 200$)	57.72	45.18	41.31	40.74
fastText (CBOW, $c = 20, d = 300$)	54.55	42.62	38.85	38.36
fastText (skipgram, $c = 5, d = 300$)	69.91	60.90	49.74	48.74
trained on full Wikipedia corpora				
fastText (skipgram, $c = 5, d = 300$)	73.77	66.63	48.61	48.09

Table 3: Spearman's correlation for monolingual similarity on each dataset, for each method considered. The best performance on each dataset is shown in boldface.

on language-specific tools, respectively, of these methods.

For the rest of the paper, "our model" refers to the model with an embedding size of 300 and window size of 20. Since changing the window and embedding sizes does not consistently lead to improvements for DUONG2016, and has a negative impact on precision@1, we continue to use the best parameter settings from Duong et al. (2016) for this method.

5.2 Monolingual Word Similarity

Here we evaluate the quality of cross-lingual word representations in a monolingual setting. We compare cross-lingual embeddings from our proposed model and DUONG2016. We further consider monolingual embeddings from fastText, a well-known method to learn embeddings that uses sub-word information, as a baseline. We consider several parameter settings for fastText. In particular, we consider the best parameter settings for DUONG2016 (CBOW, $c = 48, d = 200$), the best parameter settings for our model (CBOW, $c = 20$, $d = 300$), and commonly-used fastText settings (skipgram, $c = 5$, $d = 300$, and 5 negative samples). In addition, we consider three corpus sizes to train fastText: 5 million sentences (i.e., the same amount of monolingual text that DUONG2016 and our proposed method are trained on), 10 million sentences (the total amount of text in both languages that DUONG2016 and our proposed method are trained on), and full Wikipedia corpora. For the full Wikipedia corpora we only consider the commonly-used parameter settings.

Following Duong et al. (2016), we consider English and German for these experiments. We use three datasets for evaluation: English WordSim353 (WS-en, Finkelstein et al., 2002), German WordSim353 (WS-de, Luong et al., 2015), and Stanford Rare Words (RW-en Luong et al., 2013). We use cosine as the similarity score. The number of OOVs in WS-en and WS-de is very low (none for WS-en, and two for WS-de). For these datasets, we therefore report results only for in-vocabulary items. For RW-en, however, roughly 25% of the test pairs include an OOV. For this dataset we therefore also report results considering both in-vocabulary words and OOVs (referred to as "RW-en+OOV"). Because DUONG2016 is not capable of forming representations for OOVs, in such cases we assign these test pairs the average cosine similarity score over test pairs that are in-vocabulary.

Table 3 shows the results. For each dataset, our proposed model outperforms DUONG2016, and also fastText, in all configurations considered. These results indicate that a cross-lingual signal can be used to not only form a cross-lingual shared space, but also to enhance the quality of monolingual embeddings. Note that DUONG2016 improves over fastText on WS-en and WS-de, but not on RW-en (or RW-en+OOV). This indicates that sub-word information is particularly important for forming representations for low-frequency words.

5.3 Document Classification

Here we consider an extrinsic evaluation which uses cross-lingual word embeddings in a downstream task, specifically cross-lingual document

Model	Target language							
	Chinese	French	German	Italian	Japanese	Russian	Spanish	Average
DUONG2016	54.12	87.82	86.95	73.88	71.12	50.15	77.90	71.71
LASER	70.98	78.03	86.25	70.20	60.95	67.25	79.30	73.28
mBERT	76.9	72.06	80.2	68.9	56.5	73.7	72.6	71.55
Our Model	69.55	86.45	90.22	72.90	74.62	53.30	78.47	75.07
XLM_{ft}UDA	93.32	96.05	96.95	-	-	89.07	96.8	-

Table 4: Accuracy on the MLDoc zero-shot cross-lingual document classification task, for each model and target language, with English as the source language. The average accuracy over all target languages is also shown.

classification. This task is motivated by the situation where sufficient labelled training data is not available for a low-resource language. We consider zero-shot classification, i.e., we train a classifier and tune parameters on a rich-resource source language, and then apply the classifier directly to documents in a low-resource target language.

Following previous work (e.g., Artetxe and Schwenk, 2019; Wu and Dredze, 2019), we use the MLDoc dataset (Schwenk and Li, 2018), which is a subset of the RCV1/RCV2 datasets (Lewis et al., 2004) with balanced classes for training, development, and test sets for the following languages: Chinese, English, French, German, Italian, Japanese, Spanish, and Russian. It has 1000 documents in each of the training and development sets, and 4000 documents in the test set, for each language. Following Artetxe and Schwenk (2019), we use English as the source language, and the other languages as target languages.

To build corpora to train embeddings, again following previous work (Duong et al., 2016; Klementiev et al., 2012), we first randomly sample $400k$ sentences for each of the source and target language from RCV1/RCV2,[6] and then combine these in-domain corpora with larger Wikipedia corpora. We use the Wikipedia corpora described in Section 4.

We represent documents as the average of their words' embeddings, where the embeddings are learned by our proposed approach from the corpora described above. We then use a feed-forward classifier (LASER, Artetxe and Schwenk, 2019), which has been previously applied to cross-lingual document classification, with one hidden layer of 10 hidden units, a learning rate of 0.001, dropout

set to 0.2, and a batch-size of 12, as suggested by Artetxe and Schwenk.

We compare our approach against several benchmarks. First we consider the same approach described above, but using embeddings from DUONG2016 instead of our proposed approach. In this case, embeddings for OOVs are not available, and so OOVs are simply ignored in forming document representations. We further consider two strong benchmark approaches — LASER (Artetxe and Schwenk, 2019) and mBERT (Devlin et al., 2019) — that are widely used for comparison (e.g., Wu and Dredze, 2019; Patidar et al., 2019; Keung et al., 2019). Artetxe and Schwenk recently improved their model, and reported updated results.[7] We use these improved results for comparison. We use mBERT results reported by Wu and Dredze (2019).

Results are shown in Table 4. None of the approaches considered performs best for all languages. However, in terms of the average accuracy over all target languages, our proposed model performs better than DUONG2016, LASER and mBERT. It is worth noting that our model is trained on only 5.4 million sentences in each language, and does not require a parallel corpus. Artetxe and Schwenk (2019), the next best method in terms of average accuracy, on the other hand, is trained on 225 million parallel sentences. Furthermore, our model outperforms mBERT — a very large language model-based approach — on average, and for all target languages except Chinese and Russian. The current state-of-the-art for MLDOC is XLM_{ft} UDA (Lai et al., 2019). This model is pre-trained for 15 languages, but not Italian and Japanese, and so results are not available for these languages. XLM_{ft} UDA does however substantially out-perform our proposed model on the other

---

[6]We sampled 80k documents for both the source and target languages, and then sampled $400k$ sentences. For Spanish, Italian, Russian and Chinese we use all of their RCV2 documents because the total number of documents available for these languages is less than $80k$.

[7]https://github.com/facebookresearch/LASER/tree/master/tasks/mldoc

languages, but also requires a large parallel corpus for training.

6 Conclusions

In this paper we proposed an approach to learning cross-lingual word embeddings that incorporates sub-word information during training, and relies on only monolingual corpora and a bilingual dictionary. This approach could be particularly well-suited to lower-resource, morphologically-rich languages, for which large parallel corpora are not available.

We evaluated our proposed approach, on a variety of simulated lower-resource languages, for the tasks of BLI, monolingual word similarity, and document classification. Our results on BLI and monolingual word similarity indicated that incorporating sub-word information during training enhances the quality of the resulting cross-lingual, as well as monolingual, representations. For zero-shot cross-lingual document classification, incorporating sub-word information again led to improvements, and our proposed model outperformed benchmark approaches that have substantially higher resource requirements for training. Code and data to reproduce these results has been made available.[8]

In future work, we plan to evaluate our proposed approach on truly lower-resource languages to determine the impact of smaller training corpora and bilingual dictionaries on the performance of cross-lingual word embeddings. It would also be interesting to consider the morphological richness of languages in this analysis. We further intend to investigate using alternative approaches to forming sub-word representations, such as byte-pair encoding, as well as incorporating positional embeddings into our model (e.g., Grave et al., 2018), to determine their impact on the quality of the resulting cross-lingual embeddings. Finally we plan to evaluate our proposed approach on further extrinsic tasks, such as POS tagging and named entity recognition, focusing on lower-resource languages.

Acknowledgments

This work is financially supported by the Natural Sciences and Engineering Research Council of Canada, the New Brunswick Innovation Foundation, and the University of New Brunswick. This research was enabled in part by support provided by ACENET (https://www.ace-net.ca/) and Compute Canada (www.computecanada.ca).

---

[8]https://github.com/Consl3411/XLing_Subword

References

Rami Al-Rfou', Bryan Perozzi, and Steven Skiena. 2013. Polyglot: Distributed word representations for multilingual NLP. In *Proceedings of the Seventeenth Conference on Computational Natural Language Learning*, pages 183–192, Sofia, Bulgaria. Association for Computational Linguistics.

Mikel Artetxe, Gorka Labaka, and Eneko Agirre. 2017. Learning bilingual word embeddings with (almost) no bilingual data. In *Proceedings of the 55th Annual Meeting of the Association for Computational Linguistics (Volume 1: Long Papers)*, pages 451–462, Vancouver, Canada. Association for Computational Linguistics.

Mikel Artetxe, Gorka Labaka, and Eneko Agirre. 2018a. Generalizing and improving bilingual word embedding mappings with a multi-step framework of linear transformations. In *Proceedings of the Thirty-Second AAAI Conference on Artificial Intelligence*, pages 5012–5019.

Mikel Artetxe, Gorka Labaka, and Eneko Agirre. 2018b. A robust self-learning method for fully unsupervised cross-lingual mappings of word embeddings. In *Proceedings of the 56th Annual Meeting of the Association for Computational Linguistics (Volume 1: Long Papers)*, pages 789–798, Melbourne, Australia. Association for Computational Linguistics.

Mikel Artetxe and Holger Schwenk. 2019. Massively multilingual sentence embeddings for zero-shot cross-lingual transfer and beyond. *Transactions of the Association for Computational Linguistics*, 7:597–610.

Timothy Baldwin, Jonathan Pool, and Susan Colowick. 2010. PanLex and LEXTRACT: Translating all words of all languages of the world. In *Coling 2010: Demonstrations*, pages 37–40, Beijing, China. Coling 2010 Organizing Committee.

Piotr Bojanowski, Edouard Grave, Armand Joulin, and Tomas Mikolov. 2017. Enriching word vectors with subword information. *Transactions of the Association for Computational Linguistics*, 5:135–146.

Aditi Chaudhary, Chunting Zhou, Lori Levin, Graham Neubig, David R. Mortensen, and Jaime Carbonell. 2018. Adapting word embeddings to new languages with morphological and phonological subword representations. In *Proceedings of the 2018 Conference on Empirical Methods in Natural Language Processing*, pages 3285–3295, Brussels, Belgium. Association for Computational Linguistics.

Danqi Chen and Christopher Manning. 2014. A fast and accurate dependency parser using neural networks. In *Proceedings of the 2014 Conference on*

Empirical Methods in Natural Language Processing (EMNLP), pages 740–750, Doha, Qatar. Association for Computational Linguistics.

Alexis Conneau and Guillaume Lample. 2019. Cross-lingual language model pretraining. In *Advances in Neural Information Processing Systems*, pages 7057–7067.

Jacob Devlin, Ming-Wei Chang, Kenton Lee, and Kristina Toutanova. 2019. BERT: Pre-training of deep bidirectional transformers for language understanding. In *Proceedings of the 2019 Conference of the North American Chapter of the Association for Computational Linguistics: Human Language Technologies, Volume 1 (Long and Short Papers)*, pages 4171–4186, Minneapolis, Minnesota. Association for Computational Linguistics.

Long Duong, Hiroshi Kanayama, Tengfei Ma, Steven Bird, and Trevor Cohn. 2016. Learning crosslingual word embeddings without bilingual corpora. In *Proceedings of the 2016 Conference on Empirical Methods in Natural Language Processing*, pages 1285–1295, Austin, Texas. Association for Computational Linguistics.

Lev Finkelstein, Evgeniy Gabrilovich, Yossi Matias, Ehud Rivlin, Zach Solan, Gadi Wolfman, and Eytan Ruppin. 2002. Placing search in context: The concept revisited. *ACM Transactions on Information Systems*, 20(1):116–131.

Stephan Gouws and Anders Søgaard. 2015. Simple task-specific bilingual word embeddings. In *Proceedings of the 2015 Conference of the North American Chapter of the Association for Computational Linguistics: Human Language Technologies*, pages 1386–1390, Denver, Colorado. Association for Computational Linguistics.

Edouard Grave, Piotr Bojanowski, Prakhar Gupta, Armand Joulin, and Tomas Mikolov. 2018. Learning word vectors for 157 languages. In *Proceedings of the Eleventh International Conference on Language Resources and Evaluation (LREC 2018)*, Miyazaki, Japan. European Language Resources Association (ELRA).

Pratik Jawanpuria, Arjun Balgovind, Anoop Kunchukuttan, and Bamdev Mishra. 2019. Learning multilingual word embeddings in latent metric space: A geometric approach. *Transactions of the Association for Computational Linguistics*, 7:107–120.

Armand Joulin, Piotr Bojanowski, Tomas Mikolov, Hervé Jégou, and Edouard Grave. 2018. Loss in translation: Learning bilingual word mapping with a retrieval criterion. In *Proceedings of the 2018 Conference on Empirical Methods in Natural Language Processing*, pages 2979–2984, Brussels, Belgium.

Phillip Keung, Yichao Lu, and Vikas Bhardwaj. 2019. Adversarial learning with contextual embeddings for zero-resource cross-lingual classification and NER. In *Proceedings of the 2019 Conference on Empirical Methods in Natural Language Processing and the 9th International Joint Conference on Natural Language Processing (EMNLP-IJCNLP)*, pages 1355–1360, Hong Kong, China. Association for Computational Linguistics.

Alexandre Klementiev, Ivan Titov, and Binod Bhattarai. 2012. Inducing crosslingual distributed representations of words. In *Proceedings of COLING 2012*, pages 1459–1474, Mumbai, India. The COLING 2012 Organizing Committee.

Guokun Lai, Barlas Oguz, and Veselin Stoyanov. 2019. Bridging the domain gap in cross-lingual document classification. *arXiv preprint arXiv:1909.07009*.

Guillaume Lample, Alexis Conneau, Marc'Aurelio Ranzato, Ludovic Denoyer, and Hervé Jégou. 2018. Word translation without parallel data. In *6th International Conference on Learning Representations, ICLR 2018*.

David D Lewis, Yiming Yang, Tony G Rose, and Fan Li. 2004. Rcv1: A new benchmark collection for text categorization research. *Journal of machine learning research*, 5(Apr):361–397.

Thang Luong, Hieu Pham, and Christopher D. Manning. 2015. Bilingual word representations with monolingual quality in mind. In *Proceedings of the 1st Workshop on Vector Space Modeling for Natural Language Processing*, pages 151–159, Denver, Colorado. Association for Computational Linguistics.

Thang Luong, Richard Socher, and Christopher Manning. 2013. Better word representations with recursive neural networks for morphology. In *Proceedings of the Seventeenth Conference on Computational Natural Language Learning*, pages 104–113, Sofia, Bulgaria. Association for Computational Linguistics.

Tomas Mikolov, Kai Chen, Greg Corrado, and Jeffrey Dean. 2013a. Efficient estimation of word representations in vector space. In *1st International Conference on Learning Representations, ICLR 2013, Scottsdale, Arizona, USA, May 2-4, 2013, Workshop Track Proceedings*.

Tomas Mikolov, Quoc V. Le, and Ilya Sutskever. 2013b. Exploiting similarities among languages for machine translation. *CoRR*, abs/1309.4168.

Aitor Ormazabal, Mikel Artetxe, Gorka Labaka, Aitor Soroa, and Eneko Agirre. 2019. Analyzing the limitations of cross-lingual word embedding mappings. In *Proceedings of the 57th Annual Meeting of the Association for Computational Linguistics*, pages 4990–4995, Florence, Italy. Association for Computational Linguistics.

Mayur Patidar, Surabhi Kumari, Manasi Patwardhan, Shirish Karande, Puneet Agarwal, Lovekesh Vig, and Gautam Shroff. 2019. From monolingual to multilingual FAQ assistant using multilingual co-training. In *Proceedings of the 2nd Workshop on Deep Learning Approaches for Low-Resource NLP (DeepLo 2019)*, pages 115–123, Hong Kong, China. Association for Computational Linguistics.

Jeffrey Pennington, Richard Socher, and Christopher Manning. 2014. GloVe: Global vectors for word representation. In *Proceedings of the 2014 Conference on Empirical Methods in Natural Language Processing (EMNLP)*, pages 1532–1543, Doha, Qatar. Association for Computational Linguistics.

Sebastian Ruder, Ivan Vuliundefined, and Anders Søgaard. 2019. A survey of cross-lingual word embedding models. *Journal of Artificial Intelligence Research*, 65(1):569–630.

Holger Schwenk and Xian Li. 2018. A corpus for multilingual document classification in eight languages. In *Proceedings of the Eleventh International Conference on Language Resources and Evaluation (LREC 2018)*, Miyazaki, Japan. European Language Resources Association (ELRA).

Rico Sennrich, Barry Haddow, and Alexandra Birch. 2016. Neural machine translation of rare words with subword units. In *Proceedings of the 54th Annual Meeting of the Association for Computational Linguistics (Volume 1: Long Papers)*, pages 1715–1725, Berlin, Germany. Association for Computational Linguistics.

Anders Søgaard, Sebastian Ruder, and Ivan Vulić. 2018. On the limitations of unsupervised bilingual dictionary induction. In *Proceedings of the 56th Annual Meeting of the Association for Computational Linguistics (Volume 1: Long Papers)*, pages 778–788, Melbourne, Australia. Association for Computational Linguistics.

Ivan Vulić, Goran Glavaš, Roi Reichart, and Anna Korhonen. 2019. Do we really need fully unsupervised cross-lingual embeddings? In *Proceedings of the 2019 Conference on Empirical Methods in Natural Language Processing and the 9th International Joint Conference on Natural Language Processing (EMNLP-IJCNLP)*, pages 4407–4418, Hong Kong, China. Association for Computational Linguistics.

Ivan Vulić and Marie-Francine Moens. 2013. Cross-lingual semantic similarity of words as the similarity of their semantic word responses. In *Proceedings of the 2013 Conference of the North American Chapter of the Association for Computational Linguistics: Human Language Technologies*, pages 106–116, Atlanta, Georgia. Association for Computational Linguistics.

Ivan Vulić and Marie-Francine Moens. 2016. Bilingual distributed word representations from document-aligned comparable data. *Journal of Artificial Intelligence Research*, 55:953–994.

Shijie Wu and Mark Dredze. 2019. Beto, bentz, becas: The surprising cross-lingual effectiveness of BERT. In *Proceedings of the 2019 Conference on Empirical Methods in Natural Language Processing and the 9th International Joint Conference on Natural Language Processing (EMNLP-IJCNLP)*, pages 833–844, Hong Kong, China. Association for Computational Linguistics.

Chao Xing, Dong Wang, Chao Liu, and Yiye Lin. 2015. Normalized word embedding and orthogonal transform for bilingual word translation. In *Proceedings of the 2015 Conference of the North American Chapter of the Association for Computational Linguistics: Human Language Technologies*, pages 1006–1011, Denver, Colorado. Association for Computational Linguistics.

Yi Zhu, Ivan Vulić, and Anna Korhonen. 2019. A systematic study of leveraging subword information for learning word representations. In *Proceedings of the 2019 Conference of the North American Chapter of the Association for Computational Linguistics: Human Language Technologies, Volume 1 (Long and Short Papers)*, pages 912–932, Minneapolis, Minnesota. Association for Computational Linguistics.

Semantic Structural Decomposition for Neural Machine Translation

Elior Sulem[*]
Dept. of Computer and Information Science
University of Pennsylvania
eliors@seas.upenn.edu

Omri Abend   **Ari Rappoport**
Dept. of Computer Science
The Hebrew University of Jerusalem
oabend|arir@cs.huji.ac.il

Abstract

Building on recent advances in semantic parsing and text simplification, we investigate the use of semantic splitting of the source sentence as preprocessing for machine translation. We experiment with a Transformer model and evaluate using large-scale crowd-sourcing experiments. Results show a significant increase in fluency on long sentences on an English-to-French setting with a training corpus of 5M sentence pairs, while retaining comparable adequacy. We also perform a manual analysis which explores the tradeoff between adequacy and fluency in the case where all sentence lengths are considered.[1]

1 Introduction

In this paper, we apply a semantic decomposition approach for Neural Machine Translation (NMT) and demonstrate that it can tackle two of the main limitations of state-of-the-art NMT. The first is the translation of long sentences, which is a recurrent issue arising in NMT evaluation (Sutskever et al., 2014; Cho et al., 2014; Pouget-Abadie et al., 2014; Su et al., 2018; Currey and Heafield, 2018). The second limitation is that current research in NMT mostly focuses on translating single sentences to single sentences, and is evaluated accordingly. However, Li and Nenkova (2015) showed that using several sentences to translate a source sentence is sometimes the preferable option. Therefore, the simplicity of the output could be an important quality marker for translation.

In our model, each source sentence is split (or decomposed) into semantic units, namely scenes,

building on the Direct Semantic Splitting algorithm (DSS; Sulem et al., 2018b) that uses the Universal Conceptual Cognitive Annotation (UCCA; Abend and Rappoport, 2013) scheme for semantic representation. Scenes are then translated separately and concatenated for generating the final translation output, which may consist of several sentences.

Our main experiments use the state-of-the-art Transformer model (Vaswani et al., 2017) in English-to-French settings. We also include experiments with other MT architectures and training set sizes, and evaluate our results using the crowd-sourcing protocol of Graham et al. (2016) (§4). We obtain a significant increase in fluency on sentences longer than 30 words on the newstest2014 test corpus for English-to-French translation, with a training corpus of 5M sentence pairs, without degrading adequacy. Considering all sentence lengths, we observe a tradeoff between fluency and adequacy. We explore it using a manual analysis, suggesting that the decrease in adequacy is partly due to the loss of cohesion resulting from the splitting (§6).

We then proceed to investigate the case of simulated low-resource settings as well as the effect of other sentence splitting methods, including Split-and-Rephrase models (Aharoni and Goldberg, 2018; Botha et al., 2018) (§7). The latter yield considerably lower scores than the use of simple semantic rules, supporting the case for corpus-independent simplification rules.

2 Related Work

Sentence segmentation for MT. Segmenting sentences into sub-units, based on punctuation and syntactic structures, and recombining their output has been explored by a number of statistical MT works (Xiong et al., 2009; Goh and Sumita, 2011; Sudoh et al., 2010). In NMT, Pouget-Abadie et al. (2014) segmented the source using ILP, tackling English-to-French neural translation. They con-

---

*Proceedings of the Ninth Joint Conference on Lexical and Computational Semantics (*SEM)*, pages 50–57
Barcelona, Spain (Online), December 12–13, 2020

cluded that segmentation improves overall translation quality but quality may decrease if the segmented fragments are not well-formed. The concatenation may sometimes degrade fluency and result in errors in punctuation and capitalization. Kuang and Xiong (2016) attempted to find split positions such that no reordering will be necessary in the target side for Chinese-English. We differ from these approaches in using a separate text simplification module that can be applied to different kinds of MT systems, and using a semantically-motivated segmentation. Moreover, we allow the final output to be composed of several sentences, taking into account the structural simplicity aspect of translation quality (Li and Nenkova, 2015).

Text Simplification for MT. Sentence splitting, which goes beyond segmentation and denotes the conversion of one sentence into one or several sentences, is the main structural operation studied in Text Simplification (TS). While MT preprocessing was one of the main motivations for the first automatic simplification system (Chandrasekar et al., 1996), only few works empirically explored the usefulness of simplification techniques for MT.

Mishra et al. (2014) used sentence splitting as a preprocessing step for Hindi-to-English translation with a dependency parser and additional modules for gerunds and shared arguments. Štajner and Popović (2016) performed structural and lexical simplification as part of a preprocessing step for English-to-Serbian MT. Manual correction is carried out before translation. Štajner and Popović (2018) investigated the use of TS as a processing step for NMT, focusing on syntax-based rules that address relative clauses (Siddhathan, 2011) for English-to-German and English-to-Serbian translation. Investigating the translation of 106 out of 1000 sentences that have been modified by simplification, they find that the automatic simplification of English relative clauses can improve translation only if simplifications are quality-controlled or corrected in post-processing. We differ from this work in using semantic rules and by translating independently each of the obtained sentences.

3 Semantic Decomposition

UCCA (Universal Cognitive Conceptual Annotation; Abend and Rappoport, 2013) is a semantic annotation scheme rooted in typological and cognitive linguistic theory (Dixon, 2010b,a; Langacker, 2008). It aims to represent the main semantic phe-

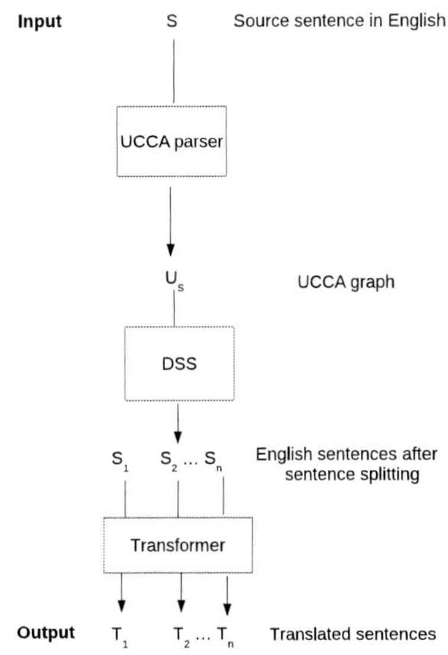

Figure 1: SemSplit pipeline. After the application of the Direct Semantic Splitting, which requires UCCA parsing, each of resulted sentences is independently translated using a Transformer system, previously trained on English-French parallel data. The obtained translations are directly concatenated, forming the final output.

nomena in the text, abstracting away from syntax.

Formally, UCCA structures are directed acyclic graphs whose nodes (or *units*) correspond either to the leaves of the graph or to several elements viewed as a single entity according to some semantic or cognitive consideration. A *scene* is UCCA's notion of an event or a frame, and is a unit that corresponds to a movement, an action or a state which persists in time. Every scene contains one main relation, which can be either a Process or a State. Scenes may contain one or more Participants, interpreted in a broad sense to include locations and destinations. For example, the sentence "John went home" has a single scene whose Process is "went". The two Participants are "John" and "home".

Scenes can provide additional information about an established entity (Elaborator scenes), commonly participles or relative clauses. For example, "(child) who went home" is an Elaborator scene in "The child who went home is John". A scene may also be a Participant in another scene. For example, "John went home" in the sentence: "He said John went home". In other cases, scenes are annotated as parallel scenes (H), which are flat structures and may include a Linker (L), as in: "When$_L$ [he arrives]$_H$, [he will call them]$_H$".

For UCCA parsing, we use TUPA, a transition-based parser (Hershcovich et al., 2017) (specifically, the TUPA$_{BiLSTM}$ model).

We build on the DSS rule-based semantic splitting method (Sulem et al., 2018b), and use Rule #1 which targets parallel scenes. We further explore the use of the additional kinds of scenes in Section 7 for less conservative sentence splitting. In Rule #1, parallel scenes of a given sentence are extracted, split into different sentences and concatenated according to the order of appearance. More formally, given a decomposition of a sentence S into parallel scenes $Sc_1, Sc_2, \cdots Sc_n$ (indexed by the order of the first token), we obtain the following rule, where "|" is the sentence delimiter:

$$S \longrightarrow Sc_1|Sc_2|\cdots|Sc_n$$

As UCCA allows argument sharing between scenes, the rule may duplicate the same sub-span of S across sentences. For example, the rule will convert "He came back home and played the piano" into "He came back home"|"He played the piano.".

Using UCCA-based sentence splitting in our model is motivated by the corpus-based analysis presented in Sulem et al. (2015) where it is shown that a scene in English is generally translated to a scene in French.

4 Experimental Setup

Corpora We experiment on the full English-French training data provided in the WMT setting (Bojar et al., 2014), which corresponds to about 39M sentence pairs after cleaning.[2] We refer to this setting as the FullTrain Setting. We also experiment on the LessTrain Setting where less training data is involved by removing the large UN Corpus and the 10^9 French-English Corpus from the training data, obtaining a new training corpus of about 5M sentence pairs. The development set is Newstest 2013, that consists of 3000 sentences. The test set is Newstest2014, consisting of 3003 sentences.

Systems To investigate the use of semantic structural decomposition for NMT, we propose a two-step method. First, the original sentence is split into several sentences the DSS rule (see § 3), implemented with the UCCA software.[3] Then, each of the obtained sentences is translated separately

by the OpenNMT-py implementation of the Transformer (Vaswani et al., 2017).[4] The translated sentences are concatenated to form the final output. We name the combined system Transformer Sem-Split and compare it to the Transformer Baseline, where no splitting is performed. The pipeline architecture is summarized in Figure 1.

The Transformer is trained for 200K training steps, both in the FullTrain and the LessTrain settings. The development data was used for selecting the model with the highest accuracy (where perplexity was used in cases of ties). The system was evaluated on the development data every 10K steps.

For comparison, we also implement our system in the case where the Transformer is replaced by another NMT system, namely a two-layers LSTM model and the Moses phrase-based machine translation system (Koehn et al., 2007). The neural model, also implemented with OpenNMT-py, is trained and validated in the same way as the Transformer. For Moses, the default model is used in a single setting (LessTrain) with MGIZA word alignment,[5] and KenLM language model (Heafield, 2011) using the monolingual data provided in WMT 2014, and MERT tuning on the development set. Here too we compare the combined systems to baseline systems which do not perform decomposition.

4.1 Evaluation Using Crowdsourcing

In addition to the limitations of BLEU evaluation (Papineni et al., 2002) in the context of MT (Callison-Burch et al., 2006, and much subsequent work), BLEU may correlate negatively with output quality in cases that involve sentence splitting (Sulem et al., 2018a). We therefore evaluate using crowdsourcing, and follow the protocol proposed by Graham et al. (2016). Evaluation was carried out using Amazon Mechanical Turk.[6] See Appendix A for a detailed description.

5 Results

The results in both FullTrain and LessTrain settings are presented in Table 1.

In terms of fluency, LessTrain Transformer Sem-Split ranks first in this setting and significantly outperforms the corresponding baseline system (52.5 vs. 42.5, $p < 10^{-4}$).[7] For Moses too, the use

---

[2]Cleaning, tokenization and truecasing as well as detokenization and detruecasing of the outputs are performed using the Moses tools: http://www.statmt.org/moses/.

[3]https://github.com/danielhers/ucca

[4]https://github.com/OpenNMT/OpenNMT-py

[5]https://github.com/moses-smt/mgiza

[6]https://www.mturk.com/

[7]Significance is computed using the Wilcoxon one-sided rank sum test applied on the standardized scores, following Graham et al. (2016).

System		Adequacy		Fluency	
		All	Long	All	Long
Transformer	Baseline	48.8	48.0	57.1	49.4
	SemSplit	40.0	28.7	43.5	37.1
LSTM	Baseline	41.2	50.1	43.2	46.8
	SemSplit	33.1	34.7	39.3	37.5
Transformer	Baseline	47.5	41.7	42.5	39.6
	SemSplit	39.8	40.1	52.5	52.1
LSTM	Baseline	40.6	37.5	47.3	52.9
	SemSplit	36.8	34.9	46.6	44.5
Moses	Baseline	40.1	45.4	38.1	30.1
	SemSplit	34.9	43.2	40.2	50.4

Table 1: Raw system adequacy and fluency scores of the SemSplit systems and the baselines on the FullTrain (top) and LessTrain (bottom) settings. For each system, the raw score is presented, both when considering every sentence length (**All**) and when focusing on sentences longer than 30 words (**Long**).

System		Adequacy	Fluency
Transformer	Baseline	47.0	47.5
	SemSplit$_{1+2}$	29.7	32.5
	NeuralWiki-Split	12.9	6.0
	NeuralWEB-SPLIT	4.1	5.1
LSTM	Baseline	40.6	38.2
	SemSplit$_{1+2}$	24.3	34.2
Transformer	Baseline	50.6	55.1
	SemSplit$_{1+2}$	25.3	39.1
LSTM	Baseline	45.6	46.4
	SemSplit$_{1+2}$	31.9	31.0
Moses	Baseline	38.2	38.3
	SemSplit	30.8	23.5

Table 2: Raw system adequacy and fluency scores of the SemSplit$_{1+2}$ systems and the baselines on the FullTrain (top) and LessTrain (bottom) setting.

of semantic sentence splitting increases fluency (40.2 vs. 38.1), but not significantly. On the other hand, where splitting is used as preprocessing, adequacy scores decrease. In particular, LessTrain Transformer Baseline significantly outperforms the SemSplit counterpart (47.5 vs. 39.8, $p < 10^{-4}$).

For sentences longer than 30, SemSplit Transformer in the LessTrain setting significantly outperforms the baseline in terms of fluency (52.1 vs. 39.6, $p = 0.02$), with only a non-significant (small) degradation in adequacy (41.7 vs. 40.1, $p = 0.46$).

6 Manual Analysis

To further zoom in on the obtained adequacy scores, we decompose adequacy into two dimensions: preservation of semantic content in the level of scenes and the cohesion of the text (i.e., whether the different scenes are cohesively linked together). To do so, we manually annotate a sample of 150 sentences from the original test set with a similar proportion of sentences in different length categories as the original corpus, and assess the semantic preservation at the scene-level for each of the extracted scenes, as well as the sentence-level cohesion (see Appendix B for the protocol).

For LessTrain, we find that 66.2% of the scenes

are deemed equally preserved by the SemSplit and Baseline systems. On the other hand, 20.9% of the scenes are better preserved by the baseline and 10.7% of the scenes are better preserved by the SemSplit system. Averaging over scenes that belong to the same sentence, we find that 68% of the sentences are either better preserved by SemSplit or equally preserved. Regarding cohesion, SemSplit and the Baseline have a comparable cohesion for 59% of the sentences. The Baseline has a better cohesion for 36% of the sentences, while it is improved by SemSplit in 5% of the cases.

The analysis suggests that cohesion has a central role in the decrease (and the non-increase for long sentences) of the adequacy scores. Therefore the tradeoff between adequacy and fluency observed when all sentence lengths are considered can be explained by a tradeoff between the cohesion and structural simplicity aspects of translation quality.

The different aspects of the translation quality are further illustrated in Table 3, where two input and output examples are presented, focusing on the LessTrain setting. In example (1), the SemSplit output is similar to the Baseline one at the lexical level but differs in its structure, the SemSplit system behaving as a cross-lingual simplifier at the structural level. On the other hand, linkers such as "so" are not translated in the case of SemSplit. In example (2), the word "interference" is correctly translated by SemSplit, while it is translated into "ingérence" ("intervention") in French, which is wrong in this context.

7 Additional Experiments

We first explore the performance of the proposed system in low-resource machine translation, by following the approach of Hoang et al. (2018) and randomly select 1M and 100K sentence pairs from the entire English-French training set, defining the 1MTrain and 100KTrain settings respectively. Tuning and testing remain as before.

The resulted raw scores for the 1MTrain and 100KTrain settings are presented in Appendix D, Table 4 . We observe that while in 1MTrain, the SemSplit models obtain low results compared to the respective baselines, the SemSplit models obtain higher fluency in 100KTrain, though not significantly.

Second, to further explore the sentence splitting component, we replicate our model, separating both parallel and embedded scenes before the

(1) **Input:**	Hamas has defended its use of tunnels in the fight against Israel, stating that the aim was to capture Israeli soldiers so they could be exchanged for Palestinian prisoners.
Baseline (LessTrain)	**Output:** Le Hamas a défendu son utilisation de tunnels dans la lutte contre Israël, affirmant que l'objectif était de capturer des soldats israéliens afin qu'ils puissent être échangés contre des prisonniers palestiniens.
	Literal translation: Hamas has defended its use of tunnels in the fight against Israel, stating that the aim was to capture Israeli soldiers so they could be exchanged for Palestinian prisoners.
SemSplit (LessTrain)	**Output:** Le Hamas a défendu son utilisation de tunnels dans la lutte contre Israël. Le Hamas a déclaré que l'objectif était de capturer des soldats israéliens. Ils pourraient être échangés contre des prisonniers palestiniens.
	Literal translation: Hamas has defended its use of tunnels in the fight against Israel. Hamas stated that the aim was to capture Israeli soldiers. They could be exchanged for Palestinian prisoners.
(2) **Input:**	Douglas Kidd of the National Association of Airline Passengers said he believes interference from the devices is genuine even if the risk is minimal.
Baseline (LessTrain)	**Output:** Douglas., de l'Association nationale des compagnies aériennes, a déclaré qu'il considérait que l'ingérence des appareils était réelle, même si le risque était minimal.
	Literal translation: Douglas., from the Association National of the companies airline, claimed that he believed that the intervention of the devices was genuine, even if the risk is minimal.
SemSplit (LessTrain)	**Output:** Douglas., de l'Association nationale des compagnies aériennes, a déclaré qu' il estimait que l'interférence avec les appareils était réelle. Le risque est minimal.
	Literal translation: Douglas., from the Association national of the companies airline, claimed that he believed the interference with the devices was genuine. The risk is minimal.

Table 3: Input and output examples for the Baseline and SemSplit system in the LessTrain setting, together with an English literal translation of the French outputs.

translation. We use Rule #2 from the DSS system (Sulem et al., 2018b) addressing Elaborator scenes (See Appendix C), which we further extend to also include Participant scenes. We denote the resulting system with Transformer SemSplit$_{1+2}$. We also compare the model with two additional sentence splitting systems, where DSS is replaced with the Seq2Seq Copy 512 model for Split-and-Rephrase (Aharoni and Goldberg, 2018) trained on the WEB-SPLIT corpus (Narayan et al., 2017) (version 1.0), and the same model trained on the WikiSplit corpus (Botha et al., 2018). Each of the obtained new sentences is translated by the FullTrain Transformer system. Finally the translated sentences are directly concatenated. The resulting systems are denoted with Transformer NeuralWEB-SPLIT and Tranformer NeuralWiki-Split.

The results for the FullTrain and LessTrain settings are presented in Table 2. As in the case where only the first rule is used, adequacy scores decrease following splitting. On the other hand, in this case the SemSplit models do not have higher fluency scores than their corresponding baselines, probably because of the more aggressive splitting compared to #Rule 1 alone. For both adequacy and fluency, the Split-and-Rephrase models obtain very low scores. Observing their outputs, we find many wrong splits and word repetitions at the splitting phase, which affects the final output. As this trend is not observed on the standard WEB-SPLIT test corpus, these results may suggest a domain adaptation effect, which supports the case for corpus-independent sentence splitting.

8 Conclusion

This work investigates the application of semantic structural decomposition for NMT, proposing an intermediate way between sentence segmentation used in MT and TS preprocessing, where each of the semantic components is separately translated. Using the Transformer and large-scale crowd-sourcing evaluation, we obtain an increase in fluency on long sentences on an English-to-French setting without significantly lowering adequacy. We further observe increased fluency when evaluating on all the sentences, albeit at the cost of adequacy. Future work concerns the recombination of the output sentences, inserting the linkage between them, so as not to lose semantic content.

Aknowledgments

We would like to thank the annotators for participating in our evaluation experiments and in the UCCA annotation. This work was partially supported by the Israel Science Foundation (grant No.929/17) and by the HUJI Cyber Security Research Center in conjunction with the Israel National Cyber Bureau in the Prime Minister's Office.

References

Omri Abend and Ari Rappoport. 2013. Universal Conceptual Cognitive Annotation (UCCA). In *Proc. of ACL-13*, pages 228–238.

Omri Abend, Shai Yerushalmi, and Ari Rappoport. 2017. UCCAApp: Web-application for syntactic and semantic phrase-based annotation. In *Proc. of ACL'17, System Demonstrations*, pages 109–114.

Roee Aharoni and Yoav Goldberg. 2018. Split and rephrase: Better evaluation and a stronger baseline. In *Proc. of ACL'18 (Short papers)*, pages 719–728.

Ondrej Bojar, Christian Buck, Christian Federmann, Barry Haddow, Philipp Koehn, Johannes Leveling, Christof Monz, Pavel Pecina, Matt Post, Herve Saint-Amand, Radu Soricut, Lucia Specia, and Aleš Tamchyna. 2014. Findings of the 2014 workshop on statistical machine translation. In *Proceedings of the Ninth Workshop on Statistical Machine Translation*, pages 12–58, Baltimore, Maryland, USA. Association for Computational Linguistics.

Jan A. Botha, Manaal Faruqui, John Alex, Jason Baldridge, and Dipanjan Das. 2018. Learning to split and rephrase from Wikipedia edit history. In *Proc. of EMNLP'18 (Short papers)*, pages 732–737.

Chris Callison-Burch, Miles Osborne, and Philipp Koehn. 2006. Re-evaluating the role of BLEU in machine translation. In *Proc. of EACL'06*, pages 249–256.

Raman Chandrasekar, Christine Doran, and Bangalore Srinivas. 1996. Motivations and methods for sentence simplification. In *Proc. of COLING'96*, pages 1041–1044.

Kyunghyun Cho, Bart van Merriënboer, Dzmitry Bahdanau, and Yoshua Bengio. 2014. On the properties of neural machine translation: Encoder–decoder approaches. In *Proc. of Eighth Workshop on Syntax, Semantics and Structure in Statistical Translation*.

Anna Currey and Kenneth Heafield. 2018. Multi-source syntactic neural machine translation. In *Proc. of EMNLP'18*, pages 2961–2966.

Robert M.W. Dixon. 2010a. *Basic Linguistic Theory: Grammatical Topics*, volume 2. Oxford University Press.

Robert M.W. Dixon. 2010b. *Basic Linguistic Theory: Methodology*, volume 1. Oxford University Press.

Chooi-Ling Goh and Eiichiro Sumita. 2011. Splitting long input sentences for phrase-based statistical machine translation. In *Proc. of ANLP'11*, pages 802–805.

Yvette Graham, Timothy Baldwin, Alistair Moffat, and Justin Zobel. 2016. Can machine translation be evaluated by the crowd alone? *Natural Language Engineering*, 1(1):1–28.

Kenneth Heafield. 2011. KenLM: Faster and smaller language model queries. In *Proc. of the Sixth Workshop on Statistical Machine Translation*.

Daniel Hershcovich, Omri Abend, and Ari Rappoport. 2017. A transition-based directed acyclic graph parser for UCCA. In *Proc. of ACL'17*, pages 1127–1138.

Cong Duy Vu Hoang, Philipp Koehn, Gholamreza Haffari, and Trevor Cohn. 2018. Iterative back-translation for neural machine translation. In *Proc. of the 2nd Workshop on Neural Machine Translation and Generation*, pages 18–24.

Philipp Koehn, Hieu Hoang, Alexandra Birch, Chris Callison-Buch, Marcello Federico, Nicola Bertoldi, Brooke Cowan, Wade Shen, Christine Moran, Richard Zens, Chris Dyer, Ondřej Bojar, Alexandra Constantin, and Evan Herbst. 2007. Moses: open source toolkit for statistical machine translation. In *Proc. of ACL'07 on interactive poster and demonstration sessions*, pages 177–180.

Shaoui Kuang and Deyi Xiong. 2016. Automatic long sentence segmentation for neural machine translation. In *Natural Language Understanding and Intelligent Applications: 5th CCF Conference on Natural Language Processing and Chinese Computing, NLPCC 2016, and 24th International Conference on Computer Processing of Oriental Languages, IC-CPOL 2016*, pages 162–174.

Ronald W. Langacker. 2008. *Cognitive Grammar: A Basic Introduction*. Oxford University Press, USA.

Junyi Jessi Li and Ani Nenkova. 2015. Detecting content-heavy sentences: A cross-language case study. In *Proc. of EMNLP'15*, pages 1271–1281.

Kshitij Mishra, Ankush Soni, Rahul Sharma, and Dipti Misra Sharma. 2014. Exploring the effects of sentence simplification on Hindi to English Machine Translation systems. In *Proc. of the Workshop on Automatic Text Simplification: Methods and Applications in the Multilingual Society*, pages 21–29.

Shashi Narayan, Claire Gardent, Shay B. Cohen, and Anastasia Shimorina. 2017. Split and rephrase. In *Proc. of EMNLP'17*, pages 617–627.

Kishore Papineni, Salim Roukos, Todd Ward, and Wei-Jing Zhu. 2002. BLEU: a method for automatic evaluation of machine translation. In *Proc. of ACL'02*, pages 311–318.

Jean Pouget-Abadie, Dzmitry Bahdanau, Bart van Merriënboer, Kyunghyun Cho, and Yoshua Bengio. 2014. Overcoming the curse of sentence length for neural machine translation with automatic segmentation. In *Proc. of the Eighth Workshop on Syntax, Semantics and Structure in Statistical Translation*, pages 78–85.

Advaith Siddhathan. 2011. Text simplification using typed dependencies: A comparison of the robustness of different generation strategies. In *Proc. of the 13th European Workshop on Natural Language Generation*, pages 2–11. Association of Computational Linguistics.

Sanja Štajner and Maja Popović. 2016. Can text simplification help machine translation. *Baltic J. Modern Computing*, 4:230–242.

Jinsong Su, Jiali Zeng, Deyi Xiong, Yang Liu, Mingxuan Wang, and Jun Xie. 2018. A hierarchy-to-sequence attentional neural machine translation. *IEEE/ACM Transactions on Audio, Speech, and Language Processing*, 26(3).

Katsuhito Sudoh, Kevin Duh, Hajime Tsukada, Tsutomu Hirao, and Masaaki Nagata. 2010. Divide and translate: Improving long distance reordering in statisticxal machine translation. In *Proc. of the Joint 5th Workshop on Statistical Machine Translation and MetricsMATR*, pages 418–427.

Elior Sulem, Omri Abend, and Ari Rappoport. 2015. Conceptual annotations preserve structure across translations. In *Proc. of 1st Workshop on Semantics-Driven Statistical Machine Translation (S2Mt 2015)*, pages 11–22.

Elior Sulem, Omri Abend, and Ari Rappoport. 2018a. BLEU is not suitable for the evaluation of text simplification. In *Proc. of EMNLP*, pages 738–744.

Elior Sulem, Omri Abend, and Ari Rappoport. 2018b. Simple and effective text simplification using semantic and neural methods. In *Proc. of ACL*, pages 162–173.

Ilya Sutskever, Oriol Vinyals, and Quôc Lê. 2014. Sequence to sequence learning with neural networks. In *Proc. of NIPS*.

Ashish Vaswani, Noam Shazeer, Niki Parmar, Jakob Uszkoreit, Llion Jones, Aidan Gomez, Lukasz Kaiser, and Illia Polosukhin. 2017. Attention is all you need. In *Proc. of NIPS*.

Sanja Štajner and Maja Popović. 2018. Improving machine translation of English relative clauses with automatic text simplification. In *Proc. of the INLG 2018 First Workshop on Automatic Text Adaptation (ATA)*.

Hao Xiong, Wenwen Xu, Haitao Mi, Yang Liu, and Qun Liu. 2009. Sub-sentence division for tree-based machine translation. In *Proc. od ACL'09 (Short papers)*, pages 137–140.

Appendix A: Crowdsourcing Evaluation Protocol

We follow the protocol proposed by Graham et al. (2016) for evaluation via Amazon Mechanical Turk[8] and use their pre-processing and post-processing software[9]. Adequacy (where the output is compared to the reference) and fluency (where only the output appears) are evaluated independently, according to a 100-point slider, in different experiments. Each of the experiments is composed of 10 HITs (Human Intelligence Tasks) where each HIT includes 100 French sentences which are compared to the reference in the case of adequacy and separately evaluated in the case of fluency. These 100 sentences include 70 MT system outputs extracted randomly from the test set, 10 reference translations, corresponding to 10 of the 70 system outputs, 10 bad reference translations, corresponding to a different 10 of the 70 system outputs and 10 repeat MT system outputs, drawn from the remaining 50 of the original 70 system outputs. The role of the references, bad references and repeat outputs is to control the quality of the evaluation and to not consider ratings from annotators who don't pass the threshold, based on these two main assumptions (see (Graham et al., 2016) for more details):

A: When a consistent judge is presented with a set of assessments for translations from two systems, one of which is known to produce better translations than the other, the score sample of the better system will be significantly greater than that of the inferior system.

B: When a consistent judge is presented with a set of repeat assessments, the score sample across the initial presentations will not be significantly different from the score sample across the second presentations. We here require that each HIT will be answered by 10 different annotators, who are self-assessed native French speakers.

Main setting (§4 and §5): In each of the two crowdsourcing experiments, which correspond respectively to the evaluation of adequacy and fluency in the case where only Rule #1 is applied, we include 10 systems: 4 Transformer systems, namely Transformer SemSplit in both FullTrain and LessTrain settings and the corresponding baselines; 4 LSTM systems (LSTM SemSplit in the two settings and the corresponding baselines) and 2 phrase-based systems (Moses in the LessTrain setting and its corresponding baseline).

---

[8] https://www.mturk.com/
[9] https://github.com/ygraham/crowd-alone

Low resource setting (§7): In each of the adequacy and fluency experiments, 12 systems are involved: the Transformer SemSplit, LSTM SemSplit and Moses SemSplit systems and their corresponding baselines, each implemented in both 1MTrain and 100KTrain settings.

Splitting exploration setting (§7): In each of the adequacy and fluency experiments, we include 12 systems: 6 Transformer systems, namely Transformer SemSplit$_{1+2}$ in both FullTrain and LessTrain settings, the corresponding baselines, as well as the two neural splitting systems, 4 LSTM systems (LSTM SemSplit$_{1+2}$ in the two settings and the corresponding baselines) and 2 phrase-based systems (Moses in the LessTrain setting and its corresponding baseline).

Appendix B: Manual Analysis Protocol

We perform a manual result analysis of an extract of the data, using the following protocol. First, we sub-sample 150 sentences from the original test set (3003 sentences), such that it includes the same proportion of sentences that contain 0 to 10 words (18% of sentences), 10 to 20 words (35% of the sentences), 20 to 30 words (28%), 30 to 40 words (14%), 40 to 50 words (4%) and more than 50 words (1%), as in the original corpus. Then, to abstract away from possible parsing errors, the new corpus is manually annotated by a single expert UCCA annotator using the UCCAApp annotation tool (Abend et al., 2017). For each of the 150 sentences, each scene segmentation (according to the UCCA manual annotation) is compared to the Transformer SemSplit output and the Transformer Baseline output for this sentence by a another annotator with high proficiency in both English and French (one of the authors of the paper) to analyze the relative preservation of the input scenes in the two systems. We use a 3 point Likert scale for the comparison, assessing if the SemSplit scene preservation is worse, similar or better, compared to the baseline. In the same way, the cohesion of the outputs (defined as the links between their different parts) is also compared using a 3 point Likert scale.

Appendix C: Rule #2 in Direct Semantic Splitting (Sulem et al., 2018b)

Minimal Centers in UCCA (Abend and Rappoport, 2013): With respect to units which are not scenes, the category Center denotes the semantic head. For example, "dogs" is the center of the expression "big brown dogs", and "box" is the center of "in the box". There could be more than one Center in a unit, for example in the case of coordination, where all conjuncts are Centers. Sulem et al. (2018b) defined the minimal center of a UCCA unit u to be the UCCA graph's leaf reached by starting from u and iteratively selecting the child tagged as Center.

Rule #2: Given a sentence S, the second rule extracts Elaborator scenes and corresponding minimal centers. The Elaborator scenes are then concatenated to the original sentence where the embedded scenes, except for the minimal center they elaborate are removed. Pronouns such as "who", "which" and "that" are also removed.

Formally, if $\{(Sc_1, C_1) \cdots (Sc_n, C_n)\}$ are the Elaborator scenes of S and their corresponding minimal centers, the rewrite is

$$S \longrightarrow S - \bigcup_{i=1}^{n}(Sc_i - C_i)|Sc_1| \cdots |Sc_n$$

where $S - A$ is S without the unit A. For example, in the case of Elaborator scenes, this rule converts the sentence "He observed the planet which has 14 known satellites" to "He observed the planet| Planet has 14 known satellites.".

After the extraction of Parallel scenes and Elaborator scenes, the resulting simplified Parallel scenes are placed before the Elaborator scenes.

Appendix D: Low-resource Settings

System		Adequacy	Fluency
Transformer$_{1M}$	Baseline	56.4	69.6
	SemSplit	47.1	64.0
LSTM$_{1M}$	Baseline	52.3	66.5
	SemSplit	46.0	65.5
Moses$_{1M}$	Baseline	45.3	65.6
	SemSplit	38.6	61.2
Transformer$_{100K}$	Baseline	29.9	56.5
	SemSplit	29.8	57.6
LSTM$_{100K}$	Baseline	37.1	56.7
	SemSplit	29.9	60.0
Moses$_{100K}$	Baseline	39.3	60.4
	SemSplit	34.5	61.2

Table 4: Raw system adequacy and fluency scores of the SemSplit systems and the baselines on the 1MTrain (top) and 100KTrain (bottom) settings.

Token Sequence Labeling vs. Clause Classification for English Emotion Stimulus Detection

Laura Oberländer and **Roman Klinger**
Institut für Maschinelle Sprachverarbeitung, University of Stuttgart
Pfaffenwaldring 5b, 70569 Stuttgart, Germany
{laura.oberlaender, roman.klinger}@ims.uni-stuttgart.de

Abstract

Emotion stimulus detection is the task of finding the cause of an emotion in a textual description, similar to target or aspect detection for sentiment analysis. Previous work approached this in three ways, namely (1) as text classification into an inventory of predefined possible stimuli ("Is the stimulus category *A* or *B*?"), (2) as sequence labeling of tokens ("Which tokens describe the stimulus?"), and (3) as clause classification ("Does this clause contain the emotion stimulus?"). So far, setting (3) has been evaluated broadly on Mandarin and (2) on English, but no comparison has been performed. Therefore, we analyze whether clause classification or token sequence labeling is better suited for emotion stimulus detection in English. We propose an integrated framework which enables us to evaluate the two different approaches comparably, implement models inspired by state-of-the-art approaches in Mandarin, and test them on four English data sets from different domains. Our results show that token sequence labeling is superior on three out of four datasets, in both clause-based and token sequence-based evaluation. The only case in which clause classification performs better is one data set with a high density of clause annotations. Our error analysis further confirms quantitatively and qualitatively that clauses are not the appropriate stimulus unit in English.

1 Introduction

Research in emotion analysis from text focuses on classification, i.e., mapping sentences or documents to emotion categories based on psychological theories (e.g., Ekman (1992), Plutchik (2001)). While this task answers the question *which* emotion is expressed in a text, it does not detect the textual unit, which reveals *why* the emotion has been developed. For instance, in the example *"Paul is angry because he lost his wallet."* it remains hidden that *lost his wallet* is the reason for experiencing the emotion of anger. This stimulus, e.g., an event description, a person, a state of affairs, or an object enables deeper insight, similar to targeted or aspect-based sentiment analysis (Jakob and Gurevych, 2010; Yang and Cardie, 2013; Klinger and Cimiano, 2013; Pontiki et al., 2015, 2016, i.a.). This situation is dissatisfying for (at least) two reasons. First, detecting the emotions expressed in social media and their stimuli might play a role in understanding why different social groups change their attitude towards specific events and could help recognize specific issues in society. Second, understanding the relationship between stimuli and emotions is also compelling from a psychological point of view, given that emotions are commonly considered responses to relevant situations (Scherer, 2005).

Models which tackle the task of detecting the stimulus in a text have seen three different problem formulations in the past: (1) Classification into a predefined inventory of possible stimuli (Mohammad et al., 2014), similarly to previous work in sentiment analysis (Ganu et al., 2009), (2) classification of precalculated or annotated clauses as containing a stimulus or not (Gui et al., 2016, i.a.), and (3) detecting the tokens that describe the stimulus, e.g., with IOB labels (Ghazi et al., 2015, i.a.). We follow the two settings in which the stimuli are not predefined categories (2+3, cf. Figure 1).

These two settings have their advantages and disadvantages. The clause classification setting is more coarse-grained and, therefore, more likely to perform well than the token sequence labeling setting, but it might miss the exact starting and endpoints of a stimulus span and needs clause annotations or a syntactic parse with the risk of error

*Proceedings of the Ninth Joint Conference on Lexical and Computational Semantics (*SEM)*, pages 58–70
Barcelona, Spain (Online), December 12–13, 2020

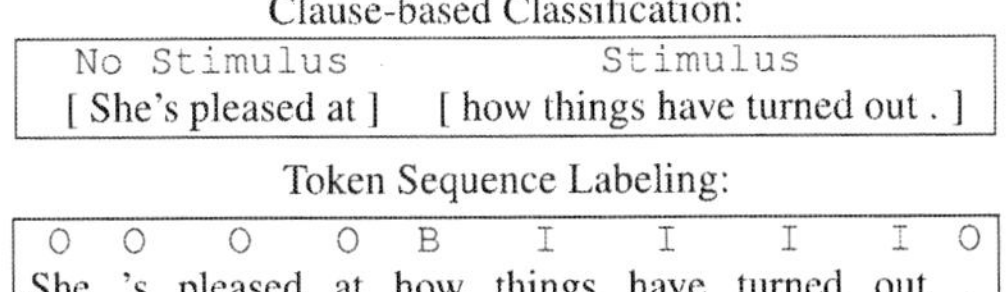

Figure 1: Different formulations for emotion stimulus detection.

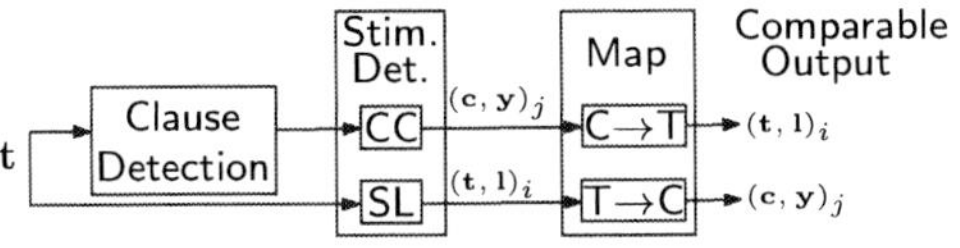

Figure 2: Framework for emotion stimulus detection. Tokens t are split into clauses for clause class. Mapping ensures that both methods result in clause classifications $(t, l)_i$ and token sequences with labels $(c, y)_j$.

propagation. The token sequence labeling setting might be more challenging, but has the potential to output more exactly which tokens belong to the stimulus. Further, sequence labeling is a more standard machine learning setting than a pipeline of clause detection and classification.

These two different formulations are naturally evaluated in two different ways and have not been compared before, to the best of our knowledge. Therefore, it remains unclear which task formulation is more appropriate for English. Further, the most recent approaches have been evaluated only on Mandarin Chinese, with the only exception being the *EmotionCauseAnalysis* dataset being considered by Fan et al. (2019), but not in comparison to token sequence labeling. No other English emotion stimulus data sets have been tackled with clause classification methods. We hypothesize that clauses are not appropriate units for English, as Ghazi et al. (2015) already noted that: "such granularity [is] too large to be considered an emotion stimulus in English". A similar argument has been brought up during the development of semantic role labeling methods: Punyakanok et al. (2008) stated that "argument[s] may span over different parts of a sentence".

Our contributions are as follows: (1) we develop an integrated framework that represents different formulations for the emotion stimulus detection task and evaluate these on four available English datasets; (2) as part of this framework, we propose a clause detector for English which is required to perform stimulus detection via clause classification in a real-world setting; (3) show that token

sequence labeling is indeed the preferred approach for stimulus detection in most available English datasets; (4) show in an error analysis that this is mostly because clauses are not the appropriate unit for stimuli in English. Finally, (5), we make our implementation and annotations for both clauses and tokens available at http://www.ims.uni-stuttgart.de/data/emotion-stimulus-detection.

The remainder of the paper is organized as follows. We first introduce our integrated framework of stimulus detection which enables us to evaluate clause classification and token sequence labeling in a comparable manner (Section 2). We then turn to the experiments (Section 3) in which we analyze results on four different English data sets. Section 4 discusses typical errors in detail, which leads to a better understanding of how stimuli are formulated in English. We conclude in Section 6.

2 An Integrated Framework for Stimulus Detection

The two approaches for open-domain stimulus detection, namely, clause classification and token sequence labeling, have not been compared on English. We propose an integrated framework (Figure 2) which takes tokens t as input, splits this sequence into clauses and classifies them (clause detection can be bypassed if manual annotations of clauses are available). The token sequence labeling does not rely on clause annotations. The output, either clauses c with classifications y ($y \in \{\text{yes}, \text{no}\}^n$) or tokens t with labels l are then mapped to each other to enable a comparative evaluation. We explain these steps in the following subsections.

2.1 Clause Extraction

The clause classification methods rely on representing an instance as a sequence of clauses. Clauses in English grammar are defined as the smallest grammatical structures that contain a subject and a predicate, and can express a complete proposition (Kroeger, 2005). We show our algorithm to detect clauses in Algorithm 1.

To mark the segments that would potentially approximate clauses, we rely on the constituency parse tree of the token sequence (Line 2). For that reason, we use the Berkeley Neural Parser (Kitaev and Klein, 2018). As illustrated by Feng et al. (2012) and Tafreshi and Diab (2018) we also do that by segmenting the constituency parse tree of the instance (Line 9) at the borders of constituents

---
Algorithm 1: Clause Extraction

Input: text
Output: Clauses **c**
1   $\mathbf{t} \leftarrow$ tokenize(text)
2   tree $\leftarrow$ parse($\mathbf{t}$)   // constituency parse
3   gaps $\leftarrow \{0, |\mathbf{t}|\}$ // potential clause bounds
4   segments $\leftarrow \varnothing$ // initial set of segments
5   **foreach** *node n in tree* **do**
6   **if** label(n) $\in$ *S, SBAR, SBARQ, INV, SQ*
7       $\ell \leftarrow$ first token leaf that n governs
8       $r \leftarrow$ last token leaf that n governs
9   gaps = gaps $\cup \{\text{idx}_\ell, \text{idx}_r + 1\}$
10   **foreach** *adjacent pair (i, j) in sort(gaps)* **do**
11   segments = segments $\cup \, \mathbf{t}[i : j]$
12   **repeat**
13   **foreach** s_i **in** *segments* **do**
14   **if** $s_i \sim= /\char`^[\char`^\text{A-za-z0-9}]+\$/$
15         $s_{i-1} = s_{i-1} \, \| \, s_i$
16   segments = segments$\backslash s_i$
17   **if** $|s_i| \leq 3$
18         $s_{i+1} = s_i \, \| \, s_{i+1}$
19   segments = segments$\backslash s_i$
20   **until** *convergence*
21   **return** *segments*

```
                        S
                       / \
                  SBARQ   N
                   / \    |
                  a   b   c

gaps = {0, |a b c|} = {0, 3}
Go over nodes tagged S, SBAR, ...
    On node SBARQ (a b)
        Add idx_ℓ (0) to gaps, new gaps: {0, 3}
        Add idx_r + 1 (2) to gaps, new gaps: {0, 3, 2}
    On node S (a b c)
        Add idx_ℓ (0) to gaps, new gaps: {0, 3, 2}
        Add idx_r + 1 (3) to gaps, new gaps: {0, 3, 2}
segments = ∅
For each pair i, j in sorted gaps ({0, 2, 3})
    i=0, j=2
        Append tokens[0:2] (a b) to segments, new seg-
ments: [a b]
    i=2, j=3
        Append tokens[2:3] (c) to segments, new seg-
ments: [a b, c]
Return segments: [a b, c]
```

Figure 3: Example for the application of Algorithm 1.

labeled as clause-type (Bies et al., 1995). We then join the segments until convergence heuristically based on punctuation (Line 12). We illustrate the algorithm in the example in Figure 3.

2.2 Stimulus Detection

Our goal is to compare sequence labeling and clause classification. To attribute the performance of the model to the formulation of the task, we keep the differences between the models at a minimum. We therefore first discuss the model components and then how we put them together.

Our models are composed of four layers. As **Embedding Layer**, we use pretrained embeddings to embed each token in the instance $s = t_1 \ldots t_n$ to obtain $\vec{e}_1, \ldots, \vec{e}_n$. For the **Encoding Layer**, we use a bidirectional LSTM which outputs a sequence of hidden states $\vec{h}_1, \ldots, \vec{h}_n$. In an additional **Attention Layer**, each word or clause is represented as the concatenation of its embedding and a weighted average over other words or clauses in the instance: $\vec{u}_i = [\vec{h}_i; \sum_{j=1}^n a_{i,j} \cdot \vec{h}_j]$. The weights $a_{i,j}$ are calculated as the dot-product between $\vec{h}_i$ and every other word, and by normalizing the scores using softmax $\vec{a}_i = \text{softmax}(\vec{h}_i^T \cdot \vec{h}_j)$. We concatenate all representations to obtain the final representation vector $\vec{s}$. The **Output Layer** is different for the two different task formulations (sequence labeling vs. single softmax). For the case of the single softmax, the input to the classifier is the representation of the clause obtained on the previous layer and the classifier output is defined as $\vec{o}_i = \text{softmax}(W \cdot \text{ReLU}(\text{Dropout}(h(\vec{s}))))$. When labels are not predicted independently from each other but rather in a sequential manner, we use a linear-chain conditional random field (Lafferty et al., 2001). It takes the sequence of probability vectors from the previous layer $\vec{u}_1, \vec{u}_2, \ldots$ and outputs a sequence of labels $\vec{y}_1, \vec{y}_2, \ldots$. The score of the labeled sequence is defined as the sum of the probabilities of individual labels and the transition probabilities: $s(y_{1:n}) = \sum_{i=1}^n \vec{u}_i(y_i) + \sum_{i=2}^n T[y_{i-1}, y_i]$, where the matrix T that contains the transition probabilities between one label and another (i.e., $T[i, j]$ represents the probability that a token labeled i is followed by a token labeled j). At prediction time, the most likely sequence is chosen with the Viterbi algorithm (Viterbi, 1967).

With these components, we can now put together the actual models which we use for stimulus detection. We compare three different models, one for token sequence labeling (SL) and two for clause classification (CC). The model architectures are illustrated in Figure 4.

Token Sequence Labeling (SL). In this model, we formulate emotion stimulus detection as token sequence labeling with the IOB alphabet (Ramshaw and Marcus, 1995). As embeddings, we use word-level GloVe embeddings (Pennington et al., 2014). The sequence-to-sequence architecture comprises a bidirectional LSTM, an attention layer and the CRF output layer.

Independent Clause Classification (ICC). This

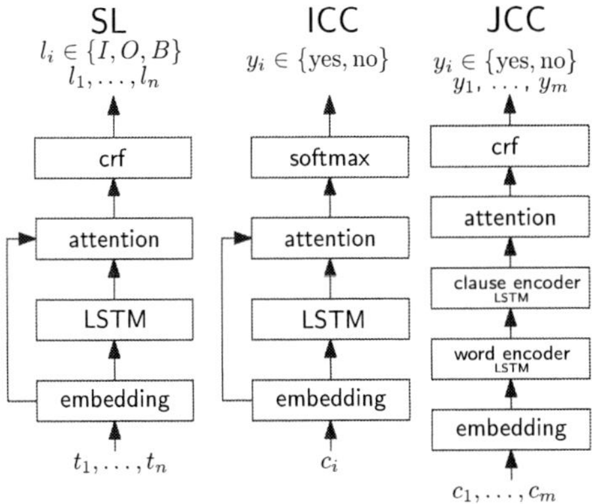

Figure 4: Comparable model architectures.

model, similarly proposed by Cheng et al. (2017), takes the clauses from the clause detector (or from annotated data) and classifies them as containing the stimulus or not. The model has a similar architecture to the one before, with the exception of the final classifier, which is a single softmax to output a single label. The training objective is to minimize the cross-entropy loss. This model does not have access to clauses other than the one it predicts for.

Joint Clause Classification (JCC). In this model, the neural architecture we employ is slightly different from before to enable it to make a prediction for clauses in the context of all clauses. It comprises multiple LSTM modules as word-level encoders, one for each clause. The LSTM at the word-level encodes the tokens of one clause into one representation. The next layer is a clause-level encoder based on two bidirectional LSTMs, where the clause representations are learned and updated by integrating the relations between multiple clauses. After we obtain the final clause representation for each clause, we perform sequence labeling with a CRF *on the clause level*. The training objective is to minimize the negative log-likelihood loss across all clauses. This implementation follows the architecture by Xia et al. (2019), with the change of the upper layer, which is, in our case, an LSTM clause encoder and not a transformer, to keep the architecture comparable across our different formulations. Therefore, this is comparable to all other hierarchical models proposed for the task (Ding et al., 2019; Xu et al., 2019; Xia and Ding, 2019).

2.3 Mapping between Task Formulations

The last component of our integrated framework maps the different representations of each formulation of emotion stimulus detection between each other, namely clause classifications to token sequence labeling and vice versa. We obtain clause classifications from token label sequences ($T \to C$ in Figure 2) by accepting any clause that has at least one token being labeled as B or I as a stimulus clause. The other way around, clause classes are mapped to tokens ($C \to T$) in such a way that the first token of a stimulus clause is a B and all the remaining tokens in the respective clause are I. Tokens from clauses that do not correspond to a stimulus all receive O labels.

3 Experiments and Results

We now put the models to use to understand the differences between sequence labeling and clause classification for English emotion stimulus detection and the suitability of clauses as the unit of analysis.

3.1 Data Sets

We base our experiments on four data sets.[1] For each data set, we report the size, the number of stimulus annotations and statistics for tokens and clauses in Table 1.

EmotionStimulus. This data set proposed by Ghazi et al. (2015) is constructed based on FrameNet's *emotion-directed* frame.[2] The authors used FrameNet's annotated data for 173 emotion lexical units, grouped the lexical units into seven basic emotions using their synonyms and built a dataset manually annotated with both the emotion stimulus and the emotion. The corpus consists of 820 sentences with annotations of emotion categories and stimuli. The rest of 1,594 sentences only contain an emotion label. For this dataset, we see the lowest average number of clauses for which all tokens correspond to a stimulus (μ w. all S/I in Table 1). This result shows that the stimuli annotations rarely align with the clause boundaries.

ElectoralTweets. Frame Semantics also inspires a dataset of social media posts (Mohammad et al., 2014). The corpus consists of 4,056 tweets of which 2,427 contain emotion stimulus annotations on the token level. The annotation was performed via crowdsourcing. The tweets are the shortest instance type in length and have a higher average of clauses per instance than the *GoodNewsEveryone* or the *EmotionStimulus* datasets. They also show

---

[1]Corpora which we do not consider for our experiments are discussed in the related work section.

[2]https://framenet2.icsi.berkeley.edu/fnReports/data/ frameIndex.xml?frame=Emotion_directed

Data set	Size	Stimuli	Tokens				Clauses			
			μ	σ	μS/I	μS/C	Total	w. S	μ I	μ w. all S/I
EmotionStimulus	2,414	820	7.29	5.20	0.12	0.11	5,818	1,117	2.41	0.05
ElectoralTweets	4,056	2,427	6.22	4.00	0.20	0.17	13,612	3,295	3.36	0.34
GoodNewsEveryone	5,000	4,798	7.27	3.67	0.55	0.50	9,190	6,301	1.84	0.52
Emotion Cause Ana.	2,655	2,580	8.48	5.20	0.20	0.10	19,473	2,897	7.33	0.33

Table 1: Data sets available for the Emotion Stimulus Detection task in English. Size: number of annotated instances, Stimuli : number of instances with stimuli annotated; μ, σ: mean/standard deviation of length of stimuli in tokens; μS/I: mean number of stimulus tokens per instance; μS/C: mean number of stimulus tokens per clause; Total: total number of clauses, w. S: number of clauses that contain a stimulus; μ I: average number of clauses per instance; μ w. all S/I: average number of clauses in which all tokens correspond to annotated stimuli.

the same mean of stimulus tokens per instance as *EmotionCauseAnalysis* with a slightly higher mean for the number of clauses in which all tokens correspond to stimulus annotations.

GoodNewsEveryone. The data set by Bostan et al. (2020) consists of news headlines. From a total of 5000 instances, 4,798 contain a stimulus. The headlines have the shortest stimuli in token count. Similar to the *ElectoralTweets*, they also have a high average stimulus token density in clauses. This set has the lowest mean number of clauses per instance (μ I in Table 1).

EmotionCauseAnalysis (Gao et al., 2017) comparably annotate English and Mandarin texts on the clause level and the token level. In our work, we use the English subset, which is the only English corpus annotated for stimuli both at the clause level and at the token level. This dataset has the fewest instances without stimuli among all the others. It also has the longest instances and stimuli. The mean of stimuli tokens annotated per clause is comparable to *EmotionStimulus* despite having a higher mean of stimuli tokens per instance. In the upcoming experiments, we use the clause annotations and not automatically recognized clauses with Algorithm 1 as input to our framework.

3.2 Clause Identification Evaluation

Before turning to the actual evaluation of the emotion stimulus detection methods, we evaluate the quality of the automatic clause detection. For an intrinsic evaluation, we annotate 50 instances from each test corpus in each data set with two annotators trained on the clause extraction task in two iterations. The two annotators are graduate students and have different scientific backgrounds: computational linguistics (A1) and computer science with a specialization in computer vision (A2). Each student annotated 50 instances of each dataset from the datasets we use in the same order. As an environment for the annotation process, we used a simple spreadsheet application. We did this small annotation experiment as an inner check for our understanding of the clause extraction task. None of the annotators is a native English speaker; A1 is a native speaker of a Romance language, and A2 a German speaker. The inter-annotator agreement is shown in Table 2. We achieve an acceptable average agreement of κ=.65.

We now turn to the question if annotated clauses (as an upper bound to an automatic system) align well with annotated stimuli (**Stimuli vs. Anno. Clauses** in Table 2). The evaluation is based on recall (i.e., measuring for how many stimuli a clause exists), either for the whole stimulus (exact), or for the left or the right boundary. We see that except for the corpus *EmotionStimulus*, the right boundaries match better than the left.

Turning to extracted clauses instead of annotated ones (**Extra. vs. Anno. Clauses**) we first evaluate the automatic extraction algorithm. We obtain F_1 values between 0.76% and 0.80%, which we consider acceptable though they also show that error propagation could occur.

For the actual extrinsic evaluation, if clause boundaries are correctly found for annotated stimuli (**Stimuli vs. Extra. Clauses**), we see that the results are only slightly lower than for the gold annotations, except for *EmotionStimulus*. Therefore, we do not expect to see error propagation due to an imperfect extraction algorithm for most data sets.

These results suggest that clauses are not an appropriate unit for stimuli in English. Still, we do not know yet if the clause detection task's simplicity outweighs these disadvantages in contrast to token sequence labeling. We turn to answer this in the following.

| | Intrinsic | | | | | | | Extrinsic | | |
| | IAA | Stimuli vs. Anno. Clauses | | | Extra. vs. Anno. Clauses | | | Stimuli vs. Extra. Clauses | | |
Dataset	κ	Exact	Left	Right	Precision	Recall	F1	Exact	Left	Right
EmotionCauseAnalysis	0.60	0.60	0.35	0.86	0.77	0.75	0.76	0.59	0.36	0.84
GoodNewsEveryone	0.77	0.62	0.29	0.90	0.87	0.76	0.80	0.61	0.27	0.89
EmotionStimulus	0.59	0.47	0.83	0.11	0.86	0.72	0.76	0.17	0.26	0.07
ElectoralTweets	0.63	0.56	0.39	0.63	0.82	0.78	0.80	0.54	0.43	0.60

Table 2: Evaluation of Clause Detection. Note that for *EmotionCauseAnalysis*, the clauses stem from the annotation provided in the original data and not from our automatic detection method.

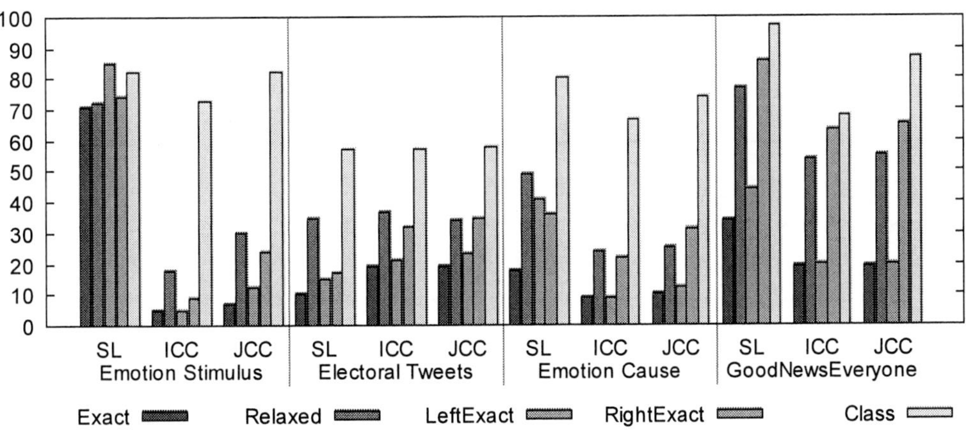

Figure 5: Results of the three different models across four different datasets

3.3 Stimulus Detection Evaluation

3.3.1 Evaluation Procedure

We evaluate the quality of all models with five different measures. Motivated by the formulation of *clause classification*, we (1) evaluate the prediction on the clause level with precision, recall, and F_1. For the *sequence labeling* evaluation, we use four variations. (2) *Exact*, where we consider a consecutive token sequence to be correct if a gold annotation exists that exactly matches, (3) *Relaxed*, where an overlap of one token with a gold annotation is sufficient, (4) *Left-Exact* and (5) *Right-Exact*, where at least the most left/right token in the prediction needs to have a gold-annotated counterpart.

One might argue that sequence labeling evaluation is unfair for the clause classification, as it is more fine-grained than the actual prediction method. However, for transparency across methods and analysis of advantages and disadvantages of the different methods, we use this approach in addition to clause classification evaluation.

We split the data for each set randomly into three sets: 80% train, 10% dev, and 10% test. We use dropout with a probability of 0.5, train with Adam (Kingma and Ba, 2015) with a base learning rate of 0.003, and a batch size of 10. At test time, we select the model with the best validation accuracy after 50 epochs with a patience of 10 epochs. All models use embedding sizes of 300 and hidden state sizes of 100 (Pennington et al., 2014). We do not tune hyperparameters for any of the architectures and implement all models with the AllenNLP library (Gardner et al., 2018).

3.3.2 Results

We now study the performance of the different models on the English data sets. Figure 5 summarizes the results. (Precision and recall values are available in Table 7 in Appendices.)

Which of the modeling approaches performs best on English data? If we only compare the absolute numbers in F_1, we see that the clause classification evaluation (Class) shows the highest result across all models and data set. The only exception is the *EmotionStimulus* data, in which the Left-Exact evaluation is slightly higher. When we rely on this evaluation score, we see that the token sequence labeling method shows a superior result to the classification methods in two data sets, namely *GoodNewsEveryone* and *EmotionCauseAnalysis*. On *ElectoralTweets* and *EmotionStimulus*, the re-

Ann./Pred.	Error types	SL				ICC				JCC				Sum
		ET	GNE	ES	ECA	ET	GNE	ES	ECA	ET	GNE	ES	ECA	
	Early stop	0	4	1	3	0	6	2	7	0	5	1	4	33
	Late stop	11	9	10	8	19	30	7	25	17	31	13	22	202
	Early start & stop	0	3	0	1	9	11	5	1	6	10	3	2	51
	Early start	152	16	0	6	192	73	9	164	220	58	3	159	1052
	Late start	28	3	0	1	3	8	1	0	2	7	1	0	54
	Late start & stop	2	1	0	0	0	2	0	1	0	1	0	1	8
	Contained	0	0	0	0	0	0	0	1	0	0	0	2	3
	Multiple	143	189	11	260	47	24	9	11	37	34	4	0	769
	Surrounded	9	10	0	5	19	31	28	43	22	33	26	28	254
	False Negative	231	160	59	228	126	112	10	97	85	50	1	81	1240
	False Positives	10	18	2	14	78	92	11	38	60	73	4	26	426
	All	586	413	83	526	493	389	82	388	449	302	56	325	4092

Table 3: Counts for each error type for each model across all data sets.

sults are *en par* across all methods with this evaluation measure. We find this surprising to some degree, as this evaluation is more natural for the classification tasks (ICC and JCC) than for sequence labeling (SL), which requires the mapping step.

As this suggests that clauses are not the appropriate unit, it is worth comparing these results with the Exact evaluation measure, which evaluates on the token-sequence level. We observe that token sequence labeling outperforms both clause classification methods on three of the four data sets, with *ElectoralTweets* being the only exception with the shortest textual instances and the highest number of clauses in which all tokens correspond to stimulus annotation (see Table 1). Therefore, we conclude that token sequence labeling is superior to clause classification on (most of our) English data sets.

Do clause classification models perform better on the left or the right side of the stimulus clause? Given the evaluation of the clause detection, we expect the right boundary to be better found for *GoodNewsEveryone* and *EmotionCauseAnalysis* and the left boundary for *EmotionStimulus*. Surprisingly, this is not entirely true – the right boundary is found with higher F_1 on all data sets, not only on those where the clauses are better aligned with the stimulus' right boundary. Nevertheless, the effect is more reliable for *GoodNewsEveryone*, as expected.

Does token sequence labeling perform better on the left or the right side of the stimulus clause? We can ask this similar question for token sequence labeling, though it might be harder to motivate than in the classification setting. Non-surprisingly, such a clear pattern cannot be observed. For *ElectoralTweets* and *EmotionCauseAnalysis*, the difference between the left and right match is minimal. For *GoodNewsEveryone*, it can be observed to a lesser extent than for the classification approaches, and for *EmotionStimulus*, the left boundary is better found than the right boundary. It seems that for the longer sequences in *EmotionStimulus* and *EmotionCauseAnalysis*, the beginning of the stimulus span is easier to find than for shorter sequences.

Is joint prediction of clause labels beneficial? This hypothesis can be confirmed; however, the differences are of a different magnitude depending on the data set. For *GoodNewsEveryone*, the effect is more substantial than for the other corpora. *ElectoralTweets* shows the smallest difference.

4 Error Analysis

In the following, we analyze the error types made by the different models on all data sets and investigate in which ways SL improves over the ICC and JCC models. We hypothesize that the higher flexibility of token-based sequence labeling leads to different types of errors than the clause-based classification models.

For quantitative analysis, we define different error types, illustrated in Table 3 with different symbols as abbreviations. The top bar illustrates the gold span, while the bottom corresponds to the predicted span. The error types illustrated with symbols correspond to false positives; are false negatives. All other error types correspond to either both false positive and false negative in a strict evaluation setting or true positives in one of

Err	Example	Model	Data set
	Steve talked to me a lot | **about being abandoned** | **and the pain** | that caused.	JCC	ECA
	No what I told about **the way** | **they treated you** **and me** | made him angry.	SL	ECA
	Fuck Mitt Romney | and Fuck Barack Obama | ... God got me !!!!!	ICC	ET
	Maurice Mitchell **wants** | **you to do more than vote**.	ICC	GNE
	And he started | to despair **that his exploration was going** | **to be entirely unsuccessful ...**	ICC	ECA
	Deeply ashamed of my wayward notions, | I tried my best to contradict myself.	ICC	ES
	Anyone else find it weird | I get excited about stuff like the **RNC** tonight ?! | # polisciprobs	SL	ET
	Doesn't he do it well | said the girl following with admiring eyes, | every movement of him.	JCC	ECA
	If he feared | that **some** **terrible secret might evaporate from them**, | it was a mania with him.	SL	ECA
	I was furious | **because the Mac XL wasn't real** said Hoffman.	SL	ECA
	With such obvious delight **in food**, it 's hard | to see how Blanc remains so slim.	SL	ES
	Triad Thugs Use Clubs **to Punish Hong Kong** ' s **Protesters**.	JCC	GNE
	I'm glad to see you | so happy Lupin	ICC	ES

Figure 6: Examples for error types for different models and data sets. Extracted clauses are separate by │.

the relaxed evaluation settings.

Do ICC and JCC particularly miss starting or end points of the stimulus annotation? We see in Table 3 that for *Late stop* ▬, CC models make considerably more mistakes across all datasets. ICC does so on ET and ECA, while JCC makes more mistakes on GNE and ES. For data sets in which stimulus annotations end with a clause, errors of this type are less likely. These results are more prominent for *Early start & stop* ▬.

Do all methods have similar issues with finding the whole consecutive stimulus? We see this in the error type *Multiple* ▬. When the CC models make this mistake, it can be attributed to the automatic fine-grained clause extraction, which can cause a small clause within a gold span to become a false negative. However, we see that SL shows higher numbers of this issue than CC. This result is also reflected in the surprisingly low number of *Contained* (▬) – if the prediction is completely inside a gold annotation, the gold annotation tends to be long, and this increases the chance that it is (wrongly) split into multiple predictions.

How do the error types differ across *models*? The *Early Start (& Stop)* and *Surrounded* (▬, ▬, ▬) counts show differences across the different types of models. Presumably, the clause classification models do have difficulties in finding the left boundary, and they are more prone to "start early" than the token sequence labeling models. This might be due to gold spans starting in the middle of a clause which is predicted to contain the stimulus.

How do the error types differ across *data sets*? The results and error types differ across data sets (see particularly ▬, ▬, ▬). This points out

what we have seen in the evaluation already: The structure of a stimulus depends on the domain and annotation. The least challenging data set is *EmotionStimulus* with the lowest numbers of errors across all models. This result is caused by most sentences having similar syntactic trees, all stimuli are explicit and mostly introduced in a similar way.

For qualitative analyses, Figure 6 shows one example of each type of error described above. In the first example, the JCC model does not learn to include the second part of the coordination – "and the pain". In the second example, similarly, the SL model misses the right part of the coordination. For most cases of independent clauses that we inspect, we see a common pattern for both types of models, which is that the prediction stops while encountering coordinating conjunctions. In the sixth example, the prediction span includes the emotion cue. This issue could be solved by doing sequence labeling instead or by informing the model of the presence of other semantic roles. These examples raise the following question: would improved clause segmentation lead to improvements for the clause-classification models across all data sets?

5   Related Work

The task of detecting the stimulus of an expressed emotion in text received relatively little attention.

Next to the corpora we mentioned so far, the *REMAN* corpus (Kim and Klinger, 2018) consists of English excerpts from literature, sampled from Project Gutenberg. The authors consider triples of sentences as a trade-of between longer passages and sentences. Further, Neviarouskaya and Aono (2013) annotated English sentences on the token level.

Besides English and Mandarin, Russo et al. (2011) developed a method for the identification of Italian sentences that contain an emotion cause phrase. Yada et al. (2017) annotate Japanese sentences on newspaper articles, web news articles, and Q&A sites. Table 8 in Appendices shows which corpora and methods have been used and compared in previous work for the available English and Chinese sets. We see that the methods applied on the Chinese sets are not evaluated on the English sets.

Lee et al. (2010) firstly investigated the interactions between emotions and the corresponding stimuli from a linguistic perspective. They publish a list of linguistic cues that help in identifying emotion stimuli and develop a rule-based approach. Chen et al. (2010) build on top of their work to develop a machine learning method. Li and Xu (2014) implement a rule-based system to detect the stimuli in Weibo posts and further inform an emotion classifier with the output of this system. Other approaches to develop rules include manual strategies (Gao et al., 2015), bootstrapping (Yada et al., 2017) and the use of constituency and dependency parsing (Neviarouskaya and Aono, 2013).

All recently published state-of-the-art methods for the task of emotion stimulus detection via clause classification are evaluated on the Mandarin data by Gui et al. (2016). They include multi-kernel learning (Gui et al., 2016) and long short-term memory networks (LSTM) (Cheng et al., 2017). Gui et al. (2017) propose a convolutional multiple-slot deep memory network (ConvMS-Memnet), and Li et al. (2018) a co-attention neural network model, which encodes the clauses with a co-attention based bi-directional long short-term memory into high-level input representations, which are further passed into a convolutional layer. Ding et al. (2019) proposed an architecture with components for "position augmented embedding" and "dynamic global label" which takes the relative position of the stimuli to the emotion keywords and use the predictions of previous clauses as features for predicting subsequent clauses. Xia et al. (2019) integrate the relative position of stimuli and evaluate a transformer-based model that classifies all clauses jointly within a text. Similarly, Yu et al. (2019) proposes a word-phrase-clause hierarchical network. The transformer-based model achieves state of the art, however, it is shown that the RNN based encoders are very close in performance (Xia et al.,

2019). Therefore, we use a comparable model that is grounded on the same concept of a hierarchical setup with LSTMs as encoders. Further, there is a strand of research which jointly predicts the clause that contains the emotion stimulus together with its emotion cue (Wei et al., 2020; Fan et al., 2020). However, the comparability of methods across data sets has been limited in previous work, as Table 8 in the appendices shows.

6   Conclusion

We contributed to emotion stimulus detection in two ways. Firstly, we evaluated emotion stimulus detection across several English annotated data sets. Secondly, we analyzed if the current standard formulation for stimulus detection on Mandarin Chinese is also a good choice for English.

We find that the domain and annotation of the data sets have a large impact on the performance. The worst performance of the token sequence labeling approach is obtained on the crowdsourced data set *ElectoralTweets*. The well-formed sentences of *EmotionStimulus* pose fewer difficulties to our models than tweets and headlines. We see that the sequence labeling approaches are more appropriate for the phenomenon of stimulus mentions in English. This shows in the evaluation of the comparably coarse-grained clause level and is also backed by our error analysis.

For future work, we propose closer investigation of whether other smaller constituents might represent the stimulus better for English and a check of whether the strong results for the sequence labeling hold for other languages. Notably, the clause classification setup has its benefits, and this might lead to a promising setting as joint modeling or as a filtering step to finding parts of the text which might contain a stimulus mention. Another step is to investigate if the emotion stimulus and the emotion category classification benefit from joint modeling in English as it has been shown for Mandarin (Chen et al., 2018).

Acknowledgments

This research has been conducted within the project SEAT (Structured Multi-Domain Emotion Analysis from Text, KL 2869/1-1), funded by the German Research Council (DFG). We thank Enrica Troiano, Evgeny Kim, Gabriella Lapesa, and Sean Papay for fruitful discussions and feedback on earlier versions of the paper.

References

Ann Bies, Mark Ferguson, Karen Katz, Robert Mac-Intyre, Victoria Tredinnick, Grace Kim, Mary Ann Marcinkiewicz, and Britta Schasberger. 1995. Bracketing guidelines for Treebank II style Penn Treebank project. Online: http://languagelog.ldc.upenn.edu/myl/PennTreebank1995.pdf.

Laura Ana Maria Bostan, Evgeny Kim, and Roman Klinger. 2020. GoodNewsEveryone: A corpus of news headlines annotated with emotions, semantic roles, and reader perception. In *Proceedings of The 12th Language Resources and Evaluation Conference*, pages 1554–1566, Marseille, France. European Language Resources Association.

Ying Chen, Wenjun Hou, Xiyao Cheng, and Shoushan Li. 2018. Joint learning for emotion classification and emotion cause detection. In *Proceedings of the 2018 Conference on Empirical Methods in Natural Language Processing*, pages 646–651, Brussels, Belgium. Association for Computational Linguistics.

Ying Chen, Sophia Yat Mei Lee, Shoushan Li, and Chu-Ren Huang. 2010. Emotion cause detection with linguistic constructions. In *Proceedings of the 23rd International Conference on Computational Linguistics (Coling 2010)*, pages 179–187, Beijing, China. Coling 2010 Organizing Committee.

Xiyao Cheng, Ying Chen, Bixiao Cheng, Shoushan Li, and Guodong Zhou. 2017. An emotion cause corpus for chinese microblogs with multiple-user structures. *ACM Transactions on Asian and Low-Resource Language Information Processing*, 17(1):6:1–6:19.

Zixiang Ding, Huihui He, Mengran Zhang, and Rui Xia. 2019. From independent prediction to re-ordered prediction: Integrating relative position and global label information to emotion cause identification. In *Proceedings of the AAAI Conference on Artificial Intelligence*, pages 6343–6350.

Paul Ekman. 1992. An argument for basic emotions. *Cognition & emotion*, 6(3-4):169–200.

Chuang Fan, Hongyu Yan, Jiachen Du, Lin Gui, Lidong Bing, Min Yang, Ruifeng Xu, and Ruibin Mao. 2019. A knowledge regularized hierarchical approach for emotion cause analysis. In *Proceedings of the 2019 Conference on Empirical Methods in Natural Language Processing and the 9th International Joint Conference on Natural Language Processing (EMNLP-IJCNLP)*, pages 5614–5624, Hong Kong, China. Association for Computational Linguistics.

Chuang Fan, Chaofa Yuan, Jiachen Du, Lin Gui, Min Yang, and Ruifeng Xu. 2020. Transition-based directed graph construction for emotion-cause pair extraction. In *Proceedings of the 58th Annual Meeting of the Association for Computational Linguistics*, pages 3707–3717, Online. Association for Computational Linguistics.

Song Feng, Ritwik Banerjee, and Yejin Choi. 2012. Characterizing stylistic elements in syntactic structure. In *Proceedings of the 2012 Joint Conference on Empirical Methods in Natural Language Processing and Computational Natural Language Learning*, pages 1522–1533, Jeju Island, Korea. Association for Computational Linguistics.

Gayatree Ganu, Noemie Elhadad, and Amélie Marian. 2009. Beyond the stars: Improving rating predictions using review text content. In *Twelfth International Workshop on the Web and Databases (WebDB 2009)*.

Kai Gao, Hua Xu, and Jiushuo Wang. 2015. A rule-based approach to emotion cause detection for chinese micro-blogs. *Expert Systems with Applications*, 42(9):4517–4528.

Qinghong Gao, Jiannan Hu, Ruifeng Xu, Gui Lin, Yulan He, Qin Lu, and Kam-Fai Wong. 2017. Overview of NTCIR-13 ECA task. In *Proceedings of the 13th NTCIR Conference on Evaluation of Information Access Technologies*, pages 361–366, Tokyo, Japan.

Matt Gardner, Joel Grus, Mark Neumann, Oyvind Tafjord, Pradeep Dasigi, Nelson F. Liu, Matthew Peters, Michael Schmitz, and Luke Zettlemoyer. 2018. AllenNLP: A deep semantic natural language processing platform. In *Proceedings of Workshop for NLP Open Source Software (NLP-OSS)*, pages 1–6, Melbourne, Australia. Association for Computational Linguistics.

Diman Ghazi, Diana Inkpen, and Stan Szpakowicz. 2015. Detecting emotion stimuli in emotion-bearing sentences. In *International Conference on Intelligent Text Processing and Computational Linguistics*, pages 152–165. Springer.

Lin Gui, Jiannan Hu, Yulan He, Ruifeng Xu, Qin Lu, and Jiachen Du. 2017. A question answering approach for emotion cause extraction. In *Proceedings of the 2017 Conference on Empirical Methods in Natural Language Processing*, pages 1593–1602, Copenhagen, Denmark. Association for Computational Linguistics.

Lin Gui, Dongyin Wu, Ruifeng Xu, Qin Lu, and Yu Zhou. 2016. Event-driven emotion cause extraction with corpus construction. In *Proceedings of the 2016 Conference on Empirical Methods in Natural Language Processing*, pages 1639–1649, Austin, Texas. Association for Computational Linguistics.

Niklas Jakob and Iryna Gurevych. 2010. Extracting opinion targets in a single and cross-domain setting with conditional random fields. In *Proceedings of the 2010 Conference on Empirical Methods in Natural Language Processing*, pages 1035–1045. Association for Computational Linguistics.

Evgeny Kim and Roman Klinger. 2018. Who feels what and why? annotation of a literature corpus with semantic roles of emotions. In *Proceedings of the 27th International Conference on Computational Linguistics*, pages 1345–1359. Association for Computational Linguistics.

Diederik P. Kingma and Jimmy Ba. 2015. Adam: A method for stochastic optimization. In *3rd International Conference on Learning Representations, ICLR 2015, San Diego, CA, USA, May 7-9, 2015, Conference Track Proceedings*.

Nikita Kitaev and Dan Klein. 2018. Constituency parsing with a self-attentive encoder. In *Proceedings of the 56th Annual Meeting of the Association for Computational Linguistics (Volume 1: Long Papers)*, pages 2676–2686, Melbourne, Australia. Association for Computational Linguistics.

Roman Klinger and Philipp Cimiano. 2013. Bidirectional inter-dependencies of subjective expressions and targets and their value for a joint model. In *Proceedings of the 51st Annual Meeting of the Association for Computational Linguistics (Volume 2: Short Papers)*, pages 848–854, Sofia, Bulgaria. Association for Computational Linguistics.

Paul R. Kroeger. 2005. *Analyzing grammar: An introduction*. Cambridge University Press.

John Lafferty, Andrew McCallum, and Fernando Pereira. 2001. Conditional random fields: Probabilistic models for segmenting and labeling sequence data. In *International Conference on Machine Learning*, pages 282–289.

Sophia Yat Mei Lee, Ying Cohen, Shoushan Li, and Chu-Ren Huang. 2010. Emotion cause events: Corpus construction and analysis. In *Proceedings of the Seventh International Conference on Language Resources and Evaluation (LREC'10)*, pages 1121–1128, Valletta, Malta. European Language Resources Association (ELRA).

Weiyuan Li and Hua Xu. 2014. Text-based emotion classification using emotion cause extraction. *Expert Systems with Applications*, 41(4):1742–1749.

Xiangju Li, Kaisong Song, Shi Feng, Daling Wang, and Yifei Zhang. 2018. A co-attention neural network model for emotion cause analysis with emotional context awareness. In *Proceedings of the 2018 Conference on Empirical Methods in Natural Language Processing*, pages 4752–4757, Brussels, Belgium. Association for Computational Linguistics.

Saif Mohammad, Xiaodan Zhu, and Joel Martin. 2014. Semantic role labeling of emotions in tweets. In *Proceedings of the 5th Workshop on Computational Approaches to Subjectivity, Sentiment and Social Media Analysis*, pages 32–41, Baltimore, Maryland. Association for Computational Linguistics.

Alena Neviarouskaya and Masaki Aono. 2013. Extracting causes of emotions from text. In *Proceedings of the Sixth International Joint Conference on Natural Language Processing*, pages 932–936, Nagoya, Japan. Asian Federation of Natural Language Processing.

Jeffrey Pennington, Richard Socher, and Christopher Manning. 2014. Glove: Global vectors for word representation. In *Proceedings of the 2014 Conference on Empirical Methods in Natural Language Processing (EMNLP)*, pages 1532–1543, Doha, Qatar. Association for Computational Linguistics.

Robert Plutchik. 2001. The nature of emotions human emotions have deep evolutionary roots, a fact that may explain their complexity and provide tools for clinical practice. *American Scientist*, 89(4):344–350.

Maria Pontiki, Dimitris Galanis, Haris Papageorgiou, Ion Androutsopoulos, Suresh Manandhar, Mohammad AL-Smadi, Mahmoud Al-Ayyoub, Yanyan Zhao, Bing Qin, Orphée De Clercq, Véronique Hoste, Marianna Apidianaki, Xavier Tannier, Natalia Loukachevitch, Evgeniy Kotelnikov, Nuria Bel, Salud María Jiménez-Zafra, and Gülşen Eryiğit. 2016. SemEval-2016 task 5: Aspect based sentiment analysis. In *Proceedings of the 10th International Workshop on Semantic Evaluation (SemEval-2016)*, pages 19–30, San Diego, California. Association for Computational Linguistics.

Maria Pontiki, Dimitris Galanis, Haris Papageorgiou, Suresh Manandhar, and Ion Androutsopoulos. 2015. SemEval-2015 task 12: Aspect based sentiment analysis. In *Proceedings of the 9th International Workshop on Semantic Evaluation (SemEval 2015)*, pages 486–495, Denver, Colorado. Association for Computational Linguistics.

Vasin Punyakanok, Dan Roth, and Wen-tau Yih. 2008. The importance of syntactic parsing and inference in semantic role labeling. *Computational Linguistics*, 34(2):257–287.

Lance Ramshaw and Mitch Marcus. 1995. Text chunking using transformation-based learning. In *Third Workshop on Very Large Corpora*, pages 82–94.

Irene Russo, Tommaso Caselli, Francesco Rubino, Ester Boldrini, and Patricio Martínez-Barco. 2011. EMOCause: An easy-adaptable approach to extract emotion cause contexts. In *Proceedings of the 2nd Workshop on Computational Approaches to Subjectivity and Sentiment Analysis (WASSA 2.011)*, pages 153–160, Portland, Oregon. Association for Computational Linguistics.

Klaus R. Scherer. 2005. What are emotions? And how can they be measured? *Social Science Information*, 44(4):695–729.

Shabnam Tafreshi and Mona Diab. 2018. Sentence and clause level emotion annotation, detection, and classification in a multi-genre corpus. In *Proceedings of the Eleventh International Conference on Language Resources and Evaluation (LREC 2018)*, pages 1246–1251, Miyazaki, Japan. European Language Resources Association (ELRA).

Andrew J. Viterbi. 1967. Error bounds for convolutional codes and an asymptotically optimum decoding algorithm. *IEEE Transactions on Information Theory*, 13(2):260–269.

Penghui Wei, Jiahao Zhao, and Wenji Mao. 2020. Effective inter-clause modeling for end-to-end emotion-cause pair extraction. In *Proceedings of the 58th Annual Meeting of the Association for Computational Linguistics*, pages 3171–3181, Online. Association for Computational Linguistics.

Rui Xia and Zixiang Ding. 2019. Emotion-cause pair extraction: A new task to emotion analysis in texts. In *Proceedings of the 57th Annual Meeting of the Association for Computational Linguistics*, pages 1003–1012, Florence, Italy. Association for Computational Linguistics.

Rui Xia, Mengran Zhang, and Zixiang Ding. 2019. RTHN: A RNN-Transformer Hierarchical Network for Emotion Cause Extraction. In *Proceedings of the Twenty-Eighth International Joint Conference on Artificial Intelligence (IJCAI-19)*, pages 5285–5291, Macao, China. International Joint Conferences on Artificial Intelligence.

Bo Xu, Hongfei Lin, Yuan Lin, Yufeng Diao, Lian Yang, and Kan Xu. 2019. Extracting emotion causes using learning to rank methods from an information retrieval perspective. *IEEE Access*, 7:15573–15583.

Ruifeng Xu, Jiannan Hu, Qin Lu, Dongyin Wu, and Lin Gui. 2017. An ensemble approach for emotion cause detection with event extraction and multi-kernel svms. *Tsinghua Science and Technology*, 22(6):646–659.

Shuntaro Yada, Kazushi Ikeda, Keiichiro Hoashi, and Kyo Kageura. 2017. A bootstrap method for automatic rule acquisition on emotion cause extraction. In *2017 IEEE International Conference on Data Mining Workshops (ICDMW)*, pages 414–421.

Bishan Yang and Claire Cardie. 2013. Joint inference for fine-grained opinion extraction. In *Proceedings of the 51st Annual Meeting of the Association for Computational Linguistics (Volume 1: Long Papers)*, pages 1640–1649, Sofia, Bulgaria. Association for Computational Linguistics.

Xinyi Yu, Wenge Rong, Zhuo Zhang, Yuanxin Ouyang, and Zhang Xiong. 2019. Multiple level hierarchical network-based clause selection for emotion cause extraction. *IEEE Access*, 7:9071–9079.

A Appendix

| Data | Model | SL Evaluation | | | | | | | | | | | | CC Evaluation | | |
| | | Exact | | | Relaxed | | | Left-Exact | | | Right-Exact | | | Clause | | |
		P	R	F$_1$	P	R	F$_1$	P	R	F$_1$	P	R	F$_1$	P	R	F$_1$
EmotionStimulus	SL	69	73	71	69	74	72	100	74	85	100	59	74	81	83	82
	ICC	03	26	05	10	100	18	03	26	05	05	44	09	82	70	73
	JCC	05	12	07	21	42	30	12	10	12	17	46	24	84	80	82
ElectoralTweets	SL	15	07	10	41	30	35	52	09	15	42	11	17	100	40	57
	ICC	12	47	19	22	100	37	13	47	21	21	74	32	59	59	59
	JCC	14	30	19	25	54	34	15	48	23	28	47	35	59	57	58
EmotionCauseAnalysis	SL	16	20	18	42	60	49	76	29	41	83	23	36	99	68	80
	ICC	05	35	09	14	100	24	05	35	09	13	82	22	79	64	67
	JCC	06	29	10	18	40	25	11	15	12	35	29	31	82	68	74
GoodNewsEveryone	SL	39	30	34	66	92	77	79	30	44	86	86	86	96	99	97
	ICC	15	29	19	37	100	54	15	29	20	48	92	63	71	67	68
	JCC	16	25	19	40	90	55	17	25	20	54	82	65	82	93	87

Figure 7: Results of the three different models across the five different datasets

| | Models | Papers | Data sets and Annotation Approach | | | | | |
| | | | Categorical Class. & Sequence Lab. | Sequence Labeling | | | Clause Class. | |
			ET (en)	ES (en)	REMAN (en)	GNE (en)	ECA (en)	EDCE (zh)
Methods	CRF	Ghazi et al. (2015)		+				
	BiLSTM-CRF	Kim and Klinger (2018)			+			
	BiLSTM-CRF	Bostan et al. (2020)				+		
	SVM	Mohammad et al. (2014)	+					
	CRF	Gao et al. (2017)					+	
	LSTM	Cheng et al. (2017)						
	JMECause	Chen et al. (2018)						
	multi-kernel SVM	Xu et al. (2017)						+
	Multi-Kernel	Gui et al. (2016)						+
	ConvMS-Memnet	Gui et al. (2017)						+
	CANN	Li et al. (2018)						+
	PAE-DGL	Ding et al. (2019)						+
	HCS	Yu et al. (2019)						+
	Ranking	Xu et al. (2019)						+
	Hierarchical BiLSTM	Xia and Ding (2019)						+
	RTHN	Xia et al. (2019)						+
	Our work	**Ours (2020)**	+	+		+	+	
	TransECPE	Fan et al. (2020)						+
	RankCP	Wei et al. (2020)						+

Figure 8: Mapping of previous state-of-the-art methods to data sets. + indicates that we are aware of a publication which reports on the method being evaluated on the respective data set and a — indicates our assumption that no reported results exist with the respective method being evaluated on the respective data set. ET corresponds to *ElectoralTweets*, ES to *EmotionStimulus*, GNE to *GoodNewsEveryone*, whereas the other data set are as being introduced above.

Knowledge Graphs meet Moral Values

Ioana Hulpuș[1], Jonathan Kobbe[1], Heiner Stuckenschmidt[1], Graeme Hirst[2]
[1]University of Mannheim
[2]Department of Computer Science, University of Toronto
{ioana,jonathan,heiner}@informatik.uni-mannheim.de,
gh@cs.toronto.edu

Abstract

Operationalizing morality is crucial for understanding multiple aspects of society that have moral values at their core – such as riots, mobilizing movements, public debates, etc. Moral Foundations Theory (MFT) has become one of the most adopted theories of morality partly due to its accompanying lexicon, the Moral Foundation Dictionary (MFD), which offers a base for computationally dealing with morality. In this work, we exploit the MFD in a novel direction by investigating how well moral values are captured by KGs. We explore three widely used KGs, and provide concept-level analogues for the MFD. Furthermore, we propose several Personalized PageRank variations in order to score all the concepts and entities in the KGs with respect to their relevance to the different moral values. Our promising results help to progress the operationalization of morality in both NLP and KG communities.

1   Introduction

Many of the choices that we make in daily life, such as political stance or position in debates on ideological topics, are influenced by our moral values (Sagi and Dehghani, 2014; Wolsko et al., 2016; Amin et al., 2017). Besides, moral values and moral judgments are central to decision making and cultural cohesion (Dehghani et al., 2016). The last years have seen an increasing interest in operationalizing the concept of morality as defined by psychologists, particularly from the NLP, social media, and communication communities, into an effort of extracting the latent moral dimension of texts.

Tweets (Garten et al., 2016; Araque et al., 2020), newspaper articles (Bowman et al., 2014), as well as scientific articles (Clifford and Jerit, 2013) or religious sermons (Graham et al., 2009) have been targeted for moral analysis. Lately, this line of research has been widely motivated by the rise of social media campaigns such as #BlackLivesMatter and #MeToo, which have a very strong moral load. People take different stances with respect to such matters depending on their understanding and hierarchy of moral values, and can lead to clashes of visions even within the same culture. The general assumption is that the words used in discussions on such topics reveal the moral values of the discussants.

One of the most widely adopted theories of morality is the Moral Foundations Theory (MFT) (Haidt and Joseph, 2004; Graham et al., 2013). MFT proposes at least five moral foundations, each one consisting on the one side of virtues and on the other side of vices: (1) **the care/harm foundation** which deals with the sensitivity towards the suffering of others; (2) **the fairness/cheating foundation** covering aspects of reciprocity and motivations to be fair; (3) **the loyalty / betrayal foundation** covering aspects of in-group cooperation, and the intuition of being loyal to one's group; (4) **the authority/subversion foundation** which is related to the innate intuition of endorsing hierarchies that we find just; (5) **the purity / degradation foundation** which deals with our innate drive of preferring cleanliness of body and soul over hedonism.

The Moral Foundations Dictionary (MFD) (Graham et al., 2009) has been proposed as a lexicon to guide the assessment of the moral foundations of the MFT in texts. It consists of a set of words and lemmas for each vice and virtue of each foundation and has become an essential resource for operationalizing moral values.

Nevertheless, being a word-level lexicon, this resource comes with several limitations. First, the natural ambiguity of language means that some

71

*Proceedings of the Ninth Joint Conference on Lexical and Computational Semantics (*SEM)*, pages 71–80
Barcelona, Spain (Online), December 12–13, 2020

of the words and lemmas provided can have other meanings than the ones related to the moral foundations. For instance, the stem *subver** covers the ambiguous word *subversion*, which besides the meaning related to the *authority / subversion* foundation, it is used with a completely different meaning in software development.

Second, it contains a limited set of lemmas and words, particularly focusing on those whose main meaning is the one related to the corresponding moral foundation. This, on the one side, means that more ambiguous synonyms are not contained, and on the other side, it means that very specific rarely used words are contained. These effects lead to a high precision with poor recall, which is not necessarily the preferred strategy in many scenarios.

Moreover, it only contains uni-grams, and the entries are associated with either vice or virtue, without a score for the strength of the association. However, this lexicon has been widely exploited lately, and several approaches have been proposed to overcome these weaknesses, for instance, by extending it or by its projection into continuous spaces.

In this work, we investigate a new direction, that of projecting the MFD lexicon on knowledge graphs (KGs) with the purpose of scoring all entities and concepts therein with respect to their relevance for each moral foundation. We envision multiple benefits from this endeavor. First, it overcomes the ambiguity and incompleteness limitations. Second, entities and concepts in KGs oftentimes strongly relate to moral values. For example, *Rebecca Reichmann Tavares* is a UN diplomat promoting race relations and human rights, a position highly related to the Fairness/Cheating moral foundation. Similarly, the concept *History of Human Rights* is also highly related to the same moral foundation. Such concepts and entities are not part of the MFD, but their mentioning can help the detection of moral foundations expressed by the texts.

Third, the usefulness of KGs for many tasks resides in the fact that they provide factual knowledge such as relations between entities. Still, an important drawback of current KGs is their weak representation of common sense knowledge. For example, the fact that the concept of "crime" is generally bad and undesirable cannot be derived from current KGs although such common sense knowledge is crucial, for example, for understand-

ing arguments: To understand that an argument claiming that *racism leads to crime* is an argument against racism, it is necessary to understand that crime is *bad* or a *vice*. In this work, we propose a means of adding a moral dimension to KGs, and hence extend them with common-sense "intuition" of morality[1].

2 Related Work

The main target of this work is to investigate how the moral foundations characterized by the MFD are captured in KGs, with the purpose of scoring each entity and concept in the KGs with respect to their relevance to the moral foundations. Therefore, we are particularly interested in the way previous literature uses the MFD.

Some works (Graham et al., 2009; Clifford and Jerit, 2013; Teernstra et al., 2016; Lin et al., 2018) simply use MFD counts either on their own or as features in supervised classifiers for determining the moral values expressed by text. Works that try to overcome the issues related to the simple counts of lexicon hits embed the moral values in continuous spaces. Dehghani et al. (2016) and Kaur and Sasahara (2016) generate vectors for words based on a Latent Semantic Analysis (LSA) (Deerwester et al., 1990) methodology. Then, for each moral value, a vector in the same space is obtained by adding up all the vectors of the modeled lexicon words. Garten et al. (2016), Nokhiz and Li (2017) and Xie et al. (2019) use Word2Vec (Mikolov et al., 2013) or GloVe (Pennington et al., 2014) models to embed the words of the lexicon, and then either aggregate these vectors to produce a vector representation of each moral value, or they keep each of these vectors separate and use different strategies for determining the moral values expressed by novel embedded texts (such as k-nearest neighbor).

Other works that go into a direction more related to ours extend the MFD lexicon by using WordNet (Rezapour et al., 2019; Araque et al., 2020), and then manually curate the results with human annotators (Rezapour et al., 2019) or extend the annotations with values for valence and arousal (Araque et al., 2020). However, the methods differ from our approach as the results of these works are still word-level lexicons, while our moral value relevance annotation is done at a synset rather than

---

[1] All resources created in this work, as well as all relevance scores for the KGs, are available at `https://github.com/dwslab/Morality-in-Knowledge-Graphs`.

word level. For example, MoralStrength (Araque et al., 2020) is built by manually expanding the MFD with new words from the same WordNet synsets.

The only work that acknowledges that entities from Wikipedia/DBpedia also carry a moral load is that of Lin et al. (2018). They use Wikipedia abstracts and DBpedia properties in order to generate features of the entities mentioned in text and use these features together with the textual features in order to classify the texts based on their moral values. However, they do not provide a moral value score of the specified entities, and they do not look into linking the MFD to the knowledge base.

With respect to WordNet, this work is related to another research direction, that of automatically creating sense-level lexicons starting from word-level lexicons. Two commonly used such lexicons are SentiWordNet (Baccianella et al., 2010) and +/–EffectWordNet (Choi and Wiebe, 2014). The first one is a sense-level lexicon providing WordNet synsets with prior sentiment polarity annotations. +/–EffectWordNet provides annotations for synsets that express negative or positive effects over entities. Our work of annotating WordNet synsets as well as other KG concepts with scores reflecting their relevance to moral values is complementary to the previously mentioned lexicons, as they bring in the dimension of morality.

In our work, we investigate how moral values are captured in KGs such as DBpedia, WordNet, and ConceptNet. We use the same intuition across all three KGs: if terms in the MFD can be linked to corresponding concepts in the KG, then the semantic relations contained in the KGs can be exploited to score all the other concepts with respect to their relevance to the moral values. These relevance scores can subsequently be used, for example, for expanding the lexicon. Alternatively, they can be used directly as features in applications aiming at classifying texts based on moral values.

Another important motivation for our work is that KGs have the benefit of providing structured knowledge, but most of the time, this knowledge is factual (e.g., DBpedia) or lexical (e.g., WordNet). Most KGs, ConceptNet being one exception, lack in common sense knowledge. And knowledge such as what is generally accepted as morally good or bad is also missing in ConceptNet. This work is a step in the direction of enriching KGs with such common-sense knowledge.

3   Approach

The core idea of our approach is to map the MFD lexicon to a KG, and subsequently score all entities in the KG with respect to their relevance to moral values. We are taking a layered approach to the moral foundations, as we are interested in scoring the relevance on three levels: (1) the **moral trait level**, in which we are interested in the relevance of concepts with respect to each moral trait (virtue / vice). Hence, each concept obtains 10 scores, two (virtue and vice) for each moral foundation. (2) **the moral foundation level** that scores each concept with respect to the five moral foundations; and (3) the **the moral polarity level** that scores each concept with respect to its relevance to vices and virtues.

As a measure of relevance in KGs, we use Personalized PageRank (Haveliwala, 2003)(PPR). Our work consists of two main steps: first, we manually link the MFD entries to entries in the KGs. Then, we use these KG entries as seeds for running PPR. We now describe both steps in more detail.

3.1   Linking the MFD to KGs

We manually link each entry in the lexicon to the corresponding concept(s) in the KGs. This step involves disambiguation judgments. Also, multiple concepts can be linked to the same lexicon entry, as long as they are related to the corresponding moral value.

Linking to WordNet 3.1 (WN)   The concepts in WN which we focus on are the synsets. As each synset has a specific meaning, we aim to only link to concepts that are truly relevant for the respective moral foundation. For example, the word *fair* occurs as a synonym for *just* which is relevant for the moral foundation of *fairness/Cheating*, but also as a *gathering of producers to promote business*. Thus, we manually decided for each synset, which contains an entry of the MFD lexicon, whether it relates to the moral foundation or not.

Linking to ConceptNet (CN)   In CN, the concepts are only disambiguated with respect to their part of speech. As this kind of disambiguation is not needed for linking the entries and in order to obtain a graph that is less sparse, we collapsed all concepts that only differ in their part of speech. Further, we remove so-called *External Concepts*, which are links to other resources such as WordNet as well as all isolated nodes. For classifying the specific moral traits and the moral polarity, we remove such relations between concepts that express a semantic difference: *Antonym, DistinctFrom, NotCapableOf, NotDesires, NotHasProperty*. For linking to ConceptNet, we check which single word concepts match the lexicon entries and manually verify these links to avoid nonsense (i.e., *Churchill* matches *church**, but we do not expect it to be an intended cue word for *purity/sanctity*). As this way of linking often includes inflected forms of words (i.e. *care** also includes *cares, cared, caring* and even *careth*), we further ignore *DerivedFrom* and *FormOf* relations in our leave-one-out evaluation.

Linking to DBpedia For linking the lexicon entries to concepts in DBpedia, we use the following process: we check in Wikipedia for articles whose name is the lexicon entry. If such an article exists, it is related to the moral value, and it is not a disambiguation page, then we add the link to the sense lexicon. If the formed URL is redirected, we check if the redirected article is related to the moral value. If so, then we add it to the sense lexicon. If an article or a redirected page does not exist, but a disambiguation page, then we check each disambiguation article listed in the disambiguation page and select the ones that are related to the moral trait. This is the case, for instance, for the term *shelter* with Wikipedia disambiguation page www.wikipedia.org/wiki/Shelter. This page provides many disambiguation options for the term, including *Shelter_(building)*, *Animal_shelter*, *Homeless_shelter* which we add to the lexicon, but also others that we deem unrelated to the intended meaning of the MFD, for example, multiple locations such as *Port_Shelter* - a harbor in Hong Kong, multiple films, albums, singles, novels, video games, and others that we do not add to the lexicon. In Wikipedia, it is often the case that an article is the default for a particular word, but that a Wikipedia disambiguation page also exists for the same word. If that is the case, we add the default article if it is related to the moral trait, and also check the disambiguation page, and manually select from all the disambiguation articles the ones that are related to the moral trait. We then map all the collected Wikipedia articles to their corresponding DBpedia resources.

The exact number of concepts that we obtain in this process for each moral trait and each KG are shown in Table 1. We use these concepts as seeds for computing relevance scores of all the concepts

Moral value	MFD	WN	CN	DBpedia
A-virtue	43	77	391	44
A-vice	27	74	285	28
C-virtue	16	66	361	53
C-vice	35	121	304	31
F-virtue	26	40	145	36
F-vice	18	46	180	24
L-virtue	28	48	260	34
L-vice	22	39	203	15
P-virtue	34	22	269	19
P-vice	46	52	482	40
General	29	82	343	26
Total	324	667	3223	350

Table 1: Number of concepts per moral trait.

in the KG, as described in the following section.

3.2 Personalized PageRank for Moral Value Relevance Scoring

We use Personalized PageRank as a measure of relevance in KGs. Relations in KGs are typed and directed. However, the relations are semantic. Therefore for each relation, one can consider that another relation in the opposite direction also exists. For example, for each *occupationOf* relation, the *hasOccupation* relation can be defined, pointing in the opposite direction. Since PPR is working on directed networks, but we want the random walker to be able to also follow incoming edges, we add for each relation with type t in the KGs, an additional, opposite relation whose type we set to inv_t.

We investigate 3 ways of computing the link probabilities in PPR: **Uniform (U)** which is the standard PPR, disregarding the edge types; **Type-Uniform (TU)**: the random walker chooses uniformly at random one of the available edge types; Then, for the chosen type, it chooses uniformly at random one of the edges with that particular type; **Type exclusivity (TE)**: the random walker first chooses an edge type uniformly at random. Then, among the edges of that type, it chooses which one to take according to the exclusivity of the edge. Exclusivity (Hulpuş et al., 2015) is a measure of relation importance that provides higher scores to relation types with low cardinality for both source and target nodes.

On the **moral trait level**, we consider each of the 10 classes of traits in the MFD individually, excluding the *general* class whose entries are not split according to their polarity. For each trait, we run a PPR process where the teleport probability is distributed uniformly to the seeds of the trait. Consequently, each concept in the KG receives 10

Class	Uniform			Type-Uniform			Type-Exclusivity		
	WN	CN	DBpedia	WN	CN	DBpedia	WN	CN	DBpedia
A-virtue	.58	.87	.42	.55	.86	.39	.55	.86	.46
A-vice	.50	.72	.39	.50	.72	.43	.50	.72	.32
C-virtue	.77	.98	.46	.77	.96	.40	.76	.96	.46
C-vice	.66	.86	.32	.64	.87	.42	.65	.86	.35
F-virtue	.73	.95	.44	.68	.94	.50	.68	.93	.53
F-vice	.54	.96	.79	.52	.96	.71	.52	.96	.67
L-virtue	.50	.85	.26	.52	.85	.26	.54	.95	.29
L-vice	.49	.96	.13	.54	.96	.13	.54	.93	.13
P-virtue	.59	.91	.53	.64	.92	.53	.64	.88	.47
P-vice	.46	.88	.52	.46	.88	.55	.46	.85	.55
Overall	.59	.89	.43	.59	.89	.44	.59	.88	.44

Table 2: Prediction accuracy for all moral traits, KGs and PR methods

scores for each PPR method.

On the **moral foundation level**, we score all concepts with respect to their relevance to the five moral foundations. We create the set of seeds for each foundation by merging the corresponding sets of vice and virtue seeds. One PPR process is run for each foundation, as well as on the *general morality* class, therefore each concept in the KG receives 6 scores for each PPR method. As previously, the teleport probability of the PPR process is shared uniformly by the seeds.

On the **moral polarity level**, we create the set of seeds for each of the two classes (vices and virtues) by merging the vice seeds and the virtue seeds of all foundations, respectively. Therefore, we provide each concept with two scores for each PPR method.

4 Experiments and Discussion

We evaluate the prediction on each level independently. Similarly to Xie et al. (2019), we use a leave-one-out evaluation. Specifically, for each seed concept of a class, we run an additional PPR process for that class when the targeted seed concept is left out of the teleport vector. Then, we check the relevance score the targeted seed concept obtains in this PPR process and compare it to its relevance scores for the other classes.

To measure the accuracy of the prediction, we take a very straightforward approach and consider a hit when the targeted seed concept achieves the maximum relevance score for the class to which it belongs when it is left out. Therefore, we compute the accuracy for a class c as the percent of seed concepts of c that obtained the maximum score across all classes for class c, when their score for class c is computed as their PPR score when left out of the seed set.

4.1 Results of Moral Trait Prediction

Table 2 shows the results obtained for each PPR version, per trait as well as overall, for each of the three KGs. Since there are 10 classes, a random baseline assignment would obtain, on average, a .10 score. Therefore, all methods manage to perform substantially better than random on all KGs.

Regarding the methods, we observe that the scores differ between the classes, particularly for DBpedia. For example, the Uniform PPR achieves a .79 score for class Fairness-vice on DBpedia, the Type Uniform PPR achieves .71, and the Type-Exclusivity .67. The class Authority-vice is also handled very differently by the three methods on DBpedia. On the other KGs, the different PPR methods do not show significant differences, with their performances being most similar on Concept-Net. Indeed, DBpedia provides many relation types with varied cardinality, so it is not surprising that methods that treat relation types differently obtain significantly different results on this KG. However, interestingly, the overall results of all the three methods are very similar, including on DBpedia.

With respect to KGs, ConceptNet is in a strong lead over both WordNet and DBpedia, with all methods obtaining scores between .72 and .98 on the individual moral traits. All methods perform worse on WordNet with .59 overall scores. These values are similar to the highest scores obtained by Xie et al. (2019) when running their leave-one-out classification of moral traits, specifically where the MFD entries are embedded using the Google N-grams corpus (Lin et al., 2012) and the classification is done with a Centroid model.

DBpedia captures the moral traits the worst among the three KGs, with a wide range of values across different classes and an overall score of .43 or .44 depending on the method. This perfor-

True class				Predicted class						
	A-virtue	A-vice	C-virtue	C-vice	F-virtue	F-vice	L-virtue	L-vice	P-virtue	P-vice
A-virtue	.58*	.08	.05	.01	.03	.01	.04	.09	**.10**	.00
A-vice	.07	.50*	.01	.09	.05	.03	.03	**.15**	.03	.04
C-virtue	.03	.00	.77*	.05	**.06**	.02	.05	.02	.02	.00
C-vice	.03	**.07**	.02	.66*	.02	.03	.02	.07	.02	.05
F-virtue	.00	.05	**.08**	.00	.73*	.00	.05	.05	.05	.00
F-vice	.04	.02	.02	.07	.02	.54*	.07	**.15**	.04	.02
L-virtue	.08	.04	.06	.08	.04	.06	.50*	**.10**	.02	.00
L-vice	.00	.10	.05	.08	.05	.05	**.13**	.49*	.05	.00
P-virtue	**.18**	.00	.05	.00	.05	.00	.00	.00	.59*	.14
P-vice	.00	.06	.02	.12	.04	.12	.02	.02	**.15**	.46*

Table 3: Confusion matrix of moral trend prediction on WordNet, for Uniform PPR

True class				Predicted class						
	A-virtue	A-vice	C-virtue	C-vice	F-virtue	F-vice	L-virtue	L-vice	P-virtue	P-vice
A-virtue	.46*	**.14**	.05	.00	.09	.05	.05	.05	.09	.02
A-vice	.11	.32*	.00	**.18**	.04	.11	.04	.11	.04	.07
C-virtue	**.12**	.02	.46*	.08	.08	.04	.00	.08	.04	.08
C-vice	.03	.06	**.16**	.35*	.03	.03	.03	**.16**	.00	.13
F-virtue	**.11**	.00	.05	.03	.53*	.08	.05	.03	.08	.03
F-vice	**.12**	.00	.00	.00	.08	.67*	.08	.00	.08	.00
L-virtue	.12	.03	.09	.00	.12	**.26**	.29*	.03	.06	.00
L-vice	.00	**.20**	.13	**.20**	.13	.13	.00	.13*	.00	.07
P-virtue	.10	.05	.00	.05	.05	.00	.00	.00	.47*	**.26**
P-vice	.00	.1	.02	.00	.05	.02	.02	.02	**.20**	.55*

Table 4: Confusion matrix for the prediction of moral traits on DBpedia, for Type-Exclusivity PPR

mance is still better than all the methods proposed by Xie et al. (2019) when training the MFD lexicon entry embeddings on the COHA corpus[2].

Regarding the different moral traits, several scores stand out, particularly the almost random performance of all methods on DBpedia for the Loyalty-vice class. As seen in Table 1, we managed to identify only 15 DBpedia concepts for this class. Among them, many are also present in the set of concepts of other moral traits. For instance, `dbpedia.org/resource/Apostasy` also belongs to the Authority-vice and to the Purity-vice classes, while three concepts related to MFD entry *abandon* are also part of the seed concepts of Care-vice. Among the MFD entries that only occur in this class, for many, we did not find a corresponding concept in DBpedia, for instance, *imposter, jilt*, miscreant, renegate*. The confusion matrix shown in Table 4 reveals that more entries of the Loyalty-vice class achieve higher relevance with respect to the Authority-vice and Care-vice traits rather than with respect to the Loyalty vice trait. Also on WordNet, Loyalty-vice prediction is relatively often mistaken for Authority-vice and Care-vice, as seen in the confusion matrix of Table 3.

As seen in Tables 3 and 4, in both WordNet and DBpedia, vices are usually confused with vices of another foundation, and virtues with virtues of other foundations, and when that is not the case, then a vice is confused with a virtue of the same dimension and the other way round. An exception is the prediction of Loyalty-virtue on DBpedia, which is often mistaken for Fairness-Vice. This is likely due to their shared MFD lexicon entry *segregation*, for which we encounter 7 concepts in DBpedia.

4.2 Results of Moral Foundation Prediction

Table 5 shows the results obtained on the moral dimension level, for each PPR version, per class as well as overall, for each of the three KGs. Since we consider 6 classes, a random baseline achieves on average .17, therefore again, all methods on all KGs significantly outperform this trivial baseline.

The Overall results come to reinforce our conclusion from the previous analysis that the treatment of relation types in the PPR process is only beneficial for DBpedia. As expected, the results of this prediction are better than of the moral-trait prediction, and this improvement is particularly strong on DBpedia.

Among the foundations, the Authority/Subversion foundation achieves under average scores on all methods on all KGs, while the Care/Harm foundation is correctly predicted more often than average by all methods on all KGs. The

[2] https://www.english-corpora.org/coha/

	Uniform			Type-Uniform			Type-Exclusivity		
Class	WN	CN	DBpedia	WN	CN	DBpedia	WN	CN	DBpedia
Authority / Subversion	.60	.76	.45	.58	.76	.48	.58	.75	.49
Care / Harm	.72	.93	.53	.71	.92	.54	.71	.92	.55
Fairness / Cheating	.59	.96	.55	.59	.96	.55	.59	.96	.53
Loyalty / Betrayal	.59	.90	.35	.59	.90	.33	.61	.90	.37
Purity / Degradation	.54	.87	.61	.53	.89	.63	.53	.87	.63
General morality	.71	.92	.68	.70	.91	.76	.68	.90	.72
Overall	.64	.88	.52	.63	.88	.53	.63	.87	.54

Table 5: Accuracy for all moral foundations, KGs and PPR methods

	Authority / Subversion	Care / Harm	Fairness / Cheating	Loyalty / Betrayal	Purity / Degradation	General morality
Authority / Subversion	.60*	.09	.05	**.11**	.07	.07
Care / Harm	.05	.72*	.04	**.07**	.05	.06
Fairness / Cheating	.06	.06	.59*	.09	.06	**.14**
Loyalty / Betrayal	**.13**	.11	.10	.59*	.03	.03
Purity / Degradation	.07	.11	.04	.00	.54*	**.24**
General morality	.04	.05	.05	.01	**.15**	.71*

(a) KG: WordNet; Method: Uniform PPR

	Authority / Subversion	Care / Harm	Fairness / Cheating	Loyalty / Betrayal	Purity / Degradation	General morality
Authority / Subversion	.49*	.08	**.13**	.10	.08	.11
Care / Harm	.10	.55*	**.11**	.10	.10	.04
Fairness / Cheating	.08	.03	.53*	**.17**	.03	.15
Loyalty / Betrayal	.14	.14	**.16**	.37*	.04	.14
Purity / Degradation	.07	.02	.05	.05	.63*	**.19**
General morality	.00	.00	**.20**	.00	.08	.72*

(b) KG: DBpedia; Method: Type-Exclusivity PPR

Table 6: Confusion matrices for predicting the moral foundation

ConceptNet prediction of the Fairness/Cheating dimension stands out through its very high scores. The prediction of the Loyalty/Betrayal foundation stands out for its poor scores on DBpedia. On the other side, the Purity/Degradation foundation is the foundation predicted best on DBpedia, achieving a score even higher than WordNet's prediction. Also the general morality class is captured quite well by all KGs, including on DBpedia, where its prediction is more accurate than on WordNet.

In Table 6, we present the confusion matrix of predicting the foundations for DBpedia and Word-Net. As previously, since ConceptNet has very high scores, the confusion matrix is not conclusive, so we do not report it. Interestingly, in DBpedia, only Purity/Degradation is not mostly confused with Fairness/Cheating.

4.3 Results of Moral Polarity Prediction

Table 7 shows the results obtained on the moral polarity level, for each PPR version, per class as well as overall, for each of the three KGs. For this prediction, the random baseline would achieve, on average, a .5 score. Again, all methods achieve for all KGs significantly higher scores than the random baseline. On DBpedia, the prediction of virtues achieves slightly higher scores than the prediction of vices, while on WordNet and ConceptNet, the opposite holds. In ConceptNet, the prediction of vices vs. virtues achieves very high scores of .96 and .97, respectively. For comparison, Xie et al. (2019) report .93 accuracy on predicting the polarity when using Google N-grams embeddings and a 5-NN model. With COHA embeddings, the highest accuracy is .80, obtained with the Centroid model.

4.4 Qualitative Analysis

To also give an intuition of how our approach scores concepts that are not seeds, we also report the top 10 highest scored concepts that are not seeds, for the fairness/cheating and the authority/subversion foundations in Table 8.

WordNet concepts found for fairness/cheating are quite reasonable, while for subversion, there are some false positives (*jurisprudence, loyalty*). In ConceptNet, we overall find similar concepts for fairness/cheating, while some are on the wrong side, such as *bias, prejudice, fair, equal, judge*. In the authority/subversion foundation, often, the same concepts are scored high for both the vice

Class	Uniform			Type-Uniform			Type-Exclusivity		
	WN	CN	DBpedia	WN	CN	DBpedia	WN	CN	DBpedia
Virtue	.84	.96	.74	.81	.96	.74	.82	.96	.75
Vice	.86	.97	.72	.85	.97	.73	.83	.97	.73
Overall	.85	.96	.73	.83	.97	.74	.83	.96	.74

Table 7: Accuracy for moral polarity, KGs and PPR methods

F-virtue	F-vice	A-virtue	A-vice
equitable, just	subjective	servile	resistance
nonpartisan, nonpartizan	unprincipled	position, situation	unorthodox
democratic	partiality, partisanship	attitude, mental attitude	jurisprudence, law
mutual, reciprocal	disposition, inclination	follower	intractability, intractableness
disposition, inclination	act upon, influence	admirer, champion	dissent, resist
broad-minded	omission	reputable	loyalty, trueness
ism, philosophical system	corrupt	honorable, honourable	bad hat, mischief-maker
conformance, conformity	intolerant	tenderness, warmness	uncontrolled
true, truthful	ideology, political orientation	pious	provocative
just	advantage, vantage	courteous	disloyal, unpatriotic

(a) WN: For space reasons, we only show the two first words of each synset.

F-virtue	F-vice	A-virtue	A-vice
justify	judgment	ranke	heresy
bias	nonstandard	slang	ick
fair minded	inequality	person	legal
fair mindedly	judge	us	disagreement
prejudice	raptophilia	computing	outlaw
fair mindedness	out of proportion	detraditionalize	defier
just	fair	historical	law
philosophy	nonsegregational	maternal	person
right	separate	honourable	obedience
nonjustificational	equal	honorarium	us

(b) CN

F-virtue	F-vice	A-virtue	A-vice
National debt of the United States	Frank Stanford	Obedience to Authority: An Experimental View	Jerome Brailey
Freedom of Religion	Persecution of Ahmadis	What Comes After Goodbye	Petty treason
Work motivation	Princelings	Supermatism	Siege of Lier (1582)
Coretta Scott King	Racial wage gap in the United States	Standings	Private Lies (book)
Al-Baqara 256	Blacklisting	Robert Holden (author)	Descent
A Critique of Pure Tolerance	Shunning	Filial piety	Version Control Example
Zechariah Chafee	United States	Blondes (John Stewart album)	Sedation
Horizontal inequality	Mick Moore (political economist)	Emil Hassler	Civil Rights Act of 1968
Life estate	Barbara Risman	United States	Universum (band)
Human rights in the Middle East	Lahore Grammar School Multan	Legal Legitimacy	The Politics of Religious Apostasy

(c) DBpedia

Table 8: Top-10 non-seed concepts for every KB

and virtue (*us*), while some that are rather on the wrong side (*detraditionalize, obedience, law*).

DBpedia ranks high entities that are much different from those of WordNet and ConceptNet. While the high scores of some entities are not easily understandable (*i.e. National debt of the United States, Frank Stanford*), others nicely capture some background knowledge about the entities: i.e., *Coretta Scott King* and *Zechariah Chafee* both espoused civil rights. Interestingly, just as for ConceptNet, the *United States* is scored as highly relevant for multiple traits. This is because many DBpedia concepts that we linked to the MFD through the disambiguation pages are related to the United States, for instance, *segregation* (Fairness-vice) has been linked among others to *Housing_segregation_in_the_United_States* and *Residential_segregation_in_the_United_States*.

5 Conclusion

In this work, we investigated how moral traits, foundations, and polarity based on the MFT are captured in three widely used KGs. Our analysis reveals big differences between the three explored KGs, both quantitatively and qualitatively. ConceptNet achieves high accuracies at predicting the class of seeds in a leave-one-out evaluation. The results on WordNet are well aligned with results obtained by related work in a similar evaluation. Lastly, the seed class prediction accuracy of DBpedia scores last among the three datasets, but still significantly higher than random, and it comes with the advantage of dealing with entities such as people and organizations.

All KGs manage to accurately discriminate between virtues and vices, which is already a great step towards automatically *telling the good from the bad*. The more complex problem of predicting the foundation and the granular trait can still undergo substantial improvements, particularly on WordNet and DBpedia. However, given that our method is completely unsupervised, using just Personalized PageRank, we conclude that there is great potential in bringing morality common-sense into knowledge graphs. As future work, we are committed to further analyzing our approach, particularly on applications such as classification of texts with respect to moral values.

Acknowledgments

This work has been funded by the Deutsche Forschungsgemeinschaft (DFG) within the project ExpLAIN, Grant Number STU 266/14-1, as part of the Priority Program "Robust Argumentation Machines (RATIO)" (SPP-1999), as well as by the Natural Sciences and Engineering Research Council of Canada.

References

Avnika B Amin, Robert A Bednarczyk, Cara E Ray, Kala J Melchiori, Jesse Graham, Jeffrey R Huntsinger, and Saad B Omer. 2017. Association of moral values with vaccine hesitancy. *Nature Human Behaviour*, 1(12):873–880.

Oscar Araque, Lorenzo Gatti, and Kyriaki Kalimeri. 2020. Moralstrength: Exploiting a moral lexicon and embedding similarity for moral foundations prediction. *Knowledge-Based Systems*, 191:105184.

Stefano Baccianella, Andrea Esuli, and Fabrizio Sebastiani. 2010. SentiWordNet 3.0: An enhanced lexical resource for sentiment analysis and opinion mining. In *Proceedings of the Seventh International Conference on Language Resources and Evaluation (LREC'10)*, Valletta, Malta. European Language Resources Association (ELRA).

Nicholas Bowman, Robert Joel Lewis, and Ron Tamborini. 2014. The morality of may 2, 2011: A content analysis of us headlines regarding the death of osama bin laden. *Mass Communication and Society*, 17(5):639–664.

Yoonjung Choi and Janyce Wiebe. 2014. +/-EffectWordNet: Sense-level lexicon acquisition for opinion inference. In *Proceedings of the 2014 Conference on Empirical Methods in Natural Language Processing (EMNLP)*, pages 1181–1191, Doha, Qatar. Association for Computational Linguistics.

Scott Clifford and Jennifer Jerit. 2013. How words do the work of politics: Moral foundations theory and the debate over stem cell research. *The Journal of Politics*, 75(3):659–671.

Scott Deerwester, Susan T Dumais, George W Furnas, Thomas K Landauer, and Richard Harshman. 1990. Indexing by latent semantic analysis. *Journal of the American society for information science*, 41(6):391–407.

Morteza Dehghani, Kate Johnson, Joe Hoover, Eyal Sagi, Justin Garten, Niki Jitendra Parmar, Stephen Vaisey, Rumen Iliev, and Jesse Graham. 2016. Purity homophily in social networks. *Journal of Experimental Psychology: General*, 145(3):366.

Justin Garten, Reihane Boghrati, Joe Hoover, Kate M Johnson, and Morteza Dehghani. 2016. Morality between the lines: Detecting moral sentiment in text. In *Proceedings of IJCAI 2016 workshop on Computational Modeling of Attitudes*.

Jesse Graham, Jonathan Haidt, Sena Koleva, Matt Motyl, Ravi Iyer, Sean P Wojcik, and Peter H Ditto. 2013. Moral foundations theory: The pragmatic validity of moral pluralism. In *Advances in experimental social psychology*, volume 47, pages 55–130. Elsevier.

Jesse Graham, Jonathan Haidt, and Brian A Nosek. 2009. Liberals and conservatives rely on different sets of moral foundations. *Journal of personality and social psychology*, 96(5):1029.

Jonathan Haidt and Craig Joseph. 2004. Intuitive ethics: How innately prepared intuitions generate culturally variable virtues. *Daedalus*, 133(4):55–66.

T. H. Haveliwala. 2003. Topic-sensitive pagerank: a context-sensitive ranking algorithm for web search. *IEEE Transactions on Knowledge and Data Engineering*, 15(4):784–796.

Ioana Hulpuş, Narumol Prangnawarat, and Conor Hayes. 2015. Path-based semantic relatedness on linked data and its use to word and entity disambiguation. In *The Semantic Web - ISWC 2015*, pages 442–457, Cham. Springer International Publishing.

Rishemjit Kaur and Kazutoshi Sasahara. 2016. Quantifying moral foundations from various topics on twitter conversations. In *2016 IEEE International Conference on Big Data (Big Data)*, pages 2505–2512.

Ying Lin, Joe Hoover, Gwenyth Portillo-Wightman, Christina Park, Morteza Dehghani, and Heng Ji. 2018. Acquiring background knowledge to improve moral value prediction. In *2018 IEEE/ACM International Conference on Advances in Social Networks Analysis and Mining (ASONAM)*, pages 552–559.

Yuri Lin, Jean-Baptiste Michel, Erez Aiden Lieberman, Jon Orwant, Will Brockman, and Slav Petrov. 2012. Syntactic annotations for the Google books NGram corpus. In *Proceedings of the ACL 2012 System Demonstrations*, pages 169–174, Jeju Island, Korea. Association for Computational Linguistics.

Tomas Mikolov, Kai Chen, Greg Corrado, and Jeffrey Dean. 2013. Efficient estimation of word representations in vector space. *arXiv preprint arXiv:1301.3781*.

Pegah Nokhiz and Fengjun Li. 2017. Understanding rating behavior based on moral foundations: The case of yelp reviews. In *2017 IEEE International Conference on Big Data (Big Data)*, pages 3938–3945.

Jeffrey Pennington, Richard Socher, and Christopher Manning. 2014. GloVe: Global vectors for word representation. In *Proceedings of the 2014 Conference on Empirical Methods in Natural Language Processing (EMNLP)*, pages 1532–1543, Doha, Qatar. Association for Computational Linguistics.

Rezvaneh Rezapour, Saumil H. Shah, and Jana Diesner. 2019. Enhancing the measurement of social effects by capturing morality. In *Proceedings of the Tenth Workshop on Computational Approaches to Subjectivity, Sentiment and Social Media Analysis*, pages 35–45, Minneapolis, USA. Association for Computational Linguistics.

Eyal Sagi and Morteza Dehghani. 2014. Moral rhetoric in twitter: A case study of the u.s. federal shutdown of 2013. *Cognitive Science*, 36.

Livia Teernstra, Peter van der Putten, Liesbeth Noordegraaf-Eelens, and Fons Verbeek. 2016. The morality machine: Tracking moral values in tweets. In *Advances in Intelligent Data Analysis XV*, pages 26–37, Cham. Springer International Publishing.

Christopher Wolsko, Hector Ariceaga, and Jesse Seiden. 2016. Red, white, and blue enough to be green: Effects of moral framing on climate change attitudes and conservation behaviors. *Journal of Experimental Social Psychology*, 65:7–19.

Jing Yi Xie, Renato Ferreira Pinto Junior, Graeme Hirst, and Yang Xu. 2019. Text-based inference of moral sentiment change. In *Proceedings of the 2019 Conference on Empirical Methods in Natural Language Processing and the 9th International Joint Conference on Natural Language Processing (EMNLP-IJCNLP)*, pages 4654–4663, Hong Kong, China. Association for Computational Linguistics.

Natural Language Inference with Mixed Effects

William Gantt*
Department of Computer Science
University of Rochester
wgantt@cs.rochester.edu

Benjamin Kane*
Department of Computer Science
University of Rochester
bkane2@cs.rochester.edu

Aaron Steven White
Department of Linguistics
University of Rochester
aaron.white@rochester.edu

Abstract

There is growing evidence that the prevalence of disagreement in the raw annotations used to construct natural language inference datasets makes the common practice of aggregating those annotations to a single label problematic. We propose a generic method that allows one to skip the aggregation step and train on the raw annotations directly without subjecting the model to unwanted noise that can arise from annotator response biases. We demonstrate that this method, which generalizes the notion of a *mixed effects model* by incorporating *annotator random effects* into any existing neural model, improves performance over models that do not incorporate such effects.

1 Introduction

A common method for constructing natural language inference (NLI) datasets is (i) to generate text-hypothesis pairs using some method—commonly, crowd-sourced hypothesis elicitation given a text from some existing resource (Bowman et al., 2015; Williams et al., 2018) or automated text-hypothesis generation (Zhang et al., 2017); (ii) to collect crowd-sourced judgments about inference from the text to the hypothesis; and (iii) to aggregate the possibly multiple annotations provided for a single text-hypothesis pair into a single label. This final step follows common practice across annotation tasks in NLP; but for NLI in particular, there is growing evidence that it is problematic due to disagreement among annotators that is not captured by the probabilistic outputs of standard NLI models (Pavlick and Kwiatkowski, 2019).

One way to capture this disagreement would be to directly model the variability in the raw annotations. But this approach presents a challenge: it can

Figure 1: Distribution of [-50, 50] slider ratings (by annotator) for the same 20 NLI pairs in Pavlick and Kwiatkowski's dataset (batch 1, described in their §3).

be difficult to assess how much disagreement arises from disagreement about the interpretation of a text-hypothesis pair and how much is due to biases that annotators bring to the task. Such biases can be extreme. For instance, Figure 1 plots the distribution by annotator of [-50, 50] ratings—with -50 clear contradiction and 50 clear entailment—for the same 20 NLI pairs in Pavlick and Kwiatkowski's dataset. Despite describing responses to the same items, the distributions are quite variable, suggesting variability in how annotators approach the task. This difference in approach may be relatively shallow—e.g. given some true label (or distribution thereon), annotators merely differ in their mapping of that value to the response scale—or they may be quite deep—e.g. annotators differ in how they interpret the relationship between texts and hypotheses.

We investigate both of these possibilities within a *mixed effects modeling* framework (Gelman and Hill, 2014). The core idea is to incorporate annotator-specific parameters into standard NLI models that either (i) merely modify the output of a standard classification/regression head or (ii) modify the parameters of the head itself. These two options correspond to the mixed effects modeling concepts of *random intercepts* and *random slopes*, respectively. For the same reason that such *random effects* can be incorporated into effectively any generalized linear model in a modular way, our components can be be similarly incorporated into any NLI model. We describe how this can be done for a simple RoBERTa-based NLI model.

We find (i) that models containing only random intercepts outperform both standard models and models containing random slopes when annotators are known; and (ii) that when annotators are not known, performance drops precipitously for both random effects models. Together, these findings suggest that those building NLI datasets should provide annotator information and that those developing NLI systems should incorporate random effects into their models.

2 Extended Task Definition

In the standard supervised setting, NLI datasets are (graphs of) functions from text-hypothesis pairs $\langle T_i, H_i \rangle \in \Sigma^* \times \Sigma^*$ to inference labels $y_i \in \mathcal{Y}$—where $\mathcal{Y}$ is commonly {*contradicted, neutral, entailed*} or {*not-entailed, entailed*}, but may also be a finer-grained (e.g. five-point) ordinal scale (Zhang et al., 2017) or bounded continuous scale (Chen et al., 2020). The NLI task is to produce a single label from $\mathcal{Y}$ given a text-hypothesis pair.

We extend this setting by assuming that NLI datasets are (graphs of) functions from text-hypothesis pairs *and* annotator identifiers $a_i \in \mathcal{A}$ to inference labels and that the NLI task is to produce a single label given a text-hypothesis pair and an annotator identifier. A particular model need not make use of the annotator information during training and may similarly ignore it at evaluation time. Though many existing datasets do not provide annotator information, it is trivial for a dataset creator to add (even *post hoc*), and so this extension could feasibly be applied to any existing dataset.

3 Models

We assume some encoder that maps from $\langle T_i, H_i \rangle \in \Sigma^* \times \Sigma^*$ to $\langle \mathbf{x}_{T_i}, \mathbf{x}_{H_i} \rangle \in \mathbb{R}^M \times \mathbb{R}^N$ independently of annotator a_i, and we focus mainly on the mapping from $\mathbf{z}_i \equiv \langle \mathbf{x}_{T_i}, \mathbf{x}_{H_i} \rangle$ and a_i to y_i.

We consider two types of model: one containing only *annotator random intercepts* and another additionally containing *annotator random slopes*. The first assumes that differences among annotators are relatively shallow—e.g. given some true label for a pair (or distribution thereon), annotators have their own specific way of mapping that value to a response—and the second assumes that the differences among annotators are deeper—e.g. annotators differ in how they interpret the relation between texts and hypotheses. This distinction is independent of the labels $\mathcal{Y}$: regardless of whether the labels are discrete or continuous, random effects can be incorporated. In the language of generalized linear mixed models, the *link functions* are the only thing that changes. We consider two label types: three-way ordinal and bounded continuous.

Annotator random intercepts amount to annotator specific bias terms $\boldsymbol{\rho}_{a_i}$ on the raw predictions of a classification/regression head. Unlike standard *fixed* bias terms, however, what makes these terms random intercepts is that they are assumed to be distributed according to some prior distribution with unknown parameters. This assumption models the idea that annotators are sampled from some population, and it yields 'adaptive regularization' (McElreath, 2020), wherein the biases for annotators who provide few labels will be drawn more toward the central tendency of the prior.

Random intercepts for categorical outputs can take two forms, depending on whether the model enforces ordinality constraints—as linked logit models do (Agresti, 2014)—or not. Since most common categorical NLI models do not enforce ordinality constraints, we do not enforce them here, assuming that the model has some independently tunable function $h_{\boldsymbol{\theta}} : \mathbb{R}^M \times \mathbb{R}^N \to \mathbb{R}^{|\mathcal{Y}|}$ that produces potentials for each label and that:

$$f(y_i \mid \mathbf{z}_i, \boldsymbol{\theta}, \boldsymbol{\rho}_{a_i}) = \text{softmax}\left(h_{\boldsymbol{\theta}}(\mathbf{z}_i) + \boldsymbol{\rho}_{a_i}\right)$$

where $\boldsymbol{\rho}_{a_i} \sim \mathcal{N}(\mathbf{0}, \boldsymbol{\Sigma})$ with unknown $\boldsymbol{\Sigma}$.

Random intercepts for continuous outputs are effectively shifting terms on the single value predicted by some independently tunable function $h : \mathbb{R}^M \times \mathbb{R}^N \to \mathbb{R}$. If the continuous output is furthermore bounded, a squashing function g is necessary. In the bounded case, we assume that the variable—scaled to $(0, 1)$—is distributed Beta (following Sakaguchi and Van Durme, 2018) with mean μ_i and precision $\nu_i = \exp\left(\rho_{a_i 1} + \nu_0\right)$.

MegaVeridicality
▶ *Someone knew that something happened.*
That thing happened.
▶ *Someone thought that something happened.*
That thing happened.

MegaNegRaising
▶ *Someone didn't think that something happened.*
That person thought that thing didn't happen.
▶ *Someone didn't know that something happened.*
That person knew that thing didn't happen.

Table 1: NLI sentence pairs from MegaVeridicality and MegNegRaising. ▶ indicates the line is a text, and the following line is its corresponding hypothesis. Hypotheses in green indicate that the context entails the hypothesis; those in red indicate that it does not.

$$\mu_i = g\left(h_{\boldsymbol{\theta}}(\mathbf{z}_i) + \rho_{a_i 2}\right)$$

$$\alpha_i; \ \beta_i = \mu_i \nu_i; \ (1 - \mu_i)\nu_i$$

$$f(y_i \mid \mathbf{z}_i, \boldsymbol{\theta}, \boldsymbol{\rho}_{a_i}; \nu_0) = \mathrm{Beta}(y_i \mid \alpha_i, \beta_i)$$

where $\rho_{a_i} \sim \mathcal{N}(\mathbf{0}, \boldsymbol{\Sigma})$ with unknown $\boldsymbol{\Sigma}$. This implies that $\nu_i \sim \log \mathcal{N}(\nu_0, \sigma_{11}^2)$ with unknown ν_0.

The precision parameter ν_i controls the shape of the Beta: with small ν_i, a_i tends to give responses near 0 and 1 (whichever is closer to μ_i); with large ν_i, a_i tends to give responses near μ_i.

Annotator random slopes amount to annotator-specific classification/regression heads h_{ϕ_i}. We swap these heads into the above equations in place of $h_{\boldsymbol{\theta}}$. As for the random intercept parameters, we assume that the annotator-specific parameters ϕ_i, which we refer to as the annotator random slopes, are distributed $\phi_i \sim \mathcal{N}(\boldsymbol{\theta}, \boldsymbol{\Sigma})$ with unknown $\boldsymbol{\theta}, \boldsymbol{\Sigma}$. One way to think about this model is that $h_{\boldsymbol{\theta}}$ produces prototypical interpretation around which annotators' actual interpretations are distributed.

4 Experiments

We compare models both with and without random effects when fit to NLI datasets conforming to the extended setting described in §2. The model without random intercepts (the *fixed model*) simply ignores annotator information—effectively locking ρ_{a_i} to 0 for all annotators a_i.

Encoder All models use pretrained RoBERTa (Liu et al., 2019) as their encoder. We use the basic LM pretrained versions (no NLI fine-tuning).

Data To our knowledge, the only NLI datasets that both publicly provide annotator identifiers and are large enough to train an NLI system are MegaVeridicality (MV; White and Rawlins, 2018; White et al., 2018), which contains three-way categorical annotations aimed at assessing whether different predicates give rise to veridicality inferences

in different syntactic structures, and MegaNegRaising (MN; An and White, 2020), which contains bounded continuous [0, 1] annotations aimed at assessing whether different predicates give rise to neg(ation)-raising inferences in different syntactic structures. Table 1 shows example pairs from each dataset. Both datasets contain 10 annotations per text-hypothesis pair from 10 different annotators. MV contains 3,938 pairs (39,380 annotations) with 507 distinct annotators, and MN contains 7,936 pairs (79,360 annotations) with 1,108 distinct annotators. In both datasets, each pair is constructed to include a particular main clause predicate and a particular syntactic structure. To test each model's robustness to lexical and structure variability, we use this information to construct folds of the cross-validation (see **Evaluation**).

Classification/Regression Heads We consider heads with one hidden affine layer followed by a rectifier. We use a hidden layer size of 128 and the default RoBERTa-base input size of 768.

Training All models were implemented in Py-Torch 1.4.0 and were trained for a maximum of 25 epochs on a single Nvidia GeForce GTX 1080 Ti GPU, with early stopping upon a change in average per-epoch loss of less than 0.01. We use Adam optimization (lr=0.01, β_1=0.9, β_2=0.999, ϵ=10^{-7}) and a batch size of 128. All code is publicly available.

Loss We use the negative log-likelihood of the observed values under the model as the loss.

Evaluation We evaluate all of our models using 5-fold cross-validation. We consider four partitioning methods: (i) RANDOM: completely random partitioning; (ii) PREDICATE: partitioning by the main clause predicate found in the text (a particular main clause predicate occurs in one and only one partition); (iii) STRUCTURE: partitioning by the syntactic structure found in the text (a particular structure occurs in one and only one partition); and (iv) ANNOTATOR: a particular annotator occurs in one and only one partition. For the first three methods, we ensure that each annotator occurs in every partition, so that random intercepts and random slopes for that annotator can be estimated. For the ANNOTATOR method, where we do not have an estimate for the random effects of annotators in the held-out data, we use the mean of the prior.[1]

We report mean accuracy on held-out folds for the categorical data (MV); and following Chen et al.

---

[1]We additionally experimented with marginalizing over the random effects, but the results did not differ.

Model	RANDOM		PREDICATE		STRUCTURE		ANNOTATOR	
	Acc	*Corr*	*Acc*	*Corr*	*Acc*	*Corr*	*Acc*	*Corr*
Fixed	1.00	0.35	0.92	0.23	0.83	0.27	0.91	**0.31**
Random Intercepts	1.15	**1.53**	**1.13**	**1.53**	**1.05**	**1.53**	**0.98**	0.20
Random Slopes	**1.17**	1.42	**1.13**	1.42	0.82	1.41	0.42	0.05

Table 2: Mean of the rescaled accuracy (categorical data) and rank correlation (bound continuous data) across cross-validation folds for each partitioning method ($\text{score}_{\text{mod}}$ from §4). Bolded values are best in column.

(2020), we report mean rank correlation on held-out folds for the bounded continuous data (MN). To make these metrics comparable, we report them relative to the performance of both a baseline model and the best possible fixed model.

$$\text{score}_{\text{mod}} = \frac{\text{raw-score}_{\text{mod}} - \text{raw-score}_{\text{base}}}{\text{raw-score}_{\text{best}} - \text{raw-score}_{\text{base}}}$$

For the categorical data, the baseline model predicts the majority class across all pairs, and the best possible fixed model predicts the majority class across annotators for each pair. Similarly, for the bounded continuous data, the baseline model predicts the mean response across all pairs, and the best possible fixed model predicts the mean response across annotators for each pair.[2]

These relative scores are 0 when the model does not outperform the baseline and 1 when the model performs as well as the best possible fixed model. It is possible for a random effects model to obtain a score of greater than 1 by leveraging annotator information or less than 0 if it overfits the data.

5 Results

Table 2 shows the results. The random intercepts models reliably outperform the fixed models in all cross-validation settings except ANNOTATOR in Bonferroni-corrected Wilcoxon rank-sum tests ($ps<0.05$). Indeed, they tend to reliably outperform even the best possible fixed model, having rescaled scores above 1. The random slopes models, while in many cases comparable to the random intercepts models, confer no additional benefit over them. In the one instance in which the random slopes model performs best (the random partition for categorical data), the advantage relative to the random intercepts model is not statistically significant.

Consistent with Pavlick and Kwiatkowski's findings, these results suggest that variability in annotators' responding behavior is substantial; otherwise, it would not be possible for the random effects models to outperform the best possible fixed model, and we would not expect the observed drops in performance when annotator information is removed. But this variability is likely relatively shallow: if these differences were due to deeper differences in annotators' interpretation of the pair, we would expect this to manifest in better performance by the random slopes models, as the latter subsumes the random intercepts model and can leverage the additional power of annotator-specific classification or regression heads. Of course, it remains a live possibility that the encoder we used does not extract features that are linearly related to the relevant interpretive variability, and so further investigation of random slopes models with different encoders may be warranted (see Geva et al., 2019).

Contrasting the results on ordinal and bounded continuous data, the fixed model tends to perform better on ordinal data than on bounded continuous data. A similar trend is not seen for the random effects models. Indeed, the random intercepts model performs substantially better on the bounded continuous data under all settings except for ANNOTATOR. These results could be due to the link function we used for the bounded continuous data: the fixed model consistently learned small values for the precision parameter ν_0, resulting in sparse (bimodal) beta distributions. But the fact that the random intercepts model reliably outperforms the best possible fixed model implies that any tweaks to the link function would not bring the fixed model up to the level of the random intercepts model.

6 Analysis

To understand how annotator biases tend to pattern with ordinal and bounded continuous scales, we investigate the mean ρ_a for each annotator a in the random intercepts models across folds under the RANDOM partition method. Figure 2 plots the distribution of biases across categorical annotators when the fixed effect potentials—$h_\theta(\mathbf{z}_i)$ in the equations in §3—are set to 0: softmax(ρ_a). This distribution can be thought of as an indicator of

---

[2]Rank correlation is technically undefined when one of the variables is constant. For the purposes of computing $\text{score}_{\text{mod}}$ for the bounded continuous data, we treat raw-score$_{\text{base}}$ as 0.

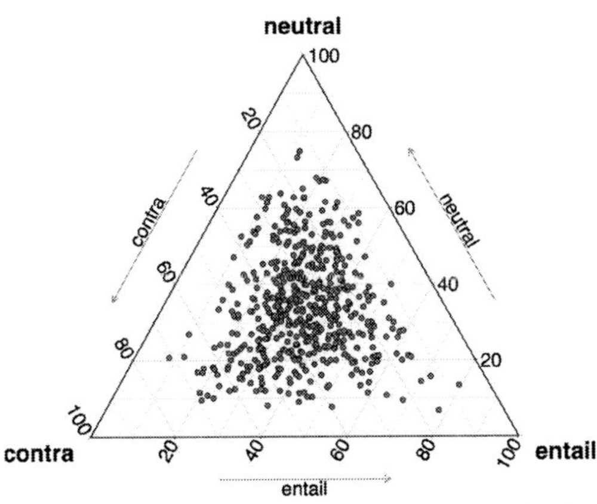

Figure 2: Distribution of biases across categorical annotators when fixed effect potentials set to **0**.

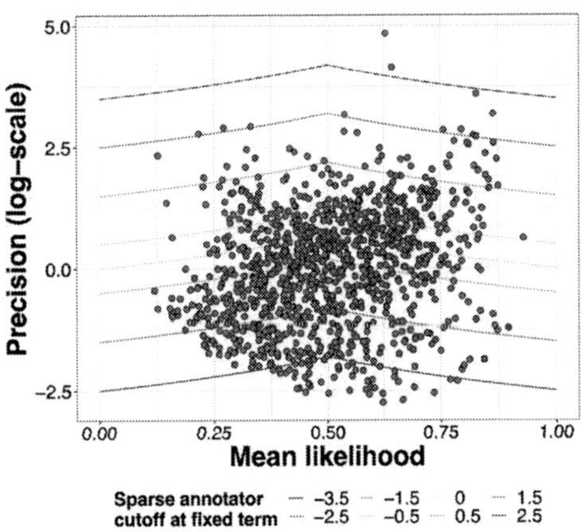

Figure 3: Distribution of biases across bounded continuous annotators when fixed effect potentials set to **0**.

how an annotator would respond in the absence of any correct answer. We see the most variability in terms of annotators' biases for or against neutral: the interquartile range for *neutral* biases is [0.23, 0.42] compared to [0.24, 0.41] for *contradiction* and [0.25, 0.40] for *entailment*. Interestingly, these biases do not reflect the fact that the scale is ordinal: if they did, we would expect more positive correlations between adjacent values; but *neutral* biases are more strongly rank anticorrelated with *contradiction* ($r = -0.57$) and *entailment* ($r = -0.48$) than *contradiction* is with *entailment* ($r = -0.35$). This finding suggests that three-value "ordinal" NLI scales are better thought of as nominal.

Figure 3 plots the analogous distribution for the bounded continuous annotators, with the y-axis showing ρ_{a1} and the x-axis showing $\text{logit}^{-1}(\rho_{a2})$. The lines behind the points show, for particular values of $h_{\boldsymbol{\theta}}(\mathbf{z}_i)$, the ρ_{a1} at which the distribution for a particular annotator becomes sparse—i.e. where $\alpha, \beta < 1$—heavily favoring responses very near zero or one, rather than the mean. We see a weak rank correlation ($r = 0.24$, $p < 0.05$) between precision and annotators' biases to give responses nearer to one, suggesting that one-biased annotators tend to give less sparse responses. This correlation might, in part, explain the poor performance of the bounded continuous models in the ANNOTATOR cross-validation setting.

7   Related Work

The models developed here are closely related to models from Item Response Theory (IRT). IRT has been used to assess annotator quality (Hovy et al., 2013, 2014; Rehbein and Ruppenhofer, 2017; Paun et al., 2018a,b; Zhang et al., 2019; Felt et al., 2018) and various properties of an item (Passonneau and

Carpenter, 2014; Sakaguchi and Van Durme, 2018; Card and Smith, 2018), including difficulty (Lalor et al., 2016, 2018, 2019). Other non-IRT-based work attempts to measure the relationship between annotator disagreement and item difficulty (Plank et al., 2014; Kalouli et al., 2019).

Other recent work focuses on incorporating annotator information in modeling annotator-generated text. Geva et al. (2019) find that concatenating annotator IDs as input features to a BERT-based text generation model yields improved performance on several datasets. Although we reach similar conclusions about the importance of annotator information in this work, our approach differs in at least one critical respect: by explicitly distinguishing linguistic input from annotator information, our model cleanly separates the linguistic representations from representations of the annotators interpreting or producing those representations. This clean separation is of potential benefit not only to those interested in using NLI models (or deep learning architectures more generally) in an experimental (psycho)linguistics setting, where distinguishing the two sorts of representations can be crucial, but also to those interested in possibly quite substantial reductions in model size.

8   Conclusion

We find (i) that models containing only random intercepts outperform standard models when annotators are known, and (ii) that models that further contain random slopes do not yield any additional benefit. These results indicate that, though differences among NLI annotators' response behavior are important to model, these differences may not be particularly deep, limited to the ways in which annotators use the response scale, but not relating to deeper interpretive differences.

Acknowledgments

This research was supported by the University of Rochester, DARPA AIDA, DARPA KAIROS, IARPA BETTER, and NSF-BCS (1748969). The U.S. Government is authorized to reproduce and distribute reprints for Governmental purposes. The views and conclusions contained in this publication are those of the authors and should not be interpreted as representing official policies or endorsements of DARPA or the U.S. Government.

References

Alan Agresti. 2014. *Categorical Data Analysis*. John Wiley & Sons.

Hannah An and Aaron White. 2020. The lexical and grammatical sources of neg-raising inferences. *Proceedings of the Society for Computation in Linguistics*, 3(1):220–233.

Samuel R. Bowman, Gabor Angeli, Christopher Potts, and Christopher D. Manning. 2015. A large annotated corpus for learning natural language inference. In *Proceedings of the 2015 Conference on Empirical Methods in Natural Language Processing*, pages 632–642, Lisbon, Portugal. Association for Computational Linguistics.

Dallas Card and Noah A. Smith. 2018. The importance of calibration for estimating proportions from annotations. In *Proceedings of the 2018 Conference of the North American Chapter of the Association for Computational Linguistics: Human Language Technologies, Volume 1 (Long Papers)*, pages 1636–1646, New Orleans, Louisiana. Association for Computational Linguistics.

Tongfei Chen, Zhengping Jiang, Adam Poliak, Keisuke Sakaguchi, and Benjamin Van Durme. 2020. Uncertain natural language inference. In *Proceedings of the 58th Annual Meeting of the Association for Computational Linguistics*, pages 8772–8779, Online. Association for Computational Linguistics.

Paul Felt, Eric Ringger, Kevin Seppi, and Jordan Boyd-Graber. 2018. Learning from measurements in crowdsourcing models: Inferring ground truth from diverse annotation types. In *International Conference on Computational Linguistics*.

Andrew Gelman and Jennifer Hill. 2014. *Data Analysis Using Regression and Multilevel/Hierarchical Models*. Cambridge University Press, New York City.

Mor Geva, Yoav Goldberg, and Jonathan Berant. 2019. Are we modeling the task or the annotator? an investigation of annotator bias in natural language understanding datasets. In *Proceedings of the 2019 Conference on Empirical Methods in Natural Language Processing and the 9th International Joint Conference on Natural Language Processing (EMNLP-IJCNLP)*, pages 1161–1166, Hong Kong, China. Association for Computational Linguistics.

Dirk Hovy, Taylor Berg-Kirkpatrick, Ashish Vaswani, and Eduard Hovy. 2013. Learning whom to trust with MACE. In *Proceedings of the 2013 Conference of the North American Chapter of the Association for Computational Linguistics: Human Language Technologies*, pages 1120–1130, Atlanta, Georgia. Association for Computational Linguistics.

Dirk Hovy, Barbara Plank, and Anders Søgaard. 2014. Experiments with crowdsourced re-annotation of a POS tagging data set. In *Proceedings of the 52nd Annual Meeting of the Association for Computational Linguistics (Volume 2: Short Papers)*, pages 377–382, Baltimore, Maryland. Association for Computational Linguistics.

Aikaterini-Lida Kalouli, Annebeth Buis, Livy Real, Martha Palmer, and Valeria de Paiva. 2019. Explaining simple natural language inference. In *Proceedings of the 13th Linguistic Annotation Workshop*, pages 132–143, Florence, Italy. Association for Computational Linguistics.

John P. Lalor, Hao Wu, Tsendsuren Munkhdalai, and Hong Yu. 2018. Understanding deep learning performance through an examination of test set difficulty: A psychometric case study. In *Proceedings of the 2018 Conference on Empirical Methods in Natural Language Processing*, pages 4711–4716, Brussels, Belgium. Association for Computational Linguistics.

John P. Lalor, Hao Wu, and Hong Yu. 2016. Building an evaluation scale using item response theory. In *Proceedings of the 2016 Conference on Empirical Methods in Natural Language Processing*, pages 648–657, Austin, Texas. Association for Computational Linguistics.

John P. Lalor, Hao Wu, and Hong Yu. 2019. Learning latent parameters without human response patterns: Item response theory with artificial crowds. In *Proceedings of the 2019 Conference on Empirical Methods in Natural Language Processing and the 9th International Joint Conference on Natural Language Processing (EMNLP-IJCNLP)*, pages 4249–4259, Hong Kong, China. Association for Computational Linguistics.

Yinhan Liu, Myle Ott, Naman Goyal, Jingfei Du, Mandar Joshi, Danqi Chen, Omer Levy, Mike Lewis, Luke Zettlemoyer, and Veselin Stoyanov. 2019. RoBERTa: A Robustly Optimized BERT Pretraining Approach. *arXiv:1907.11692 [cs]*. ArXiv: 1907.11692.

Richard McElreath. 2020. *Statistical Rethinking: A Bayesian course with examples in R and Stan*. CRC Press.

Rebecca J. Passonneau and Bob Carpenter. 2014. The benefits of a model of annotation. *Transactions of the Association for Computational Linguistics*, 2:311–326.

Silviu Paun, Bob Carpenter, Jon Chamberlain, Dirk Hovy, Udo Kruschwitz, and Massimo Poesio. 2018a. Comparing Bayesian models of annotation. *Transactions of the Association for Computational Linguistics*, 6:571–585.

Silviu Paun, Jon Chamberlain, Udo Kruschwitz, Juntao Yu, and Massimo Poesio. 2018b. A probabilistic annotation model for crowdsourcing coreference. In *Proceedings of the 2018 Conference on Empirical Methods in Natural Language Processing*, pages 1926–1937, Brussels, Belgium. Association for Computational Linguistics.

Ellie Pavlick and Tom Kwiatkowski. 2019. Inherent disagreements in human textual inferences. *Transactions of the Association for Computational Linguistics*, 7:677–694.

Barbara Plank, Dirk Hovy, and Anders Søgaard. 2014. Linguistically debatable or just plain wrong? In *Proceedings of the 52nd Annual Meeting of the Association for Computational Linguistics (Volume 2: Short Papers)*, pages 507–511, Baltimore, Maryland. Association for Computational Linguistics.

Ines Rehbein and Josef Ruppenhofer. 2017. Detecting annotation noise in automatically labelled data. In *Proceedings of the 55th Annual Meeting of the Association for Computational Linguistics (Volume 1: Long Papers)*, pages 1160–1170, Vancouver, Canada. Association for Computational Linguistics.

Keisuke Sakaguchi and Benjamin Van Durme. 2018. Efficient online scalar annotation with bounded support. In *Proceedings of the 56th Annual Meeting of the Association for Computational Linguistics (Volume 1: Long Papers)*, pages 208–218, Melbourne, Australia. Association for Computational Linguistics.

Aaron Steven White and Kyle Rawlins. 2018. The role of veridicality and factivity in clause selection. In *Proceedings of the 48th Annual Meeting of the North East Linguistic Society*, pages 221–234, Amherst, MA. GLSA Publications.

Aaron Steven White, Rachel Rudinger, Kyle Rawlins, and Benjamin Van Durme. 2018. Lexicosyntactic inference in neural models. In *Proceedings of the 2018 Conference on Empirical Methods in Natural Language Processing*, pages 4717–4724, Brussels, Belgium. Association for Computational Linguistics.

Adina Williams, Nikita Nangia, and Samuel Bowman. 2018. A broad-coverage challenge corpus for sentence understanding through inference. In *Proceedings of the 2018 Conference of the North American Chapter of the Association for Computational Linguistics: Human Language Technologies, Volume 1 (Long Papers)*, pages 1112–1122, New Orleans, Louisiana. Association for Computational Linguistics.

Sheng Zhang, Rachel Rudinger, Kevin Duh, and Benjamin Van Durme. 2017. Ordinal common-sense inference. *Transactions of the Association for Computational Linguistics*, 5:379–395.

Yi Zhang, Zachary Ives, and Dan Roth. 2019. Evidence-based trustworthiness. In *Proceedings of the 57th Annual Meeting of the Association for Computational Linguistics*, pages 413–423, Florence, Italy. Association for Computational Linguistics.

On the Systematicity of Probing Contextualized Word Representations: The Case of Hypernymy in BERT

Abhilasha Ravichander[◇*] , **Eduard Hovy**[◇], **Kaheer Suleman**[♡]
Adam Trischler[♡♠], **Jackie Chi Kit Cheung**[♠]
[◇]Carnegie Mellon University, Pittsburgh, PA
[♡]Microsoft Research, Montreal, Canada [♠]McGill University, Montreal, Canada
{aravicha, ehovy}@cs.cmu.edu
{adam.trischler, kasulema}@microsoft.com
{jcheung}@cs.mcgill.ca

Abstract

Contextualized word representations have become a driving force in NLP, motivating widespread interest in understanding their capabilities and the mechanisms by which they operate. Particularly intriguing is their ability to identify and encode conceptual abstractions. Past work has probed BERT representations (Devlin et al., 2019) for this competence, finding that BERT can correctly retrieve noun hypernyms in cloze tasks. In this work, we ask the question: *do probing studies shed light on systematic knowledge in BERT representations?* As a case study, we examine hypernymy knowledge encoded in BERT representations. In particular, we demonstrate through a simple consistency probe that the ability to correctly retrieve hypernyms in cloze tasks, as used in prior work, does not correspond to systematic knowledge in BERT. Our main conclusion is cautionary: even if BERT demonstrates high probing accuracy for a particular competence, it does not necessarily follow that BERT 'understands' a concept, and it cannot be expected to systematically generalize across applicable contexts.[1]

1 Introduction

Hierarchical representations of concepts play a central role in reasoning and understanding natural language (Wellman and Gelman, 1992). They have long been studied as a core NLP objective in their own right through tasks requiring the identification of hypernyms (Hearst, 1992; Snow et al., 2005, 2006), and as components for use in downstream

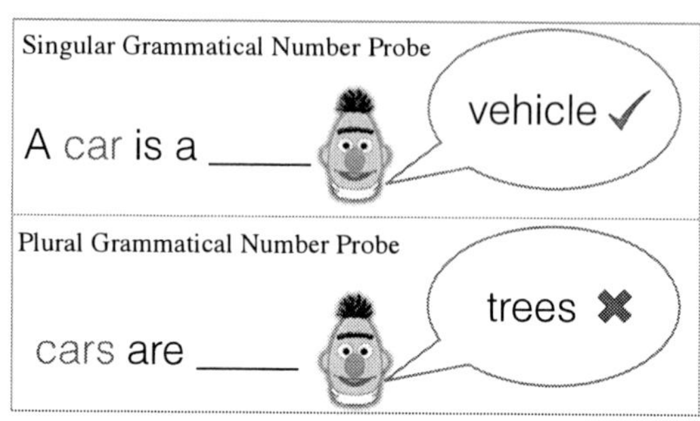

Figure 1: Illustration of BERT's inconsistent predictions on singular and plural hypernymy probes.

NLP tasks, such as recognizing textual entailment (RTE), metaphor detection, text generation and question answering (QA) (Girju et al., 2003; Dagan et al., 2006; Prager et al., 2008; Mirkin et al., 2009; Akhmatova and Dras, 2009; Mohler et al., 2013; Biran and McKeown, 2013; Yahya et al., 2013). Recently, Pretrained Language Models (PLMs), such as BERT (Devlin et al., 2019), have emerged as a popular and successful approach to a variety of NLP tasks. Thus, there has been community interest in evaluating their representations for the 'knowledge' they contain, including information about concept abstraction (Ettinger, 2020; Talmor et al., 2019; Jiang et al., 2020; Petroni et al., 2019).

We distinguish research that investigates knowledge encoded in BERT through two broad perspectives: *instrumentative* and *agentive*. We view the instrumentative perspective as treating PLMs *as a tool* to mine or store knowledge, like hypernym-hyponym and other relations, from text (Petroni et al., 2019; Jiang et al., 2020; Bouraoui et al., 2019; Bosselut et al., 2019; Madaan et al., 2020). The primary purpose of these investigations is to identify effective techniques to extract information from PLMs for use in downstream pipelines. In contrast, a growing body of work adopts an agentive perspective (Ettinger et al., 2018; Talmor et al., 2019),

---

* Part of this work was done during an internship at Microsoft Research.

[1]Diagnostic framework available at https://github.com/AbhilashaRavichander/probe-generalization.

Proceedings of the Ninth Joint Conference on Lexical and Computational Semantics (*SEM), pages 88–102
Barcelona, Spain (Online), December 12–13, 2020

treating PLMs as Artificial Intelligence (AI) agents and analyzing their linguistic competencies and world knowledge, sometimes through tasks such as natural language inference (Williams et al., 2018; Wang et al., 2018) or story completion (Zellers et al., 2018, 2019; Mostafazadeh et al., 2016).

In this work, we examine the agentive perspective, focusing specifically on the validity of conclusions drawn from probing studies. A popular approach to probing knowledge in pre-trained language models is the *zero-shot masked-LM* probing task. For example, given the statement 'A robin is a [MASK]', a PLM that produces the correct completion 'bird' is considered successful.[2] Past work has studied this competency in BERT (Ettinger, 2020), offering BERT's ability to correctly retrieve noun hypernyms in cloze tasks as evidence that it successfully encodes hypernymy information.

But to what extent does this knowledge of hypernymy generalize? Among many systematic generalization abilities desirable in PLMs, we select the following two. (1) Syntagmatic generalization: A model that has knowledge of a fact will be able to correctly answer queries about it and apply it across different contexts; (2) Paradigmatic generalization: A model with a particular competency will be able to generalize to novel cues and items. We implement these generalization requirements through a set of diagnostic probing tasks, in which a model must demonstrate consistency in applying its knowledge across different selective contexts, and by generalizing in trained probe settings to novel, unseen items belonging to the same semantic category or relation.

In particular, we focus on the setting of Ettinger (2020), which demonstrates that BERT is "very strong at associating nouns with hypernyms." We propose consistency tasks to illuminate the limits and generality of this ability, as illustrated in Figure 1. Our consistency tasks combine related zero-shot probes in such a way that a model that succeeds on one probe, if it is drawing on a systematic, general ability, should also succeed on the paired probe. Our evaluation with a grammatical number consistency task sheds light on the fragility of BERT's ability to associate correct noun hypernyms and demonstrates that pre-trained LMs have considerable room for improvement to reach a human-like level of understanding. [3]

Contributions: We demonstrate success on a hypernymy probing benchmark does not necessarily correspond to a systematic conceptual understanding of the phenomena in BERT, as discovered by probes. We further formulate evaluation protocols for characterizing the generalizability of PLM knowledge, in order to draw more reliable conclusions from probing studies.[4]

2 Experimental Methodology

Saussure (1916) expounds on syntagmatic relations, studying how words acquire relations based on the ways in which they are chained together in language context. The syntagmatic relation is based on groups of terms, in this case the hyponym and hypernym that are communicated together. In this work, we study whether PLM probes generalize syntagmatically, by evaluating the ability of models to produce correct predictions for hyponym-hypernym items across both singular and plural contexts. We also examine the ability of probes to generalize *paradigmatically*, that is, do probing studies uncover paradigms embedded in text (in this case the relations between items and their abstractions)?[5]

2.1 Syntagmatic Generalization

Knowledge in BERT is often studied using zero-shot probes (Ettinger, 2020; Talmor et al., 2019) in a *masked LM format*. In this construction, a PLM is queried by a natural language prompt designed to exercise a particular competence; for example, '*A robin is a [MASK]*' to evaluate knowledge of hypernymy. The word assigned the highest probability at the masked position is considered the PLM's answer.

In this work, we design diagnostics to examine how systematically this "knowledge" generalizes. We consider two kinds of diagnostics—(1) Consistency: We evaluate a PLM's ability to consistently answer queries reflecting the same conceptual understanding. We use a simple number consistency

---

[2] We refer to such probes henceforth as zero-shot masked LM probes, since they require no training and use BERT's masked-LM component to fill in the answer.

[3] Consistency tasks can be considered complementary to the control tasks proposed by Hewitt and Liang (2019). While control tasks test attribution, consistency tasks test validity.

[4] Our study is based on probes in English.

[5] This distinction is concerned with the axis of generalization of probes. In our syntagmatic generalization probes, we are concerned with different lexico-syntactic contexts where a model can demonstrate its knowledge of hypernymy. In the paradigmatic generalization probes, we are concerned with generalizing to novel hypernym/hyponym pairs.

check for hypernymy. Queries with hyponyms are replaced by their plural forms ; e.g. '*A robin is a [MASK]*' is perturbed as '*robins are [MASK]*'. Agents drawing on a general taxonomic reasoning ability should be able to correctly answer queries in both forms. (2) Contextual: We examine a PLM's ability to recognize the correct abstraction for a hyponym in context; e.g. '*A robin perches in its nest.*' is replaced with '*A [MASK] perches in its nest.*', where the hypernym *bird* is an acceptable substitution. Agents that understand concept instantiations should identify the correct abstraction.

2.1.1 Probes

Consistency Probes: In this paper, we adopt a *zero-shot cloze formulation* where hypernymy knowledge is in the form of triples $< x, y, t_{1...n} >$. Here, x is a hyponym, y is a hypernym and t_i is a cloze-style prompt consisting of a sequence of tokens, two of which are placeholders for the hyponym and hypernym (e.g., "A x is a y"). The final probe replaces x with the surface form of the hyponym, and lets the model predict the missing hypernym y (e.g., 'A robin is a ___').

Contextualized Probes: We further define a *contextual probe* formulation, wherein hypernymy knowledge is in the form of triples $< x, y, t_{1...n} >$. Here, x is a hyponym, y is a hypernym and t_i is a sequence of tokens, one of which is the hyponym y. The final probe asks the model to predict an appropriate hypernym x in the place of y in t_i. (e.g.., 'A ___ perches in its nest.').

2.1.2 Datasets

LM DIAGNOSTIC: We use the NEG-136 diagnostic constructed by Ettinger (2020), selecting the affirmative contexts to test models' use of hypernym information. Test items are drawn from a human study conducted by Fischler et al. (1983), wherein subject words are 18 concrete nouns and hypernyms belong to nine superordinate categories (Battig and Montague, 1969).[6] The final diagnostic set consists of 18 prompts.

LM DIAGNOSTIC EXTENDED: In this work, we additionally expand LM DIAGNOSTIC to construct a larger diagnostic set. For each superordinate category (Battig and Montague, 1969), we extract hyponyms from WordNet (Fellbaum, 1998a) such that they are nouns, not named entities, and

---

[6]bird, insect, fish, vehicle, tool, building, tree, flower, vegetable

only have a single sense in WordNet. This enables us to construct an expanded diagnostic set of 576 prompts. Statistics of both datasets, as well as sample queries, are reported in Table 1.

For each query in both datasets, we construct grammatical number consistency probes. Each query is perturbed to contain both the subject hyponym and target hypernym in plural form. Additionally, we construct contextual probes for each subject hyponym and target hypernym. These manually-crafted probes examine a PLM's abilities to identify correct abstractions for concepts in context. Each query consists of a sentential context collected from Wikipedia that contains the *hyponym* but not the hypernym, so as not to give easy cues to the LM. Each sentential context also satisfies the following additional requirements: (a) permissive of the abstraction (for example, the context *"The New York Public Library was built in the 1890's"* permits the *building* abstraction, but *"The New York Public Library fired John"* does not), (b) selective of the correct hypernym (for example, the context of the target item 'robin' in *"The charity began preservation efforts to save the robin"* is applicable to other categories besides the correct hypernym category '*bird*'—such as the '*insect*' category), and (c) upward entailing of the correct hypernym abstraction (for example, *"The largest salmon caught in the lake was 150cm"* does not entail *"The largest fish caught in the lake was 150cm"*).

2.2 Paradigmatic Generalization

We also examine conceptual generalization of the hypernymy relations: does hypernymy present a systematic pattern in the contextualized embedding space that enables generalization to novel items? To study this, we follow the popular probing methodology of training classifiers to predict hypernym relations from contextualized representations, with no task-specific fine-tuning.

Broadly, the task can be defined as follows. Given a pair of words a_1 and a_2, each grounded in a sentential context, s_1 and s_2, respectively, the goal is to describe whether a_1 and a_2 are in a hypernymy relation. For example, <building> is a hypernym of <skyscraper>, but <vehicle> is not. To examine generalization, we construct probing datasets with two settings: one where hypernyms are seen during training but hyponyms remain entirely unseen (SEEN), and one where both hyponyms and hypernyms in the tests are unseen during training

(UNSEEN). All datasets are constructed to enable three-fold cross-validation.[7] In all cases, each train instance is provided with multiple contexts from Wikipedia but test sets only feature one context per hyponym-hypernym pair.

2.2.1 Probes

We follow the work on diagnostic classifiers (Shi et al., 2016; Adi et al., 2017; Conneau et al., 2018; Hupkes et al., 2018; Liu et al., 2019; Shwartz and Dagan, 2019) and construct minimal embed-interact-predict probes to assess taxonomic knowledge in pretrained representations.

Embed: We embed each word in the hypernymy pair using the embedding model to obtain $\langle w_1, w_2 \rangle$. These representations can either be functions of the word itself (in static embeddings) or functions of the entire sentence (in contextualized embeddings).

Interact: Following Vu and Shwartz (2018), we concatenate the representations w_1, w_2 with their difference $w_2 - w_1$, and their element-wise product $w_1 \odot w_2$ to form representation $\vec{x}$.

Predict: We then apply a softmax classifier over the formed representation-
$$\vec{o} = softmax(W \cdot ReLU(Dropout(h(\vec{x}))))$$
where h is a 300-dimensional hidden layer, dropout probability = 0.2, $W \in \mathcal{R}^{n \times 300}$, and $n=2$.

2.2.2 Datasets

We select hyponym-hypernym pairs from LM DIAGNOSTIC EXTENDED. For each dataset, we pair both the hyponym and the hypernym with sentential contexts from Wikipedia.[8] We construct challenging negative examples by choosing hypernyms that belong to the same superordinate category [9] and which are not hypernyms of the word itself. We construct the datasets to meet the following specifications: (1) All datasets are balanced so that simple accuracy can be used as an evaluation metric, (2) Target pairs do not appear across train/test partitions to mitigate lexical memorization (Levy et al., 2015), (3) Negative examples should be similar words, so that simply exploiting distributional simi-

---

[7]Statistics of these datasets can be found in the appendix, Table 5 and Table 6.

[8]For both hyponyms and hypernyms, contextualized word representations are extracted using 'context embeddings' (Coenen et al., 2019). The input to BERT is a sequence of tokens from the sentential context and the output consists of a sequence of vectors corresponding to the input tokens. To obtain a representation for a hyponym or hypernym in a sentential context, we construct the average of the output vectors for the tokens in the hyponym or hypernym.

[9]animals, plant, object

larity does not work, (4) All examples are grounded in phrasal or sentential context.

3 Syntagmatic Generalization

3.1 Metrics

We consider the following rank-based metrics:

Open vocabulary accuracy: We compute mean precision@k (Open Voc.) where for a given hyponym, the value is 1 if the hypernym is ranked in the top k results and 0 otherwise. We report results with both $k = 1$ and $k = 5$. In the open vocabulary setting, the candidate list is BERT's vocabulary.

Singular accuracy: For a given hyponym, the query is posed in the singular form (e.g., 'A robin is a [MASK]'), and PLMs are evaluated on their ability to identify the correct hypernym from the nine Fischler categories, where the category assigned the highest probability by the PLM is considered the answer, as in prior work. The value is 1 if the correct hypernym is the top result and 0 if not.

Plural accuracy: For a given hyponym, the query is posed in the plural form (e.g., 'Robins are [MASK]'), and PLMs are evaluated on their ability to identify the correct hypernym from the nine Fischler categories in plural form, where the category assigned the highest probability by the PLM is considered the answer. The value is 1 if the correct hypernym is the top result and 0 if not.

Contextual accuracy: For a given hyponym, PLMs are evaluated on their ability to identify the correct hypernym in context, evaluated over the nine Fischler categories in singular form.

Paired Singular-Plural accuracy: For a given hyponym item, PLMs are evaluated on their ability to identify the correct hypernym in both singular and plural probes, over a candidate space of the nine Fischler categories. The value is 1 if the correct hypernym is the top answer in both cases.

Paired Aggregate accuracy: For hyponyms with a contextual probe, PLMs are evaluated on their ability to identify the correct hypernym in singular, plural and contextual probes, evaluated over the nine Fischler categories. The value is 1 if the correct answer is the top answer in all three cases.

3.2 Baselines and Models

We compare to the following baselines:

Dataset	Format	# Examples	Example
LM DIAGNOSTIC (Ettinger, 2020)	Zero-shot Cloze	18	A robin is a [MASK]
LM DIAGNOSTIC EXTENDED Singular	Zero-shot Cloze	576	A robin is a [MASK[
LM DIAGNOSTIC EXTENDED Plural	Zero-shot Cloze	576	Robins are [MASK[
LM DIAGNOSTIC EXTENDED Contextual	Zero-shot Cloze	186	Through use of an awl [TOOL] , the surgeon creates tiny fractures in the subchondral bone plate

Table 1: Statistics of zero-shot cloze probing datasets to study syntagmatic generalization.

Model	Open Voc. k=1	Open Voc. k=5	Singular	Plural	Contextual	Paired Singular-Plural	Paired Aggregate
			LM DIAGNOSTIC				
Majority	-	-	11.11	11.11	11.11	11.11	11.11
word2vec	0.0	50.0	83.33	100.0	-	83.33	-
GloVe	0.0	27.78	88.89	100.0	-	88.89	-
FastText	0.0	0.0	22.22	16.67	-	0.0	-
BERT-control	0.0	11.11	44.44	55.56	-	38.89	-
BERT	38.89	100.0	**100.0**	77.78	66.67	**77.78**	50.0
			LM DIAGNOSTIC EXTENDED				
Majority	-	-	22.92	22.92	31.72	22.92	31.72
word2vec	3.47	18.06	60.59	54.69	-	43.75	-
GloVe	0.35	3.3	58.16	50.17	-	35.24	-
FastText	0.0	0.0	12.15	11.11	-	1.91	-
BERT-control	0.35	2.08	30.56	39.76	-	20.66	-
BERT	23.09	48.96	**67.53**	44.1	73.66	**36.63**	33.33

Table 2: Performance of models on syntagmatic generalization probes. In the open Voc. k=1 and open Voc. k=5, we report mean precision@k, when the candidate list is BERT's vocabulary. We report accuracy(%) for singular, plural and contextual probes, where the candidate list is the nine superordinate categories (Battig and Montague, 1969)-bird, insect, fish, vehicle, tool, building, tree, flower, vegetable- in singular, plural and singular forms respectively. Paired singular-plural accuracy(%) is performance on identifying the correct hypernym in both singular and plural probes. Paired aggregate accuracy(%) is performance on identifying the correct hypernym in singular, plural and contextual probes, if a contextual probe for the hyponym exists.

Majority: Simple majority baseline quantifying the performance of a model that always predicts the majority class in the test set.

Static embedding: For each hyponym, we extract the static embedding with minimum cosine distance to the embedding of the hyponym word, amongst the Fischler categories. We evaluate the following word embeddings. (1) word2vec (Mikolov et al., 2013): Word embeddings are the hidden representations of a feedforward network trained to predict words in a fixed surrounding window to a particular word. We use the 300-dimension English word vectors trained on the Google News corpus. (2) GloVe (Pennington et al., 2014): GloVe embeddings are generated through training models to estimate the log-probability of word-pair co-occurence. We use 300-dimensional GloVe vectors trained on 6B tokens of text. (3) Fast-Text (Bojanowski et al., 2017): FastText vectors extend word2vec with sub-word information. We use 300-dimensional vectors trained on Wikipedia.

BERT-control (Devlin et al., 2019): Following Talmor et al. (2019), we define a simple BERT control which does not include relation information in the probe. Each query consists of the hyponym word followed by the *'[MASK]'* token (e.g., *'robin [MASK]'*) and the probability assigned by the PLM to the candidate list is computed.

BERT (Devlin et al., 2019): Bidirectional Encoder Representations from Transformers (BERT) is based on the transformer architecture (Vaswani et al., 2017) and is trained with both a cloze-style and next-sentence prediction objective.

3.3 Results

Table 2 displays performance scores of BERT on zero-shot probing tasks. We observe that in agreement with prior work, BERT achieves impressive results on the LM DIAGNOSTIC dataset in the open vocabulary setting, providing the right hypernym as the top answer for 38.89% of samples, and within the top 5 answers for 100.0% of samples. However, the LM DIAGNOSTIC consists of only 18

Prompt	Open Predictions	Singular Predictions	Plural Prompt	Plural Predictions
		LM DIAGNOSTIC		
A robin is a [MASK]	**robin**, bird, pigeon	**bird**, flower, tree	**robins are [MASK]**	**flowers**, birds, trees
A trout is a [MASK]	fish, trout, fishery	fish, bird, tool	trout are [MASK]	fish, trees, birds
A car is a [MASK]	**car**, vehicle, driver	**vehicle**, building, tool	**cars are [MASK]**	**trees**, vehicles, fish
		LM DIAGNOSTIC EXTENDED		
An aircraft is a [MASK]	**glider**, helicopter, aircraft	**vehicle**, bird, building	**aircraft are [MASK]**	**fish**, trees, buildings
A bumblebee is an [MASK]	**insect**, animal, airplane	**insect**, bird, flower	**bumblebees are [MASK]**	**birds**, insects, flowers
A bedbug is an [MASK]	**animal**, insect, object	**insect**, tool, vegetable	**bedbugs are [MASK]**	**fish**, flowers, insects

Table 3: Examples of BERT predictions for hypernymy relations with divergences highlighted in red, and samples with inconsistent predictions **in bold**. In the open vocabulary setting, the candidate list is BERT's vocabulary. In the singular probe setting, the candidate list is the nine superordinate categories from (Battig and Montague, 1969). In the plural setting, the candidate list is the nine categories from (Battig and Montague, 1969) in plural form, and the query is converted to the plural form.

such queries, and we observe that this performance drops considerably on the expanded diagnostic dataset LM DIAGNOSTIC EXTENDED (N=576), with the right hypernym being the top answer for only 23.09% of samples and within the top 5 answers for only 48.96% of samples.[10] We further observe that in both diagnostic datasets, BERT performance scores on plural probes are often lower than singular probes. The examples answered correctly in both plural and singular form in the LM DIAGNOSTIC EXTENDED dataset constitute approximately *half* what a standard singular zero-shot probe might lead a practitioner to believe. This is problematic, since if BERT possesses systematic 'knowledge' as discovered by probes, it ought to generalize in robust ways across our diagnostics.

Table 3 features BERT predictions on both diagnostic datasets, with divergences highlighted. We observe that in the open vocabulary setting, BERT predicts correct abstractions not included within the LM DIAGNOSTIC categories. To further estimate the kinds of errors that occur in BERT predictions for hypernymy, we sample 50 diagnostic tests from LM DIAGNOSTIC EXTENDED. We observe that in 10% of the examples, the model predicts the hyponym word itself (e.g., 'A yacht is a yacht.'). In 14% of examples, the model prediction is a valid hypernym that is not included in the Fischler categories. In 30% of diagnostic tests,

BERT predicts a generic hypernym, often a part-of-speech (e.g., 'An imaret is a noun.') and in a further 12% BERT predicts a subword fragment of the hyponym as a hypernym, but this prediction is incorrect (e.g., 'A penknife is a pen.') We speculate that hypernyms often do occur in such patterns in the training data (for example, a *steamboat* is a *boat*), making such tests particularly difficult for BERT.[11] Finally, for 34% of the predictions the source of error is unknown; however, for 17.6% of these tests BERT defaults to predicting 'horse' and for 11.8% BERT predicts 'dog', suggesting that BERT may be assigning a higher prior to certain tokens when the prompt is unfamiliar. Table 3 further displays BERT predictions in the closed vocabulary setting. Surprisingly, we observe that BERT identifies hypernyms incorrectly in plural probes, even for frequently occurring hyponyms such as 'car', predicting 'cars are trees'.

3.4 Frequency and Memorization Effects

When does BERT fail to recognize hypernyms in the zero-shot probe setting? What role does term frequency play in this ability? We investigate two hypothesized failure modes. (1) Rare hyponym: How does BERT probe performance vary with term frequency? To examine this, we consider the frequency statistics of each hyponym in the LM DIAGNOSTIC EXTENDED diagnostic, and examine those where the hypernym relation is correctly identified by BERT. We observe that correctly recognized hyponyms tend to be significantly more frequent than unrecognized ones, occurring on average 5098.15 times in Wikipedia, compared with

---

[10] However, the open vocabulary setting of Ettinger (2020) suffers from the limitation that since there are many correct hypernyms for any target word, models may be unfairly penalized in this setting for predicting a hypernym not present in the diagnostic. For this reason, we further consider the closed vocabulary setting (Singular, Plural, Contextual and Paired Singular-Plural in Table 2), where we examine probabilities assigned by the PLM to the nine hypernym categories defined in Battig and Montague (1969).

[11] Headed noun-noun compounds in English are likely to be right-headed (Williams, 1981).

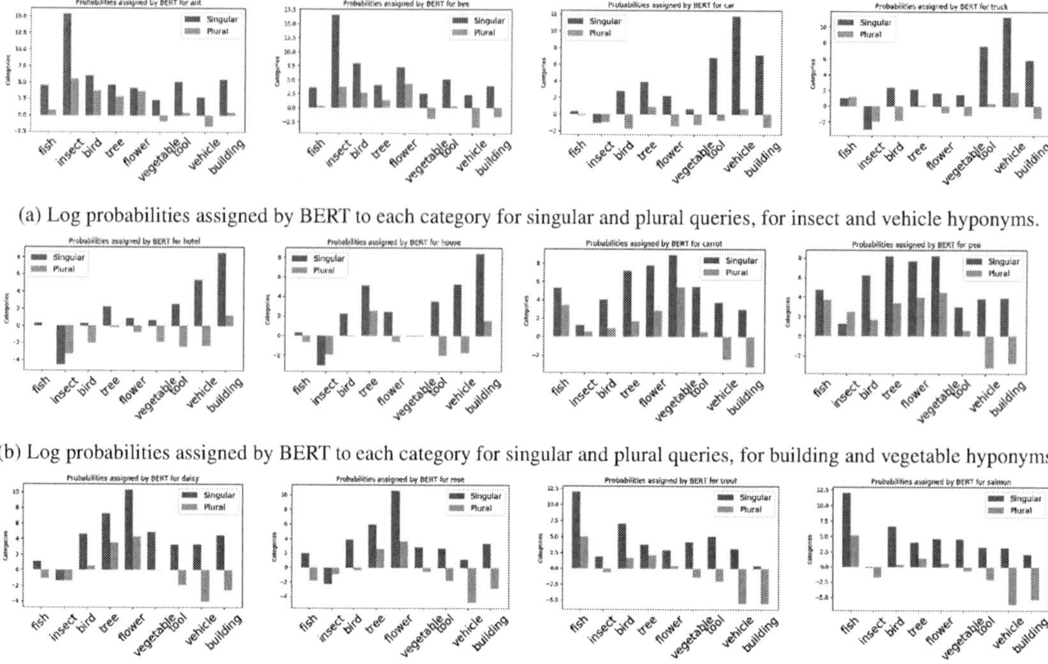

(a) Log probabilities assigned by BERT to each category for singular and plural queries, for insect and vehicle hyponyms.

(b) Log probabilities assigned by BERT to each category for singular and plural queries, for building and vegetable hyponyms.

(c) Log probabilities assigned by BERT to each category for singular and plural queries, for flower and fish hyponyms.

Figure 2: Category-wise log probability predicted by BERT for singular and plural probes.

4359.55 times for unrecognized hyponyms.[12] (2) Pattern Matching: To examine this, we extract co-occurrence patterns between hyponym and hypernym for all pairs in LM DIAGNOSTIC EXTENDED. Of all the hyponym-hypernym pairs that are known to have occurred in the template *"[hyponym] is a [hypernym]"* on Wikipedia, we can predict the hypernymy relation correctly at 78.34%, considerably higher than the average performance on the diagnostic. These results suggest BERT may be acting as a sophisticated n-gram index, and be strong at retrieving facts it has explicitly seen before in the training data.

3.5 Singular and Plural Probes

What happens when a query is posed to BERT with plural number instead of singular? Figure 2 illustrates the probabilities assigned by BERT to each category for both singular and plural probes in the LM DIAGNOSTIC. We observe that in all cases, the correct answer is predicted with greater confidence when the probe is singular. We next

Dataset	Seen Hypernyms	Unseen Hypernyms
Majority	50.00	50.00
Static Partial	56.32 ± 1.56	56.09 ± 4.21
Static	62.46 ± 3.99	58.15 ± 4.24
BERT Partial	48.36 ± 3.1	47.48 ± 4.98
BERT Context	**92.81** ± 0.81	**58.48** ± 1.74

Table 4: BERT results on hypernymy detection in SEEN and UNSEEN probing settings. Static is the summary of the best performance across word2vec, FastText and GloVe representations. The partial baseline for each representation, is the performance of a probing classifier trained only on the representation of the hypernym.

analyze errors in model predictions in singular vs. plural probes. We find that overall 7.4% of tests are predicted correctly only in plural form, 30.9% only in singular form, *only 36.63% in both singular and plural forms*, and 25% in neither.

4 Paradigmatic Generalization

Representations: We use the following representations in the encode-embed-predict architecture described in §2.2.1: For static representation baselines, we use word2vec, GloVe and FastText, and for our contextualized representation we study BERT. Detailed descriptions of the architectures can be found in §3.2

---

[12]We conduct a Shapiro-Wilk test for normality, allowing us to reject the null hypothesis of the frequency distributions being normal. We thus perform a Kruskal-Wallis non-parametric significance test, and find that recognized hyponyms tend to be statistically significantly more frequent (p<0.05).

Baselines: (1) Majority baseline: Performance of classifier that always predicts the majority class in the test set. (2) Partial: Partial-input baselines have revealed biases in Natural Language Inference (Tsuchiya, 2018; Gururangan et al., 2018; Poliak et al., 2018) and Question-Answering (Kaushik and Lipton, 2018) datasets. Levy et al. (2015) discuss the propensity of classifiers to rely on 'protoypical hypernyms' in hypernymy detection datasets, and not to solve the detection task. To control for potential dataset biases caused by the selection of items in the study, for each model we train a partial counterpart baseline, which is only provided the hypernym as input. If the dataset is unbiased in this aspect, partial baselines should achieve similar performance to a random classifier.

Results: Table 4 reports performance on SEEN and UNSEEN settings in our probing task. All experiments are done with 3-fold cross validation. We observe that all partial input baselines achieve near-random performance. Further, we observe that in the UNSEEN setting, probing classifier performance decreases considerably, indicating a lack of a systematic hypernymy function in BERT representations discoverable by the probing classifier. Thus, we determine that this class of probes does not generalize paradigmatically. Notably, we observe that a majority of the errors made by the probing classifiers is falsely detecting pairs as hypernyms, accounting for 79.4% of errors. Additionally, we observe that probing task design can considerably affect the conclusions drawn about whether a representation encodes any given property, emphasizing a need for careful consideration of design choices.

5   Related Work

There has been considerable interest in probing the capabilities of PLMs (Rogers et al., 2020). Much recent work focuses on the grammatical and syntactic capabilities of BERT (Hewitt and Manning, 2019; Liu et al., 2019; Swayamdipta et al., 2019; Goldberg, 2019; Wolf, 2019; Coenen et al., 2019; Tenney et al., 2019; Warstadt et al., 2019; Kim et al., 2019). In contrast, our focus is on probing studies that aim to uncover "knowledge" in BERT. There have been several such studies: Forbes et al. (2019) study physical commonsense encoded in BERT. Da and Kasai (2019) probe BERT for its understanding of object attributes, finding that it learns physical concrete norms (*is made of wood*) better than abstract ones (*is strong*). Wallace et al. (2019)

find a 'surprising degree of numeracy' is present in contextualized word representations. Talmor et al. (2019) probe BERT for capabilities at particular types of symbolic reasoning, such as comparison, conjunction and composition.

Our work focuses specifically on the validity of conclusions drawn from such probing studies that aim to discover knowledge in BERT, using the setting of Ettinger et al. (2018) as a case-study. We further distinguish between the instrumentative and agentive perspectives on probing. For example, there has been considerable research attention focused on querying language models for their encoded information (Petroni et al., 2019; Jiang et al., 2020; Bosselut et al., 2019), which we consider as an instrumentative effort using PLMs as a tool. Our focus in this work is instead on agentive studies, and our conclusion is that the probes we study should not be used to reveal evidence of some systematic knowledge or competence in PLMs— although PLMs can still be utilized as tools to *extract* such knowledge from text.

Closest to our work, Kassner and Schütze (2020) find that PLMs do not differentiate between negated and non-negated statements. Negation is a notoriously hard phenomenon for neural NLP models (Morante and Sporleder, 2012; Fancellu et al., 2016; Naik et al., 2018); our work demonstrates that even affirmative factual knowledge that can be extracted from BERT does not systematically generalize. Our work is also closely related to recent challenge set construction efforts, which aim to serve as sanity checks on the knowledge and commonsense capabilities of models (Marelli et al., 2014; Naik et al., 2018; Glockner et al., 2018; Ribeiro et al., 2020). For example, McCoy et al. (2019) show that BERT finetuned for the natural language inference task, relies heavily on shallow heurestics instead of acquiring adequate commonsense knowledge. Our work is complementary, demonstrating through a simple consistency task that BERT's capabilities, as discovered through probes, may not correspond to some systematic general ability.

Our work examines, in particular, hypernymy knowledge encoded in BERT representations. The identification of hypernyms is studied extensively in cognitive science and philosophy. Some prominent theories include Rosch's category theory (Rosch and Lloyd, 1978) and Tversky's category resemblance approach (Tversky, 1977). This work does not account for either of these interpretations of hypernymy, but instead relies on prior cognitive studies on category norms (Fischler et al., 1983; Battig and Montague, 1969) and relations defined with these super-ordinate categories in WordNet (Fellbaum, 1998b; Oltramari et al.). Additionally, our work ties into the rich history on modeling hypernymy in NLP systems (Lin, 1998; Weeds and Weir, 2003; Baroni et al., 2012; Rimell, 2014; Roller et al., 2014; Weeds et al., 2014; Shwartz et al., 2015; Vulić and Mrkšić, 2018) and evaluating distributional semantic models on their ability to represent it (Baroni and Lenci, 2011; Santus et al., 2015, 2016; Necsulescu, 2011; Vyas and Carpuat, 2017).

6 Discussion and Summary

We briefly discuss our findings and offer some guiding principles for future work.

Frequency and Memorization Effects: We find that BERT is particularly vulnerable to low-frequency phenomena in the training data, and succeeds at examples in the probe which have explicitly occurred in the training data. We speculate based on this evidence that BERT may just be memorizing the vast amount of training data it has been exposed to, rather than performing any kind of deeper reasoning.

Caution with cloze-style probes: BERT's Masked-LM format lends itself easily to cloze-style probes, which consider filling in a missing token correctly as evidence of PLM knowledge. Despite the accessibility of this format to investigate the behavior of PLMs, we speculate that, by design, the model is expected to fill in tokens whose context matches the provided template. The designer of the probing task may include templates to extract knowledge based on their intuitions, which (1) may or may not be the right template to extract the targeted kind of knowledge, (2) may provide enough inductive bias that it is unclear if the model understands the relation or understands how to match a particular template (which has been chosen so well based on the practitioners knowledge that it mimics the model actually understanding the deeper phenomena). We speculate that data-driven methods (Jiang et al., 2020; Bouraoui et al., 2019) can be designed to mitigate (2), but will exacerbate (1).

Dual Perspectives on PLMs: In this work, we characterize two perspectives on uncovering knowledge in PLMs: instrumentative and agent-based. We emphasize that while systematicity is a necessary requirement for agent-based analysis, as ideally we would like AI agents to reason like humans do, it is not necessary from an instrumentative perspective if the representations offer utility for a downstream task.

Implications for future work: In this work, we provide an investigation of current approaches to probing contextualized representations. Our tests for systematic generalization present a clearer picture of the conclusions that can be drawn from probing studies. We find that 'knowledge' discovered by standard probes does not serve to illuminate a systematic, general competence in the underlying PLMs. We suggest that future studies carefully evaluate the generalizability of their methods, and always be accompanied by consistency checks and controls to ensure that claims based on model behavior are made as reliable as possible.

Acknowledgements

We would like to thank Ali Emami, Ian Porada, Yanai Elazar, Alessandro Sordoni, Aakanksha Naik, Maria Ryskina and Shruti Rijhwani, for invaluable discussion related to the paper. We also thank the anonymous reviewers for their valuable suggestions. The last author is supported by the Canada CIFAR AI Chair program.

References

Yossi Adi, Einat Kermany, Yonatan Belinkov, Ofer Lavi, and Yoav Goldberg. 2017. Fine-grained analysis of sentence embeddings using auxiliary prediction tasks. In *International Conference on Learning Representations*.

Elena Akhmatova and Mark Dras. 2009. Using hypernymy acquisition to tackle (part of) textual entailment. In *Proceedings of the 2009 Workshop on Applied Textual Inference (TextInfer)*, pages 52–60, Suntec, Singapore. Association for Computational Linguistics.

Marco Baroni, Raffaella Bernardi, Ngoc-Quynh Do, and Chung-chieh Shan. 2012. Entailment above the word level in distributional semantics. In *Proceedings of the 13th Conference of the European Chapter of the Association for Computational Linguistics*, pages 23–32. Association for Computational Linguistics.

Marco Baroni and Alessandro Lenci. 2011. How we blessed distributional semantic evaluation. In *Proceedings of the GEMS 2011 Workshop on GEometrical Models of Natural Language Semantics*, pages 1–10. Association for Computational Linguistics.

William F Battig and William E Montague. 1969. Category norms of verbal items in 56 categories a replication and extension of the connecticut category norms. *Journal of experimental Psychology*, 80(3p2):1.

Or Biran and Kathleen McKeown. 2013. Classifying taxonomic relations between pairs of Wikipedia articles. In *Proceedings of the Sixth International Joint Conference on Natural Language Processing*, pages 788–794, Nagoya, Japan. Asian Federation of Natural Language Processing.

Piotr Bojanowski, Edouard Grave, Armand Joulin, and Tomas Mikolov. 2017. Enriching word vectors with subword information. *Transactions of the Association for Computational Linguistics*, 5:135–146.

Antoine Bosselut, Hannah Rashkin, Maarten Sap, Chaitanya Malaviya, Asli Çelikyilmaz, and Yejin Choi. 2019. Comet: Commonsense transformers for automatic knowledge graph construction. In *Proceedings of the 57th Annual Meeting of the Association for Computational Linguistics (ACL)*.

Zied Bouraoui, Jose Camacho-Collados, and Steven Schockaert. 2019. Inducing relational knowledge from bert.

Andy Coenen, Emily Reif, Ann Yuan, Been Kim, Adam Pearce, Fernanda Viégas, and Martin Wattenberg. 2019. Visualizing and measuring the geometry of bert.

Alexis Conneau, German Kruszewski, Guillaume Lample, Loïc Barrault, and Marco Baroni. 2018. What you can cram into a single $&!#* vector: Probing sentence embeddings for linguistic properties. In *Proceedings of the 56th Annual Meeting of the Association for Computational Linguistics (Volume 1: Long Papers)*, pages 2126–2136, Melbourne, Australia. Association for Computational Linguistics.

Jeff Da and Jungo Kasai. 2019. Cracking the contextual commonsense code: Understanding commonsense reasoning aptitude of deep contextual representations. In *Proceedings of the First Workshop on Commonsense Inference in Natural Language Processing*, pages 1–12, Hong Kong, China. Association for Computational Linguistics.

Ido Dagan, Oren Glickman, and Bernardo Magnini. 2006. The pascal recognising textual entailment challenge. In *Machine learning challenges. evaluating predictive uncertainty, visual object classification, and recognising tectual entailment*, pages 177–190. Springer.

Jacob Devlin, Ming-Wei Chang, Kenton Lee, and Kristina Toutanova. 2019. BERT: Pre-training of deep bidirectional transformers for language understanding. In *Proceedings of the 2019 Conference of the North American Chapter of the Association for Computational Linguistics: Human Language Technologies, Volume 1 (Long and Short Papers)*, pages 4171–4186, Minneapolis, Minnesota. Association for Computational Linguistics.

Allyson Ettinger. 2020. What bert is not: Lessons from a new suite of psycholinguistic diagnostics for language models. *Transactions of the Association for Computational Linguistics*, 8:34–48.

Allyson Ettinger, Ahmed Elgohary, Colin Phillips, and Philip Resnik. 2018. Assessing composition in sentence vector representations. In *Proceedings of the 27th International Conference on Computational Linguistics*, pages 1790–1801, Santa Fe, New Mexico, USA. Association for Computational Linguistics.

Federico Fancellu, Adam Lopez, and Bonnie Webber. 2016. Neural networks for negation scope detection. In *Proceedings of the 54th Annual Meeting of the Association for Computational Linguistics (Volume 1: Long Papers)*, pages 495–504, Berlin, Germany. Association for Computational Linguistics.

Christiane Fellbaum. 1998a. Towards a representation of idioms in WordNet. In *Usage of WordNet in Natural Language Processing Systems*.

Christiane Fellbaum. 1998b. *WordNet: An Electronic Lexical Database*. Bradford Books.

Ira Fischler, Paul A Bloom, Donald G Childers, Salim E Roucos, and Nathan W Perry Jr. 1983. Brain potentials related to stages of sentence verification. *Psychophysiology*, 20(4):400–409.

Maxwell Forbes, Ari Holtzman, and Yejin Choi. 2019. Do neural language representations learn physical commonsense? *arXiv preprint arXiv:1908.02899*.

Roxana Girju, Manju Putcha, and Dan Moldovan. 2003. Discovery of manner relations and their applicability to question answering. In *Proceedings of the ACL 2003 Workshop on Multilingual Summarization and Question Answering*, pages 54–60, Sapporo, Japan. Association for Computational Linguistics.

Max Glockner, Vered Shwartz, and Yoav Goldberg. 2018. Breaking NLI systems with sentences that require simple lexical inferences. In *Proceedings of the 56th Annual Meeting of the Association for Computational Linguistics (Volume 2: Short Papers)*, pages 650–655, Melbourne, Australia. Association for Computational Linguistics.

Yoav Goldberg. 2019. Assessing bert's syntactic abilities. *arXiv preprint arXiv:1901.05287*.

Suchin Gururangan, Swabha Swayamdipta, Omer Levy, Roy Schwartz, Samuel R Bowman, and Noah A Smith. 2018. Annotation artifacts in natural language inference data. *arXiv preprint arXiv:1803.02324*.

Marti A Hearst. 1992. Automatic acquisition of hyponyms from large text corpora. In *Proceedings of the 14th conference on Computational linguistics-Volume 2*, pages 539–545. Association for Computational Linguistics.

John Hewitt and Percy Liang. 2019. Designing and interpreting probes with control tasks. In *Proceedings of the 2019 Conference on Empirical Methods in Natural Language Processing and the 9th International Joint Conference on Natural Language Processing (EMNLP-IJCNLP)*, pages 2733–2743.

John Hewitt and Christopher D Manning. 2019. A structural probe for finding syntax in word representations. In *Proceedings of the 2019 Conference of the North American Chapter of the Association for Computational Linguistics: Human Language Technologies, Volume 1 (Long and Short Papers)*, pages 4129–4138.

Dieuwke Hupkes, Sara Veldhoen, and Willem Zuidema. 2018. Visualisation and'diagnostic classifiers' reveal how recurrent and recursive neural networks process hierarchical structure. *Journal of Artificial Intelligence Research*, 61:907–926.

Zhengbao Jiang, Frank F. Xu, Jun Araki, and Graham Neubig. 2020. How can we know what language models know? *Transactions of the Association for Computational Linguistics*, 8:423–438.

Nora Kassner and Hinrich Schütze. 2020. Negated and misprimed probes for pretrained language models: Birds can talk, but cannot fly. In *Proceedings of the 58th Annual Meeting of the Association for Computational Linguistics*, pages 7811–7818, Online. Association for Computational Linguistics.

Divyansh Kaushik and Zachary C. Lipton. 2018. How much reading does reading comprehension require? a critical investigation of popular benchmarks. In *Proceedings of the 2018 Conference on Empirical Methods in Natural Language Processing*, pages 5010–5015, Brussels, Belgium. Association for Computational Linguistics.

Najoung Kim, Roma Patel, Adam Poliak, Patrick Xia, Alex Wang, Tom McCoy, Ian Tenney, Alexis Ross, Tal Linzen, Benjamin Van Durme, Samuel R. Bowman, and Ellie Pavlick. 2019. Probing what different NLP tasks teach machines about function word comprehension. In *Proceedings of the Eighth Joint Conference on Lexical and Computational Semantics (*SEM 2019)*, pages 235–249, Minneapolis, Minnesota. Association for Computational Linguistics.

Omer Levy, Steffen Remus, Chris Biemann, and Ido Dagan. 2015. Do supervised distributional methods really learn lexical inference relations? In *Proceedings of the 2015 Conference of the North American Chapter of the Association for Computational Linguistics: Human Language Technologies*, pages 970–976, Denver, Colorado. Association for Computational Linguistics.

Dekang Lin. 1998. An information-theoretic definition of similarity. In *Proceedings of the Fifteenth International Conference on Machine Learning*, pages 296–304.

Nelson F Liu, Matt Gardner, Yonatan Belinkov, Matthew E Peters, and Noah A Smith. 2019. Linguistic knowledge and transferability of contextual representations. In *Proceedings of the 2019 Conference of the North American Chapter of the Association for Computational Linguistics: Human Language Technologies, Volume 1 (Long and Short Papers)*, pages 1073–1094.

Aman Madaan, Dheeraj Rajagopal, Yiming Yang, Abhilasha Ravichander, Eduard Hovy, and Shrimai Prabhumoye. 2020. Eigen: Event influence generation using pre-trained language models.

Marco Marelli, Stefano Menini, Marco Baroni, Luisa Bentivogli, Raffaella Bernardi, and Roberto Zamparelli. 2014. A SICK cure for the evaluation of compositional distributional semantic models. In *Proceedings of the Ninth International Conference on Language Resources and Evaluation (LREC-2014)*, pages 216–223, Reykjavik, Iceland. European Languages Resources Association (ELRA).

Tom McCoy, Ellie Pavlick, and Tal Linzen. 2019. Right for the wrong reasons: Diagnosing syntactic heuristics in natural language inference. In *Proceedings of the 57th Annual Meeting of the Association for Computational Linguistics*, pages 3428–3448, Florence, Italy. Association for Computational Linguistics.

Tomas Mikolov, Ilya Sutskever, Kai Chen, Greg S Corrado, and Jeff Dean. 2013. Distributed representations of words and phrases and their compositionality. In *Advances in neural information processing systems*, pages 3111–3119.

Shachar Mirkin, Lucia Specia, Nicola Cancedda, Ido Dagan, Marc Dymetman, and Idan Szpektor. 2009. Source-language entailment modeling for translating unknown terms. In *Proceedings of the Joint Conference of the 47th Annual Meeting of the ACL and the 4th International Joint Conference on Natural Language Processing of the AFNLP: Volume 2-Volume 2*, pages 791–799. Association for Computational Linguistics.

Michael Mohler, David Bracewell, Marc Tomlinson, and David Hinote. 2013. Semantic signatures for example-based linguistic metaphor detection. In *Proceedings of the First Workshop on Metaphor in*

NLP, pages 27–35, Atlanta, Georgia. Association for Computational Linguistics.

Roser Morante and Caroline Sporleder. 2012. Modality and negation: An introduction to the special issue. *Computational Linguistics*, 38(2):223–260.

Nasrin Mostafazadeh, Nathanael Chambers, Xiaodong He, Devi Parikh, Dhruv Batra, Lucy Vanderwende, Pushmeet Kohli, and James Allen. 2016. A corpus and cloze evaluation for deeper understanding of commonsense stories. In *Proceedings of the 2016 Conference of the North American Chapter of the Association for Computational Linguistics: Human Language Technologies*, pages 839–849, San Diego, California. Association for Computational Linguistics.

Aakanksha Naik, Abhilasha Ravichander, Norman Sadeh, Carolyn Rose, and Graham Neubig. 2018. Stress test evaluation for natural language inference. In *Proceedings of the 27th International Conference on Computational Linguistics*, pages 2340–2353, Santa Fe, New Mexico, USA. Association for Computational Linguistics.

Silvia Necsulescu. 2011. Automatic acquisition of possible contexts for low-frequent words. In *Proceedings of the Second Student Research Workshop associated with RANLP 2011*, pages 121–126, Hissar, Bulgaria. Association for Computational Linguistics.

Alessandro Oltramari, Aldo Gangemi, Nicola Guarino, and Claudio Masolo. Restructuring wordnet's top-level: The ontoclean approach.

Jeffrey Pennington, Richard Socher, and Christopher Manning. 2014. Glove: Global vectors for word representation. In *Proceedings of the 2014 conference on empirical methods in natural language processing (EMNLP)*, pages 1532–1543.

Fabio Petroni, Tim Rocktäschel, Sebastian Riedel, Patrick Lewis, Anton Bakhtin, Yuxiang Wu, and Alexander Miller. 2019. Language models as knowledge bases? In *Proceedings of the 2019 Conference on Empirical Methods in Natural Language Processing and the 9th International Joint Conference on Natural Language Processing (EMNLP-IJCNLP)*, pages 2463–2473, Hong Kong, China. Association for Computational Linguistics.

Adam Poliak, Jason Naradowsky, Aparajita Haldar, Rachel Rudinger, and Benjamin Van Durme. 2018. Hypothesis only baselines in natural language inference. In *Proceedings of the Seventh Joint Conference on Lexical and Computational Semantics*, pages 180–191, New Orleans, Louisiana. Association for Computational Linguistics.

John Prager, Jennifer Chu-Carroll, Eric W Brown, and Krzysztof Czuba. 2008. Question answering by predictive annotation. In *Advances in Open Domain Question Answering*, pages 307–347. Springer.

Marco Tulio Ribeiro, Tongshuang Wu, Carlos Guestrin, and Sameer Singh. 2020. Beyond accuracy: Behavioral testing of NLP models with CheckList. In *Proceedings of the 58th Annual Meeting of the Association for Computational Linguistics*, pages 4902–4912, Online. Association for Computational Linguistics.

Laura Rimell. 2014. Distributional lexical entailment by topic coherence. In *Proceedings of the 14th Conference of the European Chapter of the Association for Computational Linguistics*, pages 511–519.

Anna Rogers, Olga Kovaleva, and Anna Rumshisky. 2020. A primer in bertology: What we know about how bert works. *arXiv preprint arXiv:2002.12327*.

Stephen Roller, Katrin Erk, and Gemma Boleda. 2014. Inclusive yet selective: Supervised distributional hypernymy detection. In *Proceedings of COLING 2014, the 25th International Conference on Computational Linguistics: Technical Papers*, pages 1025–1036, Dublin, Ireland. Dublin City University and Association for Computational Linguistics.

Eleanor Rosch and Barbara Bloom Lloyd. 1978. Cognition and categorization.

Enrico Santus, Alessandro Lenci, Tin-Shing Chiu, Qin Lu, and Chu-Ren Huang. 2016. Nine features in a random forest to learn taxonomical semantic relations. In *Proceedings of the Tenth International Conference on Language Resources and Evaluation (LREC'16)*, pages 4557–4564, Portorož, Slovenia. European Language Resources Association (ELRA).

Enrico Santus, Frances Yung, Alessandro Lenci, and Chu-Ren Huang. 2015. EVALution 1.0: an evolving semantic dataset for training and evaluation of distributional semantic models. In *Proceedings of the 4th Workshop on Linked Data in Linguistics: Resources and Applications*, pages 64–69, Beijing, China. Association for Computational Linguistics.

Ferdinand de Saussure. 1916. Course in general linguistics (trans. wade baskin). *London: Fontana/Collins*, page 74.

Xing Shi, Inkit Padhi, and Kevin Knight. 2016. Does string-based neural mt learn source syntax? In *Proceedings of the 2016 Conference on Empirical Methods in Natural Language Processing*, pages 1526–1534.

Vered Shwartz and Ido Dagan. 2019. Still a pain in the neck: Evaluating text representations on lexical composition. *Transactions of the Association for Computational Linguistics*, 7:403–419.

Vered Shwartz, Omer Levy, Ido Dagan, and Jacob Goldberger. 2015. Learning to exploit structured resources for lexical inference. In *Proceedings of the Nineteenth Conference on Computational Natural Language Learning*, pages 175–184, Beijing, China. Association for Computational Linguistics.

Rion Snow, Daniel Jurafsky, and Andrew Y Ng. 2005. Learning syntactic patterns for automatic hypernym discovery. In *Advances in neural information processing systems*, pages 1297–1304.

Rion Snow, Daniel Jurafsky, and Andrew Y. Ng. 2006. Semantic taxonomy induction from heterogenous evidence. In *Proceedings of the 21st International Conference on Computational Linguistics and 44th Annual Meeting of the Association for Computational Linguistics*, pages 801–808, Sydney, Australia. Association for Computational Linguistics.

Swabha Swayamdipta, Matthew Peters, Brendan Roof, Chris Dyer, and Noah A Smith. 2019. Shallow syntax in deep water. *arXiv preprint arXiv:1908.11047*.

Alon Talmor, Yanai Elazar, Yoav Goldberg, and Jonathan Berant. 2019. olmpics – on what language model pre-training captures.

Ian Tenney, Patrick Xia, Berlin Chen, Alex Wang, Adam Poliak, R Thomas McCoy, Najoung Kim, Benjamin Van Durme, Samuel R Bowman, Dipanjan Das, et al. 2019. What do you learn from context? probing for sentence structure in contextualized word representations. *arXiv preprint arXiv:1905.06316*.

Masatoshi Tsuchiya. 2018. Performance impact caused by hidden bias of training data for recognizing textual entailment. In *Proceedings of the Eleventh International Conference on Language Resources and Evaluation (LREC-2018)*, Miyazaki, Japan. European Languages Resources Association (ELRA).

Amos Tversky. 1977. Features of similarity. *Psychological review*, 84(4):327.

Ashish Vaswani, Noam Shazeer, Niki Parmar, Jakob Uszkoreit, Llion Jones, Aidan N Gomez, Łukasz Kaiser, and Illia Polosukhin. 2017. Attention is all you need. In *Advances in Neural Information Processing Systems*, pages 5998–6008.

Tu Vu and Vered Shwartz. 2018. Integrating multiplicative features into supervised distributional methods for lexical entailment. In *Proceedings of the Seventh Joint Conference on Lexical and Computational Semantics*, pages 160–166, New Orleans, Louisiana. Association for Computational Linguistics.

Ivan Vulić and Nikola Mrkšić. 2018. Specialising word vectors for lexical entailment. In *Proceedings of the 2018 Conference of the North American Chapter of the Association for Computational Linguistics: Human Language Technologies, Volume 1 (Long Papers)*, pages 1134–1145, New Orleans, Louisiana. Association for Computational Linguistics.

Yogarshi Vyas and Marine Carpuat. 2017. Detecting asymmetric semantic relations in context: A case-study on hypernymy detection. In *Proceedings of the 6th Joint Conference on Lexical and Computational Semantics (* SEM 2017)*, pages 33–43.

Eric Wallace, Yizhong Wang, Sujian Li, Sameer Singh, and Matt Gardner. 2019. Do NLP models know numbers? probing numeracy in embeddings. In *Proceedings of the 2019 Conference on Empirical Methods in Natural Language Processing and the 9th International Joint Conference on Natural Language Processing (EMNLP-IJCNLP)*, pages 5307–5315, Hong Kong, China. Association for Computational Linguistics.

Alex Wang, Amanpreet Singh, Julian Michael, Felix Hill, Omer Levy, and Samuel Bowman. 2018. GLUE: A multi-task benchmark and analysis platform for natural language understanding. In *Proceedings of the 2018 EMNLP Workshop BlackboxNLP: Analyzing and Interpreting Neural Networks for NLP*, pages 353–355, Brussels, Belgium. Association for Computational Linguistics.

Alex Warstadt, Yu Cao, Ioana Grosu, Wei Peng, Hagen Blix, Yining Nie, Anna Alsop, Shikha Bordia, Haokun Liu, Alicia Parrish, Sheng-Fu Wang, Jason Phang, Anhad Mohananey, Phu Mon Htut, Paloma Jeretic, and Samuel R. Bowman. 2019. Investigating BERT's knowledge of language: Five analysis methods with NPIs. In *Proceedings of the 2019 Conference on Empirical Methods in Natural Language Processing and the 9th International Joint Conference on Natural Language Processing (EMNLP-IJCNLP)*, pages 2877–2887, Hong Kong, China. Association for Computational Linguistics.

Julie Weeds, Daoud Clarke, Jeremy Reffin, David Weir, and Bill Keller. 2014. Learning to distinguish hypernyms and co-hyponyms. In *Proceedings of COLING 2014, the 25th International Conference on Computational Linguistics: Technical Papers*, pages 2249–2259. Dublin City University and Association for Computational Linguistics.

Julie Weeds and David Weir. 2003. A general framework for distributional similarity. In *Proceedings of the 2003 conference on Empirical methods in natural language processing*, pages 81–88.

Henry M Wellman and Susan A Gelman. 1992. Cognitive development: Foundational theories of core domains. *Annual review of psychology*, 43(1):337–375.

Adina Williams, Nikita Nangia, and Samuel Bowman. 2018. A broad-coverage challenge corpus for sentence understanding through inference. In *Proceedings of the 2018 Conference of the North American Chapter of the Association for Computational Linguistics: Human Language Technologies, Volume 1 (Long Papers)*, pages 1112–1122, New Orleans, Louisiana. Association for Computational Linguistics.

Edwin Williams. 1981. On the notions" lexically related" and" head of a word". *Linguistic inquiry*, 12(2):245–274.

Thomas Wolf. 2019. Some additional experiments extending the tech report" assessing berts syntactic abilities" by yoav goldberg. Technical report.

Mohamed Yahya, Klaus Berberich, Shady Elbassuoni, and Gerhard Weikum. 2013. Robust question answering over the web of linked data. In *Proceedings of the 22nd ACM international conference on Conference on information & knowledge management*, pages 1107–1116. ACM.

Rowan Zellers, Yonatan Bisk, Roy Schwartz, and Yejin Choi. 2018. SWAG: A large-scale adversarial dataset for grounded commonsense inference. In *Proceedings of the 2018 Conference on Empirical Methods in Natural Language Processing*, pages 93–104, Brussels, Belgium. Association for Computational Linguistics.

Rowan Zellers, Ari Holtzman, Yonatan Bisk, Ali Farhadi, and Yejin Choi. 2019. HellaSwag: Can a machine really finish your sentence? In *Proceedings of the 57th Annual Meeting of the Association for Computational Linguistics*, pages 4791–4800, Florence, Italy. Association for Computational Linguistics.

Fold	#Train	#Dev	#Test
1	6164	206	232
2	7936	92	112
3	5892	222	219

Table 5: Statistics of UNSEEN dataset to study paradigmatic generalization.

Fold	#Train	#Dev	#Test
1	6682	176	148
2	6556	182	144
3	6582	164	154

Table 6: Statistics of SEEN dataset to examine paradigmatic generalization.

A   Datasets for Paradigmatic Generalization

Table 5 and Table 6 summarize the dataset statistics of the unseen and seen datasets respectively. We perform 3-fold cross validation.

Topology of Word Embeddings: Singularities Reflect Polysemy

Alexander Jakubowski
Heinrich Heine University
Düsseldorf
`jakubowskialexander`
`@gmail.com`

Milica Gašić
Heinrich Heine University
Düsseldorf
`gasic`
`@hhu.de`

Marcus Zibrowius
Heinrich Heine University
Düsseldorf
`marcus.zibrowius`
`@cantab.net`

Abstract

The manifold hypothesis suggests that word vectors live on a submanifold within their ambient vector space. We argue that we should, more accurately, expect them to live on a *pinched* manifold: a singular quotient of a manifold obtained by identifying some of its points. The identified, singular points correspond to polysemous words, i.e. words with multiple meanings. Our point of view suggests that monosemous and polysemous words can be distinguished based on the topology of their neighbourhoods. We present two kinds of empirical evidence to support this point of view: (1) We introduce a topological measure of polysemy based on persistent homology that correlates well with the actual number of meanings of a word. (2) We propose a simple, topologically motivated solution to the SemEval-2010 task on *Word Sense Induction & Disambiguation* that produces competitive results.

1 Introduction

Static word embeddings attempt to represent words by vectors in a high-dimensional vector space $\mathbb{R}^n$ in such a way that words of similar meaning are represented by (cosine) similar vectors, and vice versa. According to the manifold hypothesis, we should expect these vectors to lie within a lower-dimensional **word space** $\mathcal{W}$, a subspace of $\mathbb{R}^n$ that resembles a manifold. To what extent this hypothesis is true in this and other contexts is the subject of ongoing research (Fefferman et al., 2016). In this paper, we argue and demonstrate that for the word space $\mathcal{W}$, polysemy is a principal obstruction to any strict interpretation of the manifold hypothesis.

That polysemy presents a serious obstacle to the creation of adequate word vector representations is clear from the outset. Take, for example, a polysemous word like "mole". We would want the vectors representing "birthmark" and "counterspy" to be similar to the vector of "mole", but *not* similar to each other. This is impossible. In order for similarity of vectors to accurately encode similarity in meaning, we need vectors representing meanings, not words.

Let us therefore hypothesize a **space of meanings** $\mathcal{M}$ that accurately represents all possible meanings and their similarities. Our argument is a simple topological observation based on the relationship between this space $\mathcal{M}$ and the word space $\mathcal{W}$. For an idealised language, where there is a bijection between meanings and words, these two spaces would agree. For a natural language, however, multiple points of $\mathcal{M}$ get identified with a single point of $\mathcal{W}$. This process corresponds to a topological construction that we refer to as **pinching** (see Figure 2). It is easy to see that a space resulting from pinching cannot be a manifold. Thus, even if the space of meanings $\mathcal{M}$ satisfies the manifold hypothesis perfectly, the pinched space $\mathcal{W}$ cannot satisfy the hypothesis near polysemous words.[1]

Based on this intuition, and using tools from Topological Data Analysis, we introduce a measure for the polysemy of a word based on its vector embedding. Our experiments show that this **topological polysemy** (TPS) correlates well with the actual number of meanings that a word has. In addition, we present an approach to the SemEval-2010 task on *Word Sense Induction & Disambiguation* (task 14) (Manandhar et al., 2010). This approach is independent of TPS, but based on the same ideas. Despite its simplicity, it is almost on par with the best performing algorithm within the

---

[1]It may appear that a similar complication arises from synonyms, multiple words with a single meaning. However, synonyms are irrelevant for our analysis; see the discussion at the end of Section 3.1.

103

*Proceedings of the Ninth Joint Conference on Lexical and Computational Semantics (*SEM)*, pages 103–113
Barcelona, Spain (Online), December 12–13, 2020

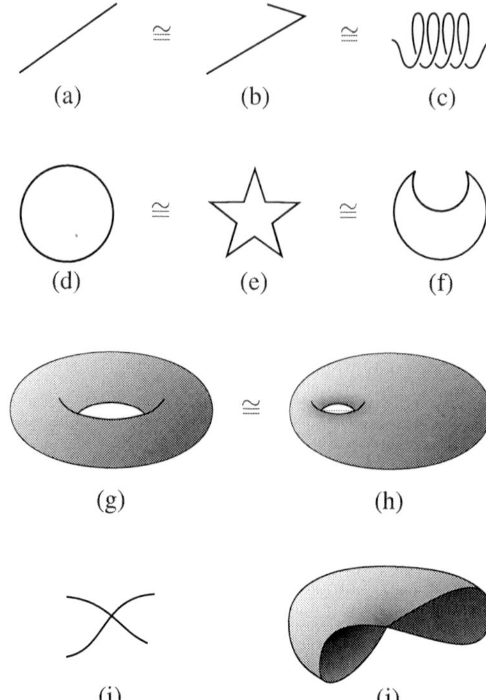

Figure 1: Some subspaces of $\mathbb{R}^3$: various deformations of an open line segment (a, b, c), deformations of a circle (d, e, f), a torus (g) and a deformation of the torus (h), two intersecting line segments (i), and a surface with a figure eight as boundary (j)

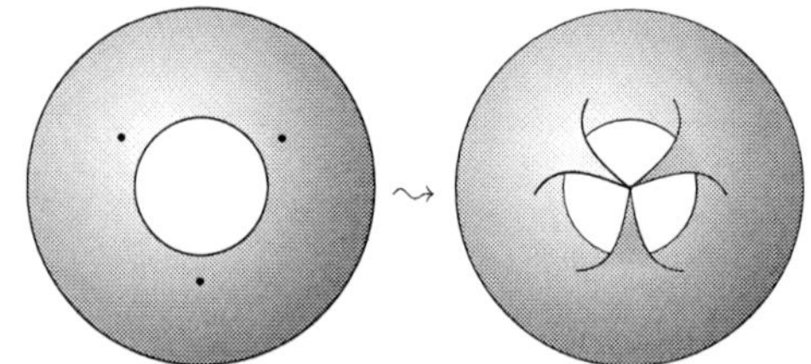

Figure 2: The effect of pinching on the torus (example (g) from Figure 1): before *(left)* and after the identification of three marked points to a singular point *(right)*

2010 challenge, and outperforms far more complicated approaches.

We see these experimental results as strong evidence that our interpretation of the word space $\mathcal{W}$ as a pinched manifold is more adequate than a more naïve view of $\mathcal{W}$ as an actual manifold.

2 Background

2.1 Topology

A space, for us, is a topological space. Readers unfamiliar with the notion may simply think of metric spaces, or indeed of subspaces of euclidean space $\mathbb{R}^n$. Two such spaces are considered equivalent, or **homeomorphic**, if they can be deformed into each other. We will not make this precise here, but we hope that Figure 1, in which homeomorphic spaces are connected by the symbol "$\cong$", gives a clear intuition. As flexible as this notion may appear, the deformations considered do keep certain properties of a space invariant. Crucially, homeomorphic spaces always have the same number of connected components and the same number of holes. Topo-

logists have developed a myriad of more subtle invariants that allow us to decide whether two spaces are homeomorphic. We refer to Hatcher (2002) for an introduction into this vast field.

Two kinds of spaces will be important for us: manifolds and pinched manifolds. A (topological) **manifold** is a space in which each point has a neighbourhood homeomorphic to an open ball of $\mathbb{R}^d$ for some d (cf. Hatcher, 2002, § 3.3).[2] We call d the local dimension of the manifold at that point. The spaces (a), (b) and (c) in Figure 1 are manifolds since each point has a neighbourhood homeomorphic to an open interval in $\mathbb{R}^1$, and so are the spaces (d), (e), (f). The spaces (g) and (h) are manifolds because each point has a neighbourhood homeomorphic to an open disk in $\mathbb{R}^2$. Space (i), on the other hand, is not a manifold, because the point of intersection has no neighbourhood homeomorphic to an open ball of any dimension, and neither is space (j), because the manifold condition is violated at all boundary points. The spaces "without corners", i.e. examples (a), (c), (d), (g) and (h) in Figure 1 are not only topological manifolds but even *differentiable* manifolds, but this distinction will be of no importance to us.

By a **pinched manifold**, we will mean a space obtained from a manifold by marking a finite number of points in different colours, and identifying ("glueing together") all points of the same colour, as illustrated in Figure 2. In a pinched manifold, the neighbourhoods of most points still look like open balls, but the neighbourhoods of the identified points look like several balls glued together at their centres. We will call these identified points **singular points**.

Singular points can thus easily be distinguished from non-singular points by the topology of their neighbourhoods. More precisely, we can distin-

---

[2]Manifolds are moreover required to be *Hausdorff*, a technical condition that all metric spaces satisfy.

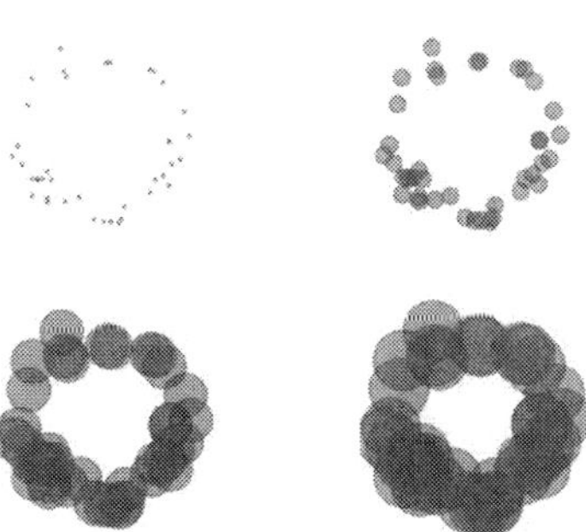

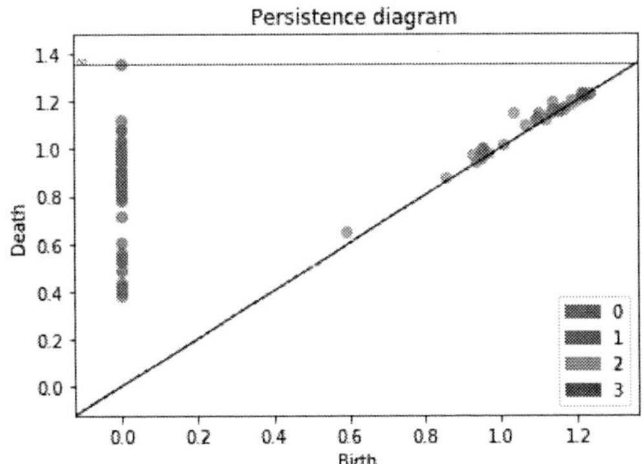

Figure 3: Points noisily sampled from the unit circle *(top left)* and the corresponding spaces $\mathcal{W}_r$ for different radii r

Figure 4: An example of a persistence diagram, summarizing the persistent homology of some point cloud $\mathcal{W}_0$ in degrees $i = 0, 1, 2$ and 3. Each dot encodes the life span of a distinct feature. Features of different degrees are displayed in different colours, as indicated in the lower right corner. For the computations in this paper, we will focus on the degree zero features, i.e. on connected components, indicated in red. As all of these are already present in the point cloud $\mathcal{W}_0$, they all have horizontal coordinate equal to zero. Their vertical coordinates are the radii at which different components merge

guish them by counting the number of connected components of their **punctured neighbourhoods**: neighbourhoods of a point from which the point itself has been removed. The punctured neighbourhood of a non-singular point is a single punctured ball, and thus is connected, at least in dimensions $d \geq 2$. The punctured neighbourhood of a singular point obtained by identifying $k > 1$ points, on the other hand, is a disjoint union of k punctured balls, and thus has several connected components. Thus, in dimensions $d \geq 2$, a point is singular if and only if small punctured neighbourhoods of it have more than one connected component.

Puncturing the neighbourhood, i.e. removing the centre, is crucial for this distinction. The unpunctured neighbourhoods of singular and non-singular points are not distinguishable by the usual topological invariants. (In technical terms, the neighbourhoods of both types of points are *contractible*.)

2.2 Topological data analysis

Topological data analysis (TDA) is an instrument for extracting topological information from a point cloud, that is a finite set of vectors $\mathcal{W}_0 = \{p_1, p_2, \ldots, p_N\} \subset \mathbb{R}^n$. The point cloud itself is trivial from a topological point of view. The fundamental assumption of TDA is that the vectors of $\mathcal{W}_0$ are not randomly distributed but instead are sampled from some underlying space $\mathcal{W} \subset \mathbb{R}^n$ which – unlike the point cloud itself – is topologically interesting. A human immediately recognises that the points in Figure 3 have been sampled from a circle. TDA provides algorithms that encode this intuition, and extend it to higher dimensions.

One such algorithm is **persistent homology**.

The basic idea is to replace $\mathcal{W}_0$ with the union $\mathcal{W}_r$ of all open balls of a certain radius r centred at the points of $\mathcal{W}_0$. As we vary this radius, we obtain a sequence of spaces, starting for $r = 0$ with the point cloud itself and ending at some high value of r with a space in which all balls are merged into a single big blob. We compute certain topological invariants, the so-called Betti numbers b_i, for each space $\mathcal{W}_r$. The Betti number b_i counts certain i-dimensional features of the space. For example, b_0 is the number of connected components and b_1 is the "number of holes"; both are equal to 1 for the two spaces in the lower half of Figure 3.

The radii at which different i-dimensional features appear and disappear can be summarized into a multiset and visualized as a two-dimensional **persistence diagram** D as in Figure 4. Each dot in this diagram encodes the life span of a distinct feature: its horizontal coordinate is the *smallest* radius r at which the feature is present in $\mathcal{W}_r$, its vertical coordinate is the *largest* radius r at which it is present. Points that lie far off the diagonal correspond to features that *persist* across a wide range of values of r, and are hence likely to reflect features of the underlying space $\mathcal{W}$. For technical reasons, every point on the diagonal is also included in the persistence diagram D with infinite multiplicity.

The **Wasserstein distance** provides a notion of distance between two such persistence diagrams, and hence a measure of similarity between different point clouds and their underlying spaces. For two diagrams D and $\tilde{D}$ it is defined as:

$$W(D, \tilde{D}) := \inf_{\eta: D \to \tilde{D}} \left(\sum_{x \in D} \|x - \eta(x)\|_\infty \right)$$

where η runs over all bijections between the two diagrams. As all points on the diagonal are included in both diagrams, such bijections always exist.

The computation of persistent homology can be restricted to a range of degrees i. In this paper, we will concentrate on persistent homology in degree $i = 0$, which is essentially a systematic application of single-linkage clustering. Computations in higher dimensions quickly become very expensive. For an in-depth discussion of the concepts mentioned in this section we recommend (Edelsbrunner and Harer, 2010).

2.3 Word vector embeddings

The distributional hypothesis states that "the meaning of words lies in their use" (Wittgenstein, 1953). This provides the basis for distributional semantics, a data driven study of word meanings. Words are modelled as vectors in such a way that (cosine) similarity of vectors corresponds to similarity in the distributions of the corresponding words in natural language, and hence to semantic similarity. In the most naïve approaches, the dimension of these vectors corresponds to the number of distinct words in the language. More sophisticated implementations in which word vectors are real-valued but of significantly smaller dimension are popularly known as **word vector embeddings**. They have proven important for various tasks of natural language processing (Collobert et al., 2011; Lubis et al., 2020).

Early word vector embeddings were constructed in latent semantic analysis using singular value decomposition. Neural methods were introduced by Bengio et al. (2003), and popularised by the algorithms word2vec (Mikolov et al., 2013a,b) and GloVe (Pennington et al., 2014). Our method of choice in this paper is fastText (Bojanowski et al., 2017), which can produce high-quality embeddings from relatively small corpora. All of these methods produce **static** embeddings: they assign to each word a single, context-independent vector.

There is, of course, a lot of existing and ongoing research to overcome the difficulties inher-ent in adequately representing polysemous words. One way to address polysemy is to produce multiple, context-dependent embeddings for the same word. The deep learning approaches mentioned above are amenable to this by incorporating heuristics (Huang et al., 2012) or non-parametric clustering (Neelakantan et al., 2014). More recently, transformer based models that exploit massive datasets have been used to produce contextualised word embeddings. Examples of these are CoVe (McCann et al., 2017), ELMo (Peters et al., 2018), and BERT (Devlin et al., 2019) and its variants ERNIE (Sun et al., 2019) and RoBERTa (Liu et al., 2019). Alternative approaches address polysemy by training multi-lingual word embeddings on multi-lingual corpora (Dufter et al., 2018; Heyman et al., 2019).

As the problem of polysemy is, at least partially, resolved in all of these more advanced approaches, we would expect the phenomenon studied in this paper to be less pronounced in the embeddings they produce. We therefore concentrate exclusively on mono-lingual static embeddings. Our analysis will not require any data beyond such an embedding.

3 The topology of the word space

3.1 The word space as a pinched manifold

In order to explain the apparent efficiency of machine learning, the **manifold hypothesis** postulates that, in general, real world data tends to live on a small-dimensional submanifold of the vector space in which it is represented (Bengio et al., 2013; Fefferman et al., 2016). For word vector embeddings, the ambient space $\mathbb{R}^n$ typically has dimension n in the range $50 \leq n \leq 300$. The hypothesis states that word vectors in fact lie on, or are densely distributed around, a submanifold $\mathcal{W} \subset \mathbb{R}^n$ of much smaller dimension. What this hypothetical **word space** $\mathcal{W}$ might look like is an intriguing question. Work of Arora et al. (2018) suggests a dimension of $\mathcal{W}$ as low as five. It is easy to imagine even smaller subspaces of $\mathcal{W}$, like a line segment connecting "cold", "cool", "lukewarm", "warm" and "hot", or a circle connecting "north", "east", "south", "west". But the global structure seems mysterious.

The manifold hypothesis has two parts: (1) that $\mathcal{W}$ is of small dimension, and (2) that $\mathcal{W}$ is a manifold.[3] It is the second statement that we would

---

[3] It may not be evident what the correct notion of "dimension" should be for arbitrary subspaces. However, there are much larger classes of spaces than manifolds to which the notion

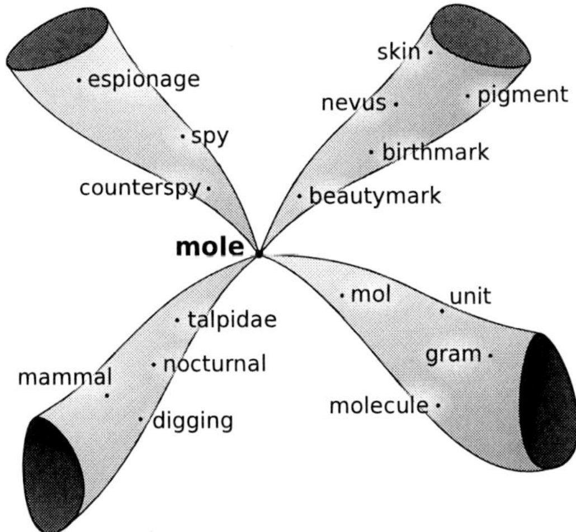

Figure 5: An idealized picture of the word space $\mathcal{W}$ near "mole": four regions of the meaning manifold are glued together to a single word

like to challenge. We argue that, in the vicinity of polysemous words, $\mathcal{W}$ cannot possibly have the structure of a manifold, i.e. it cannot resemble an open ball of any dimension. The best we can expect is that this might be true for some **space of meanings** $\mathcal{M}$ – a space that parametrizes all possible meanings that words of a given language may assume – from which $\mathcal{W}$ is obtained by identifying multiple meanings to a single word. This identification process is precisely the pinching construction discussed in Section 2.1. For example, we should expect the neighbourhood of the polysemous word "mole" in $\mathcal{W}$ to be obtained from the neighbourhoods of its different meanings in $\mathcal{M}$, all glued together as in Figure 5. Thus, even if we optimistically hypothesize the space of meanings $\mathcal{M}$ to be a manifold, the word space $\mathcal{W}$ cannot be: it is at best a *pinched* manifold. It is this hypothesis that we will pursue in the following. (If $\mathcal{M}$ has more complicated local structure, then *a fortiori* so does $\mathcal{W}$.)

The presence of synonyms in a language has no bearing on this analysis. To explain this, we need to temporarily distinguish carefully between a word w and its associated word vector $\mathbf{v}_w$. The word space $\mathcal{W}$ should more precisely be called *space of word vectors*, since this is the space in which the vectors $\mathbf{v}_w$ live, not the words themselves. Under a given word vector embedding, synonyms w and w' may get mapped to the same word vector $\mathbf{v}_w = \mathbf{v}_{w'}$. However, this does not affect the relation of the

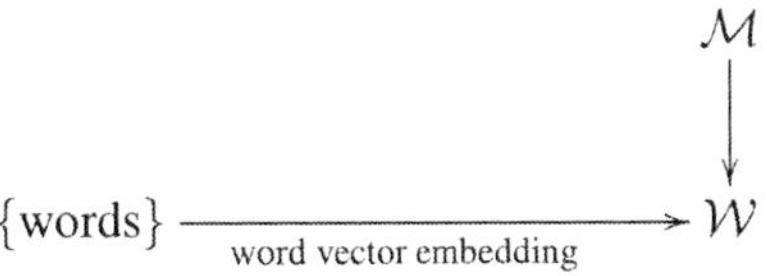

Figure 6: The relation of the space of meanings $\mathcal{M}$, the space of word vectors $\mathcal{W}$ and the set of words of a language. Synonyms may get identified under a given word vector embedding, symbolized here by the horizontal map. Multiple meanings get identified to a single word vector under the vertical map

space of meanings $\mathcal{M}$ to the space of word vectors $\mathcal{W}$ in any way. The situation is summarized in Figure 6.[4]

With this discussion out of the way, we will from now on again simplify our terminology by identifying words with their associated vectors, and refer to $\mathcal{W}$ as word space.

3.2 A topological measure of polysemy

As explained at the end of Section 2.1, we can distinguish a singular point of a pinched manifold from a non-singular point by counting the connected components of a small punctured neighbourhood of the point. What is more, the number of these components reflects the number of points that were glued together in the pinching process. Thus, according to our view of the word space $\mathcal{W}$ as a pinched quotient of the manifold of meanings $\mathcal{M}$, the number of different meanings of a word should be reflected by the number of components of a punctured neighbourhood of the word.

Of course, the relevant number of components is not directly visible from the discrete point cloud formed by the word vectors. Rather, the components can only be estimated by some form of clustering. In this section, we describe a measure of the number of components based on degree zero persistent homology, as introduced in Section 2.2.

Fix a word vector embedding, a target word w, and a neighbourhood size n. As already indicated, we will abuse language by identifying a word with its vector under the embedding in the following. The **topological polysemy** $\mathrm{TPS}_n(w)$ of w with respect to our fixed word vector embedding and our chosen neighbourhood size n is the Wasserstein

---

of dimension extends in a straight-forward manner.

[4]It is of course debatable whether the equation $\mathbf{v}_w = \mathbf{v}_{w'}$ would really hold for any pair of synonyms in practice. It seems more likely that the vectors $\mathbf{v}_w$ and $\mathbf{v}_{w'}$ would simply lie very close together.

norm of a normalized punctured neighbourhood of w. That is, $\mathrm{TPS}_n(w)$ is computed as follows:

1. Normalize all word vectors v to have L_2-norm $||v|| = 1$.

2. Consider the punctured neighbourhood $\mathcal{N}_n(w)$ consisting of the n closest neighbours of w, excluding w itself.

3. Pass to the normalized punctured neighbourhood $\mathcal{N}'_n(w)$ by translating w to lie at the origin and projecting all vectors to the unit sphere:

$$\mathcal{N}'_n(w) := \left\{ \frac{v - w}{||v - w||} \;\middle|\; v \in \mathcal{N}_n(w) \right\}$$

4. Compute the degree zero persistence diagram of $\mathcal{N}'_n(w)$.

5. $\mathrm{TPS}_n(w)$ is the Wasserstein norm of this persistence diagram, i.e. the Wasserstein distance between the computed and the empty persistence diagram.

The general normalization in Step 1 is included because word embeddings are trained only on cosine similarity; the length of each vector has no apparent meaning. The normalization allows us to compute directly with difference vectors between word vectors of high cosine similarity. The normalization in Step 3 is included because we have fixed the *cardinality* n of the neighbourhood, not its diameter. Without any normalization in this step, we would be measuring mostly the density of the word cloud around w. The normalization by projection onto the unit sphere may seem somewhat radical, but it is topologically motivated: the topological invariants we use cannot distinguish a punctured ball from its boundary sphere. (In technical terms, the punctured ball and its boundary are *homotopy equivalent*; cf. Hatcher (2002), Chapter 0.)

4 Empirical evidence

We present two pieces of empirical evidence that support our view of the word space as a pinched manifold. The experiments in Sections 4.2 and 4.3 show that the topological polysemy defined above correlates with the actual number of meanings of a word. In Section 4.4, we describe a simple approach to the SemEval-2010 task on word sense induction based on our topological intuition.

> *"Don't forget the Tatun Mountains, which shelter the town. In the old days , Tanshui folk who cultivated farms on the slopes had to walk for an hour to get to their crops. These days you can take a local mini-bus."*

Figure 7: An exemplary context of an instance of the target word "cultivate"

4.1 Experimental setup

All experiments are based on data provided with the SemEval-2010 task on *Word Sense Induction & Disambiguation* (Manandhar et al., 2010). The task is as follows: Assign a total of 8 915 **instances**, extracted from various sources including CNN and ABC, of 100 different polysemous **target words** (50 nouns and 50 verbs) to clusters based on their **context**, such that instances with different meanings get mapped to different clusters and instances with the same meaning get mapped to the same cluster. A context is simply a paragraph of text that the target word appears in. Figure 7 shows an exemplary context for an instance of the target word "cultivate". Note that labels are only provided for a test set; this is an unsupervised learning task.

The training set provided comprises 65 M occurrences of 127 151 different words. We use this corpus to train our own vector representations using the python module for fastText (Bojanowski et al., 2017). For the computation of the persistence diagrams and the Wasserstein distance we use the GUDHI library (The GUDHI Project, 2020).

4.2 Correlation of TPS with the SemEval gold standard

The SemEval data set includes a gold standard for the 100 target words. The number of clusters in this gold standard is equal to the number of true meanings of each word, as perceived by humans. Figure 8 shows our measure of polysemy $\mathrm{TPS}_{50}(w)$ for the 100 target words w plotted against these cluster counts.

Correlation coefficients between the gold standard and $\mathrm{TPS}_n(w)$ for varying neighbourhood sizes n are displayed in the first column of Table 1. We found the highest correlation for $n = 50$, equal to 0.424. Neighbourhoods consisting of just ten or less words are clearly too small to capture multiple meanings. On the other hand, for high values of n, the neighbourhoods become too large to adequately reflect the local structure of the word space around

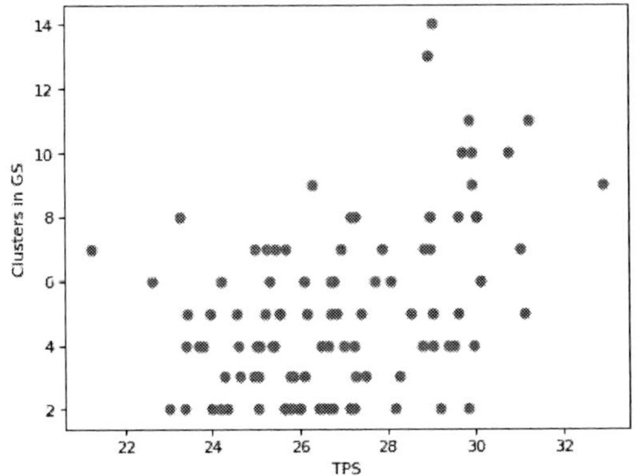

Figure 8: The topological polysemy $\mathrm{TPS}_{50}(w)$ plotted against the number of clusters in the SemEval gold standard, for the 100 SemEval target words w

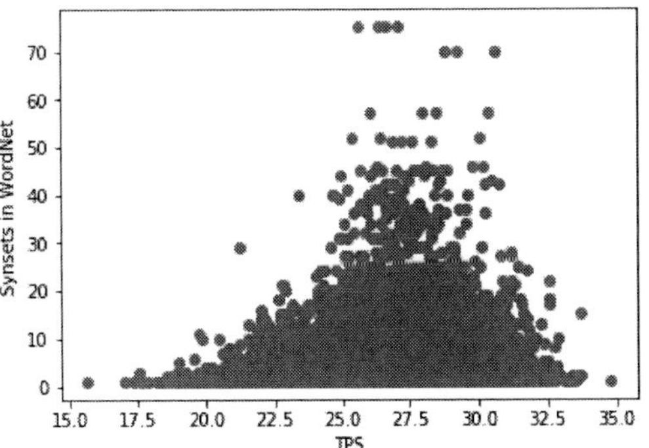

Figure 9: The topological polysemy $\mathrm{TPS}_{50}(w)$ plotted against the number of synsets in WordNet, for all 62 049 words w in the SemEval corpus that have a WordNet entry

n	TPS_n vs. GS	TPS_n vs. synsets	TPS_n vs. frequency
10	−0.001	0.122	0.002
40	0.411	0.096	−0.003
50	0.424	0.085	−0.006
60	0.414	0.076	−0.008
100	0.333	0.055	−0.013
sample size	100	62 049	127 151

Table 1: Correlations between $\mathrm{TPS}_n(w)$ and the number of meanings of w according to the SemEval gold standard (Section 4.2), the number of WordNet synsets (Section 4.3), and the frequency of w in the SemEval training corpus. The last line indicates the number of words on which the correlation is computed. The gray entry is not statistically significant, but all other entries are (p-value $< 10^{-3}$)

	GS	WordNet	TPS_{50}
sniff	3	3	27.262
reap	2	2	26.658
bow	5	14	28.533
chip	13	14	28.910
house	14	14	28.999

Table 2: Some examples of words and their corresponding cluster count in the SemEval gold standard and WordNet as well as their TPS-measure for $n = 50$

the target word. This is likewise unsurprising: recall from Section 2.1 that the manifold condition is a *local* condition around each point. Larger neighbourhoods of a point on a manifold can be arbitrarily complicated, and so can larger neighbourhoods of singular points on a pinched manifold.

The third column of Table 1 shows that $\mathrm{TPS}_n(w)$ does *not* correlate with the frequency of the words in the SemEval corpus. This is important, as frequency itself correlates with polysemy. The absence of correlation between $\mathrm{TPS}_n(w)$ and frequency strengthens our assertion that $\mathrm{TPS}_n(w)$ indeed measures polysemy.

4.3 Correlation of TPS with WordNet synsets

The correlation with the gold standard is a good indication of the validity of our method, but it is based on just 100 samples. The number of meanings, as perceived by humans, of a much larger set of words can be extracted from WordNet (Fellbaum, 1998), specifically the number of synsets associated with each word. Of course, we cannot expect the correlation between our topological polysemy and these numbers of synsets to be as high as for the SemEval gold standard. Firstly, we have trained our fastText vectors specifically on the SemEval training set, which does not capture the breadth of WordNet, and which does not comprise enough data to yield adequate embeddings for non-target words. Secondly, WordNet captures distinctions in meaning far more granular that one could hope to detect within the, say, 50 closest neighbours of a word.

Nonetheless, plotting $\mathrm{TPS}_{50}(w)$ against the number of synsets for all 62 049 words of the SemEval corpus that have a WordNet entry indicates a clear trend, see Figure 9. Correlation coefficients for varying n are included in Table 1.

4.4 The SemEval task

Our hypothesis that the word space is a manifold pinched at polysemous words also suggests the following, direct approach to the SemEval-2010 task itself, which we call **Overlap with Punctured Neighbourhood (OPN)**. Fix a neighbourhood size n. In a first step, we cluster punctured neighbourhoods of size n of the 100 target words using a common clustering algorithm like k-means or dbscan (Ester et al., 1996). The different clusters of the neighbourhood cloud obtained in this way are taken to represent different meanings of the target word. In a second step, we assign a given instance of the target word to the cluster of the neighbourhood cloud that has the highest relative word overlap with the context of that instance.

For clustering with dbscan, we found that the best results are achieved with parameter values $\text{Eps} = 0.09$ and $\text{MinPts} = 2$ and large neighbourhood sizes n. The k-means clustering algorithm requires the number k of clusters aimed for as a parameter. We experimented both with fixed values of k and with a word-dependent variable value $k(w)$, predicted using TPS as follows. Define the TPS-percentile $\%(w)$ of a target word w as

$$\%(w) := \left\lceil \frac{\text{TPS}_{50}(w) - \text{TPS}_{\min}}{\text{TPS}_{\max} - \text{TPS}_{\min}} \cdot 100 \right\rceil,$$

where $\text{TPS}_{\min}$ and $\text{TPS}_{\max}$ denote the minimum and maximum values that $\text{TPS}_{50}(\cdot)$ assumes on all target words, respectively, and where $\lceil \cdot \rceil$ denotes rounding to the next largest integer. Thus, the percentile is an integer between 0 and 100 that reflects how large $\text{TPS}_{50}(w)$ is in comparison to all other target words. The expected number of clusters $k(w)$ is defined as

$$k(w) := \begin{cases} 2 & \text{if} \quad \%(w) \leq 1 \\ \%(w) + 1 & \text{if } 1 < \%(w) < 100 \\ 100 & \text{if} \quad \%(w) = 100 \end{cases}$$

Thus, the predicted number of clusters $k(w)$ varies between 2 and 100.

The performance is commonly measured by two scores, the F-score and the V-measure, which capture to what extent a clustering agrees with the gold standard clustering. Since both scores are important, we rank different approaches based on the product of these scores. This automatically discounts the performance of trivial approaches: MFS, which assigns each occurrence to the same cluster, and 1cl1inst, which assigns each occurrence to its own cluster. Table 3 shows the results for OPN with different clustering algorithms and different parameters. For comparison, the table moreover includes the best performing models of the SemEval task, as well as some other models published since. Our best performing set-up (OPN with dbscan, $n = 5000$) achieves the second best results, outperforming much more complex methods. Note that, unlike Arora et al. (2018) and Mu et al. (2017), we do not use any additional data to train embeddings.

For OPN with k-means clustering, we found that $k = 30$ gives the best results among possible fixed values for k. As Table 3 shows, the performance of our method with the TPS-informed variable value $k(w)$ is better than the performance with this fixed value. This provides further evidence to our claim that TPS is positively correlated with the true number of meanings. A comparison of the performance of OPN with dbscan and of OPN with k-means indicates that the size n of the neighbourhood to be considered for clustering needs to be an order of magnitude larger when we do not incorporate any information from TPS. Our interpretation is that TPS witnesses the disturbance that an additional meaning causes in a small neighbourhood of a word, even when no word related to that meaning is present in the neighbourhood.

In Table 4, we single out the three best performing and the three worst performing target words with our best performing model and give the associated scores as an illustration.

5 Conclusion

In this work, we challenge the manifold hypothesis for static word vector embeddings and experimentally show that it is more accurate and helpful to view the space of word embeddings as a pinched manifold. We introduce a topological measure of polysemy that correlates well with the number of meanings of a word according to the gold standard of the SemEval-2010 task on *Word Sense Induction & Disambiguation*. We also produce a surprisingly simple, but topologically motivated solution to the task itself that achieves highly competitive results.

We stress that our measure of polysemy, TPS, is computed solely on the topology of the point cloud consisting of the vectors of a fixed word vector embedding. Of course, any solution to the described

Method	Parameters	V-Measure	F-Score	Product
UoY (Korkontzelos and Manandhar, 2010)		0.157	0.498	**0.0782**
OPN with dbscan	$n = 5000$	0.175	0.420	0.0735
OPN with dbscan	$n = 2000$	0.135	0.493	0.0666
(Mu et al., 2016)	$k = 5$	0.145	0.441	0.0639
OPN with k-means	$n = 500, k = k(w)$	0.165	0.356	0.0588
KSU KDD (Elshamy et al., 2010)		0.157	0.369	0.0579
OPN with k-means	$n = 500, k = 30$	0.161	0.352	0.0567
(Arora et al., 2018)	$k = 5$	0.115	0.464	0.0533
(Mu et al., 2016)	$k = 2$	0.073	0.571	0.0417
OPN with dbscan	$n = 500$	0.070	0.571	0.0400
(Arora et al., 2018)	$k = 2$	0.061	0.586	0.0357
1cl1inst		**0.317**	0.090	0.0285
MFS		0.000	**0.634**	0.0000

Table 3: Performance of different methods on task 14 of SemEval-2010. According to our ranking by product of V-measure and F-score, the algorithms UoY and KSU KDD were the strongest contenders in the initial challenge. The algorithms MFS and 1cl1inst in the last two rows are trivial baseline algorithms

Target word	F-Score	Precision	Recall	V-Measure	Homo-geneity	Com-pleteness	Product
presume.v	0.827	0.957	0.728	0.477	0.683	0.366	0.3945
cultivate.v	0.657	0.648	0.667	0.518	0.564	0.479	0.3403
accommodate.v	0.465	0.476	0.455	0.605	0.777	0.495	0.2813
$\vdots$							
violate.v	0.153	0.813	0.085	0.023	0.292	0.012	0.0035
root.v	0.574	0.405	0.984	0.000	0.000	1.000	0.0000
sniff.v	0.453	0.295	0.969	0.000	0.000	1.000	0.0000

Table 4: The performance of our best solution to SemEval on the three best performing vs. the three worst performing words, as evaluated according to the product of F-score and V-measure

SemEval task will also predict, in particular, the number of meanings of the target words. However, these predictions rely on access to the underlying corpus, or at least parts thereof. Similarly, the first step (clustering) of our solution to the SemEval task is performed directly on the word vectors, without recourse to any corpus. This is in sharp contrast with early clustering approaches to word sense disambiguation such as (Schütze, 1998) (which of course had to rely on far less sophisticated word vector embeddings than are now available).

A number of avenues could be pursued to further improve the results presented here. To allow a fair comparison with other solutions to the SemEval task, we have used word vector embeddings trained on a fairly small corpus. We have used only *degree zero* persistent homology. Our method of taking

the Wasserstein norm of a persistance diagram is rather crude. The elimination of noise from the embeddings could also improve the results.

We conjecture that other NLP tasks that also rely, implicitly or explicitly, on the manifold hypothesis could similarly benefit from a more refined topological analysis.

Acknowledgments

We thank Claudius Zibrowius for Figures 1, 2 and 5 and Peter Arndt, Michael Heck and Carel van Niekerk for helpful discussions. The results of this publication are part of the project DYMO, which has received funding from the European Research Council under the grant agreement no. STG2018 804636. Computational resources were provided by Google Cloud.

References

Sanjeev Arora, Yuanzhi Li, Yingyu Liang, Tengyu Ma, and Andrej Risteski. 2018. Linear algebraic structure of word senses, with applications to polysemy. *Transactions of the Association for Computational Linguistics*, 6(0):483–495.

Yoshua Bengio, Aaron Courville, and Pascal Vincent. 2013. Representation learning: A review and new perspectives. *IEEE Transactions on Pattern Analysis and Machine Intelligence*, 35(8):1798–1828.

Yoshua Bengio, Réjean Ducharme, Pascal Vincent, and Christian Jauvin. 2003. A neural probabilistic language model. *Journal of machine learning research*, 3(Feb):1137–1155.

Piotr Bojanowski, Edouard Grave, Armand Joulin, and Tomas Mikolov. 2017. Enriching word vectors with subword information. *Transactions of the Association for Computational Linguistics*, 5:135–146.

Ronan Collobert, Jason Weston, Léon Bottou, Michael Karlen, Koray Kavukcuoglu, and Pavel Kuksa. 2011. Natural language processing (almost) from scratch. *Journal of machine learning research*, 12(Aug):2493–2537.

Jacob Devlin, Ming-Wei Chang, Kenton Lee, and Kristina Toutanova. 2019. BERT: Pre-training of deep bidirectional transformers for language understanding. In *Proceedings of the 2019 Conference of the North American Chapter of the Association for Computational Linguistics: Human Language Technologies, Volume 1 (Long and Short Papers)*, pages 4171–4186, Minneapolis, Minnesota. Association for Computational Linguistics.

Philipp Dufter, Mengjie Zhao, Martin Schmitt, Alexander Fraser, and Hinrich Schütze. 2018. Embedding learning through multilingual concept induction. In *Proceedings of the 56th Annual Meeting of the Association for Computational Linguistics (Volume 1: Long Papers)*, pages 1520–1530, Melbourne, Australia. Association for Computational Linguistics.

Herbert Edelsbrunner and John Harer. 2010. *Computational Topology: An Introduction*. American Mathematical Society.

Wesam Elshamy, Doina Caragea, and William H. Hsu. 2010. Ksu kdd: Word sense induction by clustering in topic space. In *Proceedings of the 5th International Workshop on Semantic Evaluation*, SemEval '10, pages 367–370, USA. Association for Computational Linguistics.

Martin Ester, Hans-Peter Kriegel, Jörg Sander, and Xiaowei. Xu. 1996. A density-based algorithm for discovering clusters in large spatial databases with noise. In *Proceedings of the Second International Conference on Knowledge Discovery and Data Mining*, pages 226–231. Institute for Computer Science, University of Munich.

Charles Fefferman, Sanjoy Mitter, and Hariharan Narayanan. 2016. Testing the manifold hypothesis. *J. Amer. Math. Soc.*, 29(4):983–1049.

Christiane Fellbaum. 1998. *WordNet: An Electronic Lexical Database*. MIT Press, Cambridge, MA. https://wordnet.princeton.edu/.

Allen Hatcher. 2002. *Algebraic topology*. Cambridge University Press, Cambridge.

Geert Heyman, Bregt Verreet, Ivan Vulić, and Marie-Francine Moens. 2019. Learning unsupervised multilingual word embeddings with incremental multilingual hubs. In *Proceedings of the 2019 Conference of the North American Chapter of the Association for Computational Linguistics: Human Language Technologies, Volume 1 (Long and Short Papers)*, pages 1890–1902, Minneapolis, Minnesota. Association for Computational Linguistics.

Eric H. Huang, Richard Socher, Christopher D. Manning, and Andrew Y. Ng. 2012. Improving word representations via global context and multiple word prototypes. In *Association for Computational Linguistics (ACL)*, Jeju, Republic of Korea.

Ioannis Korkontzelos and Suresh Manandhar. 2010. Uoy: Graphs of unambiguous vertices for word sense induction and disambiguation. In *Proceedings of the 5th International Workshop on Semantic Evaluation*, SemEval '10, page 355–358, USA. Association for Computational Linguistics.

Yinhan Liu, Myle Ott, Naman Goyal, Jingfei Du, Mandar Joshi, Danqi Chen, Omer Levy, Mike Lewis, Luke Zettlemoyer, and Veselin Stoyanov. 2019. Roberta: A robustly optimized BERT pretraining approach.

Nurul Lubis, Michael Heck, Carel van Niekerk, and Milica Gasic. 2020. Adaptable conversational machines. *AI Magazine*, 41(3):28–44.

Suresh Manandhar, Ioannis P. Klapaftis, Dmitriy Dligach, and Sameer S. Pradhan. 2010. Semeval-2010 task 14: Word sense induction & disambiguation. In *Proceedings of the 5th International Workshop on Semantic Evaluation*, SemEval '10, pages 63–68, USA. Association for Computational Linguistics.

Bryan McCann, James Bradbury, Caiming Xiong, and Richard Socher. 2017. Learned in translation: Contextualized word vectors. In *Advances in Neural Information Processing Systems*, pages 6294–6305.

Tomas Mikolov, Kai Chen, Greg Corrado, and Jeffrey Dean. 2013a. Efficient estimation of word representations in vector space.

Tomas Mikolov, Ilya Sutskever, Kai Chen, Greg S. Corrado, and Jeff Dean. 2013b. Distributed Representations of Words and Phrases and their Compositionality. In *Advances in Neural Information Processing Systems*.

Jiaqi Mu, Suma Bhat, and Pramod Viswanath. 2016. Geometry of polysemy.

Jiaqi Mu, Suma Bhat, and Pramod Viswanath. 2017. Representing sentences as low-rank subspaces. In *Proceedings of the 55th Annual Meeting of the Association for Computational Linguistics (Volume 2: Short Papers)*, pages 629–634, Vancouver, Canada. Association for Computational Linguistics.

Arvind Neelakantan, Jeevan Shankar, Alexandre Passos, and Andrew McCallum. 2014. Efficient nonparametric estimation of multiple embeddings per word in vector space. In *Proceedings of the 2014 Conference on Empirical Methods in Natural Language Processing (EMNLP)*, pages 1059–1069, Doha, Qatar. Association for Computational Linguistics.

Jeffrey Pennington, Richard Socher, and Christopher Manning. 2014. GloVe: Global vectors for word representation. In *Proceedings of the 2014 conference on empirical methods in natural language processing (EMNLP)*, pages 1532–1543.

Matthew E. Peters, Mark Neumann, Mohit Iyyer, Matt Gardner, Christopher Clark, Kenton Lee, and Luke Zettlemoyer. 2018. Deep contextualized word representations. In *Proc. of NAACL.*

Hinrich Schütze. 1998. Automatic word sense discrimination. *Computational Linguistics*, 24(1):97–123.

Yu Sun, Shuohuan Wang, Yukun Li, Shikun Feng, Xuyi Chen, Han Zhang, Xin Tian, Danxiang Zhu, Hao Tian, and Hua Wu. 2019. ERNIE: Enhanced representation through knowledge integration. *arXiv preprint arXiv:1904.09223.*

The GUDHI Project. 2020. *GUDHI User and Reference Manual*, 3.2.0 edition. GUDHI Editorial Board.

Ludwig Josef Johann Wittgenstein. 1953. Philosophische Untersuchungen. §43.

Assessing Polyseme Sense Similarity through Co-predication Acceptability and Contextualised Embedding Distance

Janosch Haber and **Massimo Poesio**
Queen Mary University of London
{j.haber|m.poesio}@qmul.ac.uk

Abstract

Co-predication is one of the most frequently used linguistic tests to tell apart shifts in polysemic sense from changes in homonymic meaning. It is increasingly coming under criticism as evidence is accumulating that it tends to mis-classify specific cases of polysemic sense alteration as homonymy. In this paper, we collect empirical data to investigate these accusations. We asses how co-predication acceptability relates to explicit ratings of polyseme word sense similarity, and how well either measure can be predicted through the distance between target words' contextualised word embeddings. We find that sense similarity appears to be a major contributor in determining co-predication acceptability, but that co-predication judgements tend to rate less similar sense interpretations as being as unacceptable as homonym pairs, effectively misclassifying these instances. The tested contextualised word embeddings fail to predict word sense similarity consistently, but the similarities between BERT embeddings show a significant correlation with co-predication ratings. We take this finding as evidence that BERT embeddings might be better representations of context than encodings of word meaning.

1 Introduction

Polysemy is a form of lexical ambiguity which occupies a unique middle ground between *monosemy* –word forms with exactly one interpretation– and *homonymy* –word forms associated with two or more completely unrelated interpretations. Unlike monosemes, polysemes can evoke different interpretations, but unlike homonyms, polysemic sense interpretations are thought to be closely related to each other (Lyons, 1977). It is commonly assumed that most words in natural language are in fact polysemous to some degree (Falkum and Vicente, 2015), and the question whether there in fact are any proper monosemes has been the source of ongoing debate (see for example Jackendoff, 1989; Fodor, 1998). Homonyms have been a driving factor in developing contextualised language models (e.g. Peters et al., 2018; Devlin et al., 2018; Radford et al., 2019) in order to account for the different unrelated meanings some words can evoke in different contexts:

a. The match burned my fingers.

b. The match ended without a winner.

Comparing these uses of the word *match* to the various closely related interpretations of canonical polyseme *school* illuminates the conceptual difference between the two phenomena of lexical ambiguity:[1]

a. The school [building] is on fire.

b. The school [rules] has prohibited wearing hats in the classroom.

c. I have talked to the school [director, staff] about it already.

d. The school [participants] went for a visit to the cathedral.

Although the distinction is clear in theory, distinguishing monosemy, polysemy and homonymy in practice proves exceedingly difficult: At what point are interpretation nuances pronounced enough to speak of two different word senses? Is the coercion of word sense a manifestation of polysemic sense alteration or a context effect on a monosemic word form? Do word senses related through metaphor qualify as polysemes or are their interpretations a form or homonymic ambiguity? Traditionally, co-predication tests are used to provide a linguistic means to answer these questions and attempt a

---

[1]Examples taken from Ortega-Andrés and Vicente (2019)

*Proceedings of the Ninth Joint Conference on Lexical and Computational Semantics (*SEM)*, pages 114–124
Barcelona, Spain (Online), December 12–13, 2020

classification of word sense interpretations into one of the three categories. In co-predication tests, two interpretations of a word form are simultaneously invoked by the context. If this renders a felicitous construction (see Example 1), the two interpretations are considered to evoke the same sense or meaning of the word; if the reading is infelicitous (Example 2) they are considered to be derived from two different word meanings.

(1) The newspaper wasn't very interesting, so she folded it and put it away. [content/object]

(2) # The match burned my fingers but ended without a winner.

Based on a range of experiments finding that homonyms seem to be processed differently than polysemes (Frazier and Rayner, 1990; Rodd et al., 2002; Klepousniotou et al., 2008, 2012), the prevailing understanding of co-predication is that it is rendered felicitous if the different sense interpretations are activated simultaneously and can be shifted between without additional processing costs. Co-predication is thought to lead to infelicitous sentences if the different activations are not activated automatically, and cognitive effort is involved in updating the assumed meaning of a word. These hypotheses informed a number of linguistic models to define different mental representations of homonymic meaning and polysemic sense, respectively. The Generative Lexicon (Pustejovsky, 1991; Asher and Pustejovsky, 2006; Asher, 2011) for example postulates individual lexicon entries for different interpretations of a homonym, while all sense interpretations of a polyseme are represented by a single under-specified entry and therefore do not require any processing cost for sense switching. Recently, a growing body of work however came to challenge a unified, under-specified representation of polysemic sense (see Klepousniotou, 2002; Pylkkänen et al., 2006; Frisson, 2015). Klepousniotou et al. (2012) for example report that their experiments indicate that the processing of irregular polysemes resembles homonymic meaning alterations more than the sense alterations in regular polysemes, while an ongoing series of co-predication studies (e.g. Antunes and Chaves, 2003; Traxler et al., 2005; Schumacher, 2013; Filip and Sutton, 2017; Zobel, 2017; Sutton and Filip, 2018) show that not all polysemic senses can be co-predicated either, and that the co-predication of some poly-

semic interpretations can lead to infelicitous and zeugmatic expressions:[2]

a. # The newspaper fired its editor in chief and got wet from the rain. [publisher/publication]

b. # They took the door off its hinges and walked through it. [object/opening]

A recent model of polyseme sense clustering proposed by Ortega-Andrés and Vicente (2019) tries to explain why certain polyseme senses lead to infelicitous co-predication by suggesting that polyseme senses might be grouped based on their similarity. According to their grouping, closely related senses are thought to form co-activation packages that remain active for a while, allowing for cost-free sense shifting and therefore felicitous co-predication. Distantly related sense interpretations on the other hand would not co-activate and therefore require cognitive effort to be changed, much like homonynic meaning alterations.

The difficulty in assessing this hypothesis is the unavailability of a ready reference of contextualised word sense similarity for polysemes. To mitigate this, we collected human annotated data on a number of different measures of polysemic sense similarity to empirically investigate the correlation between sense similarity ratings and co-predication acceptability judgements. Specifically, we use crowdsourcing to collect i) graded co-predication acceptability judgements, ii) explicit (meta-linguistic) word sense similarity judgements, iii) word class similarity ratings, and iv) determine the similarity in a target word's contextualised embeddings derived from different models. If word sense similarity indeed governs co-activation and therefore co-predication acceptability, we expect similarity judgements to be a strong predictor for acceptability judgements. Conversely, if co-predication acceptability is a representative test of the mental processing of lexically ambiguous items, we expect acceptability judgements to be a strong predictor of similarity judgements and reliably tell apart homonyms from polysemes.

We find that sense similarity appears to be a major contributor in determining co-predication acceptability, but that co-predication judgements tend to rate less similar sense interpretations equally as unacceptable as homonym pairs, effectively misclassifying these instances. We therefore argue

---

[2]Examples from Cruse (1995)

that these findings provide both, a) support for a more hierarchical representation of polysemic sense based on sense similarity, and, b) an additional, empirically founded argument against co-predication as a prevailing test for distinguishing polysemy and homonymy. Finally, the tested contextualised word embeddings fail to predict word sense similarity consistently, but the similarities between BERT embeddings show a significant correlation with co-predication ratings.

2   Method

In order to evaluate both, i) the hypothesis that polysemic senses might form groupings based on their similarity, and ii) the prevalence of co-predication as a linguistic test for the distinction between homonymy and polysemy, we collect three human annotated measures of word sense similarity together with five word sense similarity proxies derived from computational methods. We investigate how well these different metrics distinguish homonyms from polysemes, and to what degree they can predict one another. In order to achieve a fair comparison of the different measures, we defined a fixed set of target words, sense interpretations and contexts to be used in all experiments.

2.1   Samples

Since at least Apresjan (1974), polysemes are generally considered to be either regular or irregular, depending on whether or not their sense patterns are shared with other word forms. Irregular polysemes often demonstrate a metaphorical connection between the different interpretations of their senses that does not carry over for other uses (see Example 3), regular, or systematic polysemes on the other hand exhibit the same interpretation patterns across a number of word forms (Example 4). See Moldovan (2019) for a recent in-depth discussion of this distinction.

> (3)   **[cold]** I got a cold/#hot/#tired after getting caught in the rain last week.
> The librarian gave me a cold/#hot/#tired stare when my phone rang.

> (4)   **[liquid-for-container]** He took a sip and put his beer/coffee/juice/gin/soup... back on the kitchen table.

With growing evidence that irregular polysemes might be processed differently than their regular counterparts (e.g. Klepousniotou et al., 2012), we decided to focus on regular polysemic nouns for this study. Regular polysemes can be more clearly distinguished from homonyms, maximising the impact of our findings if metrics fail to classify them correctly. With their canonical division of sense interpretations, they also allow for a clear separation of different sense interpretations, making it easier to generate contexts that unequivocally evoke the different senses. We selected ten of the systematic polysemy types compiled in Dölling (Forthcoming), with target expressions having between two and four clearly distinct but related senses, and picked one of the most frequently used expressions representing each class from his compilation.

To create sample contexts invoking the different interpretations, we followed a custom template designed to guarantee that samples could be used individually to collect graded word sense judgements, class ratings and context embedding similarity, but could also be combined into a co-predication structure without invalidating acceptability due to repetitions or temporal or logical mis-matches. Following this template, samples were created such that i) the ambiguous target expression is the subject of the sentence, ii) the context is kept as short as possible, and iii) the context invokes a certain sense as clearly as possible without mentioning that sense explicitly.[3] Besides creating clear sample sentences for our human participants, these guidelines also minimise the impact of syntactic features and compounding context effects for contextualised models, which are shown to significantly impact embeddings (see e.g. Wiedemann et al., 2019) and cloud the accessibility of meaning representations.

Two sample contexts were created for every sense interpretation of the ten polysemes, resulting in a total of 54 sentences. As an example, consider the six sample sentences of polyseme *newspaper*, generated for its three senses (1) *organisation/institution*, (2) *physical object* and (3) *information/data*:

1a The newspaper fired its editor in chief.,
1b The newspaper was sued for defamation.
2a The newspaper lies on the kitchen table.,
2b The newspaper got wet from the rain.
3a The newspaper wasn't very interesting.,
3b The newspaper is rather satirical today.

Besides the polyseme samples, we created an ad-

---

[3] As in "The school is an old building." for sense *building*. See Haber and Poesio (2020) for more details.

ditional two samples sets. The first set is made up of 15 common homonyms, with two sentences invoking their two most dominant senses each. While our focus is on polysemes, comparing ratings for the homonym samples to ratings assigned to polyseme pairs, we will be able to test the different similarity measures' performance in predicting whether an ambiguous target pair is polysemic or homonymic. The second set contains 15 pairs of synonyms meant to be used as quality control and to calibrate the rating scale. All sample sentences were rated to be acceptable by annotators recruited from Amazon Mechanical Turk (AMT)[4] in a validation experiment.

2.2 Graded Co-predication Acceptability

Traditionally, co-predication acceptability is one of the most frequently used linguistic tests for distinguishing homonyms from polysemes. Acceptability usually is determined through introspection, classifying a sentence invoking two different interpretations of the same word form as either acceptable or not. When assessed through annotator judgements, co-predication acceptability however appears to be a graded measure (Lau et al., 2014). We therefore decided to collect empirical data on graded annotator judgements, asking participants to rate the acceptability of co-predication structures combining different pairings of target word samples through conjunction reduction (Zwicky and Sadock, 1975). As an example, the previously shown *newspaper* contexts 1a and 1b where combined into co-predication sample 1ab for data collection:

1ab The newspaper fired its editor in chief and was sued for defamation.

Co-predication samples were generated for all combinations of sense interpretations, resulting in four samples for polysemes with two senses, nine for polysemes with three senses, and 16 for those with four, and a grand total of 75. We manually inspected the co-predication structures for any inconsistencies that might have emerged through the conjunction, and corrected issues with the least invasive measures possible. The samples were then distributed over 15 questionnaires so that no target expression appeared twice in any questionnaire. We added one of the homonym and synonym val-

idation samples to each questionnaire, and filled all questionnaires to a total of ten items with co-predication structures generated from random sentence pairs to obfuscate the focus on polysemes. Item order was then randomised per questionnaire.

We used AMT to collect graded co-predication accceptability judgements by asking workers to rate a given sentence using a slider labelled with "The sentence is absolutely unacceptable" on the left hand side and "The sentence is absolutely acceptable" on the right. The submitted slider positions were translated to a 100-point acceptability score ranging between 0 and 1, and stored in combination with a worker's unique ID. To improve judgement quality, we required workers to have obtained a US high school degree and reached the "AMT Master" qualification.[5] Workers were paid 0.35 USD for every completed questionnaire.

We collected between 20 and 40 judgements for each item. A total of 43 individual workers contributed to the study, with HITs taking an average of 146 seconds (median of 93). Through filtering out any submissions that rated at least two filler samples higher than 0.66 or the synonym sample lower than 0.33,[6] we excluded a total of 44 judgements. The resulting dataset features an average of 28 judgements per item.

2.3 Graded Word Sense Similarity

As a first measure of sense similarity, we collected graded annotator judgements explicitly rating the similarity of word sense interpretations as invoked by different pairings of sample sentences. In contrast to co-predication judgements, these pairwise similarity ratings are less influenced by factors like sentence order and compound consistency, but do provide a meta-linguistic signal rather than the more ecological acceptability rating derived from co-predication. Still, if word sense similarity is the driving factor in determining the mental representation of polysemic sense, we should find a strong correlation between these judgements and the previously measured co-predication judgements.

We collected word sense similarity judgements using our custom polyseme sample set, this time combining samples into sentence pairs invoking

---

[4] https://www.mturk.com/

[5] According to AMT's website, "[T]hese Workers have consistently demonstrated a high degree of success in performing a wide range of HITs across a large number of Requesters," https://www.mturk.com/worker/help

[6] Note that in co-predication the synonymity effect is lost as only one subject noun phrase remains in the conjunction.

different combinations of sense interpretations instead of joining them into a single co-predication structure. The same method as in the first experiment was used for distributing test items over questionnaires, with the distinction that now homonym, synonym and filler samples were presented as sentence pairs rather than co-predication structures as well. We highlighted target expressions in bold font and asked workers to rate the highlighted expressions using a slider labelled with "The highlighted words have a completely different meaning" on the left hand side and "The highlighted words have completely the same meaning" on the right. Qualification requirements and payment remained identical.

We collected 20 judgements for each questionnaire. 65 individual workers in total contributed to the study, with HITs taking an average of 133 seconds (median = 90). Applying the same filtering as with the co-predication samples, we removed 9 submissions and retained at least 18 judgements per item.

2.4 Word Sense Class Ratings

As a second judgement of word sense similarity, we collected categorical sense class labels. If the determining factor in whether or not word senses can be co-predicated is not specifically their distance, but whether or not both interpretations refer to the same type or class of object, the agreement in assigned sense class should be a good predictor of co-predication acceptability - and valid proxy of word sense similarity.

To collect sense class labels, AMT Workers were presented with individual sample sentences together with a list of 16 sense class labels. Class labels were derived from the descriptions of the ten polyseme's different interpretations as used in Dölling (Forthcoming) and included an "other" category label. We used the same set of polyseme samples as before, with target expression highlighted like in the second experiment. Designed to validate the other two annotation metrics, we did not include any homonym, synonym or filler items in this experiment. Workers were asked to classify the highlighted target expression by selecting all applicable labels. Submissions were stored in 16-dimensional multi-hot vectors indicating the selection of labels together with the worker's ID. We kept the same worker qualification requirements and payment regime as before and collected 15 labels for each item, incidentally provided by exactly 15 individual workers, i.e. each individual worker completed all 15 questionnaires. HIT's took an average of 178 seconds (median of 107). Classification results were not filtered, but averaged per item in order to create word sense class vectors. Pairwise sense class similarity was then calculated through the cosine between the different combinations of sense interpretations, i.e. the overlap in their averaged multi-class assignments.

The resulting dataset containing all three types of human annotations is publicly available.[7]

2.5 Word Embedding Similarity

Because the three previously described measures of word sense similarity are based on costly human-annotated labels, we were also interested in investigating how well sense similarity estimates derived from computational models would correlate with these metrics. Models of polysemy have previously been proposed in distributional semantics (see for example Boleda et al., 2012), but for the most part, such models found limited application in computational linguistics. With the recent development of context-sensitive models of word embeddings such as ELMo (Peters et al., 2018) and BERT (Devlin et al., 2018), the field however obtained a new tool to capture polysemic sense alterations, leading to a demonstrated improvement in various NLP systems. While ELMo was developed explicitly to capture a target word's context, BERT is a language model based on the encoder architecture of the Transformer model (Vaswani et al., 2017), an attention mechanism for learning the contextual relations between words. While BERT's output is usually fed to a downstream model, our aim is to see whether it is able to capture differences in word sense by using its outputs directly.

To obtain ELMo embeddings we used a pretrained model available on TensorFlow Hub[8] and extracted target word vectors from the LSTM's second layer hidden state, which has previously been shown to encode more semantic information than the character-level first layer or the LSTM's first layer (Ethayarajh, 2019; Haber and Poesio, 2020). For the investigation of BERT's embeddings we used the output of a pretrained cased model as provided by Huggingface[9] with 12 layers, a hidden

---

[7]https://github.com/dali-ambiguity/
Word-Sense-Dataset-v1
[8]https://tfhub.dev/google/ELMo/3
[9]https://huggingface.co/transformers/

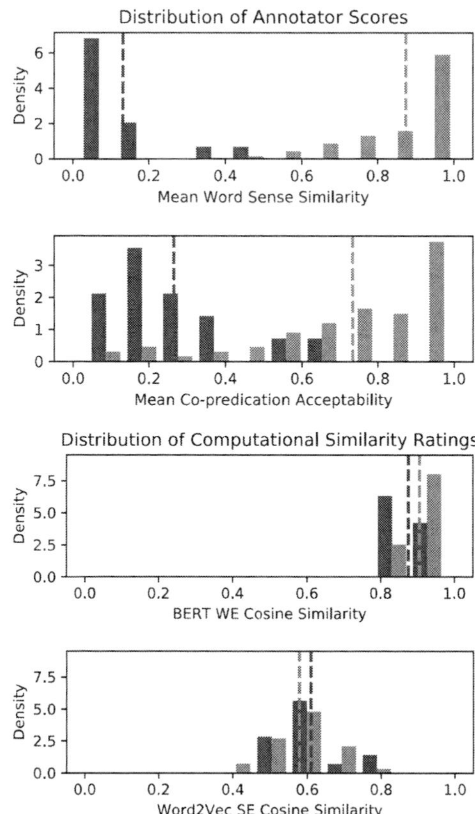

Figure 1: Distribution of human annotation ratings and computational similarity ratings for homonymic (blue) and polysemic (orange) sentence pairs, together with their means.

state size of 768 and 12 attention heads. We i) extracted and averaged sub-word vectors before pooling, ii) extracted the embedding of the [CLS] token, and iii) used the pooled sentence embedding. Lastly, we also determined a primitive contextualised sentence embedding by averaging over the sentence's token embeddings as derived from Word2Vec (Mikolov et al., 2013) pretrained on the Google News Dataset.[10]

3 Results

We report the collected data in four steps: Firstly, we inspect to what degree the different metrics and combinations thereof can predict whether a pair of target sense interpretations is polysemic or homonymic. We then investigate the correlation between the three collected annotation metrics, and

model_doc/bert.html

[10]https://code.google.com/archive/p/word2vec/

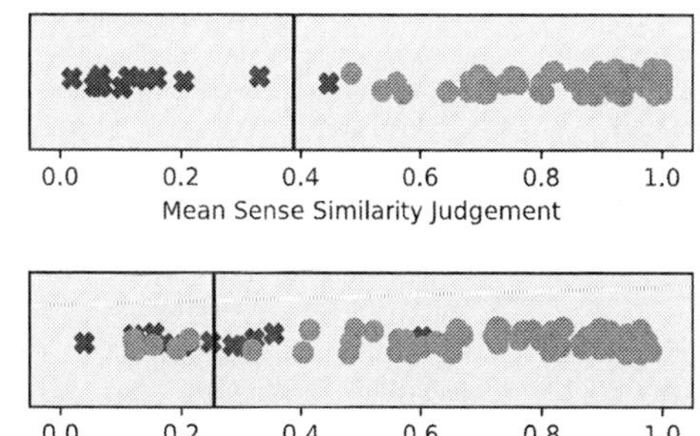

Figure 2: Classification of homonym (blue) and polyseme (orange) sample pairs based on pairwise similarity annotations and co-predication acceptability judgements.

report how well the computational measures predict the human annotations. Finally, we move to a more qualitative analysis, investigating in more detail the distribution of ratings over the different sense interpretations of a polyseme.

3.1 Predicting Ambiguity Types

The top two graphs in Figure 1 show the distribution of human annotations for homonymic (blue) and polysemic (orange) target words based on their explicit word sense similarity ratings or co-predication acceptability, respectively. Both annotation measures clearly separate the modes of the distributions, but while co-predication acceptability judgements for the tested polyseme pairs occupy the entire rating scale, explicit word sense similarity ratings only span the upper half (the lowest score is 0.48). Conversely, co-predication acceptability ratings for homonym pairs reach up to 0.67, while the highest-scoring homonym pair only reaches a similarity score of 0.44. This impacts the distribution means, which are closer to each other in the co-predication metric than in the similarity scores. The computational approaches to rating word sense similarities overall return relatively high scores for both, homonym and polyseme pairs, often only occupying the top 20% of the scale. As a result, the means of their distributions are significantly closer, as exemplified by the distributions of BERT word embedding similarity ratings for polyseme and homonym pairs in the third graph of Figure 1. The primitive Word2Vec sentence embeddings lastly assign a higher mean similarity score to homonym pairs than to polysemes (last graph).

Because co-predication acceptability judge-

| Combination | | Correlation | | Ordinary Least Squares (OLS) Regression Analysis | | | | | | Prediction | |
First Measure	Second Measure	r	p	Coef.	R^2	F-stat.	Prob.	Omnib.	Prob.	MSE	R^2
Similarity	Acceptability	0.529	2.08E-06	0.910	0.280	26.855	2.08E-06	3.756	0.153	0.040	0.208
Similarity	Classification	0.539	1.21E-06	1.091	0.291	28.320	1.21E-06	6.587	0.037	0.057	0.162
Acceptability	Similarity	0.529	2.08E-06	0.308	0.280	26.855	2.08E-06	22.297	0.000	0.014	0.149
Acceptability	Classification	0.563	3.21E-07	0.662	0.317	32.015	3.21E-07	11.321	0.003	0.050	0.301
Classification	Similarity	0.539	1.21E-06	0.267	0.291	28.320	1.21E-06	29.957	0.000	0.014	0.175
Classification	Acceptability	0.563	3.21E-07	0.479	0.317	32.015	3.21E-07	6.101	0.047	0.037	0.258
BERT WE	Similarity	0.211	0.077	0.762	0.045	3.226	0.077	14.001	0.001	0.018	-0.214
BERT WE	Acceptability	0.482	0.000	2.991	0.233	20.936	0.000	21.974	0.000	0.041	0.204
BERT WE	Classification	0.221	0.064	1.614	0.049	3.553	0.064	15.446	0.000	0.069	-0.007
BERT CLS	Similarity	-0.038	0.756	-0.390	0.001	0.097	0.756	12.775	0.002	0.019	-0.298
BERT CLS	Acceptability	0.271	0.023	4.832	0.073	5.448	0.023	13.459	0.001	0.049	0.033
BERT CLS	Classification	0.051	0.672	1.075	0.003	0.181	0.672	17.604	0.000	0.073	-0.051
BERT SE	Similarity	-0.007	0.955	-0.067	0.000	0.003	0.955	13.383	0.001	0.020	-0.322
BERT SE	Acceptability	0.011	0.929	0.181	0.000	0.008	0.929	14.479	0.001	0.058	-0.162
BERT SE	Classification	-0.016	0.895	-0.317	0.000	0.018	0.895	17.751	0.000	0.073	-0.067
ELMo WE	Similarity	0.295	0.012	1.191	0.087	6.600	0.012	10.325	0.006	0.018	-0.188
ELMo WE	Acceptability	0.178	0.138	1.233	0.032	2.257	0.138	13.644	0.001	0.051	-0.015
ELMo WE	Classification	0.323	0.006	2.630	0.104	8.022	0.006	14.382	0.001	0.065	0.063
Word2Vec SE	Similarity	0.053	0.662	0.085	0.003	0.193	0.662	13.484	0.001	0.020	-0.305
Word2Vec SE	Acceptability	0.245	0.039	0.681	0.060	4.423	0.039	16.732	0.000	0.051	-0.006
Word2Vec SE	Classification	0.249	0.036	0.813	0.062	4.555	0.036	15.828	0.000	0.070	-0.026

Table 1: Correlations between the three different metrics of word sense similarity based on annotation judgements, and correlation between computational proxies of word sense similarity as compared to the human judgements. The first set of columns displays pairwise correlation based on Pearson's r, the second set shows the key statistics obtained from their OLS regression, and the third set contains the mean regression scores based on 5-fold cross validation.

ments show a higher overlap between the distributions of homonym and polyseme ratings than the similarity ratings, we expect similarity to be a stronger predictor in classifying target pairs as either homonyms or polysemes. To validate this intuition, we classified items through a support vector machine (SVM) with linear kernel under five-fold cross-validation. As our dataset is skewed towards polysemy samples, baseline performance is an accuracy of 0.825, achieved by assigning all samples to the polyseme class. Both classification based on similarity ratings and co-predication ratings outperform this baseline, with an accuracy of 0.988 for similarity ratings, and 0.895 for co-predication ratings, respectively. Figure 2 shows the optimal decision boundary between homonym samples (blue) and polyseme pairs (orange) calculated for the two annotation metrics. The higher overlap in homonym and polyseme ratings indeed prevents a clear delineation between the two ambiguity types. None of the computational metrics manages to outperform the baseline, and consistently apply max-class labels. Neither combining the two human annotated metrics, nor combining any of the computational metrics improves their respective classification performance over the best individual score.

3.2 Relation Between Different Annotations of Sense Similarity

In order to establish a measure of correlation between the three human annotation metrics, we consider all six combinations of metrics and i) calculate their Pearson's r, ii) perform an ordinary least squares (OLS) regression, and iii) calculate the mean squared error (MSE) of OLS predictions under five-fold cross validation. The results of these calculations are displayed in Table 1, and visualised in Figure 3. We find a moderate but significant correlation between the three human annotation metrics. Similarity judgements and co-predication acceptability judgements show the lowest correlation in the set (Pearson's r of 0.529), while acceptability judgements and categorical class similarity achieve the highest correlation (Pearson's r of 0.563). These results indicate that categorical class boundaries between referent interpretations might have a more direct influence on whether two different senses can felicitously be co-predicated than their graded similarity score. The correlation graphs in Figure 3 again display the coverage of judgements obtained for the three human annotation metrics, indicating that class similarity ratings, like co-predication acceptability, span over the full scale, while similarity judgements only cover the

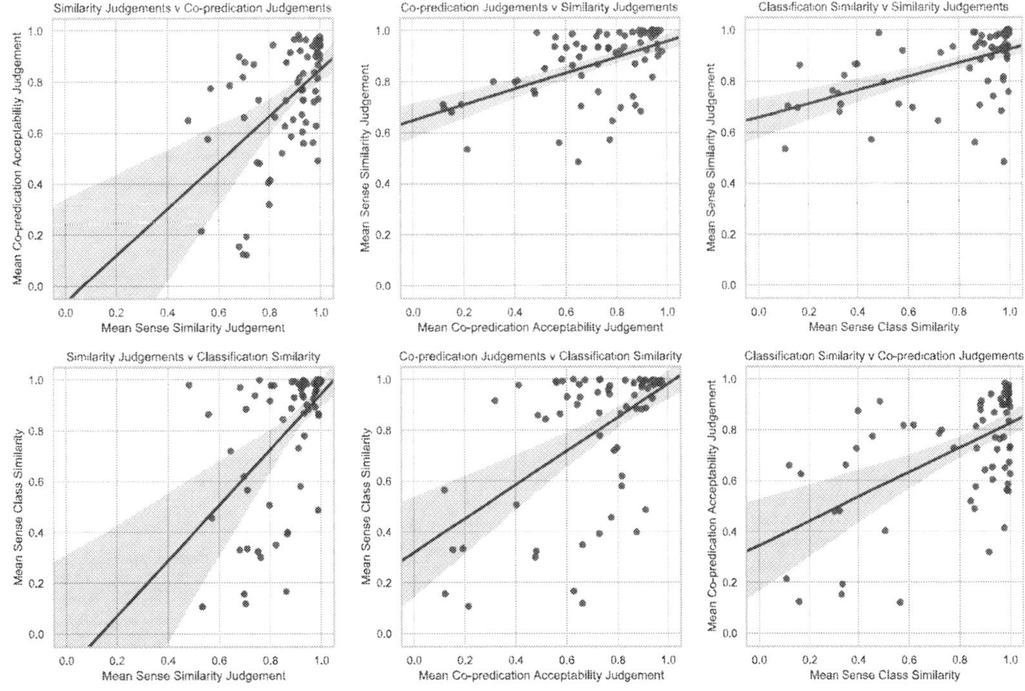

Figure 3: Correlations between polysemic target word pairs based on the three collected judgements of word sense similarity, together with their best linear fit.

top half. Here however this means that predicting co-predication ratings from similarity scores is more difficult than the inverse, leading to a higher error rate in the prediction of low-similarity items, and an overall higher mean squared error (MSE; 0.014 to 0.04). The same holds for predicting similarity class labels from similarity judgements, which is more difficult than predicting similarity judgements based on class similarity.

3.3 Relation between Computational Estimates and Human Judgements

The bottom part of Table 1 displays the results of predicting human judgements of polyseme sense similarity based on the different computational proxies. Only seven of the pairwise correlations are significant, and only the correlation between BERT contextualised word embeddings and co-predication acceptability ratings approaches a moderate degree (Pearson's r of 0.48). We argue that it was to be expected that the correlation between the similarity of BERT's contextualised embeddings and co-predication acceptability should be higher than between BERT scores and explicit similarity ratings, as BERT does not specifically capture the sense of a target word, but rather the diversity and

type of context it appears in. This way it is easier to predict whether a combined context as created by co-predication is natural to occur (and therefore more felicitous) than to directly predict the targets' sense similarity. Other notable significant pairs are ELMo word embeddings and classification similarity (Pearson's r of 0.32), ELMo and similarity ratings (r = 0.3), as well as BERT classification token similarity and co-predication acceptability (r = 0.27), indicating that BERT and ELMo might capture slightly different facets of word sense - but, as indicate above - not in such a way that combining them would improve their performance in predicting the ambiguity type of a target word pair.

3.4 Qualitative Analysis

While the correlation between explicit similarity judgements and co-predication acceptability is imperfect, our analysis reveals that judgements are more similar towards the upper end of the rating scale than at the lower end. To investigate this observation in more detail, we here analyse polyseme *newspaper*, which provides two samples to the low-similarity cluster. As mentioned before, in our experiments we assume that *newspaper* has three distinct but related sense interpretations: (1)

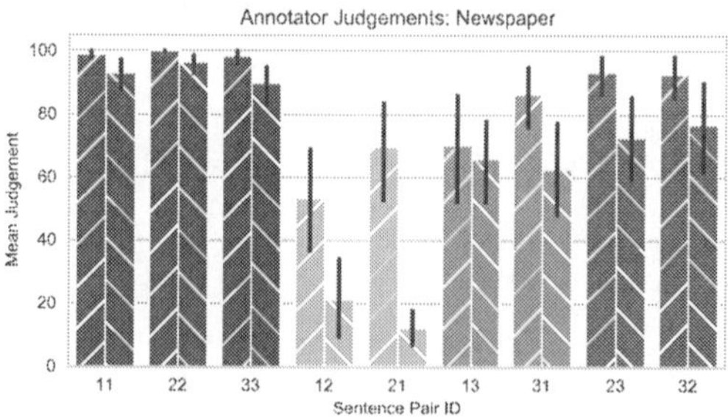

Figure 4: Mean similarity ratings (left, ascending hatch) and co-predication acceptability ratings (right, descending hatch) for the nine sense interpretation pairs of polyseme *newspaper*. The first three bars represent same-sense pairs, the other three groups the different combinations of cross-sense readings, respectively.

organisation/institution, (2) *physical object*, and (3) *information/data*. Figure 4 shows the mean similarity and acceptability ratings for the nine combinations of sense interpretations: The first three bars represent same-sense pairs 11, 22 and 33, the other three groups the different combinations of cross-sense pairs. The figure reveals that the three same-sense pairs receive equally high similarity and acceptability ratings, but while similarity ratings show a gradual decrease in scores assigned to cross-sense pairs, the co-predication acceptability scores are only gradual for more similar cross-sense pairs, and drop significantly for less similar ones. These results indicate that similarity ratings appear to be a more nuanced, continuous measure than co-predication acceptability, which can assigns extremely low scores for readings deemed to be infelicitous. A more detailed investigation of the grouping of polyseme senses and its implications for the hypothesis of hierarchical sense representation can be found in Haber and Poesio (2020).

4 Conclusion

The data collected in this study allows for a number of observations about the role of word sense similarity in the processing of homonyms and polysemes. On the one hand, graded co-predication acceptability ratings are shown to be less able to tell apart samples of homonymic and polysemic sense pairs than explicit sense similarity ratings. This supports the growing collection of studies indicating that co-predication might not be as suited a tool to distinguish different types of lexical ambiguity as traditionally assumed. On the other hand, the collected judgements of word sense similarity

indicate that polyseme sense pairs mis-classified by co-predication acceptability are overall less similar to each other than other sense pairs, and significantly so than same-sense interpretations. This to some degree vindicates co-predication as a linguistic test, suggesting that rather than distinguishing homonyms form polysemes per se, it might be a coarse indication of the underlying word sense similarity.

Our results also provide support for recent hypotheses suggesting that polyseme representation in the mental lexicon cannot be fully underspecified. During data collection, annotators rated some polysemic sense interpretations to be significantly less similar to each other than other sense pairs, and even rated some of the polyseme cross-sense co-predication samples as unacceptable. This indicates that the interpretations of polysemic words might be grouped based on their similarity, and only grouped interpretations are available for cost-free sense shifting and felicitous co-predication. Because only a single target word per type of systematic polysemy was tested here, we cannot ascertain whether sense groupings are idiosyncratic or systematic across target words of a certain polysemy type. Data for an analysis of this question can however easily be obtained by repeating our experiments with a larger set of target words. In a similar vain, we also recommend an in-depth analysis of irregular or metaphorical polysemes, which were omitted in this data collection effort.

Lastly, investigating the suitability of contextualised language models as proxies for human word sense similarity judgements, we find that the tested contextualised embeddings fail to predict word sense similarity consistently, but that the similarities between BERT embeddings show a significant correlation with co-predication acceptability ratings. We take this finding as evidence that BERT might create better encodings of complex contexts than encodings of actual word meaning, as it seems to perform well in determining whether contexts can be felicitously combined without consistently determining the similarity of word senses from these contexts first. We strongly encourage further research into determining the exact lexical semantic information available in BERT encodings in order to shed more light on this issue.

Acknowledgements

The work presented in this paper was supported by the DALI project, ERC Grant 695662. The authors would like to thank Derya Çokal and Andrea Bruera for their input, and the anonymous reviewers for their feedback.

References

Sandra Antunes and Rui Pedro Chaves. 2003. On the Licensing Conditions of Co-Predication. In *Proceedings of the 2nd International Workshop on Generative Approaches to the Lexicon*.

Juri D. Apresjan. 1974. Regular polysemy. *Linguistics*, 12:5–32.

Nicholas Asher. 2011. *Lexical Meaning in Context: A Web of Words*. Cambridge University Press.

Nicholas Asher and James Pustejovsky. 2006. A type composition logic for generative lexicon. *Journal of Cognitive Science*, 6(1).

Gemma Boleda, Sabine Schulte im Walde, and Toni Badia. 2012. Modeling regular polysemy: A study on the semantic classification of catalan adjectives. *Computational Linguistics*, 38(3):575–616.

Alan D. Cruse. 1995. Polysemy and related phenomena from a cognitive linguistic viewpoint. In Patrick Saint-Dizier and Evelyn Viegas, editors, *Computational Lexical Semantics*, Studies in Natural Language Processing, page 33–49. Cambridge University Press.

Jacob Devlin, Ming-Wei Chang, Kenton Lee, and Kristina Toutanova. 2018. BERT: Pre-training of Deep Bidirectional Transformers for Language Understanding.

Johannes Dölling. Forthcoming. Systematic Polysemy. In Daniel Gutzmann, Lisa Matthewson, Cécile Meier, Hotze Rullmann, and Thomas Ede Zimmermann, editors, *The Blackwell Companion to Semantics*. Wiley.

Kawin Ethayarajh. 2019. How contextual are contextualized word representations? comparing the geometry of bert, elmo, and gpt-2 embeddings. *Proceedings of the 2019 Conference on Empirical Methods in Natural Language Processing and the 9th International Joint Conference on Natural Language Processing (EMNLP-IJCNLP)*.

Ingrid Lossius Falkum and Augustin Vicente. 2015. Polysemy: Current perspectives and approaches. *Lingua*, 157:1–16.

Hana Filip and Peter Sutton. 2017. Singular count NPs in measure constructions. In *Semantics and Linguistic Theory*, volume 27, pages 340–357.

Jerry A. Fodor. 1998. *Concepts: Where Cognitive Science Went Wrong*. Oxford University Press.

Lyn Frazier and Keith Rayner. 1990. Taking on semantic commitments: Processing multiple meanings vs. multiple senses. *Journal of Memory and Language*.

Steven Frisson. 2015. About bound and scary books: The processing of book polysemies. *Lingua*, 157:17 – 35. Polysemy: Current Perspectives and Approaches.

Janosch Haber and Massimo Poesio. 2020. Word sense distance in human similarity judgements and contextualised word embeddings. In *Proceedings of the Probability and Meaning Conference (PaM 2020)*, pages 128–145, Gothenburg. Association for Computational Linguistics.

Ray Jackendoff. 1989. What is a concept, that a person may grasp it?1. *Mind & Language*, 4(1-2):68–102.

Ekaterini Klepousniotou. 2002. The Processing of Lexical Ambiguity: Homonymy and Polysemy in the Mental Lexicon. *Brain and Language*, 81(1-3):205–223.

Ekaterini Klepousniotou, G. Bruce Pike, Karsten Steinhauer, and Vincent Gracco. 2012. Not all ambiguous words are created equal: An EEG investigation of homonymy and polysemy. *Brain and Language*.

Ekaterini Klepousniotou, Debra Titone, and Carolina Romero. 2008. Making sense of word senses: The comprehension of polysemy depends on sense overlap.

Jey Han Lau, Alexander Clark, and Shalom Lappin. 2014. Measuring Gradience in Speakers' Grammaticality Judgements. *Proceedings of the 36th Annual Meeting of the Cognitive Science Society (CogSci 2014)*.

John Lyons. 1977. *Semantics*, volume 2. Cambridge University Press.

Tomas Mikolov, Kai Chen, Greg Corrado, and Jeffrey Dean. 2013. Efficient estimation of word representations in vector space. In *1st International Conference on Learning Representations, ICLR 2013 - Workshop Track Proceedings*.

Andrei Moldovan. 2019. Descriptions and tests for polysemy. *Axiomathes*, pages 1–21.

Marina Ortega-Andrés and Agustín Vicente. 2019. Polysemy and co-predication. *Glossa: a journal of general linguistics*, 4(1).

Matthew E. Peters, Mark Neumann, Mohit Iyyer, Matt Gardner, Christopher Clark, Kenton Lee, and Luke Zettlemoyer. 2018. Deep contextualized word representations. *CoRR*, abs/1802.05365.

James Pustejovsky. 1991. The Generative Lexicon. *Comput. Linguist.*, 17(4):409–441.

Liina Pylkkänen, Rodolfo Llinás, and Gregory L. Murphy. 2006. The representation of polysemy: Meg evidence. *Journal of cognitive neuroscience*, 18(1):97–109.

Alec Radford, Jeffrey Wu, Rewon Child, David Luan, Dario Amodei, and Ilya Sutskever. 2019. Language models are unsupervised multitask learners. *OpenAI Blog*, 1(8):9.

Jennifer Rodd, Gareth Gaskell, and William Marslen-Wilson. 2002. Making sense of semantic ambiguity: Semantic competition in lexical access. *Journal of Memory and Language*, 46(2):245 – 266.

Petra Schumacher. 2013. When combinatorial processing results in reconceptualization: toward a new approach of compositionality. *Frontiers in Psychology*, 4:677.

Peter R. Sutton and Hana Filip. 2018. Counting Construcions and Coercion: Container, Portion and Measure Interpretations. *Oslo Studies in Language*, 10(2).

Matthew J. Traxler, Brian McElree, and Martin J. Williams, Rihana S .and Pickering. 2005. Context effects in coercion: Evidence from eye movements. *Journal of Memory and Language*, 53(1):1–25.

Ashish Vaswani, Noam Shazeer, Niki Parmar, Jakob Uszkoreit, Llion Jones, Aidan N. Gomez, Łukasz Kaiser, and Illia Polosukhin. 2017. Attention is all you need. In I. Guyon, U. V. Luxburg, S. Bengio, H. Wallach, R. Fergus, S. Vishwanathan, and R. Garnett, editors, *Advances in Neural Information Processing Systems 30*, pages 5998–6008. Curran Associates, Inc.

Gregor Wiedemann, Steffen Remus, Avi Chawla, and Chris Biemann. 2019. Does bert make any sense? interpretable word sense disambiguation with contextualized embeddings.

Sarah Zobel. 2017. The sensitivity of natural language to the distinction between class nouns and role nouns. In *Semantics and Linguistic Theory*, volume 27, pages 438–458.

Arnold M. Zwicky and Jerrold M. Sadock. 1975. Ambiguity tests and how to fail them. In *Syntax and Semantics volume 4*, pages 1–36. Brill.

Fine-tuning BERT with Focus Words for Explanation Regeneration

Isaiah Onando Mulang'[1], Jennifer D'Souza[2], Sören Auer[2]
[1]University of Bonn, Bonn, Germany
{mulang}@iai.uni-bonn.de
[2]TIB Leibniz Information Centre for Science and Technology, Hannover, Germany
{jennifer.dsouza | auer}@tib.eu

Abstract

Explanation generation introduced as the WorldTree corpus (Jansen et al., 2018) is an emerging NLP task involving multi-hop inference for explaining the correct answer in multiple-choice QA. It is a challenging task evidenced by low state-of-the-art performances (below 60% in F-score) demonstrated on the task. Of the state-of-the-art approaches, fine-tuned transformer-based (Vaswani et al., 2017) BERT models have shown great promise toward continued system performance improvements compared with approaches relying on surface-level cues alone that demonstrate performance saturation. In this work, we take a novel direction by addressing a particular linguistic characteristic of the data—we introduce a novel and lightweight focus feature in the transformer-based model and examine task improvements. Our evaluations reveal a significantly positive impact of this lightweight focus feature achieving highest scores, second only to a significantly computationally intensive system.

1 Introduction

Multi-hop Inference for Explanation Regeneration (MIER) is an emerging task in NLP that concerns aggregating facts to justify the correct answer choice in multiple-choice question answering settings. The WorldTree corpus (Jansen et al., 2018) that introduced this as a community shared task (Jansen and Ustalov, 2019), was dedicated to finding systems that generate explanations for answers to elementary science questions based on the MIER paradigm.

The core task essentially entails two main steps: identification of relevant explanation facts from a given knowledge base, followed by ranking the

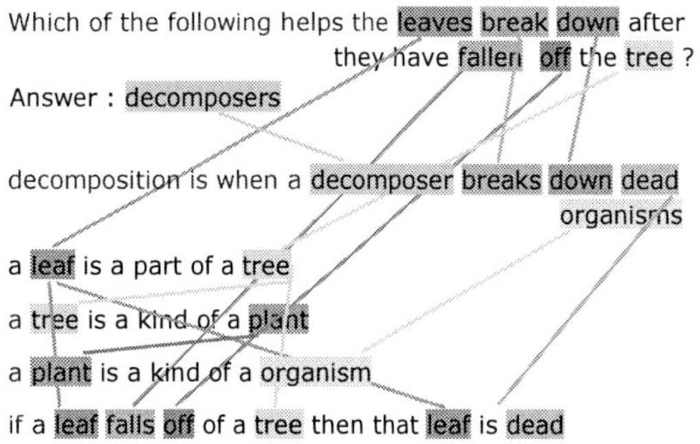

Figure 1: A elementary science question, its correct answer, and the ordered set of justification facts for the answer in the WorldTree corpus (Jansen et al., 2018) depicted as a subgraph of lexical matches.

selected facts as a logically coherent paragraph. Figure 1 shows an example data instance from the WorldTree corpus (Jansen et al., 2018) that defines this task. It is basically a question, its correct answer, and a set of ordered facts that justify the correct answer choice. Depicted in the figure, as a subgraph, is a crucial characteristic feature of the data: that there are lexical overlaps between the question, the correct answer, and the explanation facts. In this respect, however, there are two notable caveats: 1) *distractors*—the lexical overlaps can also exist with irrelevant facts to the QA. E.g., given the KB fact: *a decomposer is usually a bacterium or fungus*, it has a lexical match to the answer, but it is not relevant to the explanation. Similarly, at least 13 other such matching irrelevant facts can be found in the WorldTree corpus (2018) knowledge base. And 2) *multi-hop inference of valid explanation facts*—not all the relevant explanation facts have a direct lexical match to the QA pair, some of the facts are lexically connected to the other valid explanation facts. E.g., the fact *a plant is a kind of an organism* has no lexical relation to the question or to the answer, but it does to the

*Proceedings of the Ninth Joint Conference on Lexical and Computational Semantics (*SEM), pages 125–130*
Barcelona, Spain (Online), December 12–13, 2020

first explanation fact, hence this entails multihop inference from the QA to the explanation fact to another explanation fact. As such, selecting the set of relevant explanation facts, demands extra effort beyond direct lexical matches with the QA.

In light of these caveats in the data, the task presents itself as a fairly complex inference task, where traditional methods for QA that are based on simple fact matching have proved inadequate (Clark et al., 2013; Jansen et al., 2016). Given the lexical match characteristic of the data, a slightly adapted application of *tf-idf* algorithm (Chia et al., 2019), unsurprisingly demonstrates high performance near that of state-of-the-art neural models.

The MIER task defined in the WorldTree corpus (Jansen et al., 2018) was introduced for the first time as a shared task at TextGraph-13 (Jansen and Ustalov, 2019). The state-of-the-art system (Das et al., 2019) employed a fine-tuned BERT-based model in an extended computationally intensive architecture. Generally, the performance of these fine-tuned transformer models depends on how related the data is to the original pretraining data and how best the input representation can be encoded. To this end, in this work, concentrating exclusively on enhancing the lexical match between a question, answer, and explanation, we encode a novel lightweight feature based on the psycholinguistic concept of *focus* words that has been defined by Brysbaert et al. Loosely, a focus word can be defined as a word which is not too tangible to be experienced directly by the five natural senses (i.e., smell, touch, sight, taste, and hearing), while as well not too abstract (e.g., acquirable) that the meaning may not be illustrated without using other words. From Figure 1, as an example, the focus words are break down, fall, decompose, organism, dead. Inspired by (Jansen et al., 2017), we demonstrate for the first time the application of focus words in the context of contemporary neural-based transformer models for the task of explanation generation. We observe that employing focus words in neural-based models enhances the lexical attention capability within transformer-based BERT models and demonstrates an improvement on vanilla BERT models. In fact, among all systems for the task, we obtain the highest scores, second only to the computationally intensive system by Das et al. Thus, our successful application of focus words in elementary science explanation generation demonstrates a poignant application of a vital psycholinguistic feature in the context of a contemporary problem in Artificial Intelligence.

In our experiments, we examine two main research questions. The first assesses the optimal training experimental setting of the WorldTree corpus (2018). Specifically, **RQ1**: how does the proportion of negative training examples impact fine-tuning model performance? The second directly assesses the impact of our *focus word* feature. **RQ2**: what is the impact of the novel *focus word* feature on explanation generation in an optimal fine-tuned model? The rest of the paper is structured as follows. We define our problem in Section 2, followed by a description of the related work in Section 3. Section 4 discusses our approach, with evaluation results presented in Section 5. We conclude in Section 6.

2   Problem Definition

Given a question $q = \{w_1, w_2, .., w_{|q|}\}$, its correct answer $a = \{w_1, w_2, ..., w_{|a|}\}$, and a set of explanation facts $\mathcal{E}$ s.t. every $e \in \mathcal{E} = \{w_1, w_2, ..., w_{|e|}\}$ where w_i are words $\in V$ for some vocabulary V. Following the definition for the TextGraphs-13 MIER task (Jansen and Ustalov, 2019), the aim is to obtain, for every question and its correct answer, an ordered list of a set of facts that are coherent in discourse from a knowledge base of facts. By definition, for a question-correct answer pair (q, a), there exists a set of ordered explanation facts $\mathcal{R}_{q,a} \subseteq \mathcal{E}$ called the relevant set. For each (q, a) pair, the task aims to generate an ordered list of all the explanation facts in the knowledge base $\mathcal{E}^o$ such that $\forall e^o, e \in \mathcal{E} : e^o \in \mathcal{R}_{q,a} \wedge e \notin \mathcal{R}_{q,a}$, $rank(e^o, \mathcal{E}^o) < rank(e, \mathcal{E}^o)$. We define, for any given (q, a) pair the ordered list as $\mathcal{E}^o_{q,a} = Reorder(\{(e_k, \gamma_k) \mid e_k \in \mathcal{E}\})$ where γ_k is an associated relevance score obtained by predicting a proximity value $\Phi(q, a, e_k, \theta)$. The *Reorder* function therefore ranks the values e_k using the proximity score γ_k, where the result is a ranked list of all explanations in which the facts with higher γ_k scores are ranked higher. Φ is a regression function and θ represents the transformer model hyperparameters.

As alluded to in the Introduction, we induce novel focus word features from both the question and the answer, and the explanation facts. Adapted from Brysbaert et al., we deem as focus words $v \in V$ a word with an annotated psycholinguistic concreteness score between 3.0 and 4.2, i.e. one relegated as somewhere in between an abstract and concrete concept word which is relevant in elementary science since they often discuss phenomenon such as "evaporation," "dead," "break down," etc.

3   Related Work

(Jansen et al., 2017) attempted to jointly solve question answering as a consequence of explanation generation. They first identified the question focus words using a predetermined range of psycholinguistic concreteness scores (Brysbaert et al., 2014). Then they generate answer justifications by aggregating multiple facts from external knowledge sources (via constructs called text aggregation graphs). We leverage these concreteness scores, specifically the range between 3.0 and 4.2 that define focus words, as feature labels for the elementary science QA focus words in a transformer BERT model.

The TextGraph-13 MIER Shared Task saw two flavors of approaches to the task. The traditional approach of using hand-crafted linguistic features in an SVM ranker (D'Souza et al., 2019) and with reranking rules to correct obvious prediction errors. And, on the other hand, the most recent BERT-based rerankers over heuristically ranked data in a first stage. Banerjee tested initial ranking using two different transformer models: BERT (Devlin et al., 2018) and XLNet (Yang et al., 2019), and observe that including parts of gold explanations with question text when training for relevance as additional context offers performance improvement. Their approach included reranking the top 15 ranked facts via cosine similarity. Chia et al. explore an iterative *tf-idf* to recursively refine the results and achieve significant improvements on a baseline non-optimized tf-idf. In addition, they employ the results of this process in a BERT-based re-ranker to rank the top 64 candidates. The top-ranked system by Das et al. used fine-tuned BERT both for the initial step and the reranking. Where the first BERT model is fine-tuned on the whole set of facts in the knowledge base, the second BERT model is fine-tuned as a path ranking model. In this latter case, a BERT model is trained with chains of valid multi-hop facts from the top 25 candidates. Computing chains of multi-hop facts was a brute-force computationally exhaustive process which is not practically viable as noted by the authors. We also include results for a BERT model trained purely on just the focus words of the question/answer pairs, and the explanations. This model obtains no signals

at all from the data, an indication that focus words are best used as extra signals to the data as opposed to being utilized as standalone data by themselves.

4   Our Approach

Our approach is illustrated in Figure 2 and is described next.

4.1   Our Novel Focus Words Feature

Word concreteness ratings coming from research in psycholinguistics (Brysbaert et al., 2014) forms a good source of information to identify whether a word in a sentence reflects an abstract or a concrete real-world concept. In prior work, Jansen et al. were the first to employ the word concreteness scores to identify focus words in elementary science QA as a linking signal with relevant explanation facts. In their work, the focus words were employed to help aggregate related explanation facts, whereby the identified focus words were considered highly relevant in finding the answer to a question, hence significant for connecting justification sentences together. We borrow this insight and apply concreteness scores during finetuning BERT which we employ as a reranker (described in the next subsection). The raw annotated data with the concreteness scores is a list of 40,000 lemmas from common English.[1] As mentioned earlier, focus words are those with concreteness scores between 3.0 and 4.2 a range defined in (Berant and Liang, 2014) which reflect the degree to which a word is a focus word with abstract words and concrete words being on the extreme ends of the words spectrum. In the context of our problem domain, i.e. elementary science, we have identified that the most relevant content terms fall in the conceptual spectrum of focus words. For example the focus words measure/measurement, eat/eating, evaporate/evaporation are words that describe the relevant concepts in elementary science.

We preprocess the text using the spaCy[2] NLP toolkit for tokenization and lemmatization before retrieving concreteness scores (Brysbaert et al., 2014) for the words from the dictionary.

4.2   Finetuning BERT Ranker with Focus Words

We utilize the pretrained BERT (Devlin et al., 2018) model and fine tune it on the sentence pair scoring task with a regression function to obtain

---

[1]`http://crr.ugent.be/archives/1330`
[2]Available from `https://spacy.io/`

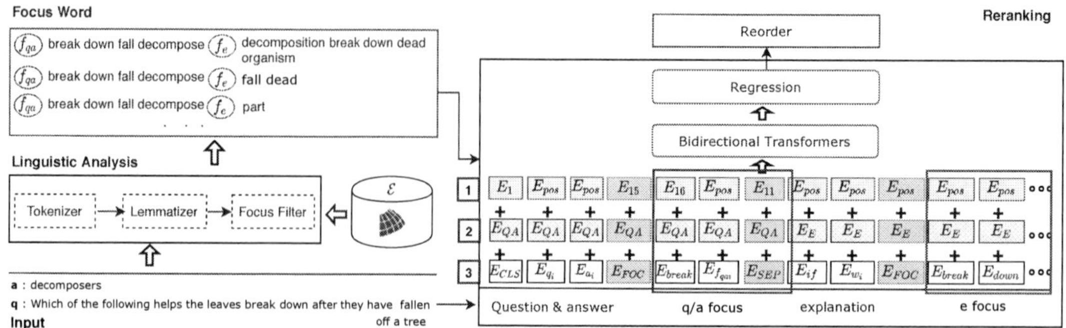

Figure 2: Fine-tuning of Transformers with Focus Word Features. Approach: The q, a are paired with each explanation in the set. This is then passed through the Focus word extractor that identifies the focus words based on concreteness scores. Input representation layers: 1) Position Embeddings; 2) Segment Embeddings; and 3) Word Embeddings.

ranking scores. Our input to the BERT model is encoded as follows: the special $[CLS]$ token is appended to the beginning of every data instance; a special token $[SEP]$ is used to separate the (q, a) pair from the explanation fact and is appended to the end of the explanation fact as well; additionally, to encode our focus word feature, we introduce a new special token $[FOC]$. Focus words are identified from the (q, a) and explanation facts, and they are listed following the text with the $[FOC]$ separator. As an example of our input, consider `[CLS] Which of the following helps leaves break down after they have fallen off a tree decomposers [FOC] break fall decompose [SEP] decomposition is when a decomposer breaks down dead organisms [FOC] decomposition decompose break down organism [SEP]`.

This is then used as input to the model which learns representations for both the (q, a) and explanation fact text fragments, and the focus word tokens. Our model architecture in Figure 2 depicts how the input is handled at the embeddings layer. For instance, to obtain a representation for a focus word at position i in the input, from the (q, a) side: the word embedding E_{qa_i} - layer 3, segment embedding E_{QA} - layer 2, and the position embedding E_{pos_i} - layer 1, are summed up into a single embedding vector. This output is then passed to the bidirectional transformer layer and finally through a regression layer to produce the score γ for the input explanation fact. Finally, all facts are sorted by γ scores in descending order.

4.2.1 Training and Hyperparameters

Our BERT model is initialized using publicly available weights from the pretrained $BERT_{BASE}$ model available in the Python package Pytorch-Transformers[3]. We use the default learning rate of 2e-5, a batch size of 32 and maximum sequence length of 512. The batch size and sequence length are unchanged for training and testing. The model was fine-tuned for 3 epochs using the Adam optimizer (Kingma and Ba, 2014).

5 Evaluation and Results

To develop and evaluate our approach, we use the TextGraphs-13 MIER Shared Task (Jansen and Ustalov, 2019) dataset and evaluation scripts, respectively.

5.1 Experimental Setup

Dataset. The TextGraph-13 MIER task used the WorldTree corpus (Jansen et al., 2018) consisting of 1,190, 264, and 1,247 training, development, and test set QA instances additionally annotated with explanations, comprising anywhere between 1 to 23 facts. The QA part of the dataset is a multiple-choice dataset, therefore, each question has upto 5 answer choices of which the correct answer is already known. A set of 4,789 candidate facts was additionally provided as the knowledge base.

Evaluation Metrics. The shared task evaluation script employed the mean Average Precision (mAP) metric.

5.2 Results and Discussion

To address **RQ1**, we perform experiments with different numbers of negative examples in the training set, starting with the whole dataset containing $\sim$4,770 negative explanation facts per (q, a).

---

[3]Accessible at `https://github.com/huggingface/transformers`

Approach	mAP	
	Dev	Test
BERT Re-ranker + inference chains (Das et al., 2019)	**58.5**	**56.3**
BERT Re-ranker + Iterated TF-IDF (Chia et al., 2019)	50.9	47.7
Iterated TF-IDF (Chia et al., 2019)	49.7	45.8
Optimized TF-IDF (Chia et al., 2019)	45.8	42.7
BERT iterative re-ranker (Banerjee, 2019)	42.3	41.3
Rules + Feature-rich SVM^{Rank} (D'Souza et al., 2019)	44.4	39.4
Generic Feature-rich SVM^{Rank} (D'Souza et al., 2019)	37.1	34.1
TF-IDF Baseline + SVM^{Rank} (Jansen and Ustalov, 2019)	–	29.6
TF-IDF Baseline	24.4	24.8
BERT + Only Focus Words + Optimized Neg Facts	0.019	0.083
BERT + Optimized Neg Facts (Ours)	**54.1**	**52.6**
BERT + Focus Words + Optimized Neg Facts (Ours)	**55.6**	**53.8**

Table 1: Mean Average Precision (mAP) percentage scores for the Elementary Science Explanation Regeneration comparing our approach (last two rows) with nine reference systems

#Neg. Examples	Dev mAP	Test mAP
~ 4770	43.21	40.11
1000	53.12	50.42
900	54.14	**52.57**
800	54.88	52.26
600	54.88	52.26

Table 2: Mean Average Precision (mAP) percentage scores of finetuning BERT over varying negative training examples

Note, by the whole dataset, we mean all the explanation facts in the knowledge base that are not annotated as valid facts for a given (q, a) instance. Table 2 shows that too many negative examples for training had a negative impact. The configuration with (~ 4770) refers to the *Vanilla BERT model* trained on each question-answer (q, a) paired with all the explanation facts. We reached an equilibrium between 600 and 900 negative explanation facts per (q, a). Thus, **RQ1** investigated obtaining an optimally trained model given the WorldTree corpus (2018) as input which we found at 900 explanation facts.

Table 1 shows the performance of our optimally trained BERT model with and without focus words for the MIER task. Addressing **RQ2**, we find that the focus tokens induces a performance improvement above 1% mAP. Overall, our model outperforms eight of the nine reference systems. It is second only to a more computationally intensive model (Das et al., 2019) where comparatively ours is significantly simpler, thereby practically viable. Separately, a model trained only on focus words

from the (q, a) and explanation facts, themselves, do not provide any substantial signals to train a useful model (see row *"BERT + Pure Focus Words + Optimised Neg Facts"* row). This affirms that the original sentence provide necessary training signals which can be further accentuated with the focus word features.

6 Conclusions

In this paper, we empirically determine that the number of negative examples in training has an impact on the fine-tuning process for the explanation regeneration task. We have presented a lightweight, nonetheless, effective solution to the problem of explanation regeneration in elementary science QA. Staying on course with the current trend of investigating neural models, we implement a BERT-based model with an additional linguistic focus words feature. Thereby with our new feature we tap deeper into the nature of data in terms of its linguistic match characteristic. We obtained a considerable improvement in task performance. Subsequently, since focus words have proven effective in our experiments, by their nature we hypothesize that attention-based models are a promising future direction for this task. In this work, we developed our system based on the MIER TextGraph-13 Shared Task (Jansen and Ustalov, 2019) definition for explanation generation, in the context of which we utilize only the correct answer for ranking explanation facts. Toward an end-to-end model, as a first step, we plan to explore the training of an optimal model with all answer choices; following which, we plan to jointly model the question answering process together with explanation generation in a feedback loop such that both tasks mutually improve each other (Pirtoaca et al., 2019), except we will test our system for elementary science QA.

References

Pratyay Banerjee. 2019. Asu at textgraphs 2019 shared task: Explanation regeneration using language models and iterative re-ranking. In *Proceedings of the Thirteenth Workshop on Graph-Based Methods for Natural Language Processing (TextGraphs-13)*, pages 78–84.

Jonathan Berant and Percy Liang. 2014. Semantic parsing via paraphrasing. In *Proceedings of the 52nd Annual Meeting of the Association for Computational Linguistics (Volume 1: Long Papers)*, pages 1415–1425, Baltimore, Maryland. Association for Computational Linguistics.

M Brysbaert, AB Warriner, and V Kuperman. 2014. Concreteness ratings for 40 thousand generally known english word lemmas. *Behavior research methods*, 46(3):904.

Yew Ken Chia, Sam Witteveen, and Martin Andrews. 2019. Red dragon AI at TextGraphs 2019 shared task: Language model assisted explanation generation. In *Proceedings of the Thirteenth Workshop on Graph-Based Methods for Natural Language Processing (TextGraphs-13)*, pages 85–89, Hong Kong. Association for Computational Linguistics.

Peter Clark, Philip Harrison, and Niranjan Balasubramanian. 2013. A study of the knowledge base requirements for passing an elementary science test. In *Proceedings of the 2013 workshop on Automated knowledge base construction*, pages 37–42. ACM.

Rajarshi Das, Ameya Godbole, Manzil Zaheer, Shehzaad Dhuliawala, and Andrew McCallum. 2019. Chains-of-reasoning at TextGraphs 2019 shared task: Reasoning over chains of facts for explainable multi-hop inference. In *Proceedings of the Thirteenth Workshop on Graph-Based Methods for Natural Language Processing (TextGraphs-13)*, pages 101–117, Hong Kong. Association for Computational Linguistics.

Jacob Devlin, Ming-Wei Chang, Kenton Lee, and Kristina Toutanova. 2018. BERT: pre-training of deep bidirectional transformers for language understanding. *CoRR*, abs/1810.04805.

Jennifer D'Souza, Isaiah Onando Mulang', and Sören Auer. 2019. Team SVMrank: Leveraging feature-rich support vector machines for ranking explanations to elementary science questions. In *Proceedings of the Thirteenth Workshop on Graph-Based Methods for Natural Language Processing (TextGraphs-13)*, pages 90–100, Hong Kong. Association for Computational Linguistics.

Peter Jansen, Niranjan Balasubramanian, Mihai Surdeanu, and Peter Clark. 2016. What's in an explanation? characterizing knowledge and inference requirements for elementary science exams. In *Proceedings of COLING 2016, the 26th International Conference on Computational Linguistics: Technical Papers*, pages 2956–2965, Osaka, Japan. The COLING 2016 Organizing Committee.

Peter Jansen, Rebecca Sharp, Mihai Surdeanu, and Peter Clark. 2017. Framing qa as building and ranking intersentence answer justifications. *Computational Linguistics*, 43(2):407–449.

Peter Jansen and Dmitry Ustalov. 2019. TextGraphs 2019 Shared Task on Multi-Hop Inference for Explanation Regeneration. In *Proceedings of the Thirteenth Workshop on Graph-Based Methods for Natural Language Processing (TextGraphs-13)*, Hong Kong. Association for Computational Linguistics.

Peter Jansen, Elizabeth Wainwright, Steven Marmorstein, and Clayton T. Morrison. 2018. Worldtree: A corpus of explanation graphs for elementary science questions supporting multi-hop inference. In *Proceedings of the 11th International Conference on Language Resources and Evaluation (LREC)*.

Diederik P. Kingma and Jimmy Ba. 2014. Adam: A method for stochastic optimization. Cite arxiv:1412.6980Comment: Published as a conference paper at the 3rd International Conference for Learning Representations, San Diego, 2015.

George Sebastian Pirtoaca, Traian Rebedea, and Stefan Ruseti. 2019. Answering questions by learning to rank-learning to rank by answering questions. In *Proceedings of the 2019 Conference on Empirical Methods in Natural Language Processing and the 9th International Joint Conference on Natural Language Processing (EMNLP-IJCNLP)*, pages 2531–2540.

Ashish Vaswani, Noam Shazeer, Niki Parmar, Jakob Uszkoreit, Llion Jones, Aidan N. Gomez, Lukasz Kaiser, and Illia Polosukhin. 2017. Attention is all you need. *CoRR*, abs/1706.03762.

Zhilin Yang, Zihang Dai, Yiming Yang, Jaime G. Carbonell, Ruslan Salakhutdinov, and Quoc V. Le. 2019. Xlnet: Generalized autoregressive pretraining for language understanding. *CoRR*, abs/1906.08237.

PISA: A Measure of Preference in Selection of Arguments
to Model Verb Argument Recoverability

Giulia Cappelli
Scuola Normale Superiore
giulia.cappelli@sns.it

Alessandro Lenci
CoLing Lab
University of Pisa
alessandro.lenci@unipi.it

Abstract

Our paper offers a computational model of
the semantic recoverability of verb arguments,
tested in particular on direct objects and Instruments. Our fully distributional model is
intended to improve on older taxonomy-based
models, which require a lexicon in addition to
the training corpus. We computed the selectional preferences of 99 transitive verbs and
173 Instrument verbs as the mean value of the
pairwise cosine similarity between their arguments (a weighted mean between all the arguments, or an unweighted mean with the top-
most k arguments). Results show that our
model can predict the recoverability of objects
and Instruments, providing a similar result to
that of taxonomy-based models but at a much
cheaper computational cost.

1 Introduction

Verb meaning, together with pragmatic and
discourse-related factors, has long been identified
as playing a major role in determining argument
optionality (Levin, 1993). Here, we specifically focus on the **semantic recoverability** of arguments,
which has often been claimed to be the key determi-
nant of object omission (Jespersen, 1927; Hopper
and Thompson, 1980; Levin, 1993; Resnik, 1993,
1996; Conklin et al., 2004; Medina, 2007; Glass,
2020). Resnik (1993, 1996) link argument recoverability to selectional preferences by means of an
experiment we detail in Section 2, and also show
that it is correlated with plausibility and typicality
judgments provided by human subjects.

The relation linking a verb to its optional argument
is a grammatical function in Resnik (1993, 1996),
such as "subject" or "direct object", but it may also
be a semantic role, such as "Instrument" or "Patient". The choice between the two depends on

computational requirements rather than on theoretical constraints.

Let us consider some examples. Recoverability
affects the grammaticality of the sentences in (1),
since the Patient of an eating event (as in (1a)) is
easily recoverable as a member of the class of edi-
bles, but there are no such strict constraints on what
one can make (as in (1b)).

(1) a.   John ate $\varnothing_{\text{object}}$.
     b.   *John made $\varnothing_{\text{object}}$.

The same applies to prepositional phrases filling
the Instrument role, albeit in a more nuanced fashion. Koenig et al. (2002, 2003, 2007) have shown
that verbs describing actions may be divided into
two classes based on whether they semantically
require an Instrument (as in (2a)) or they merely
allow it (as in (2b)). Require-Instrument verbs select for a smaller range of Instruments than Allow-
Instrument verbs: For instance, a beheading event
is very likely to involve a heavy bladed tool like
a sword, while a killing event may happen with a
much larger set of tools or even without any. While
both sentences in (2) are grammatically acceptable,
given that Instruments are syntactic adjuncts (Rissman and Rawlins, 2017), it is much easier to infer
the type of instrument used in the event depicted
in (2a) than the one in (2b), given the high recoverability of the tool used in the former from verb
meaning.

(2) a.   John beheaded the prisoner $\varnothing_{\text{Instrument}}$.
     b.   John killed the prisoner $\varnothing_{\text{Instrument}}$.

Instruments are an interesting object of study for a
number of reasons. First of all, they are arguably
underesearched with respect to recoverability if
compared to direct objects, and to our knowledge
there are no computational models of Instrument
recoverability. Moreover, this semantic role is usu-

131

*Proceedings of the Ninth Joint Conference on Lexical and Computational Semantics (*SEM), pages 131–136*
Barcelona, Spain (Online), December 12–13, 2020

ally overtly realized with prepositional phrases in English and typologically similar languages, making it very different from direct objects and a computationally challenging problem to tackle.

The first attempt to formalize the requirement that a verbal dependent be recoverable in order to be omitted was provided by Resnik (1993, 1996). Resnik's result is a probabilistic information-theoretic model of selectional constraints relying on a manually-built lexicon. In this paper, we propose a fully distributional model of argument recoverability. The crucial idea is that the more mutually similar the arguments selected by a verb are, the more recoverable they are from the meaning of the verb alone. This intuition builds upon the hypotheses and results by Resnik (1993, 1996); Koenig et al. (2007), adding a distributional dimension that those works lacked. We will show that this solution reproduces Resnik's findings about direct objects, addresses the drawbacks of Resnik's model, and is robust enough to predict the recoverability of Instruments. A model such as ours can find a wide range of applications, both in Natural Language Processing (e.g., in semantic role labeling and word sense disambiguation), in linguistic research (e.g., language acquisition and processing), and even in real-life technology (e.g., to provide robots with commonsense knowledge).

2   Related work

Given a verb-relation pair (such as the verb-object relation) Resnik (1993, 1996) formulate the *selectional preference strength* (SPS) of the verb with respect to the possible fillers in the given role (see Eq. 1) as the Kullback-Leibler divergence between the (posterior) distribution of WordNet synsets for the given verb–relation pair and the (prior) distribution of synsets participating in the given relation over all verbs in the corpus. In 1, "classes" refers to the taxonomic classes used in WordNet:

$$SPS_{v,r} = \sum_{c \in classes} p(c|v, r) \, log \frac{p(c|v, r)}{p(c|r)} \quad (1)$$

This yields higher SPS scores for verb-relation pairs admitting only a restricted range of arguments.

Resnik also defines the *selectional association* (SA) of a verb-relation-class triple as the ratio of the SPS for that class and the overall SPS of the verb-relation pair (see Eq. 2), and the SA of a verb-relation-argument triple as the highest verb-relation-class SA among those computed for each WordNet class the argument belongs to:

$$SA_{v,r,c} = \frac{p(c|v, r) \, log \frac{p(c|v,r)}{p(c|r)}}{SPS_{v,r}} \quad (2)$$

Resnik's work inspired more taxonomy-based models of SA over the years (Grishman and Sterling, 1992; Abe and Li, 1996; Ciaramita and Johnson, 2000; Clark and Weir, 2001; Alishahi and Stevenson, 2007; Padó et al., 2009), but no further refinements of the SPS itself.

Distributional Semantic Models (DSMs) (Lenci, 2018) instead tackle the main drawback of taxonomy-based models, i.e. the need for a manually-built lexicon, by requiring no other resource than the corpus they are trained on. They rely on different strategies to compute SA, such as clustering (Pereira et al., 1993), Support Vector Machines (Bergsma et al., 2008), and hybrid approaches (Schulte im Walde et al., 2008).

Erk (2007) and Erk et al. (2010) provide a cognitively plausible distributional model that proves particularly relevant for our purposes. Given a verb-relation pair, it computes the plausibility of a potential argument of the pair (i.e., the SA of the triple) via the weighted similarity between that argument and the exemplar arguments stored in the model as vectors, as shown in Eq. 3:

$$SA_{v,r}(a_0) = \sum_{a \in args(v,r)} wt_{v,r}(a) \, sim(a_0, a) \quad (3)$$

3   PISA: a novel measure of Preference In Selection of Arguments

We introduce **PISA**, our own distributional measure of **Preference In Selection of Arguments**, which we use to model argument recoverability in the spirit of Resnik's SPS. It stems from the intuition that *the vector-based SPS of a given verb-relation pair should be positively correlated with the distributional similarity of their arguments*. The simplest way to capture this notion is by computing the **semantic density** of the verb-relation pair as the mean value of the pairwise cosine similarity between the arguments of the pair. In order to take into account the fact that some arguments are more associated with a given verb-relation pair than others, it is possible to compute a **weighted** measure of semantic density. This is tantamount to averaging Erk et al. (2010)'s SA in Eq. 3 over n arguments of a given verb-relation pair:

$$PISA_{v,r} = \frac{1}{n} \sum_{i=1}^{n} SA_{v,r}(a_i) \qquad (4)$$

As in previous literature, relations in our model may be syntactic ones or semantic roles, depending on their availability in a corpus. We used only one similarity measure, cosine.

3.1 Weighted models

We assigned a weight to each argument in our equation based on the 5 weight functions below. The weight functions UNI, FRQ and IDF are taken from Erk et al. (2010):

UNI assumes a uniform distribution:

$$wt_{v,r}(a) = 1 \qquad (5)$$

FRQ is the co-occurrence frequency of a given argument with the verb-relation pair:

$$wt_{v,r}(a) = freq(a, v, r) \qquad (6)$$

IDF is inspired to the well-known Inverse Document Frequency weighting scheme, which assigns higher scores to arguments occurring with fewer verb-relation pairs:

$$wt_{v,r}(a) = \log \frac{|v,r|}{|v,r : a \in v,r|} \qquad (7)$$

LMI is the Local Mutual Information of the argument and a given verb-relation pair:

$$wt_{v,r}(a) = f(a, v, r) \log_2 \frac{p(a, v, r)}{p(a)p(v, r)} \qquad (8)$$

ENT is the entropy of the argument of a given verb-relation pair:

$$wt_{v,r}(a) = -\sum_{a \in args(v,r)} p(a) \log_2 p(a) \qquad (9)$$

with $p(x) = \frac{f(x)}{\sum_{a \in A} f(a)}$ where A is the complete set of arguments extracted. We entered in the equation only the verbs of our interest.

3.2 Unweighted models

In addition to the weighted models, we created unweighted models taking into consideration only the top/bottom k argument nouns for each verb-relation pair, sorted based on the FRQ, IDF, LMI

and ENT weighting functions. In particular we considered the top/bottom 300 nouns for the direct object relation and the top/bottom 20 for the Instrument semantic role. The parameters were determined empirically depending on the fact that our transitive verbs occur with a large number of direct objects, while our Instrument-verbs occur with a much smaller set of Instruments. Both top-k and bottom-k models were computed as not all weighting functions are directly proportional to PISA (e.g. a high IDF means that the nouns is quite selective with respect to what verbs it appears with, whereas high entropy means the opposite).

4 Experimental settings

The datasets and the scripts we used to run our model are freely available on GitHub[1].

4.1 Datasets

We tested our model on two datasets:

- 99 transitive verbs (50 recoverable-object + 49 non-recoverable-object), comprising Resnik's original 34-verb dataset, 35 recoverable-object verbs from Levin (1993), and 30 non-recoverable-object verbs we sampled among high-frequency transitive verbs.

- 173 Instrument verbs (116 recoverable-Instrument + 57 non-recoverable-Instrument), taken from Koenig et al. (2007).

4.2 Extraction of verb arguments

We extracted the arguments participating in the verb-relation pairs of our interest from ukWaC, a 2-billion token part-of-speech tagged and lemmatized corpus of English (Ferraresi et al., 2008). We limited the extraction to the head nouns of the phrases involved in a direct object or Instrument relation with each verb, excluding determiners and modifiers (e.g., *sword* instead of *a big rusty sword*). We mapped the Instrument role to PPs headed by *with* and having an Artifact as a noun argument[2], following Erk et al. (2010) in considering syntactic relations as noisy approximations of semantic roles. Since we are only interested in implicit argument alternations (Ex. (3)), we discarded sentences having an Artifact subject to avoid including inchoative/causative alternations (Ex. (4)) and instrument alternations (Ex. (5)) in our computation.

---

[1]https://github.com/ellepannitto/PISA
[2]As defined in WordNet 3.0 (Miller, 1995)

SVD	w2v	w2vf
synt.c1000	CBOW.w10	SGNS.synt.c1000
synt.c500	CBOW.w2	SGNS.synt.c500
w10	SGNS.w10	SGNS.w10
w2	SGNS.w2	SGNS.w2

Table 1: Tested embedding types (w2v = word2vec; w2vf = word2vecf).

(3)   a.   John broke the vase with a hammer.
      b.   John broke the vase.

(4)   a.   John broke the vase with a hammer.
      b.   The vase broke.

(5)   a.   John broke the vase with a hammer.
      b.   The hammer broke the vase.

4.3 Word embeddings

As for the vector representation of arguments, we a variety of 300-dimensional embeddings trained on a concatenation of ukWaC and a 2018-dump of English Wikipedia. The embeddings we tested include both SVD reduced count-based DSMs and neural embeddings created via `word2vec`[3] (Mikolov et al., 2013), testing both SGNS and CBOW models, and `word2vecf` (Levy and Goldberg, 2014). We used both window-based and syntax-based contexts, and we tested different window sizes (2 or 10) for `word2vec` and SVD models, for a total of 12 models (Table 1).

5 Results and discussion

5.1 Resnik's SPS

We tested the hypothesis that recoverable-argument verbs have higher SPS scores than non-recoverable argument verbs, by means of Mann-Whitney U tests. We replicated Resnik's experiment by calculating the SPS scores for our transitive and Instrument verbs, based on the distribution of their arguments in ukWaC. The results are consistent with our and Resnik's hypothesis.

The mean score for transitive verbs is 4.27 for recoverable-object verbs and 1.89 for non-recoverable-object verbs. The difference between the two groups is significant ($U = 264$, $n_1 = 50$, $n_2 = 49$, $P < .001$). Similarly, the mean score for Instrument verbs is 4.72 for recoverable-Instrument verbs and 3.60 for non-recoverable-Instrument verbs, and their difference is significant too ($U = 4646$, $n_1 = 116$, $n_2 = 57$, $P < .001$).

[3]https://code.google.com/archive/p/word2vec/

		weighted	top k	bot k
UNI	SVD	***	–	–
	w2v	***	–	–
	w2vf	** (***)	–	–
FRQ	SVD	***	** (***)	ns
	w2v	***	***	ns
	w2vf	***	** (***)	ns
IDF	SVD	***	** (ns)	ns (***)
	w2v	***	*** (ns)	***
	w2vf	** (***)	ns	ns
LMI	SVD	*** (**)	** (ns)	ns (**)
	w2v	***	* (ns)	*
	w2vf	*** (*)	* (ns)	* (**)
ENT	SVD	*** (*)	ns (***)	ns
	w2v	*** (**)	***	ns
	w2vf	*** (**)	* (ns)	*

Table 2: Mann-Whitney U tests comparing recoverable- and non-recoverable-argument verbs (significance levels). Whenever transitive and Instrument-verb results are different, the former are on the left and the latter on the right of the same cell

5.2 PISA

In Tables 2 to 4, we collapsed the results from the 12 distributional models into three types (see Table 1), since there are no within-group notable differences. For each group, we report the worst score. Significance levels are given as follows: *** $p \leq 0.001$, ** $p \leq 0.01$, * $p \leq 0.05$, *ns* $p > 0.05$.

As shown in Table 2, PISA can reliably separate the two groups of recoverable- and non-recoverable-argument verbs based on Mann-Whitney U tests comparing the mean score of the two groups. Looking closer at the results, it appears that the weighted versions of PISA yield highly significant results overall, while the versions using the top k nouns yield varying results depending on both the weights and the distributional spaces. The most notable pattern within the top-k models is that the word2vec spaces lead to consistently significant results, and FRQ appears to be the best-performing weight.

The same significance pattern observed for the Mann-Whitney U scores is found, with slight differences, in the Spearman correlations (Tables 3 and 4). In this case, we considered how much the ranking of our set of verbs based on PISA is similar to the ranking yielded by Resnik's SPS, since PISA is intended to improve on Resnik's methodology, while building on the same theoretical premises. Once again, the best scores come from the weighted models (especially those weighted with entropy), and the FRQ models are the best within the top-k group.

		weighted	top300	bot300
UNI	SVD	.832***	-	-
	w2v	.851***	-	-
	w2vf	.250*	-	-
FRQ	SVD	.854***	.341***	-.041 ns
	w2v	.835***	.712***	-.024 ns
	w2vf	.743***	-.368***	-.090 ns
IDF	SVD	.750***	-.328***	.211 ns
	w2v	.818***	-.388***	.457***
	w2vf	.256*	-.154 ns	.164 ns
LMI	SVD	.791***	-.385***	-.092 ns
	w2v	.711***	-.135 ns	.129 ns
	w2vf	.667***	-.092 ns	.091 ns
ENT	SVD	-.905***	.163 ns	.111 ns
	w2v	-.908***	.579***	.134 ns
	w2vf	-.911***	.254*	.320**

Table 3: Spearman correlations between PISA and Resnik scores for transitive verbs.

		weighted	top20	bot20
UNI	SVD	.404***	-	-
	w2v	.244***	-	-
	w2vf	.105 ns	-	-
FRQ	SVD	.283***	.481***	-.025 ns
	w2v	.179*	.519***	-.005 ns
	w2vf	.127 ns	.326***	.037 ns
IDF	SVD	.384***	.005 ns	.135 ns
	w2v	.242***	.09 ns	.265***
	w2vf	.082 ns	.176*	.03 ns
LMI	SVD	.170*	.152*	-.011 ns
	w2v	.134 ns	.134 ns	-.065 ns
	w2vf	.077 ns	.266***	-.013 ns
ENT	SVD	-.885***	.118 ns	.003 ns
	w2v	-.920***	.256***	.088 ns
	w2vf	-.928***	.031 ns	.334***

Table 4: Spearman correlations between PISA and Resnik scores for Instrument verbs.

6 Conclusions and future work

In this paper, we presented a novel distributional measure of semantic selectivity (PISA) and used it to quantify direct object and Instrument recoverability. Most notably, PISA achieves a degree of precision comparable with Resnik's SPS but at a much cheaper computational cost, since it does not require a taxonomy or other lexical resources external to the training corpus.

Considering the full picture provided in Tables 2 to 4, the question arises of which is the best choice amongst the various PISA variants. We believe there is no univocal answer. The simplest solution would be to choose a UNI weighted model, since it does requires neither an additional step to compute the weight nor an assessment of the optimal value of k to compute the top-k models. If one cares for their results to resemble Resnik's in the verb ranking, the most conservative solution would be to choose an ENT weighted model. If one works with a very large set of verbs, each occurring with many different arguments, the computationally most parsimonious solution would be to choose a UNI or better a FRQ top-k model.

It will be interesting to use our new measure to predict the recoverability of arguments participating in other syntactic relations or semantic roles, to see whether it generalizes to them and to what extent.

Acknowledgments

We would like to thank Ludovica Pannitto for helping us with the computational implementation of our model, Najoung Kim for her contribution to the shaping of the ideas hereby presented, and the anonymous reviewers for their comments and suggestions.

References

Naoki Abe and Hang Li. 1996. Learning Word Association Norms Using Tree Cut Pair Models.

Afra Alishahi and Suzanne Stevenson. 2007. A cognitive model for the representation and acquisition of verb selectional preferences. In *Proceedings of the Workshop on Cognitive Aspects of Computational Language Acquisition*, pages 41–48, Prague, Czech Republic. Association for Computational Linguistics.

Shane Bergsma, Dekang Lin, and Randy Goebel. 2008. Discriminative Learning of Selectional Preference from Unlabeled Text. In *Proceedings of the 2008*

Conference on Empirical Methods in Natural Language Processing, pages 59–68. Association for Computational Linguistics.

Massimiliano Ciaramita and Mark Johnson. 2000. Explaining away ambiguity: Learning verb selectional preference with Bayesian networks. In *COLING 2000 Volume 1: The 18th International Conference on Computational Linguistics*.

Stephen Clark and David Weir. 2001. Class-based probability estimation using a semantic hierarchy. In *Second Meeting of the North American Chapter of the Association for Computational Linguistics*.

Kathy Conklin, Jean-Pierre Koenig, and Gail Mauner. 2004. The role of specificity in the lexical encoding of participants. 90(1-3):221–230.

Katrin Erk. 2007. A simple, similarity-based model for selectional preferences. In *Proceedings of the 45th Annual Meeting of the Association of Computational Linguistics*, pages 216–223, Prague, Czech Republic. Association for Computational Linguistics.

Katrin Erk, Sebastian Padó, and Ulrike Padó. 2010. A Flexible, Corpus-Driven Model of Regular and Inverse Selectional Preferences. 36(4):723–763.

Adriano Ferraresi, Eros Zanchetta, Marco Baroni, and Silvia Bernardini. 2008. Introducing and evaluating ukwac, a very large web-derived corpus of english. In *In Proceedings of the 4th Web as Corpus Workshop (WAC-4*.

Lelia Glass. 2020. Verbs describing routines facilitate object omission in English. 5(1):44.

Ralph Grishman and John Sterling. 1992. Acquisition of Selectional Patterns. In *COLING 1992 Volume 2: The 15th International Conference on Computational Linguistics*.

Paul J. Hopper and Sandra A. Thompson. 1980. Transitivity in Grammar and Discourse. 56(2):251.

Otto Jespersen. 1927. *A Modern English Grammar on Historical Principles. Part III. Syntax*, volume 2. Routledge.

Jean-Pierre Koenig, Gail Mauner, and Breton Bienvenue. 2002. Class Specificity and the Lexical Encoding of Participant Information. 81(1-3):224–235.

Jean-Pierre Koenig, Gail Mauner, and Breton Bienvenue. 2003. Arguments for adjuncts. *Cognition*, 89(2):67–103.

Jean-Pierre Koenig, Gail Mauner, Breton Bienvenue, and Kathy Conklin. 2007. What with? The Anatomy of a (Proto)-Role. 25(2):175–220.

Alessandro Lenci. 2018. Distributional Models of Word Meaning. *Annual Review of Linguistics*, 4:151–171.

Beth Levin. 1993. *English Verb Classes and Alternations: A Preliminary Investigation*. University of Chicago Press.

Omer Levy and Yoav Goldberg. 2014. Dependency-based word embeddings. In *Proceedings of the 52nd Annual Meeting of the Association for Computational Linguistics (Volume 2: Short Papers)*, pages 302–308.

Tamara Nicol Medina. 2007. Learning which verbs allow object omission: Verb semantic selectivity and the implicit object construction.

Tomas Mikolov, Kai Chen, Greg Corrado, and Jeffrey Dean. 2013. Efficient estimation of word representations in vector space. *arXiv preprint arXiv:1301.3781*.

George A. Miller. 1995. WordNet: A lexical database for English. *Communications of the ACM*, 38(11):39–41.

Ulrike Padó, Matthew W. Crocker, and Frank Keller. 2009. A Probabilistic Model of Semantic Plausibility in Sentence Processing. 33(5):794–838.

Fernando Pereira, Naftali Tishby, and Lillian Lee. 1993. Distributional clustering of English words. In *Proceedings of the 31st Annual Meeting on Association for Computational Linguistics -*, pages 183–190. Association for Computational Linguistics.

Philip Resnik. 1993. *Selection and Information: A Class-Based Approach to Lexical Relationships*. IRCS Technical Reports Series. University of Pennsylvania.

Philip Resnik. 1996. Selectional constraints: An information-theoretic model and its computational realization. 61(1-2):127–159.

Lilia Rissman and Kyle Rawlins. 2017. Ingredients of Instrumental Meaning. 34(3):507–537.

Sabine Schulte im Walde, Christian Hying, Christian Scheible, and Helmut Schmid. 2008. Combining EM Training and the MDL Principle for an Automatic Verb Classification Incorporating Selectional Preferences. In *Proceedings of ACL-08: HLT*, pages 496–504. Association for Computational Linguistics.

Learning Negation Scope from Syntactic Structure

Nick McKenna
School of Informatics
University of Edinburgh
nick.mckenna@ed.ac.uk

Mark Steedman
School of Informatics
University of Edinburgh
steedman@inf.ed.ac.uk

Abstract

We present a semi-supervised model which learns the semantics of negation purely through analysis of syntactic structure. Linguistic theory posits that the semantics of negation can be understood purely syntactically, though recent research relies on combining a variety of features including part-of-speech tags, word embeddings, and semantic representations to achieve high task performance. Our simplified model returns to syntactic theory and achieves state-of-the-art performance on the task of Negation Scope Detection while demonstrating the tight relationship between the syntax and semantics of negation.

1 Introduction

Negation is a semantic phenomenon in natural language which varies significantly. For example, "Sherlock did not solve the case" contains a simple negation cued by "not." However, there are many cue words such as "without" and "nothing," and word affixes like "un-" which instantiate negation, and their effect on meaning can be different and dependent on context.

We approach the meaning of negation using a logical semantics, in which natural language negation is expressed with the negation operator on logical expressions (Horn, 1989; Horn and Wansing, 2017), such as in $\neg$SOLVE($Sherlock, case$). Further, in truth-theoretic logic the meaning of negation is simply the inverted truth value of this expression. Capturing the meaning of a negation cue in language can thus be understood as simply identifying the negated expression. This is the task of Negation Scope Detection (NSD): given a negation cue in a sentence, identify the sentence tokens which make up the negated expression.

1.1 Negation Scope Detection Task

The task of NSD has been approached in several formulations using different annotation schemes (Kim et al., 2008; Szarvas et al., 2008), but these older tasks do not define negation semantically, in contrast to the commonly accepted *SEM2012 Shared Task competition (*SEM, 2012). Under the *SEM definition cues scope over events and participants, either directly or via predicate arguments and complements. Linguistic theory explains negation semantics in terms of events, which are built from syntactic phrase structures (Huddleston and Pullum, 2005), i.e. that negation doesn't just scope over individual words, but rather whole phrases and clauses which make up events. The following examples drawn from the *SEM2012 dataset of Conan Doyle writing illustrate how scope is built from phrase structures. Cues are in **bold*** with <u>underlined</u> scope.

(1) Well, sir, I thought **no*** <u>good could come of it</u>.

Example (1) contains the main verb "thought" which takes a complement clause. This clause contains a simple verb "come" negated by its negative subject "no good." The correct negation scope covers this verb, its arguments, and its modifier "could" (leaving out the cue itself, following *SEM convention). Figure 1 (a) shows that scope corresponds to clause boundaries in the syntactic tree.

(2) He saw him once or twice but <u>he</u> is a deep one and <u>gives</u> **nothing*** <u>away</u>.

The scope in example (2) has discontinuous span. In this sentence "he" is a subject shared by two clauses in coordination, but only one of these is negated. Figure 1 (b) illustrates this. As cases add complexity it's clear that NSD requires reasoning about the underlying structure of the sentence.

*Proceedings of the Ninth Joint Conference on Lexical and Computational Semantics (*SEM), pages 137–142*
Barcelona, Spain (Online), December 12–13, 2020

1.2 Contributions

In this work we build on the theory of negation scope as a syntactic phenomenon and reframe the task of NSD as a tree tagging problem over syntactic constituents. We develop a new Structural Tree Recursive Neural Network for this task which labels scope for constituents conditioned on just the syntactic structure of the sentence, with no other features. Our model achieves the highest score to date on the *SEM2012 dataset. We further show that adding word embedding features does not improve results, demonstrating that efficient use of syntax is all you need to perform well on this task.

2 Previous Work

There have been a variety of approaches to NSD. The *SEM shared task dataset is the only resource available with semantic annotations (other NSD datasets are annotated for different goals), but there are many models which use *SEM to compare with (Morante and Blanco, 2012).

Fancellu et al. (2016) show the most recent, best-performing model on *SEM. It is a BiLSTM sequence tagging model which produces in-scope/out-of-scope classifications for each word, and jointly learns word embeddings with additional part-of-speech features for each token. However, further analysis (Fancellu et al., 2017) shows the model is over-reliant on punctuation like commas (",") which often mark scope boundaries in English and especially in Conan Doyle's older style of writing (the content of the *SEM dataset). The model does not learn a very robust semantics without these markers, yet also does not make use of the full syntactic structure of sentences. Fancellu et al. (2018) address this with a Dependency-LSTM model which processes dependency trees using encodings both for words and dependency relations. On a modified *SEM dataset this model slightly improves over the BiLSTM when they are ensembled together, showing again that the BiLSTM method lacks some structural understanding.

The original winner of *SEM, UiO_1 (Read et al., 2012), uses an SVM classifier on constituents that contain the cue. Constituents are shown to be useful, but this is not enough to capture discontinuous scopes (see example (2)) which do not align to a single constituent. Read adds extra heuristics to help with this, and Rosenberg (2013) continues from this with a comprehensive set of syntactic heuristics deployed on dependency graphs. This model performs well and demonstrates the strength of syntax by itself for capturing negation semantics.

Packard et al. (2014) and Li et al. (2010) approach NSD "in the semantic domain." Packard first induces a Minimal Recursion Semantics parse of a sentence (Copestake et al., 2005), then crawls it to identify negated predicates and arguments. Though intuitive, inducing a full parse may overshoot the problem — by itself the crawler doesn't compete because it loses much information during parsing and backtracking to sentence words. Ensembling with UiO_1 provides a boost over UiO_1 itself, which indicates that MRS parsing provides complementary information, possibly due to induction of additional structure.

3 A Structural Approach

We argue for a solution returning to syntax which makes per-word scope judgements conditioned on the full syntactic structure of the sentence. Section 1.1 discusses the theoretical basis in syntax for negation semantics and section 2 details successful models on the task. While syntax is used by several models to a degree, full trees are rarely used and recent models rely on additional features like word embeddings to achieve high performance.

Combinatory Categorial Grammar (CCG) is a nearly context-free constituency grammar capable of describing complex phenomena like coordination (Steedman, 2000). CCG also has transparency between syntax and semantics: a CCG syntactic parse may be transformed into a logical form in terms of events, similar to the Sherlock example in section 1. Steedman (2011) separately formalizes a theory for computing the polarity of lexical items using a CCG-based calculus, which encourages an automated approach to learning negation scope by example.

Figure 1(a) shows the CCG parse tree for example (1). Commonly, simple independent clauses in English form one continuous scope span, which is distinguishable in syntax. The scope of negation in (1) is simply the complement clause.

However, it is not always the case that negation scope aligns cleanly to subtrees, like in example Figure 1(b), the parse tree for sentence (2). CCG provides structural insight which alleviates this problem. In this example CCG's explicit modeling of coordination makes it straightforward to identify the subject to the left of the coordinated dependent clauses.

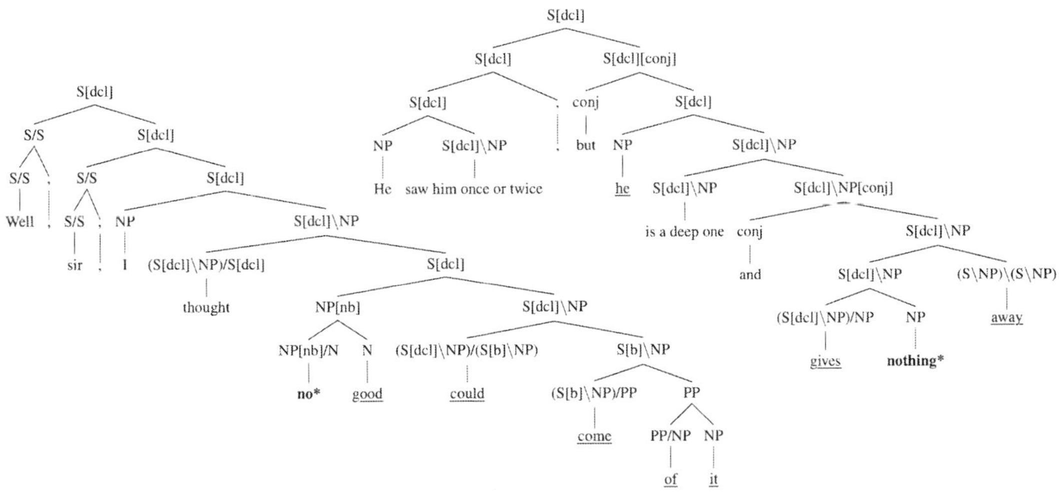

Figure 1: **(a)** (left) The cue "no" negates the subject "good" and thus scopes over the related event. This corresponds cleanly with the constituent subtree (headed by S[dcl]) which spans that text. **(b)** (right) The cue "nothing" lies in a dependent clause, lacking a subject. This can be found on the left using the CCG parse structure.

Understanding how semantics is built from phrase structures is key to our method. Analyses from additional sentences support this (see appendix for parse trees).

(3) <u>I</u> **never*** <u>hurt man or woman in my life</u> that I know of.

(4) <u>Some people</u> **without*** <u>possessing genius</u> have a remarkable power of stimulating it.

4 Methods

The Global Belief Tree Recursive Neural Network of Paulus et al. (2014) is adapted to solve this task. The GB-TRNN takes as input a binarized syntax tree (satisfied by CCG) and starting state vectors for each word in the sentence, referred to now as tree leaves. It first recursively combines constituent states from leaves to root in an upward pass, building up to a single, global state vector. Conditioned on this state, the downward pass recursively unfolds the global vector following the parse tree back down from the root to the leaves. The output for each constituent in the downward pass can be used to produce classifications conditioned on the entire tree.

We add additional syntactic target inputs in both passes and refer to this new architecture as a Structural Tree Recursive Neural Network (STRNN). These additional inputs represent the current kind of CCG combination. In the upward step the parent tag (composed category) is additionally passed in

with the two child states, while in the downward step the two child tags (decomposed categories) are passed in addition to the parent state.

The STRNN learns one embedding matrix for CCG syntactic categories $E_{Cat} \in \mathbb{R}^{|V_{CCG}| \times s}$, where V_{CCG} is the CCG category vocabulary ($\sim$400 tags) and the embedding size $s = 50$. Figure 2 shows a diagram of the STRNN.

Upward Pass. The initial state $\mathbf{u}_i$ for a leaf constituent i is the result of the transformation matrix $H \in \mathbb{R}^{(s+c) \times h}$. This consumes a category embedding and the cue feature c to produce an initial upward state $\mathbf{u}_i$ of size $h = 200$. c is a binary indicator expressing if the word is a cue. Note that only a word's CCG category and cue status are shown to the model.

The STRNN first makes an upward pass through the syntax tree. This pass recursively combines two child constituent states $\mathbf{u}_{left}$ and $\mathbf{u}_{right}$ as well as the target parent category embedding $\mathbf{s}_{parent} \in E_{Cat}$ to produce an upward state for the parent constituent $\mathbf{u}_{parent}$. A weight matrix $W^{\uparrow} \in \mathbb{R}^{(2h+s) \times h}$ is learned for this operation.

$$\mathbf{x} = [\mathbf{u}_{left} ; \mathbf{u}_{right} ; \mathbf{s}_{parent}]$$
$$\mathbf{u}_{parent} = tanh(\mathbf{x}W^{\uparrow} + \mathbf{b}^{\uparrow})$$

Downward Pass. The top level hidden state of size h, GLOBAL$^{\uparrow}$, is then transformed with the matrix $G \in \mathbb{R}^{h \times h}$ to make the GLOBAL$^{\downarrow}$ downward state following Paulus. This is recursively unfolded

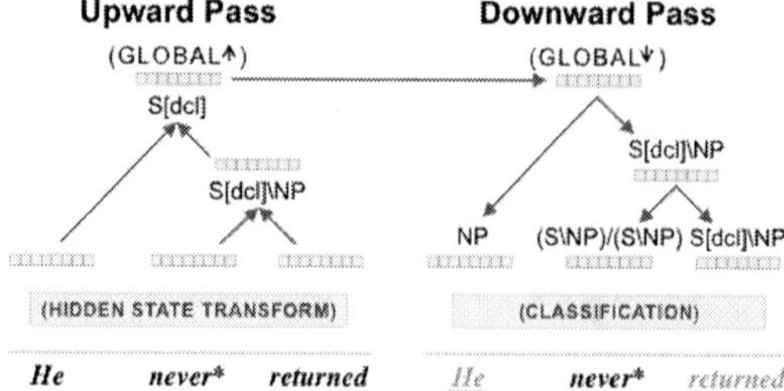

Figure 2: (Left) Upward pass: recursive composition of constituent states from leaves to root. (Right) Downward pass: recursive decomposition of constituent states from root to leaves. **NB:** The model sees only the CCG parse and cue. Word identities are hidden.

down the tree to the leaves using the learned matrix $W^\downarrow \in \mathbb{R}^{(2h+2s)\times 2h}$.

The recursive cell consumes two recurrent inputs following Paulus: the downward parent state $\mathbf{d}_{parent}$ and upward state $\mathbf{u}_{parent}$. We supply additional inputs which instruct the cell how to decompose the state vector, the target child category embeddings $\mathbf{s}_{left}, \mathbf{s}_{right} \in E_{Cat}$. The cell produces a double-wide state vector which is split into left- and right-child state vectors $\mathbf{d}_{left}$ and $\mathbf{d}_{right}$. Completing the downward pass results in a globally-informed information state $\mathbf{d}_j$ for each constituent j in the syntax tree.

$$\mathbf{x} = [\mathbf{u}_{parent} ; \mathbf{d}_{parent} ; \mathbf{s}_{left} ; \mathbf{s}_{right}]$$
$$[\mathbf{d}_{left} ; \mathbf{d}_{right}] = tanh(\mathbf{x}W^\downarrow + \mathbf{b}^\downarrow)$$

Classification. Classifications are produced using the matrix $C \in \mathbb{R}^{2h\times 2}$ and a softmax activation. C takes as input, for any tree constituent j, the concatenation of $\mathbf{u}_j$ and $\mathbf{d}_j$ vectors. This can be applied in the same way to tree leaves (words) and to any higher tree constituent to produce a scope judgement.

Optimization. The model is semi-supervised. The *SEM dataset provides supervision signal only for which words are in scope, not general constituents. However, like the GB-TRNN, the STRNN produces classifications for all tree constituents, learning the general pattern from the supervision of words. During training the Adam optimizer was used with cross-entropy loss and 0.001 initial learning rate. Regularization is important with a small training set, and we used dropout following Gal and Ghahramani (2016) with recurrent connections set to 0.2 and others 0.5.

Model	Precision	Recall	F_1
Fancellu BiLSTM	92.62	85.13	88.72
MRS *Crawler*	85.8	68.4	76.1
UiO_1	81.99	88.81	85.26
STRNN	94.81	84.04	**89.10**
STRNN + BERT	89.36	86.54	87.93
STRNN + ST	92.56	83.38	87.73
Punctuation Baseline	65.60	89.47	75.70

Table 1: Table of Scope Tokens results for the *SEM2012 Negation Scope Detection test set. "ST" is self-trained embeddings learned jointly with the task. "BERT" is with pretrained embeddings.

5 Results

Table 1 shows performance results for the STRNN and key comparison models on the *SEM2012 test corpus. The conventional *SEM test metric is the F_1 measure of individual sentence tokens predicted in-scope of the cue. Not shown here is Fancellu's Dependency-LSTM, which published results on a modified version of *SEM. The corpus consists of sentences where each word is annotated with a gold label of in-scope or out-of-scope, and the negation cue. We augment these with CCG parses (Stanojević and Steedman, 2019).

Adapted from Fancellu et al. (2017) is a naïve baseline which predicts scope within the nearest punctuation marks left and right of the cue. It performs fairly well because punctuation indicates and defines grammatical structure. Compared to the STRNN this model overpredicts things like subordinate clauses (e.g. sentence (3)) and underpredicts distant arguments separated by e.g. an appositive.

Our base syntactic model outperforms the comparison models on the task, achieving a new state of the art on this dataset. Notably, it performs at least as well as the word embedding-based model, also the highest-scoring model to date, Fancellu's BiLSTM. Figure 1 actually shows correct model output on the example sentences, demonstrating the model on a simple case and a complex coordination. Given this, it might be interesting to ablate Fancellu's BiLSTM to see if it still performs well only using embeddings for POS tags. We note that POS tags contain punctuation markers, and as discussed in section 2 this model has been found to lean heavily on punctuation. The BiLSTM would be able to take advantage of these markers in the same way as before.

Word embeddings frequently boost performance in language disambiguation tasks by incorporating many kinds of information (Mikolov et al., 2013). We tested augmented STRNN models by adding word embeddings to leaves in addition to syntax embeddings. We obtain an embedding for each word in the sentence using BERT (Devlin et al., 2019) and concatenate this word embedding with our basic syntactic vector, which includes the CCG category embedding and cue status for the given word. We then proceed as before with learning and classification. We also tested a variant with randomly initialized word vectors which are jointly learned with the task. We found that both self-trained word embeddings and pretrained BERT embeddings provided no noticeable benefit to F_1 score on the task.

The model classifies all constituents in the syntax tree. We examined local labeling decisions within trees in the development set and found that in 89.9% of cases where a parent constituent has both children classified in-scope, the model also classifies the parent in-scope. On average, a constituent has a 24.1% chance of in-scope classification. This shows the model's preference for representing scope in larger phrase structures, aligning with the syntactic theory.

5.1 Error Analysis

Development set results for the base STRNN model were analyzed and 18 difficult sentences were found with accuracy below random chance guessing. The largest group of errors (11 sentences) were likely caused by CCG parsing errors. Some have speech-like text with stuttering, parentheticals, etc, and four have improper attachments within the parse tree affecting the scoped text. A few other sentences have fine CCG parses but are very complex, including one with a 19-word noun phrase. Many of these are related to the style of the genre.

To analyze model robustness, Pearson correlations of accuracy vs several factors were calculated. Negation cues do not always take a scope (such as with interjections) so we measure with accuracy instead of F_1. No correlation with accuracy was found for sentence length, maximum tree depth, cue depth in the tree, or tree balance.

6 Conclusions

We show the STRNN model effectively predicts negation scope using syntactic parse trees. State-of-the-art performance is achieved on the *SEM2012 Shared Task without identifying individual words or extracting features beyond syntax.

This result reverts to earlier theories about the relationship between syntax and negation semantics. Both word embeddings and semantic reasoning require large resource overhead in model parameters and processing, but efficient use of syntax is all that is needed for high performance on this task.

7 Acknowledgements

This work was supported in part by ERC H2020 Advanced Fellowship GA 742137 SEMANTAX, and an Edinburgh and Huawei Technologies Research Centre award.

References

Ann Copestake, Dan Flickinger, Carl Pollard, and Ivan A Sag. 2005. Minimal recursion semantics: An introduction. *Research on language and computation*, 3(2-3):281–332.

Jacob Devlin, Ming-Wei Chang, Kenton Lee, and Kristina Toutanova. 2019. BERT: Pre-training of deep bidirectional transformers for language understanding. In *Proceedings of the 2019 Conference of the North American Chapter of the Association for Computational Linguistics: Human Language Technologies, Volume 1 (Long and Short Papers)*, pages 4171–4186, Minneapolis, Minnesota. Association for Computational Linguistics.

Federico Fancellu, Adam Lopez, and Bonnie Webber. 2016. Neural networks for negation scope detection. In *Proceedings of the 54th Annual Meeting of the Association for Computational Linguistics (Volume 1: Long Papers)*, volume 1, pages 495–504.

Federico Fancellu, Adam Lopez, Bonnie Webber, and Hangfeng He. 2017. Detecting negation scope is easy, except when it isn't. In *Proceedings of the 15th Conference of the European Chapter of the Association for Computational Linguistics: Volume 2, Short Papers*, volume 2, pages 58–63.

Federico Fancellu, Adam Lopez, and Bonnie L. Webber. 2018. Neural networks for cross-lingual negation scope detection. *CoRR*, abs/1810.02156.

Yarin Gal and Zoubin Ghahramani. 2016. A theoretically grounded application of dropout in recurrent neural networks. In *Advances in neural information processing systems*, pages 1019–1027.

Laurence Horn. 1989. *A Natural History of Negation*. University of Chicago Press.

Laurence R. Horn and Heinrich Wansing. 2017. Negation. In Edward N. Zalta, editor, *The Stanford Encyclopedia of Philosophy*, spring 2017 edition. Metaphysics Research Lab, Stanford University.

Rodney Huddleston and Geoffrey K. Pullum. 2005. *A Student's Introduction to English Grammar*. Cambridge University Press.

Jin-Dong Kim, Tomoko Ohta, and Jun'ichi Tsujii. 2008. Corpus annotation for mining biomedical events from literature. *BMC bioinformatics*, 9(1):10.

Junhui Li, Guodong Zhou, Hongling Wang, and Qiaoming Zhu. 2010. Learning the scope of negation via shallow semantic parsing. In *Proceedings of the 23rd International Conference on Computational Linguistics*, COLING '10, pages 671–679, Stroudsburg, PA, USA. Association for Computational Linguistics.

Tomas Mikolov, Scott Wen-tau Yih, and Geoffrey Zweig. 2013. Linguistic regularities in continuous space word representations. In *Proceedings of the 2013 Conference of the North American Chapter of the Association for Computational Linguistics: Human Language Technologies (NAACL-HLT-2013)*. Association for Computational Linguistics.

Roser Morante and Eduardo Blanco. 2012. *SEM2012 shared task: Resolving the scope and focus of negation. In *Proceedings of the First Joint Conference on Lexical and Computational Semantics-Volume 1: Proceedings of the main conference and the shared task, and Volume 2: Proceedings of the Sixth International Workshop on Semantic Evaluation*, pages 265–274. Association for Computational Linguistics.

Woodley Packard, Emily M Bender, Jonathon Read, Stephan Oepen, and Rebecca Dridan. 2014. Simple negation scope resolution through deep parsing: A semantic solution to a semantic problem. In *Proceedings of the 52nd Annual Meeting of the Association for Computational Linguistics (Volume 1: Long Papers)*, volume 1, pages 69–78.

Romain Paulus, Richard Socher, and Christopher D Manning. 2014. Global belief recursive neural networks. In Z. Ghahramani, M. Welling, C. Cortes, N. D. Lawrence, and K. Q. Weinberger, editors, *Advances in Neural Information Processing Systems 27*, pages 2888–2896. Curran Associates, Inc.

Jonathon Read, Erik Velldal, Lilja , and Stephan Oepen. 2012. Uio1: Constituent-based discriminative ranking for negation resolution. In *Proceedings of the First Joint Conference on Lexical and Computational Semantics - Volume 1: Proceedings of the Main Conference and the Shared Task, and Volume 2: Proceedings of the Sixth International Workshop on Semantic Evaluation*, SemEval '12, pages 310–318, Stroudsburg, PA, USA. Association for Computational Linguistics.

Sabine Rosenberg. 2013. Negation triggers and their scope. Master's thesis, Concordia University.

*SEM. 2012. *SEM2012: First joint conference on lexical and computational semantics.

Miloš Stanojević and Mark Steedman. 2019. CCG parsing algorithm with incremental tree rotation. In *Proceedings of the 2019 Conference of the North American Chapter of the Association for Computational Linguistics: Human Language Technologies, Volume 1 (Long and Short Papers)*, pages 228–239, Minneapolis, Minnesota. Association for Computational Linguistics.

Mark Steedman. 2000. *The Syntactic Process*. MIT Press, Cambridge, MA, USA.

Mark Steedman. 2011. Negation and polarity. In *Taking Scope*, pages 175–208. The MIT Press.

György Szarvas, Veronika Vincze, Richárd Farkas, and János Csirik. 2008. The bioscope corpus: Annotation for negation, uncertainty and their scope in biomedical texts. In *Proceedings of the Workshop on Current Trends in Biomedical Natural Language Processing*, BioNLP '08, pages 38–45, Stroudsburg, PA, USA. Association for Computational Linguistics.

A Visuospatial Dataset for Naturalistic Verb Learning

Dylan Ebert
Brown University
dylan_ebert@brown.edu

Ellie Pavlick
Brown University
ellie_pavlick@brown.edu

Abstract

We introduce a new dataset for training and evaluating grounded language models. Our data is collected within a virtual reality environment and is designed to emulate the quality of language data to which a pre-verbal child is likely to have access: That is, naturalistic, spontaneous speech paired with richly grounded visuospatial context. We use the collected data to compare several distributional semantics models for verb learning. We evaluate neural models based on 2D (pixel) features as well as feature-engineered models based on 3D (symbolic, spatial) features, and show that neither modeling approach achieves satisfactory performance. Our results are consistent with evidence from child language acquisition that emphasizes the difficulty of learning verbs from naive distributional data. We discuss avenues for future work on cognitively-inspired grounded language learning, and release our corpus with the intent of facilitating research on the topic.

1 Introduction

While distributional models of semantics have seen incredible success in recent years (Devlin et al., 2018), most current models lack "grounding", or a connection between words and their referents in the non-linguistic world. Grounding is an important aspect to representations of meaning and arguably lies at the core of language "understanding" (Bender and Koller, 2020). Work on grounded language learning has tended to make opportunistic use of large available corpora, e.g. by learning from web-scale corpora of image (Bruni et al., 2012) or video captions (Sun et al., 2019), or has been driven by particular downstream applications such as robot navigation (Anderson et al., 2018).

In this work, we take an aspirational look at grounded distributional semantics models, based on the type of situated contexts and weak supervision from which children are able to learn much of their early vocabulary. Our approach is motivated by the assumption that building computational models which emulate human language processing is in itself a worthwhile endeavor, which can yield both scientific (Potts, 2019) and engineering (Linzen, 2020) advances in NLP. Thus, we aim to develop a dataset that better reflects both the advantages and the challenges of humans' naturalistic learning environments. For example, unlike most vision-and-language models, children likely have the advantage of access to symbolic representations of objects and their physics prior to beginning word learning (Spelke and Kinzler, 2007). However, also unlike NLP models, which are typically trained on image or video captions with strong signal, children's language input is highly unstructured and the content is often hard to predict given only the grounded context (Gillette et al., 1999).

We make two main contributions. First (§2), using a virtual reality kitchen environment, we collect and release[1] the New Brown Corpus[2]: A dataset containing 18K words of spontaneous speech alongside rich visual and spatial information about the context in which the language occurs. Our protocol is designed to solicit naturalistic speech and to have good coverage of vocabulary items with low average ages of acquisition according to data on child language development (Frank et al., 2017). Second (§3), we use our corpus to compare several distributional semantics models, specifically comparing mod-

---

[1]https://github.com/dylanebert/nbc

[2]Our university namesake, plus paying homage to important Brown corpora in both NLP (Francis and Kucera, 1979) and Child Language Acquisition (Brown, 1973).

*Proceedings of the Ninth Joint Conference on Lexical and Computational Semantics (*SEM)*, pages 143–153
Barcelona, Spain (Online), December 12–13, 2020

els which represent the environment in terms of objects and their physics to models which represent the environment in terms of pixels. We focus on verbs, which have received considerably less attention in work on grounded language learning than have nouns and adjectives (Forbes et al., 2019). More so than nouns, verb learning is believed to rely on subtle combinations of both syntactic and grounded contextual signals (Piccin and Waxman, 2007) and thus progress on verb learning is likely to require new approaches to modeling and supervision. In our experiments, we find that strong baseline models, both feature-engineered and neural network models, perform only marginally above chance. However, comparing models reveals intuitive differences in error patterns, and points to directions for future research.

2   Data

The goal of our data collection is to enable research on grounded distributional semantics models using data that better resembles the type of input young children receive on a regular basis during language development. Doing this fully is ambitious if not impossible. Thus, we focus on a few aspects of children's language learning environment that are lacking from typical grounded language datasets and that can be emulated well given current technology: 1) spontaneous speech (i.e. as opposed to contrived image or video captions) and 2) rich information about the 3D world (i.e. physical models of the environment as opposed to flat pixels).

We develop a virtual reality (VR) environment within which we collect this data in a controlled way. Our environment data is described in Section 2.1 and our language data is described in Section 2.2. Our collection process results in a corpus of 152 minutes of concurrent video, audio, and ground-truth environment information, totaling 18K words across 18 unique speakers performing six distinct tasks each. The current data is available for download in json format at `https://github.com/dylanebert/nbc`. The code needed to implement the described environment and data recording is available at `https://github.com/dylanebert/nbc_unity_scripts`.

2.1   Environment Data Collection

2.1.1   Environment Construction

Our environment is a simple kitchen environment, implemented in Unity with SteamVR and our experiments are conducted using an HTC Vive headset. We choose to use VR as opposed to alternative interfaces for simulated interactions (e.g. keyboard or mouse control) since VR enables participants to use their usual hand and arm motions and to narrate in real time, leading to more natural speech and more faithful simulations of the actions they are asked to perform.

We design six different kitchen environments, using two different visual aesthetics (Fig. 1) with three floorplans each. This variation is so that we can test, for example, that learned representations are not overfit to specific pixel configurations or to exact hand positions that are dependent on the training environment(s) (e.g. "being in the northwest corner of the kitchen" as opposed to "being near the sink"). Each kitchen contains at least 20 common objects (not every kitchen contains every object). These objects were selected because they represent words with low average ages of acquisition (described in detail in §2.2) and were available in different Unity packages and thus could be included in the environment with different appearances. Across all kitchens, the movable objects used are: `Apple, Ball, Banana, Book, Bowl, Cup, Fork, Knife, Lamp, Plant, Spoon, Toy1:Bear|Bunny, Toy2:Doll|Dinosaur, Toy3:Truck|Plane`. The participant's hands and head are also included as movable objects. We also include the following immovable objects: `Cabinets, Ceiling, Chair, Clock, Counter, Dishwasher, Door, Floor, Fridge, Microwave, Oven, Pillar, Rug, Sink, Stove, Table, Trash Bin, Wall, Window`.

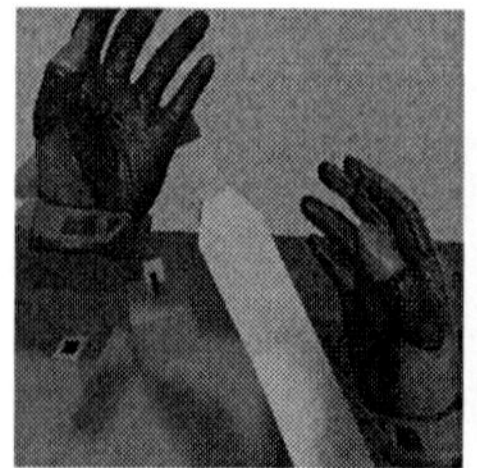

Figure 1: Screenshots of a person picking up a banana in each of our two kitchen aesthetics.

Our environments are constructed using a combination of Unity Asset Store assets and custom models. All paid assets (most objects we used) come from two packs: 3DEverything Kitchen Collection 2 and Synty Studios Simple House Interiors, from the Unity asset store[3]. These packs account for the two visual styles. VR interaction is enabled using the SteamVR Unity plugin, available for free on the Unity asset store.

2.1.2 Data Recording

During data collection, we record the physical state of each object in the environment, according to the ground-truth in-game data, at a rate of 90fps (frames per second). The Vive provides accurate motion capture, allowing us to record the physical state of the user's head and hands (Borges et al., 2018) as well. For each object, we record the physical features described in Table 1. Audio data is also collected in parallel to spatial data, using the built-in microphone. We later transcribe the audio using the Google Cloud Speech-to-Text API[4]. Word-level timestamps from the API allow us to match words to visuospatial frames. While spatial and audio data are recorded in real-time, video recording is not, since this would introduce high computational overhead and drop frames. Instead, we iterate back over the spatial data, and reconstruct/rerender the playback frame-by-frame. This approach makes it possible to render from any perspective if needed, though our provided image data is only from the original first-person perspective.

2.2 Language Data Collection

We design our protocol so as to solicit the use of vocabulary items that are known to be common among children's early-acquired words. To do this, we first select 20 nouns, 20 verbs, and 20 prepositions/adjectives which have low average ages of acquisition according to Frank et al. (2017) and which can be easily operationalized within our VR environment (e.g. *"apple"*, *"put (down)"*, *"red"*, see Appendix A for full word list). We then choose six basic tasks which the participants will be instructed to carry out within the environment. These tasks are: set the table, eat lunch, wash dishes, play with toys, describe a given object, and clean up toys. The tasks are

intended to solicit use of many of the target vocabulary items without explicitly instructing participants to use specific words, since we want to avoid coached or stilted speech as much as possible. One exception is the "describe a given object" task, in which we ask participants to describe specific objects as though a child has just asked what the object is, e.g. *"What's a spoon?"*. We use this task to ensure uniform coverage of vocabulary items across environments, so that we can construct good train/test splits across differently appearing environments. See Appendix B for details on distributing vocabulary items.

We recruited 18 participants for our data collection. Participants were students and faculty members from multiple departments involved with language research. We asked each participant to perform each of our tasks, one by one, and to narrate their actions as they went, as though they were a parent or babysitter speaking to a young child. The exact instructions given to participants before each task are shown in Appendix C. An illustrative example of the language in our corpus is the following: *"okay let's pick up the ball and play with that will it bounce let's see if we can bounce it exactly let's let it drop off the edge yes it bounced the ball bounced pick it up again..."*. The full data can be browsed at `https://github.com/dylanebert/nbc`.

Our study design was determined not to be human subjects research by the university IRB. All participants were informed of the purpose of the study and provided signatures consenting to the recording and release of their anonymized data for research purposes (consent form in Appendix D).

2.3 Comparison to Child Directed Speech

Since our stated goal was to collect data that better mirrors the distribution of language input a young child is likely to receive, we run several corpus analyses to assess whether this goal was met.

2.3.1 Vocabulary Distribution

First, we compare the distribution of vocabulary in our collected data to that observed in the Brent-Siskind Corpus (Brent and Siskind, 2001), a corpus of child-directed speech consisting of 16 English-speaking mothers speaking to their preverbal children. For reference, we also compare with the vocabulary distributions of three existing corpora which could be used for training distributional semantics models: 1) MSR-VTT (Xu et al.,

---

[3]`https://assetstore.unity.com/`
[4]`https://cloud.google.com/text-to-speech/`

Name (Type)	Description
pos (xyz)	Absolute position of object center, computed using the `transform.position` property; equivalent to position relative to an arbitrary world origin, approximately in the center of the floor.
rot (xyzw)	Absolute rotation of object, computed using the `transform.rotation` property.
vel (xyz)	Absolute velocity of object center, computed using the `VelocityEstimator` class included with SteamVR.
relPos (xyz)	Position of object's center relative to the person's head, computed using Unity's built-in `head.transform.TransformPoint(objectPosition)`.
relRot (xyzw)	Rotation of object relative to the person's head, computed by applying the inverse of the head rotation to the object rotation.
relVel (xyz)	Velocity of the object's center, from the frame of reference of the person's head
bound (xyz)	Distance from object's center to the edge of bounding box
inView (bool)	Whether or not the object was in the person's field of view, computed using Unity's `GeometryUtility` to compute if an object is in the Camera renderer bounds. This is based on the default camera's 60 degree FOV, not the wide headset FOV. The head and hands are always considered *inView*.
img_url (img)	Snapshot of the person's entire field of view as a 2D image. We compute this once per frame (as opposed to the above features which are computed once per object per frame).

Table 1: Object features recorded during data collection. Object appearance does not vary across frames; img_url does not vary across objects. All other features vary across object and frame.

2016), a large dataset of YouTube videos labeled with captions, 2) Room2Room (R2R) (Anderson et al., 2018), a dataset for instruction following within a 3D virtual world, and 3) a random sample of sentences drawn from Wikipedia. Since our primary focus is on grounded language, MSR and R2R offer the more relevant points of comparison, since each contains language aligned with some kind of grounded semantic information (raw RGB video feed for MSR and video+structured navigation map for R2R). We include Wikipedia to exemplify the type of web corpora that are ubiquitous in work on representation learning for NLP.

Figure 2 shows, for each of the five corpora, the token- and type-level frequency distributions over major word categories[5] and of individual lexical items. In terms of word categories, we see that our data most closely mirrors the distribution of child-directed speech: Both our corpus and the Brent corpus contain primarily verbs ($\sim$23% when computed at the token level) followed by pronouns ($\sim$19%) followed by nouns at around 17%. In contrast, the MSR video caption corpus and Wikipedia both contain predominantly nouns ($\sim$40%) and the R2R instruction dataset contains nouns and verbs in equal proportions ($\sim$33% each). None of the baseline corpora contain significant counts of pronouns. Additionally, in terms of specific vocabulary items, our cor-

pus contains decent coverage for many of the most frequent verbs observed in CDS, while the baseline corpora are dominated by a single verb each (*"go"* for R2R and *"be"* for MSR and Wikipedia). For nouns and adjectives, we also see better coverage of top-CDS words in our data compared to the other corpora analyzed, though we note that the difference is less obvious and that the lexical items in these categories are much more topically determined.

2.3.2 Word-Context Alignment

We next look at how well the language corresponds to the the salient objects and events in the context of its use. This property is important as it relates to how strong the "training signal" would be for a model that is attempting to learn linguistic meaning from distributional signal. It is hard to directly estimate the quality of the "training signal" available to children. However, experiments in psychology using the Human Simulation Paradigm (HSP) (Gillette et al., 1999; Piccin and Waxman, 2007) come close. In the HSP design, experimenters collect audio and video recordings of a child's normal activities (i.e. via head-mounted cameras). Given this data, adults are asked to view segments of videos and predict which words are said at given points in time. This technique is used to estimate how "predictable" language is given only the grounded (non-linguistic) input to which a child has access. Using this technique, Gillette et al. (1999) estimates that nouns can be predicted at 45% accuracy and verbs at 15% accuracy.

---

[5]We preprocess all corpora using the SpaCy 2.3.2 preprocessing pipeline with the `en_core_web_lg` model. For our data and Brent, we process the entire corpus. Since MSR, R2R, and Wikipedia are much larger, we process a random sample of 5K sentences from each.

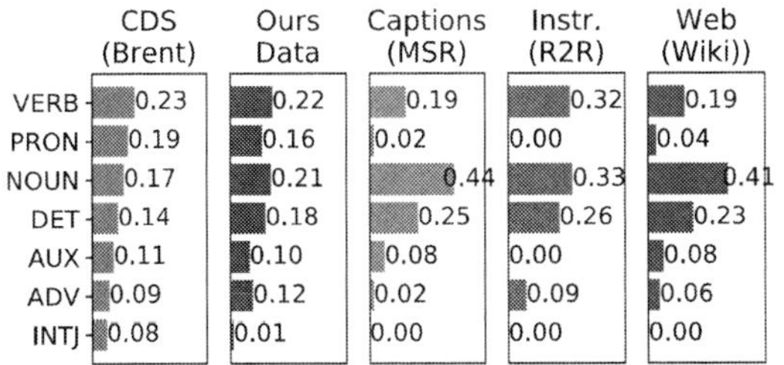

(a) Token-Level Frequency of Word Categories

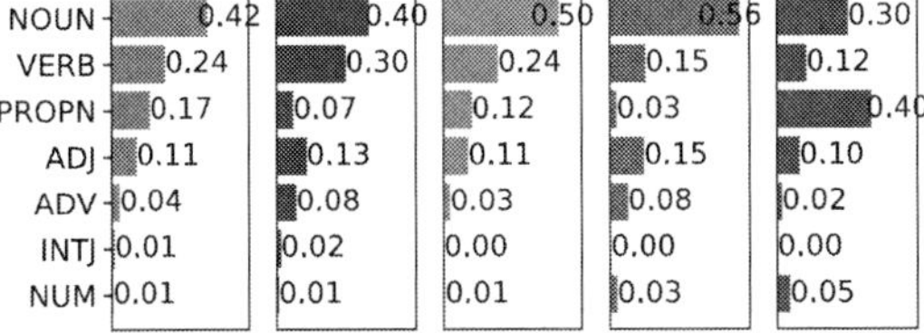

(b) Type-Level Frequency of Word Categories

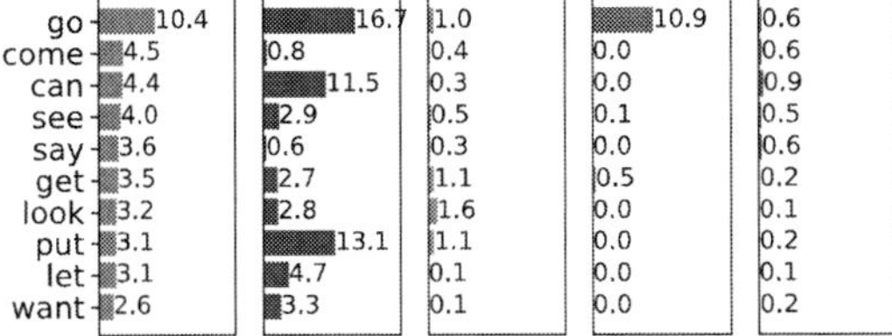

(c) Token Frequency of Individual Verbs

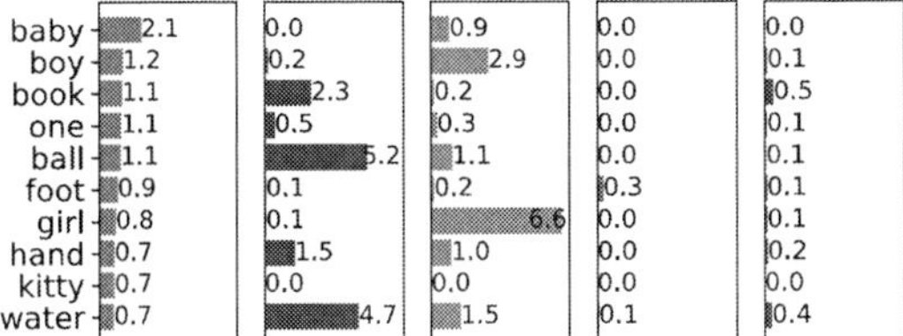

(d) Token Frequency of Individual Nouns

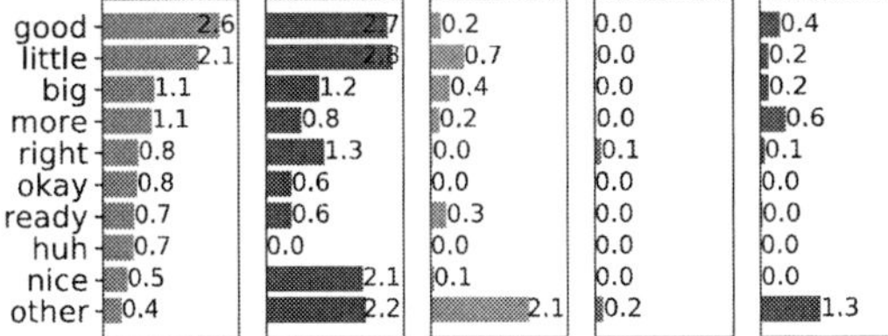

(e) Token Frequency of Individual Adjectives

Figure 2: Comparison of word category and lexical distributions. Lexical item frequencies labels are ×1000. Distributions are over the most frequent categories/words according to the Brent-Siskind corpus of child-directed speech.

While not directly comparable to our setting, this provides us with an approximate point of comparison against which to benchmark the word-to-context alignment of our collected data. Rather than try to guess the word given a video clip, we instead view a short (5 second) video clip alongside an uttered word and make a binary judgement for whether or not the clip depicts an instance of the word: e.g., *yes or no, does the clip depict an instance of "pick up"?* We chose this design over the HSP design since it provides a more interpretable measure of the quality of the training signal from the perspective of NLP and ML researchers using the data. We expect this variant of the task to yield higher numbers than the HSP design, since it does not require guessing from the entire vocabulary. We take a sample of (up to) five instances for each of our target nouns and verbs (fewer if the word occurs less often in our data) and label them in this way. We find inner annotator agreement on this task to be very high (91% when computed between two researchers on the project) and thus have a single annotator label all instances.

Table 2 shows the results of this analysis. We see the expected trend, in which grounded context is a considerably better signal of noun use than verb use. We also note there is substantial variation in training signal across verbs. For example, while some verbs (e.g. *"pick"*, *"take"*, *"hold"*) have strong signal, other verbs (*"eat"*) tend to be used in contexts sufficiently detached from the activities themselves. The noisiness of this signal is one of the biggest challenges of learning from such naturalistic data, as we will discuss further in §3.4.

3 Experiments

Using the above data, we now compare several grounded distributional semantics models (DSM) in terms of how well they encode verb meanings, focusing in particular on differences in how the environment is represented when put in to the DSM. Our hypothesis is that models will perform better if they represent the environment in terms of 3D objects and their physics rather than pixels, since work in psychology has shown that children learn to parse the physical world into objects and agents very early in life (Spelke and Kinzler, 2007), long before they show evidence of language understanding. We also explore how models vary when they have access to linguistic supervision early in the pipeline, during environment encoding, in addition to later, during language learning. We note that the models explored are intended as sim-

Nouns			Verbs		
w	N	P	w	N	P
table	81	1.0	go	238	0.0
spoon	76	1.0	put	193	0.4
banana	75	0.8	pick	162	0.8
apple	68	1.0	eat	77	0.0
cup	57	1.0	take	63	0.8
ball	54	0.6	get	43	0.4
toy	48	1.0	wash	38	0.6
fork	47	0.8	play	37	0.8
bowl	42	1.0	walk	25	0.4
knife	40	0.8	throw	25	0.6
book	25	1.0	hold	21	1.0
plant	22	1.0	drop	17	0.4
bear	18	1.0	stop	13	0.0
chair	16	0.4	give	13	0.0
doll	13	0.8	open	3	0.3
clock	12	0.6			
lamp	2	1.0			
door	2	0.0			
window	1	1.0			
Avg.	37	0.8	Avg.	64	0.4

Table 2: Estimates of training signal quality for nouns and verbs. N is the number of times the word occurs in the training data. P is the precision–given a 5 second clip in which the word is used, how often does the clip depict an instance of the word? Note that the verb *"go"* is an outlier, since it appears most often as *"going to"*.

ple instantiations to test the parameters of interest given our (small) dataset. Future work on more advanced models should no doubt yield improvements.

3.1 Preprocessing

Our raw data consists of continuous video and game-engine recordings of the environment, and parallel transcriptions of the natural language narration. To convert this into a format usable by our DSM, we perform the following preprocessing steps. This preprocessing phase is common to all the models evaluated. First, we segment the environment data into "clips". Each clip is five seconds long[6] and thus consists of 450 frames (since the VR environment recording is at 90fps), which we subsample to 50 frames (10fps). Since our grounded DSMs require associating a word w with its grounded context c, we consider the clip imme-

---

[6]The length of 5 seconds was chosen heuristically prior to model development.

diately following the utterance of w to be the context c. See earlier discussion (§2.3.2) for estimates of the signal-to-noise ratio produced by this labeling method. Training clips that are not the context of any word are discarded. We hold out two subjects' sessions (one from each visual aesthetic) for test, and use the remaining 16 subjects' sessions for training.

Finally, since this verb-learning problem proves quite challenging, we scope down our analysis to the following 14 verbs, which come from the 20 verbs specified in our initial target vocabulary (§2.2) less 6 which did not ultimately occur in our data: *"walk"*, *"throw"*, *"put (down)"*, *"get"*, *"go"*, *"give"*, *"wash"*, *"open"*, *"hold"*, *"eat"*, *"play"*, *"take"*, *"drop"*, *"pick (up)"*. Again, these words all have low average ages of acquisition (19 to 28 months) and thus should represent reasonable targets for evaluation. Nonetheless, we will see in §3.3 that models struggle to perform well on this task; we elaborate on this discussion in §4.

3.2 Models

We train and evaluate four different DSMs, each of which represent a word w in terms of its grounded context c. The parameters we vary are 1) the feature representation of c ($3.2.1) and 2) the type of supervision provided to the DSM (§3.2.2). All models share the same simple pipeline. First, we build a word-context matrix M which maps each token-level instance of w to a featurized representation of c. We then run dimensionality reduction on M. Finally, we take the type-level representation of w to be the average row vector of M, across all instances of w. All of our model code is available at `http://github.com/dylanebert/nbc_starsem`.

3.2.1 Context Encoders

Object-Based. In our Object-Based encoder, we take a feature-engineered approach intended to provide the model with a knowledge of the basic object physics likely to be relevant to the semantics of the verbs we target. Specifically, we represent each clip using four feature templates (`trajectory`, `vel`, `dist_to_head`, `relPos`), defined as follows. First, we find the "most moving object", i.e., the object with the highest average velocity over the clip. We then compute our four sets of features for this most moving object. Our `velocity` and `relPos` features are simply the `mean, min, max, start, end,` and `variance` of the object's velocity and relative position, respectively, over the clip. For our `dist_to_head` feature, for each position dimension (xyz), we compute the following values of the distance from the object's center to the participant's head: `start, end, mean, var, min, max, min_idx, max_idx,` where min/max index is the point at which min/max value was reached (recorded as a % of the way through the clip). Finally, our `trajectory` features are intended to capture the shape of the objects trajectory over the clip. To compute this, for each of position dimension (xyz), we compute four points during the clip: start, peak (max), trough (min), end. Then, if max happens before min, we consider the max to be "key point 1" (kp1) and the min to be "key point 2" (kp2), and vice-versa if the min happens before the max. We then compute the following features: `kp1-start, kp2-kp1, end-kp2, end-start.`

Pretrained CNN. To contrast with the above featured-engineered approach, we also implement an encoder based on the features extracted by a pretained CNN. Our CNN encoder has an advantage over the Object-Based encoder in that it has been trained on far more image data, but has a disadvantage in that it lacks domain-specific feature engineering. We use pretrained VGG16 (Simonyan and Zisserman, 2014), which is a 16-layer CNN trained on ImageNet that produces a 4096-dimensional vector for each image. We compute this vector for each frame in the clip, and then compute the following features along each dimension in order to get a vector representation of the full clip: `start_value, end_value, min, max, mean.`

3.2.2 Dimensionality Reduction

Given a matrix M that maps each word instance to a feature vector using one of the encoders above, we run dimensionality reduction to get a 10d vector[7] for each word instance. We consider two settings. In the unsupervised setting, we run vanilla SVD. In the supervised setting, we run supervised LDA in which the "labels" are the words uttered at the start of the clip as described in §3.1.

---

[7] 10d is chosen since we are only attempting to differentiate between 14 words, and thus our supervised LDA cannot use more than 13d.

3.3 Evaluation

We evaluate our models in terms of their precision when assigning verbs to unseen clips. Specifically, for our two heldout subjects, we partition the full session into consecutive 5-second clips, resulting in 189 clips total. For testing, unlike in training, we include all clips, even those in which the subject is not speaking. Then, for each model, we encode each clip using the model's encoder and then find the verb with the highest cosine similarity to the encoded clip. The authors then view each clip alongside the predicted verb and make a binary judgement for whether or not the verb accurately depicts the action in the clip, e.g. *yes or no, does the clip depict an instance of "pick up"?* To avoid annotation bias, all four models plus a random baseline are shuffled and evaluated together, and annotators do not know which prediction comes from which model. Annotator agreement was high (91%).

3.4 Results and Analysis

Table 3 reports our main results for each model. We compute both "strict" precision, in which a prediction is only considered correct if both annotators deemed it correct, as well as "soft" precision, in which a prediction is correct as long as one annotator deemed it correct. As the results show, no model performs especially well. Random guessing achieves 32% (soft) precision on average. The supervised Object-Based model and the unsupervised CNN model both perform a bit better (40% on average), but we note that the samples are small and we cannot call these differences significant (see 95% bootstrapped confidence intervals given in Table 3). Only the unsupervised Object-Based model stands out in that it performs significantly worse than all other models (20% soft precision). For the CNN models, we do not see a significant difference with the supervised dimensionality reduction. Figure 3 shows example clips for each encoder.

Table 4 shows a breakdown of model performance by verb. We see a few intuitive differences between the CNN-based model and the Object-Based model, discussed below. We note these observations are based on a small number of predictions, and thus should be taken only as suggestive.

Low-level actions. The Object-Based models achieve higher precision on low-level verbs like *"pick"*, *"take"*, and *"hold"*. This makes intuitive

Figure 3: Example clips, subsampled to 6 frames. **(b)** is **(a)**'s nearest-neighbor using the Object-Based model. In each of these clips, the participant picks up an object with their right hand. **(d)** is **(c)**'s nearest-neighbor using the CNN. In each, the participant is washing dishes in a similar looking sink.

	Soft	Strict
Random	0.32 (0.25–0.39)	0.23 (0.17–0.29)
Obj.	0.20 (0.14–0.25)	0.13 (0.08–0.19)
CNN	0.40 (0.33–0.47)	0.29 (0.22–0.36)
Obj+Sup.	0.40 (0.33–0.47)	0.28 (0.22–0.34)
CNN+Sup.	0.35 (0.28–0.42)	0.25 (0.19–0.31)

Table 3: Precision of each method with 95% bootstrapped CI. "Soft" means a prediction is correct as long as one annotator considers it to be so; "strict" means prediction is only considered correct if both annotators agree that it is correct.

	CNN		Obj		Obj+Sup.	
	N	Prec.	N	Prec.	N	Prec.
pick	0	0.00	1	1.00	4	1.00
take	0	0.00	3	1.00	12	0.67
hold	11	0.64	5	0.80	17	0.65
get	32	0.56	5	0.00	13	0.54
go	29	0.21	1	0.00	17	0.47
put	4	0.00	11	0.27	31	0.29
play	7	0.29	17	0.18	6	0.17
walk	16	0.44	33	0.30	26	0.15
throw	36	0.08	25	0.00	16	0.06
drop	4	0.25	16	0.06	2	0.00
eat	2	0.00	2	0.00	19	0.00
give	17	0.00	35	0.00	5	0.00
open	8	0.00	30	0.00	10	0.00
wash	23	0.48	5	0.00	11	0.00

Table 4: Analysis of model precision broken down by verb. Top-level columns are the unsupervised CNN, unsupervised obj model, and supervised obj model.[8] For each, N is the number of times the model predicts that verb. Precision is the proportion of the time that prediction was correct.

sense, since the 3D spatial features are designed to capture these types of mechanical actions, independent of the objects with which they co-occur. The 2D visual data, on the other hand, may struggle to ground a visually diverse set of objects-in-motion to these low-level mechanical actions.

Visual cues. Some actions are strongly predicted by specific objects, which are well captured by visual cues. This is most obvious in the case of *"wash"*, on which the CNN achieves higher precision than the Object-Based models. This is again intuitive as *wash* tends to co-occur with a clear view of the sink, which is a large, visually-distinct part of the field of view.

Vague actions. Actions like *"go"*, *"walk"*, and *"hold"* occur frequently, even when the language signal does not reflect it. That is, in any given clip, there is a high chance that the participant walks, goes somewhere, or holds something. Thus, mod-

els which happen to predict these verbs frequently may have artificially high accuracy. For example, the unsupervised Object-Based model only predicts *"go"* once and *"hold"* 5 times , which may contribute to the unsupervised Object-Based model performing significantly worse than random, despite seeming to capture low-level actions well.

Special cases. We note that some verbs are very difficult or impossible to detect given limitations of our data. In particular, *"give"*, *"eat"*, and *"open"* have a precision of 0 across all models, as well as in the training signal (§2.3.2). For example, *"give"* only occurs twice in our data (*"fluffy teddy bear going to give it a little hug"* and *"turn on the water give it a little sore[sic] and we can let it dry there"*), but cannot occur in its prototypical sense since there is no clear second agent to be a recipient. During instances of *"eat"* and *"open"*, participants tended to mime the actions, but the in-game physics data does not faithfully capture the semantics of these verbs (e.g., containers do not actually open). These words highlight limitations of the environment which may be addressed in future work.

4 Discussion

We compare two types of models for grounded verb learning, one based on 2D visual features and one based on 3D symbolic and spatial features. Our analysis suggests that these approaches favor in different aspects of verb semantics. One open question is how to combine these differing signals, and how to design training objectives that encourage models to chose the right sensory inputs and time scale to which to ground each verb.

We evaluated on a small set of verbs that are acquired comparably early by children. Nonetheless, our models perform only marginally better than random. This disconnect highlights an important challenge to be addressed by work on computational models of grounded language learning: Can statistical associations between words and contexts result in more than simple noun-centric image or video captioning, eventually forming general-purpose language models? While that question is still wide open, research from psychology could better inform work on grounded NLP. For example, Piccin and Waxman (2007) argues that verb learning in particular is not learned from purely grounded signal, but rather is "scaffolded" by earlier-acquired knowledge of nouns and of syntax. From this perspective, the models we explored here, which are similar to what is used for noun-learning, are far too simplistic for verb learning. More research is needed on ways to combine linguistic and grounded signal in order to learn more abstract semantic concepts.

5 Related Work

We contribute to a large body of research on learning grounded representations of language. Grounded representations have been shown to improve performance on intrinsic semantic similary metrics (Hill et al., 2017; Vulić et al., 2017) as well as to be better predictors of human brain activity (Anderson et al., 2015; Bulat et al., 2017). Much prior work has explored the augmentation of standard language modeling objectives with 2D image (Bruni et al., 2011; Kiela et al., 2017; Lazaridou et al., 2015; Silberer and Lapata, 2012; Divvala et al., 2014) and video (Sun et al., 2019) data. Recent work on detecting fine-grained events in videos is particularly relevant (Hendricks et al., 2018; Zhukov et al., 2019; Fried et al., 2020, among others). Especially relevant is the data collected by Gaspers et al. (2014), in which human subjects were asked to play simple games with a physical robot and narrate while doing so. Our data and work differs primarily in that we focus on the ability to ground to symbolic objects and physics rather than only to pixel data. Past work on "situated language learning", inspired by emergence theories of language acquisition (MacWhinney, 2013), has trained AI agents to learn language from scratch by interacting with humans and/or each other in simulated environments or games (Wang et al., 2016; Mirowski et al., 2016; Urbanek et al., 2019; Beattie et al., 2016; Hill et al., 2018; Mirowski et al., 2016),

6 Conclusion

We introduce the New Brown Corpus, a dataset of spontaneous speech aligned with rich environment data, collected in a VR kitchen environment. We show that, compared to existing corpora, the distribution of vocabulary collected is more comparable to that found in child-directed speech. We analyze several baseline distributional models for verb learning. Our results highlight the challenges of learning from naturalistic data, and outlines directions for future research.

7 Acknowledgements

This work was supported by DARPA under award number HR00111990064. Thanks to George Konidaris, Roman Feiman, Mike Hughes, members of the Language Understanding and Representation (LUNAR) Lab at Brown, and the reviewers for their help and feedback on this work.

References

Andrew James Anderson, Elia Bruni, Alessandro Lopopolo, Massimo Poesio, and Marco Baroni. 2015. Reading visually embodied meaning from the brain: Visually grounded computational models decode visual-object mental imagery induced by written text. *NeuroImage*, 120:309–322.

Peter Anderson, Qi Wu, Damien Teney, Jake Bruce, Mark Johnson, Niko Sünderhauf, Ian Reid, Stephen Gould, and Anton van den Hengel. 2018. Vision-and-Language Navigation: Interpreting visually-grounded navigation instructions in real environments. In *Proceedings of the IEEE Conference on Computer Vision and Pattern Recognition (CVPR)*.

Charles Beattie, Joel Z Leibo, Denis Teplyashin, Tom Ward, Marcus Wainwright, Heinrich Küttler, Andrew Lefrancq, Simon Green, Víctor Valdés, Amir Sadik, et al. 2016. Deepmind lab. *arXiv preprint arXiv:1612.03801*.

Emily M. Bender and Alexander Koller. 2020. Climbing towards NLU: On meaning, form, and understanding in the age of data. In *Proceedings of the 58th Annual Meeting of the Association for Computational Linguistics*, pages 5185–5198, Online. Association for Computational Linguistics.

Miguel Borges, Andrew Symington, Brian Coltin, Trey Smith, and Rodrigo Ventura. 2018. Htc vive: Analysis and accuracy improvement. In *2018 IEEE/RSJ International Conference on Intelligent Robots and Systems (IROS)*, pages 2610–2615. IEEE.

Michael R Brent and Jeffrey Mark Siskind. 2001. The role of exposure to isolated words in early vocabulary development. *Cognition*, 81(2):B33–B44.

Roger Brown. 1973. *A first language: The early stages*. Harvard U. Press.

Elia Bruni, Giang Binh Tran, and Marco Baroni. 2011. Distributional semantics from text and images. In *Proceedings of the GEMS 2011 Workshop on GEometrical Models of Natural Language Semantics*, pages 22–32, Edinburgh, UK. Association for Computational Linguistics.

Elia Bruni, Jasper Uijlings, Marco Baroni, and Nicu Sebe. 2012. Distributional semantics with eyes: Using image analysis to improve computational representations of word meaning. In *Proceedings of the 20th ACM international conference on Multimedia*, pages 1219–1228. ACM.

Luana Bulat, Stephen Clark, and Ekaterina Shutova. 2017. Speaking, seeing, understanding: Correlating semantic models with conceptual representation in the brain. In *Proceedings of the 2017 Conference on Empirical Methods in Natural Language Processing*, pages 1081–1091, Copenhagen, Denmark. Association for Computational Linguistics.

Jacob Devlin, Ming-Wei Chang, Kenton Lee, and Kristina Toutanova. 2018. Bert: Pre-training of deep bidirectional transformers for language understanding. *arXiv preprint arXiv:1810.04805*.

Santosh K Divvala, Ali Farhadi, and Carlos Guestrin. 2014. Learning everything about anything: Weblysupervised visual concept learning. In *Proceedings of the IEEE Conference on Computer Vision and Pattern Recognition*, pages 3270–3277.

Maxwell Forbes, Christine Kaeser-Chen, Piyush Sharma, and Serge Belongie. 2019. Neural naturalist: Generating fine-grained image comparisons. In *Proceedings of the 2019 Conference on Empirical Methods in Natural Language Processing and the 9th International Joint Conference on Natural Language Processing (EMNLP-IJCNLP)*, pages 708–717, Hong Kong, China. Association for Computational Linguistics.

W Nelson Francis and Henry Kucera. 1979. Brown corpus manual. *Letters to the Editor*, 5(2):7.

Michael C Frank, Mika Braginsky, Daniel Yurovsky, and Virginia A Marchman. 2017. Wordbank: An open repository for developmental vocabulary data. *Journal of child language*, 44(3):677–694.

Daniel Fried, Jean-Baptiste Alayrac, Phil Blunsom, Chris Dyer, Stephen Clark, and Aida Nematzadeh. 2020. Learning to segment actions from observation and narration. In *Proceedings of the 58th Annual Meeting of the Association for Computational Linguistics*, pages 2569–2588, Online. Association for Computational Linguistics.

Judith Gaspers, Maximilian Panzner, Andre Lemme, Philipp Cimiano, Katharina J. Rohlfing, and Sebastian Wrede. 2014. A multimodal corpus for the evaluation of computational models for (grounded) language acquisition. In *Proceedings of the 5th Workshop on Cognitive Aspects of Computational Language Learning (CogACLL)*, pages 30–37, Gothenburg, Sweden. Association for Computational Linguistics.

Jane Gillette, Henry Gleitman, Lila Gleitman, and Anne Lederer. 1999. Human simulations of vocabulary learning. *Cognition*, 73(2):135–176.

Lisa Anne Hendricks, Oliver Wang, Eli Shechtman, Josef Sivic, Trevor Darrell, and Bryan Russell. 2018. Localizing moments in video with temporal language. In *Proceedings of the 2018 Conference on Empirical Methods in Natural Language Processing*, pages 1380–1390, Brussels, Belgium. Association for Computational Linguistics.

Felix Hill, Karl Moritz Hermann, Phil Blunsom, and Stephen Clark. 2017. Understanding grounded language learning agents. *arXiv preprint arXiv:1710.09867*.

Felix Hill, Karl Moritz Hermann, Phil Blunsom, and Stephen Clark. 2018. Understanding grounded language learning agents.

Douwe Kiela, Alexis Conneau, Allan Jabri, and Maximilian Nickel. 2017. Learning visually grounded sentence representations. *arXiv preprint arXiv:1707.06320*.

Angeliki Lazaridou, Nghia The Pham, and Marco Baroni. 2015. Combining language and vision with a multimodal skip-gram model. pages 153–163.

Tal Linzen. 2020. How can we accelerate progress towards human-like linguistic generalization? In *Proceedings of the 58th Annual Meeting of the Association for Computational Linguistics*, pages 5210–5217, Online. Association for Computational Linguistics.

Brian MacWhinney. 2013. The emergence of language from embodiment. In *The emergence of language*, pages 231–274. Psychology Press.

Piotr Mirowski, Razvan Pascanu, Fabio Viola, Hubert Soyer, Andrew J Ballard, Andrea Banino, Misha Denil, Ross Goroshin, Laurent Sifre, Koray Kavukcuoglu, et al. 2016. Learning to navigate in complex environments. *arXiv preprint arXiv:1611.03673*.

Thomas B Piccin and Sandra R Waxman. 2007. Why nouns trump verbs in word learning: New evidence from children and adults in the human simulation paradigm. *Language Learning and Development*, 3(4):295–323.

Christopher Potts. 2019. A case for deep learning in semantics: Response to pater. *Language*, 95(1):e115–e124.

Carina Silberer and Mirella Lapata. 2012. Grounded models of semantic representation. In *Proceedings of the 2012 Joint Conference on Empirical Methods in Natural Language Processing and Computational Natural Language Learning*, pages 1423–1433, Jeju Island, Korea. Association for Computational Linguistics.

Karen Simonyan and Andrew Zisserman. 2014. Very deep convolutional networks for large-scale image recognition. *arXiv preprint arXiv:1409.1556*.

Elizabeth S Spelke and Katherine D Kinzler. 2007. Core knowledge. *Developmental science*, 10(1):89–96.

Chen Sun, Austin Myers, Carl Vondrick, Kevin Murphy, and Cordelia Schmid. 2019. Videobert: A joint model for video and language representation learning. *arXiv preprint arXiv:1904.01766*.

Jack Urbanek, Angela Fan, Siddharth Karamcheti, Saachi Jain, Samuel Humeau, Emily Dinan, Tim Rocktäschel, Douwe Kiela, Arthur Szlam, and Jason Weston. 2019. Learning to speak and act in a fantasy text adventure game. In *Proceedings of the 2019 Conference on Empirical Methods in Natural Language Processing and the 9th International Joint Conference on Natural Language Processing (EMNLP-IJCNLP)*, pages 673–683, Hong Kong, China. Association for Computational Linguistics.

Ivan Vulić, Daniela Gerz, Douwe Kiela, Felix Hill, and Anna Korhonen. 2017. Hyperlex: A large-scale evaluation of graded lexical entailment. *Computational Linguistics*, 43(4):781–835.

Sida I. Wang, Percy Liang, and Christopher D. Manning. 2016. Learning language games through interaction. In *Proceedings of the 54th Annual Meeting of the Association for Computational Linguistics (Volume 1: Long Papers)*, pages 2368–2378, Berlin, Germany. Association for Computational Linguistics.

Jun Xu, Tao Mei, Ting Yao, and Yong Rui. 2016. Msrvtt: A large video description dataset for bridging video and language. In *Proceedings of the IEEE Conference on Computer Vision and Pattern Recognition (CVPR)*.

Dimitri Zhukov, Jean-Baptiste Alayrac, Ramazan Gokberk Cinbis, David Fouhey, Ivan Laptev, and Josef Sivic. 2019. Cross-task weakly supervised learning from instructional videos. In *Proceedings of the IEEE Conference on Computer Vision and Pattern Recognition*, pages 3537–3545.

Find or Classify? Dual Strategy for Slot-Value Predictions on Multi-Domain Dialog State Tracking

Jian-Guo Zhang[1*] **Kazuma Hashimoto**[2†] **Chien-Sheng Wu**[2] **Yao Wan**[3]
Philip S. Yu[1] **Richard Socher**[2] **Caiming Xiong**[2]

[1] University of Illinois at Chicago, Chicago, USA
[2] Salesforce Research, Palo Alto, USA
[3] Huazhong University of Science and Technology, Wuhan, China
{jzhan51,psyu}@uic.edu, wanyao@hust.edu.cn
{k.hashimoto,wu.jason,rsocher,cxiong}@salesforce.com

Abstract

Dialog state tracking (DST) is a core component in task-oriented dialog systems. Existing approaches for DST mainly fall into one of two categories, namely, ontology-based and ontology-free methods. An ontology-based method selects a value from a candidate-value list for each target slot, while an ontology-free method extracts spans from dialog contexts. Recent work introduced a BERT-based model to strike a balance between the two methods by pre-defining categorical and non-categorical slots. However, it is not clear enough which slots are better handled by either of the two slot types, and the way to use the pre-trained model has not been well investigated. In this paper, we propose a simple yet effective dual-strategy model for DST, by adapting a single BERT-style reading comprehension model to jointly handle both the categorical and non-categorical slots. Our experiments on the MultiWOZ datasets show that our method significantly outperforms the BERT-based counterpart, finding that the key is a deep interaction between the domain-slot and context information. When evaluated on noisy (MultiWOZ 2.0) and cleaner (MultiWOZ 2.1) settings, our method performs competitively and robustly across the two different settings. Our method sets the new state of the art in the noisy setting, while performing more robustly than the best model in the cleaner setting. We also conduct a comprehensive error analysis on the dataset, including the effects of the dual strategy for each slot, to facilitate future research.

1 Introduction

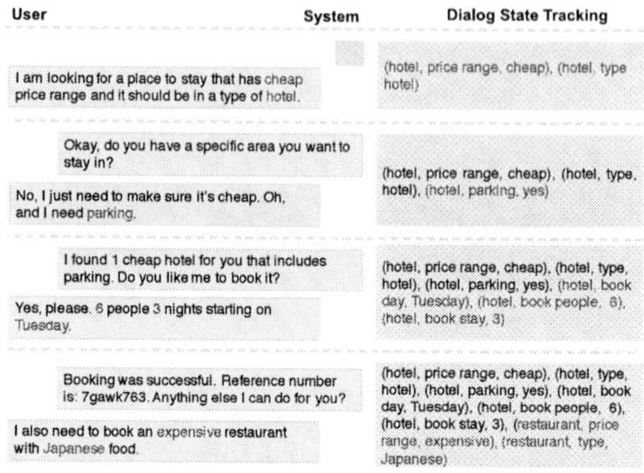

Figure 1: An example of dialog state tracking for booking a hotel and reserving a restaurant. Each turn contains a user utterance (grey) and a system utterance (orange). The dialog state tracker (green) tracks all the $< domain, slot, value >$ triplets until the current turn. Blue color denotes the new state appearing at that turn. Best viewed in color.

Virtual assistants play important roles in facilitating our daily life, such as booking hotels, reserving restaurants and making travel plans. Dialog State Tracking (DST), which estimates users' goal and intention based on conversation history, is a core component in task-oriented dialog systems (Young et al., 2013; Gao et al., 2019a). A dialog state consists of a set of $< domain, slot, value >$ triplets, and DST aims to track all the states accumulated across the conversational turns. Fig. 1 shows a dialogue with corresponding annotated turn states.

Traditional approaches for DST usually rely on hand-crafted features and domain-specific lexicon, and can be categorized into two classes (Xu and Hu, 2018; Gao et al., 2019b; Ramadan et al., 2018; Zhong et al., 2018): i.e., ontology-based and ontology-free. The ontology-based approaches (Ramadan et al., 2018; Zhong et al., 2018; Chen et al., 2020) require full access to the pre-defined ontol-

*Proceedings of the Ninth Joint Conference on Lexical and Computational Semantics (*SEM)*, pages 154–167
Barcelona, Spain (Online), December 12–13, 2020

ogy to perform classification over the candidate-value list. However, in practice, we may not have access to an ontology or only have partial ontology in the industry. Even if a full ontology exists, it is computationally expensive to enumerate all the values when the full ontology for some slots is very large and diverse (Wu et al., 2019; Xu and Hu, 2018). The ontology-free approaches (Gao et al., 2019b; Xu and Hu, 2018) find slot values directly from the input source using a copy mechanism without requiring an ontology, e.g., learning span matching with start and end positions in the dialog context. However, it is nontrivial to handle situations where values do not appear in the dialog context or have various descriptions by users.

To mitigate the above issues, recently, (Zhou and Small, 2019) introduced a question asking model to generate questions asking for values of each-domain slot pair and a dynamic knowledge graph to learn relationships between the (domain, slot) pairs. (Rastogi et al., 2020) introduced a BERT-based model (Devlin et al., 2019) to strike a balance between the two methods by pre-defining categorical and non-categorical slots. However, more studies are needed to know which slots are better handled by either of the two slot types, and the way to use the pre-trained models is not well investigated (Lee et al., 2019; Gao et al., 2019b; Rastogi et al., 2020).

Inspired by the task-oriented dialog schema design in (Rastogi et al., 2020) and the recent successful experience in locating text spans in machine reading comprehensions (Gao et al., 2019b; Asai et al., 2019). we design a simple yet effective **D**ual-**S**trategy **D**ialog **S**tate **T**racking model (**DS-DST**), which adapts a single BERT question answering model to jointly handle both the categorical and non-categorical slots, and different with previous approaches on multi-domain DST, we enable the model with direct interactions between dialog context and the slot. We decide whether a slot belongs to a non-categorical slot or a categorical slot by following the heuristics from (Rastogi et al., 2020). For example, it is common that when users book hotels, the requests for parking are usually *yes* or *no* with limited choices. These kinds of slots are defined as categorical slots, and the slot values are selected over a partial ontology. In addition, how long the user will stay has unlimited values and it can be found in the context. These kinds of slots are treated as non-categorical slots, and the values are found trough span matching in the dialog

context. Hence, the model is flexible depending on the access level to the ontology or whether the values of slots could be found directly in the dialog context.

Our contributions are summarized as follows:

• We designed a simple yet effective dual-strategy model based on BERT with strong interactions between the dialog context and domain-slot pairs.

• Our model achieves state of the art on Multi-WOZ 2.0 (Budzianowski et al., 2018) and competitive performance on MultiWOZ 2.1 (Eric et al., 2019). Our model also performs robustly across the two different settings.

• We conducted a comprehensive error analysis on the dataset, including the effects of the dual strategy for each slot, to facilitate future research.

2   Related Work

Multi-domain DST, which tracks dialog states in complicated conversations across multiple domains with many slots, has been a hot research topic during the past few years, along with the development of Dialogue State Tracking Challenges (Williams et al., 2013; Henderson et al., 2014a,b; Kim et al., 2016, 2017, 2019). Traditional approaches usually rely on hand-crafted features or domain-specific lexicon (Henderson et al., 2014c; Wen et al., 2016), making them difficult to be adapted to new domains. In addition, these approaches require a pre-defined full ontology, in which the values of a slot are constrained by a set of candidate values (Ramadan et al., 2018; Liu and Lane, 2017; Zhong et al., 2018; Lee et al., 2019; Chen et al., 2020). To tackle these issues, several methods have been proposed to extract slot values through span matching with start and end positions in the dialog context. For example, (Xu and Hu, 2018) utilizes an attention-based pointer network to copy values from the dialog context. (Gao et al., 2019b) poses DST as a reading comprehension problem and incorporates a slot carryover model to copy states from previous conversational turns. However, tracking states only from the dialog context is insufficient since many values in DST cannot be exactly found in the context due to annotation errors or diverse descriptions of slot values from users. On the other hand, pre-trained models such as BERT (Devlin et al., 2019) and GPT (Radford et al., 2018) have shown promising performances in many downstream tasks. Among them, DSTreader (Gao et al., 2019b) utilizes BERT as word embeddings for dialog contexts, SUMBT (Lee et al., 2019) employs BERT to extract representations of candidate values, and BERT-DST (Rastogi et al., 2020) adopts BERT to encode the inputs of the user turn as well as the previous system turn. Different from these approaches where the dialog context and domain-slot pairs are usually separately encoded, we employ strong interactions to encode them. [1]. Moreover, We investigate and provide insights to decide slot types and conduct a comprehensive analysis of the popular MultiWOZ datasets.

Another direction for multi-domain DST is based on generative approaches (Lei et al., 2018; Wu et al., 2019; Le et al., 2020) which generate slot values without relying on fixed vocabularies and spans. However, such generative methods suffer from generating ill-formatted strings (e.g., repeated words) upon long strings, which is common in DST. For example, the hotel address may be long and a small difference makes the whole dialog state tracking incorrect. By contrast, both the categorical (picklist-based) and non-categorical (span-based) methods can rely on existing strings rather than generating them.

3 DS-DST: a Dual Strategy for DST

Let $X = \{(U_1^{sys}, U_1^{usr}), \ldots, (U_T^{sys}, U_T^{usr})\}$ denote a set of pairs of a system utterance U_t^{sys} and a user utterance U_t^{usr} ($1 \leq t \leq T$), given a dialogue context with T turns. Each turn (U_t^{sys}, U_t^{usr}) talks about a particular domain (e.g., *hotel*), and a certain number of slots (e.g., *price range*) are associated with the domain. We denote all the N possible domain-slot pairs as $S = \{S_1, \ldots, S_N\}$, where each domain-slot pair consists of $\{s_1, \ldots, s_n\}$ tokens, e.g., *hotel-price range* includes three tokens. Let $X_t = \{(U_1^{sys}, U_1^{usr}), \ldots, (U_t^{sys}, U_t^{usr})\}$ denote the dialogue context at the t_{th} turn and X_t has $\{x_1, \ldots, x_m\}$ tokens. Our goal is to predict the values for all the domain-slot pairs in S. Here we assume that M domain-slot pairs in S are treated as non-categorical slots, and the remaining $N - M$ pairs as categorical slots. Each categorical slot has L possible candidate values (picklist), i.e., $\{V_1, \ldots, V_L\}$, where L is the size of the picklist, and each value has $\{v_1, \ldots, v_c\}$ tokens.

Bearing these notations in mind, we then propose a dual strategy model with direct interactions between dialog context and domain-slot pairs for DST. Fig. 2 shows an overview of the architecture of our proposed DS-DST model. We first utilize a pre-trained BERT (Devlin et al., 2019) to encode information about the dialogue context X_t along with each domain-slot pair in S, and obtain contextualized representations conditioned on the domain-slot information. We then design a slot gate to handle special types of values. In particular, for the non-categorical slots, we utilize a two-way linear mapping to find text spans. For the categorical slots, we select the most plausible values from the picklists based on the contextual representation.

3.1 Slot-Context Encoder

We employ a pre-trained BERT (Devlin et al., 2019) to encode the domain-slot types and dialog contexts. For the j_{th} domain-slot pair and the dialog context X_t at the t_{th} turn, we concatenate them and get corresponding representations:

$$R_{tj} = \text{BERT}\left([\text{CLS}] \oplus S_j \oplus [\text{SEP}] \oplus X_t\right), \quad (1)$$

where $[\text{CLS}]$ is a special token added in front of each sample, and $[\text{SEP}]$ is a special separator token. The outputs of BERT in Eq. (3.1) can be decomposed as $R_{tj} = [r_{tj}^{\text{CLS}}, r_{tj}^1, \ldots, r_{tj}^K]$, where r_{tj}^{CLS} is the aggregated representation of the total K sequential input tokens, and $[r_{tj}^1, \ldots, r_{tj}^K]$ are the token-level representations. They are used for slot-value predictions in the following sections, and the BERT is fine-tuned during the training process.

3.2 Slot-Gate Classification

As there are many domain-slot pairs in multi-domain dialogues, it is nontrivial to correctly predict whether a domain-slot pair appears at each turn of the dialogue. Here we follow (Wu et al., 2019; Xu and Hu, 2018) and design a slot gate classification module for our neural network. Specifically, at the t_{th} turn, the classifier makes a decision among $\{none, dontcare, prediction\}$, where *none* denotes that a domain-slot pair is not mentioned or the value is 'none' at this turn, *dontcare* implies that the user can accept any values for this slot, and *prediction* represents that the slot should be processed by the model with a real value. We utilize r_{tj}^{CLS} for the slot-gate classification, and the probability for the j_{th} domain-slot pair at the t_{th} turn is calculated as:

$$P_{tj}^{gate} = \text{softmax}(W_{gate} \cdot \left(r_{tj}^{\text{CLS}}\right)^{\top} + b_{gate}), \quad (2)$$

---

[1] Recent work on question answering has shown that the joint encoding of query-context pairs is crucial to achieving high accuracy (Qiu et al., 2019; Asai et al., 2019)

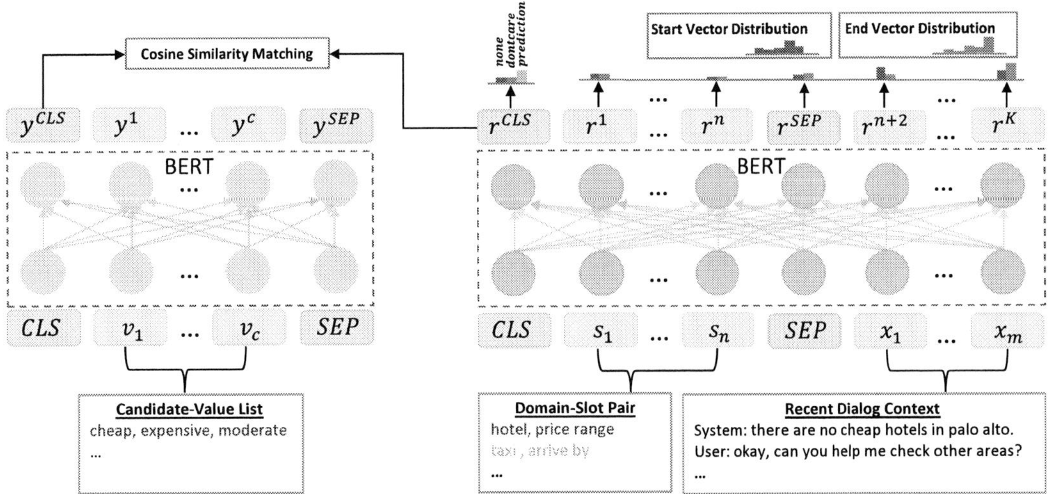

Figure 2: The architecture of our proposed DS-DST model. The left part is a fixed BERT model which acts as a feature extractor and outputs the representations of values in the candidate-value list for each categorical slot (marked in purple). The right part is the other fine-tuned BERT model which outputs representations for the concatenation of each domain-slot pair and the recent dialog context.

where W_{gate} and b_{gate} are learnable parameters and bias, respectively.

We adopt the cross-entropy loss function for the slot gate classification as follows:

$$\mathcal{L}_{gate} = \sum_{t=1}^{T} \sum_{j=1}^{N} -\log(P_{tj}^{gate} \cdot (y_{tj}^{gate})^{\top}), \quad (3)$$

where y_{tj}^{gate} is the one-hot gate label for the j_{th} domain-slot pair at the t_{th} turn.

3.3 Non-Categorical Slot-Value Prediction

For each non-categorical slot, its value can be mapped to a span with start and end position in the dialog context, e.g., slot $leave\ at$ in the $taxi$ domain has spans $4:30pm$ in the context. We take token-level representations $[r_{tj}^1, \ldots, r_{tj}^K]$ of the dialog context as input, and apply a two-way linear mapping to get a start vector α_{tj}^{start} and an end vector α_{tj}^{end}:

$$\left[\alpha_{tj}^{start}, \alpha_{tj}^{end}\right] = W_{span} \cdot \left([r_{tj}^1, \ldots, r_{tj}^K]\right)^{\top} + b_{span}, \quad (4)$$

where W_{span} and b_{span} are learnable parameters and bias, respectively.

The probability of the i_{th} word being the start position of the span is computed as: $p_{tj}^{start_i} = \frac{e^{\alpha_{tj}^{start} \cdot r_{tj}^i}}{\sum_k \alpha_{tj}^{start} \cdot r_{tj}^k}$, and the loss for the start position pre-

diction can be calculated as:

$$\mathcal{L}_{start} = \sum_{t=1}^{T} \sum_{j=1}^{M} -\log(P_{tj}^{start} \cdot (y_{tj}^{start})^{\top}), \quad (5)$$

where y_{tj}^{start} is the one-hot start position label for the j_{th} domain-slot pair at the t_{th} turn.

Similarly, we can also get the loss $\mathcal{L}_{end}$ for end positions prediction. Therefore, the total loss $\mathcal{L}_{span}$ for the non-categorical slot-value prediction is the summation of $\mathcal{L}_{start}$ and $\mathcal{L}_{end}$.

3.4 Categorical Slot-Value Prediction

Each categorical slot has several candidate values; e.g., slot $price\ range$ in the $hotel$ domain has three values $\{cheap, expensive, moderate\}$. At the t_{th} turn, for the j_{th} domain-slot pair, we first use another pre-trained BERT to get the aggregated representation of each value in the candidate list:

$$y_l^{\text{CLS}} = \text{BERT}([\text{CLS}] \oplus V_l \oplus [\text{SEP}]), \quad (6)$$

where $l \in \{1, \ldots, L\}$. Note that during the training process, this separate BERT model acts as a feature extractor and its model parameters are fixed.

We calculate the relevance score between the aggregated representation and a reference candidate by the cosine similarity (Lin et al., 2017):

$$cos(r_{tj}^{\text{CLS}}, y_l^{\text{CLS}}) = \frac{r_{tj}^{\text{CLS}} \cdot (y_l^{\text{CLS}})^{\top}}{\left\|r_{tj}^{\text{CLS}}\right\| \left\|y_l^{\text{CLS}}\right\|}, \quad (7)$$

Domain	Hotel	Train	Restaurant	Attraction	Taxi
Slots	price range type parking book stay book day book people area stars internet name	destination day departure arrive by book people leave at	food price range area name book time book day book people	area name type	leave at destination departure arrive by
Train	3381	3103	3813	2717	1654
Validation	416	484	438	401	207
Test	394	494	437	395	195

Table 1: The dataset information of MultiWOZ 2.0 and MultiWOZ 2.1. The top two rows list 5 selected domains, consisting of 30 domain-slot pairs. The last three rows show the number of dialogues for each domain.

where r_{tj}^{CLS} and y_l^{CLS} are the aggregated representations from the slot-context encoder and the reference candidate value, respectively.

During the training process, we employ a hinge loss to enlarge the difference between the similarity of r_{tj}^{CLS} to the target value and that to the most similar value in the candidate-value list:

$$\mathcal{L}_{picklist} = \sum_{t=1}^{T} \sum_{j=1}^{N-M} \max(0, \lambda - cos(r_{tj}^{\text{CLS}}, y_{target}^{\text{CLS}}) + \max_{y_l^{\text{CLS}} \neq y_{target}^{\text{CLS}}} cos(r_{tj}^{\text{CLS}}, y_l^{\text{CLS}})), \qquad (8)$$

where λ is a constant margin and $l \in \{1, \dots, L\}$, and $\mathcal{L}_{picklist}$ only requires partial ontology for DS-DST.

3.5 Training Objective

During training process, the above three modules can be jointly trained and share parameters of BERT. We optimize the summations of different losses as:

$$\mathcal{L}_{total} = \mathcal{L}_{gate} + \mathcal{L}_{span} + \mathcal{L}_{picklist}. \qquad (9)$$

For the slots that are not mentioned or the users can accept any values (i.e., slots $\in \{none, dontcare\}$) at each dialogue turn, $\mathcal{L}_{span}$ and $\mathcal{L}_{picklist}$ are set to 0 and only the slot-gate classification is optimized during the training process.

4 Experimental Setup

4.1 Datasets

We use the MultiWOZ 2.0 (Budzianowski et al., 2018) dataset and the MultiWOZ 2.1 (Eric et al., 2019) dataset. MultiWOZ 2.0 is one of the largest multi-domain dialogue corpora with seven distinct domains and over $10,000$ dialogues. Compared with the original dataset, MultiWOZ 2.1 conducts dataset correction, including correcting dialog states, spelling errors, dialogue utterance corrections, and mis-annotations to reduce several substantial noises (more details can be found in Eric et al. (2019)).

As *hospital* and *police* domains contain very few dialogues (5% of total dialogues), and they only appear in the training dataset, we ignore them in our experiments, following Wu et al. (2019). We adopt only five domains (i.e., *train, restaurant, hotel, taxi, attraction*) and obtain totally 30 domain-slot pairs in the experiments. Table 1 summarizes the domain-slot pairs and their corresponding statistics in MultiWOZ 2.0 and MultiWOZ 2.1. We follow the standard training/validation/test split strategy provided in the original datasets, and the data pre-processing script provided in Wu et al. (2019).

For MultiWOZ 2.0 and 2.1, the candidate values for the categorical slots are derived based on the ground-truth values of each slot that appeared in the partial dataset ontology. Besides, Since there are no provided ground-truth start positions and end positions for non-categorical slots in the datasets, we find the spans trough string matching between the ground truth values and the values in the dialog contexts, and we treat the start and end positions of the span which appeared at the most recent dialog turn as the ground-truth start positions and end positions.

4.2 Models

We make a comparison with several existing models [2] and introduce some of them as below:

• **SpanPtr** (Xu and Hu, 2018). It applies a RNN-based pointer network to find text spans with start and end pointers for each domain-slot pair.

• **Ptr-DST**. It is a variant based on SpanPtr with the exception that some slots are categorical slots, following DS-DST.

• **DSTreader** (Gao et al., 2019b). It models the DST from the perspective of machine reading comprehensions and applies a pre-trained BERT as initial word embeddings.

• **DSTQA** (Zhou and Small, 2019). It applies a dynamically-evolving knowledge graph and generates question asking for the values of a domain-slot

---

[2] We did not compare with (Lee et al., 2019) and (Shan et al., 2020) as the datasets preprocessing is different with other baselines and ours.

Models	MultiWOZ 2.0	MultiWOZ 2.1
SpanPtr (Xu and Hu, 2018)	30.28%	29.09%
Ptr-DST	-	42.17%
DSTreader (Gao et al., 2019b)	39.41%	36.40%*
TRADE (Wu et al., 2019)	48.62%	45.60%*
COMER (Ren et al., 2019)	45.72%	-
DSTQA w/span (Zhou and Small, 2019)	51.36%	49.67%
DSTQA w/o span[+] (Zhou and Small, 2019)	51.44%	51.17%
BERT-DST (Rastogi et al., 2020)	-	43.40%
MA-DST (Kumar et al., 2020)	-	51.04%
SST-2[+] (Chen et al., 2020)	51.17%	**55.23%**
NA-DST (Le et al., 2020)	50.52%	49.04%
DS-Span	42.59%	40.00%
DS-DST	52.24%	51.21%
DS-Picklist[+]	**54.39%**	53.30%

Table 2: Joint accuracy on the test sets of MultiWOZ 2.0 and 2.1. [+]: the models require a full ontology, and *: the results are reported by Eric et al. (2019)

pair.

- **TRADE** (Wu et al., 2019). It contains a slot gate module for slots classification and a pointer generator for states generation.

- **COMER** (Ren et al., 2019). It applies BERT as contextualized word embeddings and first generates the slot sequences in the belief state, then generates the value sequences for each slot.

- **BERT-DST** (Rastogi et al., 2020). It uses BERT to obtain schema element embeddings and encode system as well as user utterances for dialogue state tracking. Different from the original model, it incorporates a pointer-generator copying mechanism for non-categorical slots of the Multi-WOZ datasets.

- **SST-2** (Chen et al., 2020). It uses the graph neural network to incorporate slot relations and model slot interactions.

For our proposed methods, we design three variants:

- **DS-DST**. It represents our proposed dual strategy model for DST, which can simultaneously handle the non-categorical slots as well as the categorical ones. Following heuristics from (Rastogi et al., 2020), *time* and *number* related slots are treated as non-categorical slots, resulting in five slot types across four domains (nine domain-slot pairs in total), and the rest slots are treated as categorical slots (See also in Table 4). We also conduct investigations to decide domain-slot types in the experiments.

- **DS-Span**. Similar to Xu and Hu (2018); Gao et al. (2019b), it treats all domain-slot pairs as non-categorical slots, where corresponding values for each slot are extracted through text spans (string matching) with start and end positions in the dialog context.

- **DS-Picklist**. Similar to (Lee et al., 2019; Chen et al., 2020), It assumes a full ontology is available and treats all domain-slot pairs as categorical slots, where corresponding values for each slot are found in the candidate-value list (picklist).

5 Experimental Results

We evaluate all the models using the joint accuracy metric. At each turn, the joint accuracy is 1.0 if and only if all $< domain, slot, value >$ triplets are predicted correctly, otherwise 0. The score is averaged across all the turns in the evaluation set.

5.1 Joint Accuracy

Overall performance Table 2 shows the results on the test sets of two datasets. We can see that our models achieve the top performance on MultiWOZ 2.0 and competitive performance on MultiWOZ 2.1. Among these state-of-the-art results, ours are less sensitive to the dataset differences.

Comparing DS-Span and DS-DST, we can find that jointly using the non-categorical and categorical approaches is indeed helpful in multi-domain DST. When the model has access to the full ontology, DS-Picklist shows that our method could further improve the DST performance. Although DS-Picklist is higher than DS-DST, in real scenarios, it may be nontrivial to have access to the full ontology. In the paper, we jointly train the three mod-

Models	Joint Accuracy
BERT-DST (Rastogi et al., 2020)	43.40%
DS-DST	51.21%
BERT-DST-Picklist (single turn)	39.86%
BERT-DST-Picklist (whole dialog history)	46.42%
ToD-BERT (Wu et al., 2020)	48.00%
DS-Picklist	53.30%

Table 3: Joint accuracy on the test sets of MultiWOZ 2.1. BERT-DST is the model used in MultiWOZ 2.1. BERT-DST-Picklist is the original model described in (Rastogi et al., 2020), where a full ontology is required and all the slots are treated as categorical slots,. 'single turn' and 'whole dialog history' represent the Bert utterance inputs are the current dialog turn and the whole dialog history, respectively.

ules in Section 3.5, we also conduct experiments for separately training the non-categorical slots and categorical slots. DS-DST drops by 1.90% on MultiWOZ 2.1, which shows the benefits of jointly training.

Detailed comparisons with BERT related methods Compared with those methods as shown in Table 2, we can observe that DS-Span, which employs the strength of BERT, outperforms SpanPtr by 10.91%, and it outperforms COMMER and DSTreader, which also use a pre-trained BERT model as dialog context embeddings and word embeddings, respectively. DS-DST outperforms BERT-DST, which separately encodes dialog context and domain-slot pairs based on BERT, by 7.81% on MultiWOZ 2.1. The above results shows the effectiveness of our model design based on BERT, where we enforce the strong interactions between dialog context and domain-slot pairs.

To further investigate the differences and importance of strong interactions, we reproduce the original BERT-DST model described in (Rastogi et al., 2020). In addition, we compare with ToD-BERT (Wu et al., 2020), which is a large pre-trained model based on several task-oriented dialogue datasets, and it also separately encodes dialog context and domain-slot pairs. We show the results in Table 3. [3] We observe that our model is consistently much better than BERT-DST and BERT-DST-Picklist. Moreover, our models based on BERT surpass the strong ToD-BERT. We conclude that our improvements come from the strong interactions between slots and dialog context. Therefore, it is important to

---

Slot Name	DS-Span	DS-DST	DS-Picklist
hotel-type	87.92	93.97 (**+6.05**)	94.29 (**+6.37**)
attraction-name	91.16	93.81 (**+2.65**)	93.93 (**+2.77**)
restaurant-name	92.11	93.38 (+1.27)	92.89 (+0.78)
hotel-internet	92.98	97.48 (**+4.50**)	97.26 (**+4.28**)
hotel-parking	93.42	97.18 (**+3.76**)	96.99 (**+3.57**)
attraction-type	93.77	96.86 (**+3.09**)	96.91 (**+3.14**)
hotel-name	94.19	94.87 (+0.68)	94.77 (+0.58)
hotel-area	94.73	95.87 (+1.14)	95.47 (+0.74)
restaurant-area	96.23	96.86 (+0.63)	97.18 (**+0.95**)
attraction-area	96.57	96.96 (+0.39)	96.73 (+0.16)
hotel-price range	96.92	97.39 (+0.47)	96.97 (+0.05)
train-departure	96.96	98.55 (**+1.59**)	98.34 (**+1.38**)
restaurant-food	97.24	97.60 (+0.36)	97.19 (-0.05)
restaurant-price range	97.29	97.73 (+0.44)	97.69 (+0.40)
taxi-departure	97.57	98.53 (**+0.96**)	98.59 (**+1.02**)
taxi-destination	97.69	98.49 (**+0.80**)	98.24 (+0.55)
hotel-stars	97.80	97.48 (-0.32)	97.76 (-0.04)
train-destination	98.17	98.86 (**+0.69**)	98.59 (+0.42)
train-day	99.24	99.35 (+0.11)	99.33 (+0.09)
hotel-book day	99.40	99.32 (-0.08)	99.24 (-0.16)
restaurant-book day	99.40	99.57 (+0.17)	99.44 (+0.04)
train-leave at	93.43	93.30 (-0.13)	93.91 (+0.48)
train-arrive by	95.25	95.78 (+0.53)	96.59 (**+1.34**)
train-book people	97.99	97.84 (-0.15)	98.51 (+0.52)
restaurant-book time	98.56	98.44 (-0.12)	99.04 (+0.48)
taxi-leave at	98.63	98.53 (-0.10)	98.94 (+0.31)
hotel-book people	99.06	99.04 (-0.02)	99.29 (+0.23)
taxi-arrive by	99.12	99.01 (-0.11)	99.09 (-0.03)
hotel-book stay	99.25	99.25 (+0.00)	99.40 (+0.15)
restaurant-book people	99.31	99.16 (-0.15)	99.44 (+0.13)
Average Accuracy	96.38%	97.35%	97.40%

Table 4: The slot-level accuracy on the test set of MultiWOZ 2.1. '+/-' indicates absolute performance improvement/degradation compared with DS-Span. The numbers highlighted in bold indicate that the difference is significant ($p < 0.05$), tested by bootstrap resampling (Noreen, 1989). The slots above the first dashed line are categorical slots and the slots below the first dashed line are non-categorical slots for DS-DST. The last row shows the average slot accuracy.

employ strong interactions to multi-domain DST tasks.

5.2 Per Slot Accuracy

Now that we have observed that DS-DST and DS-Picklist perform much better than DS-Span, we focus on where the accuracy improvement comes from. Table 4 shows the accuracy for each slot type on the MultiWOZ 2.1 test set, and we can observe significant improvement over the DS-Span baseline for some slots, including *hotel-type, attraction-type, attraction-name, hotel-internet* and *hotel-parking*. This is because their values usually have different expressions and cannot be extracted from the dialog context, which decreases the performance of the span-based methods. In contrast, their values can be predicted directly from the candidate-value lists. Compared with other slots, these slots still have space for improvements.

---

[3]Here we did not show the results when treating all the slots as non-categorical slots, one reason is that the performances of BERT-DST-Span are much worse than BERT-DST.

Slot Name	DS-Span (#Unfound / #Relative_Turns)	DS-DST	DS-Picklist
hotel-type	667/1395	86.36%	85.91%
hotel-parking	419/1048	89.50%	86.63%
hotel-internet	421/1124	95.72%	94.54%
taxi-leave at	73/364	0.00%	43.84%
attraction-name	215/1261	70.23%	74.42%
attraction-type	270/1658	84.81%	84.07%
train-leave at	181/1164	2.21%	41.44%
hotel-area	168/1452	51.19%	58.93%
train-arrive by	125/1428	9.60%	79.20%
attraction-area	177/1620	67.23%	71.75%

Table 5: Statistics of Top-10 slots on the MultiWOZ 2.1 validation set based on (*#Unfound / #Relative_Turns*). DS-DST and DS-Picklist show percentages based on (*#Recover / #Unfound*). *#Unfound* is the number of slots whose values cannot be found through span matching in the dialog context, *#Relative_Turns* is the number of dialogue turns where the slot type is mentioned, and *#Recover* indicates the number of values correctly predicted by DS-DST or DS-Picklist.

5.3 Analysis and Discussions

Error analysis To better understand the improvement, we conducted an error analysis and inspected actual examples on the MultiWOZ 2.1 validation set. Table 5 shows the top-10 slots, according to the ratio of ground-truth slot values which cannot be found through span matching. That is, for such examples, DS-Span cannot extract the ground-truth strings, resulting in the low joint accuracy. Here, we show how well our DS-DST and DS-Picklist can correctly predict the missing values in DS-Span. As we can see in this table, the two methods dramatically reduce the errors for some slots such as *attraction-type*, *hotel-internet* and *hotel-parking*. Hence, for these kinds of slots, it is better to treat them as categorical slots. Among the top-10 slots, the *time*-related slots such as *taxi-leave at* and *train-arrive by*, which are span-based slots in DS-DST, DS-Span and DS-DST cannot perform well as there are no span matching in the dialogue context, and only few values (i.e., '*none*' and '*dontcare*') can be correctly predicted by the slot-gate classification. When the ontology is accessible, DS-Picklist can further reduce the error rates, since the predicted values can be found in the candidate-values lists.

On the other hand, we also investigated slots whose ground-truth values can be found through span matching, and we did not observe a significant difference between the three methods. This means that both the non-categorical and categorical methods perform similarly when target values are explicitly mentioned in the dialogues. Therefore,

when most of the slot values can be found directly in the dialog context, these slots can be treated as either non-categorical slots or categorical slots.

As our model relies on the slot-gate classification in Section 3.2, we also investigate the potential influence of this module. We replace this module with an oracle slot-gate classification module, and the joint accuracy is improved from 55.23% to 86.10% on the development set of MultiWOZ 2.1, which indicates that there is a great space to improve the performance with better designs of the slot-gate classification module.

Examples Table 6 shows three examples of dialogue turns in the validation set. In the first example, we can see that DS-Span cannot correctly extract the ground-truth values, because the User does not always explicitly mention '*yes*' or '*no*' when being asked about the internet or parking requests. In the second example, the User and the System are talking about a swimming pool, but they just say '*pool*' and its meaning can be inferred from the context. As a result, DS-Span can only extract '*pool*' as a value, which is not sufficient. In the third example, all the predictions are semantically correct; however, in terms of the string match, only DS-Picklist can correctly predict the value. The two other methods rely on span extraction. This is caused by formatting issues; that is, it is not always guaranteed that strings in the context satisfy desired formats, such as time expressions. Based on our analysis, future work needs to consider more relevant evaluation metrics than the widely-used

User	i am looking for an expensive place to stay on the north side of cambridge .
System	i am sorry , i haven ' t found any matches , would you like me to look for something else ?
User	i am looking for a 4 star hotel and i need free internet and parking .
Ground Truths	<hotel, internet, yes>, <hotel, stars, 4>, <hotel, parking, yes>, <hotel, type, hotel>, <hotel, area, north>, <hotel, price range, expensive>
DS-Span	**<hotel, internet, free internet>**, <hotel, stars, 4>, **<hotel, parking, internet>**, **<hotel, type, none>**, <hotel, area, north>, <hotel, price range, expensive>
DS-DST	<hotel, internet, yes>, <hotel, stars, 4>, <hotel, parking, yes>, **<hotel, type, none>**, <hotel, area, north>, <hotel, price range, expensive>
User	it's so hot today , can you help me find a good pool to visit on the north side of the city ?
System	i have 2 pools in the north area of town : jesus green outdoor pool and kings hedges learner pool . which do you prefer ?
User	kings hedges sounds nice . can i get the address please ?
Ground Truths	<attraction, area, north>, <attraction, type, swimming pool>, <attraction, name, kings hedges learner pool>
DS-Span	<attraction, area, north>, **<attraction, type, pool>**, <attraction, name, kings hedges learner pool>
DS-DST	<attraction, area, north>, <attraction, type, swimming pool>, <attraction, name, kings hedges learner pool>
User	do you happen to know of any trains leaving for cambridge this wednesday ?
System	yes . there are a total of 202 trains leaving for cambridge on wednesday . where will you be departing from ?
User	i will be leaving from norwich and i need to arrive by 8 : 15 .
System	the tr4203 is leaving from norwich to cambridge at 05 : 16 . would you like to book a ticket ?
User	sure , can you book that for 2 people and provide my reference number ?
Ground Truths	<train, arrive by, 08 : 15>, <train, departure, norwich>, <train, day, wednesday>, <train, book people, 2>, <train, destination, cambridge>
DS-Span	**<train, arrive by, 8 : 15>**, <train, departure, norwich>, <train, day, wednesday>, <train, book people, 2>, <train, destination, cambridge>
DS-DST	**<train, arrive by, 8 : 15>**, <train, departure, norwich>, <train, day, wednesday>, <train, book people, 2>, <train, destination, cambridge>
DS-Picklist	<train, arrive by, 08 : 15>, <train, departure, norwich>, <train, day, wednesday>, <train, book people, 2>, <train, destination, cambridge>

Table 6: Predicted dialog states on the MultiWOZ 2.1 validation set, bold face means incorrect prediction. The first two examples show comparisons between DS-Span and DS-DST. The last example shows comparisons between DS-Span, DS-DST and DS-Picklist.

string matching metric. For example, in the QA research community, it is investigated how to more robustly evaluate QA models (Chen et al., 2019).

Open discussions Multi-domain dialog state tracking is enjoying popularity in enhancing research on task-oriented dialog systems, to handle tasks across different domains and support a large number of services. However, it should be noted that there is much room for improvement with the popular MultiWOZ 2.0 (Budzianowski et al., 2018) and MultiWOZ 2.1 (Eric et al., 2019) datasets, due to their annotation errors, ambiguity, and inconsistency. Moreover, a potential problem is that no standard ways have been established for the evaluation of the MultiWOZ dataset. Some papers are following the pre-processing ways provided by Wu et al. (2019), while others have their own ways, which may result in unfair comparisons; for example, there are some 'none' values in the test set, and an evaluation metric without considering them will lead to higher accuracy (up to 3% in our experience). Recent work has refined the datasets to form the latest MultiWOZ 2.2 dataset with higher quality and consistency (Zang et al., 2020). We encourage providing more details of the data processing in future work, and more importantly, testing models on the test set with the higher quality.

6   Conclusion

In this paper, we have proposed a dual strategy model with strong interactions between the dialog context and domain-slot pairs for the task of multi-domain dialog state tracking. In particular, we predict the slot value via selecting over a partial ontology for categorical slots or finding values from the dialog context for non-categorical slots. Our models achieve the state of the art results on the MultiWOZ 2.0 and competitive results on the MultiWOZ 2.1. Moreover, we conduct a comprehensive analysis on the dataset to facilitate future research.

Acknowledgments

This work is supported in part by NSF under grants III-1763325, III-1909323, and SaTC-1930941. We thank Salesforce research members for their insightful discussions, and the anonymous reviewers for their helpful and valuable comments.

References

Akari Asai, Kazuma Hashimoto, Hannaneh Hajishirzi, Richard Socher, and Caiming Xiong. 2019. Learning to retrieve reasoning paths over wikipedia graph for question answering. *arXiv preprint arXiv:1911.10470*.

Paweł Budzianowski, Tsung-Hsien Wen, Bo-Hsiang Tseng, Inigo Casanueva, Stefan Ultes, Osman Ramadan, and Milica Gašić. 2018. Multiwoz-a large-scale multi-domain wizard-of-oz dataset for task-oriented dialogue modelling. *In EMNLP*.

Anthony Chen, Gabriel Stanovsky, Sameer Singh, and Matt Gardner. 2019. Evaluating question answering evaluation. In *Proceedings of the 2nd Workshop on Machine Reading for Question Answering*.

Lu Chen, Boer Lv, Chi Wang, Su Zhu, Bowen Tan, and Kai Yu. 2020. Schema-guided multi-domain dialogue state tracking with graph attention neural networks. In *AAAI*, pages 7521–7528.

Jacob Devlin, Ming-Wei Chang, Kenton Lee, and Kristina Toutanova. 2019. Bert: Pre-training of deep bidirectional transformers for language understanding. *In NAACL*.

Mihail Eric, Rahul Goel, Shachi Paul, Abhishek Sethi, Sanchit Agarwal, Shuyag Gao, and Dilek Hakkani-Tur. 2019. Multiwoz 2.1: Multi-domain dialogue state corrections and state tracking baselines. *arXiv preprint arXiv:1907.01669*.

Jianfeng Gao, Michel Galley, Lihong Li, et al. 2019a. Neural approaches to conversational ai. *Foundations and Trends® in Information Retrieval*, 13(2-3):127–298.

Shuyang Gao, Abhishek Sethi, Sanchit Aggarwal, Tagyoung Chung, and Dilek Hakkani-Tur. 2019b. Dialog state tracking: A neural reading comprehension approach. *In SIGDIAL*.

Matthew Henderson, Blaise Thomson, and Jason D Williams. 2014a. The second dialog state tracking challenge. In *SIGDIAL*.

Matthew Henderson, Blaise Thomson, and Jason D Williams. 2014b. The third dialog state tracking challenge. In *IEEE SLT*.

Matthew Henderson, Blaise Thomson, and Steve Young. 2014c. Word-based dialog state tracking with recurrent neural networks. In *SIGDIAL*.

Seokhwan Kim, Luis Fernando D'Haro, Rafael E Banchs, Jason D Williams, Matthew Henderson, and Koichiro Yoshino. 2016. The fifth dialog state tracking challenge. In *2016 IEEE Spoken Language Technology Workshop (SLT)*, pages 511–517. IEEE.

Seokhwan Kim, Luis Fernando D'Haro, Rafael E Banchs, Jason D Williams, and Matthew Henderson. 2017. The fourth dialog state tracking challenge. In *Dialogues with Social Robots*, pages 435–449. Springer.

Seokhwan Kim, Michel Galley, Chulaka Gunasekara, Sungjin Lee, Adam Atkinson, Baolin Peng, Hannes Schulz, Jianfeng Gao, Jinchao Li, Mahmoud Adada, et al. 2019. The eighth dialog system technology challenge. *arXiv preprint arXiv:1911.06394*.

Adarsh Kumar, Peter Ku, Anuj Kumar Goyal, Angeliki Metallinou, and Dilek Hakkani-Tur. 2020. Ma-dst: Multi-attention based scalable dialog state tracking. *AAAI*.

Hung Le, Richard Socher, and Steven CH Hoi. 2020. Non-autoregressive dialog state tracking. *ICLR*.

Hwaran Lee, Jinsik Lee, and Tae-Yoon Kim. 2019. Sumbt: Slot-utterance matching for universal and scalable belief tracking. *In ACL*.

Wenqiang Lei, Xisen Jin, Min-Yen Kan, Zhaochun Ren, Xiangnan He, and Dawei Yin. 2018. Sequicity: Simplifying task-oriented dialogue systems with single sequence-to-sequence architectures. In *ACL*.

Kevin Lin, Dianqi Li, Xiaodong He, Zhengyou Zhang, and Ming-Ting Sun. 2017. Adversarial ranking for language generation. In *NIPS*.

Bing Liu and Ian Lane. 2017. An end-to-end trainable neural network model with belief tracking for task-oriented dialog. *In INTERSPEECH*.

Eric W. Noreen. 1989. *Computer-Intensive Methods for Testing Hypotheses: An Introduction*. Wiley-Interscience.

Lin Qiu, Yunxuan Xiao, Yanru Qu, Hao Zhou, Lei Li, Weinan Zhang, and Yong Yu. 2019. Dynamically fused graph network for multi-hop reasoning. In *ACL*.

Alec Radford, Karthik Narasimhan, Tim Salimans, and Ilya Sutskever. 2018. Improving language understanding by generative pre-training.

Osman Ramadan, Paweł Budzianowski, and Milica Gašić. 2018. Large-scale multi-domain belief tracking with knowledge sharing. *In ACL*.

Abhinav Rastogi, Xiaoxue Zang, Srinivas Sunkara, Raghav Gupta, and Pranav Khaitan. 2020. Towards scalable multi-domain conversational agents: The schema-guided dialogue dataset. *AAAI*.

Liliang Ren, Jianmo Ni, and Julian McAuley. 2019. Scalable and accurate dialogue state tracking via hierarchical sequence generation. *EMNLP*.

Yong Shan, Zekang Li, Jinchao Zhang, Fandong Meng, Yang Feng, Cheng Niu, and Jie Zhou. 2020. A contextual hierarchical attention network with adaptive objective for dialogue state tracking. *arXiv preprint arXiv:2006.01554*.

Tsung-Hsien Wen, David Vandyke, Nikola Mrksic, Milica Gasic, Lina M Rojas-Barahona, Pei-Hao Su, Stefan Ultes, and Steve Young. 2016. A network-based end-to-end trainable task-oriented dialogue system. *In EACL*.

Jason Williams, Antoine Raux, Deepak Ramachandran, and Alan Black. 2013. The dialog state tracking challenge. In *SIGDIAL*.

Chien-Sheng Wu, Steven Hoi, Richard Socher, and Caiming Xiong. 2020. Tod-bert: Pre-trained natural language understanding for task-oriented dialogues. *arXiv preprint arXiv:2004.06871*.

Chien-Sheng Wu, Andrea Madotto, Ehsan Hosseini-Asl, Caiming Xiong, Richard Socher, and Pascale Fung. 2019. Transferable multi-domain state generator for task-oriented dialogue systems. *In ACL*.

Puyang Xu and Qi Hu. 2018. An end-to-end approach for handling unknown slot values in dialogue state tracking. *In ACL*.

Steve Young, Milica Gašić, Blaise Thomson, and Jason D Williams. 2013. Pomdp-based statistical spoken dialog systems: A review. *Proceedings of the IEEE*, 101(5):1160–1179.

Xiaoxue Zang, Abhinav Rastogi, Srinivas Sunkara, Raghav Gupta, Jianguo Zhang, and Jindong Chen. 2020. Multiwoz 2.2: A dialogue dataset with additional annotation corrections and state tracking baselines. *arXiv preprint arXiv:2007.12720*.

Victor Zhong, Caiming Xiong, and Richard Socher. 2018. Global-locally self-attentive encoder for dialogue state tracking. In *ACL*.

Li Zhou and Kevin Small. 2019. Multi-domain dialogue state tracking as dynamic knowledge graph enhanced question answering. *arXiv preprint arXiv:1911.06192*.

A Appendix

A.1 Training Details

We employ a pre-trained BERT model with the "bert-base-uncased" configuration.[4] During the fine-tuning process, we update all the model parameters using the BertAdam (Devlin et al., 2019) optimizer. The maximum input sequence length after WordPiece tokenization for BERT is set to 512. The constant margin λ is set to 0.5 for the DS-DST and DS-Picklist models. For the Multi-WOZ 2.0 and MultiWOZ 2.1 datasets, the initial learning rate is set to $1e - 4$, and the proportion for learning rate warmup is set to 0.1. The batch size is set to 16. We follow the learning rate decay mechanism as in (Lee et al., 2019), and we set the maximum number of the training epochs to 5. We check the joint accuracy on the validation set after every 1,000 iterations, and keep the best checkpoint to be used for the final evaluation on the test set.

A.2 Sample Output

We present outputs of DS-Span and DS-DST in all the turns for two dialogues (i.e., *MUL0729*, *PMUL2428*) on the validation set of the MultiWOZ 2.1. Table 7 and Table 8 show the predicted dialog states for *MUL0729* and *PMUL2428*, respectively. In Table 7, *hotel type* and *hotel internet* are predicted incorrectly by DS-Span, where the value *yes* of *hotel internet* has a different description *free wifi* in the dialog context. For this type of values, DS-Span cannot find the spans directly in the dialog context. In Table 8, DS-Span does not correctly predict the state *<taxi, departure, funky fun house>* at the 6_{th} turn.

---

[4]`https://github.com/huggingface/`
`transformers/tree/master/examples`

Turn 1	**User:**	i am looking for a train from ely to cambridge . do you have such trains ?
	Ground Truths:	<train, destination, cambridge>, <train, departure, ely>
	DS-Span:	<train, destination, cambridge>, <train, departure, ely>
	DS-DST:	<train, destination, cambridge>, <train, departure, ely>
Turn 2	**System:**	there are 70 trains do you have a date and time you would like to go ?
	User:	i would like to leave on a sunday and arrive by 11:30 .
	Ground Truths:	<train, arrive by, 11:30>, <train, destination, cambridge>, <train, departure, ely>, <train, day, sunday>
	DS-Span:	<train, arrive by, 11:30>, <train, destination, cambridge>, <train, departure, ely>, <train, day, sunday>
	DS-DST:	<train, arrive by, 11:30>, <train, destination, cambridge>, <train, departure, ely}, <train, day, sunday>
Turn 3	**System:**	tr4212 is arriving at 9:52 would that work for you ?
	User:	what time does that train depart ?
	Ground Truths:	<train, arrive by, 11:30>, <train, destination, cambridge>, <train, departure, ely>, <train, day, sunday>
	DS-Span:	<train, arrive by, 11:30>, <train, destination, cambridge>, <train, departure, ely>, <train, day, sunday>
	DS-DST:	<train, arrive by, 11:30>, <train, destination, cambridge>, <train, departure, ely>, <train, day, sunday>
Turn 4	**System:**	the train leaves at 9:35 . shall i book it for you ?
	User:	no , thank you . i would like to see if you could find a place for me to stay that would have a 4 star rating .
	Ground Truths:	<train, day, sunday>, <hotel, stars, 4>, <train, destination, cambridge>, <train, arrive by, 11:30>, <train, departure, ely>
	DS-Span:	<train, day, sunday>, <hotel, stars, 4>, <train, destination, cambridge>, <train, arrive by, 11:30>, <train, departure, ely>
	DS-DST:	<train, day, sunday>, <hotel, stars, 4>, <train, destination, cambridge>, <train, arrive by, 11:30>, <train, departure, ely>
Turn 5	**System:**	of course , there are many 4 star hotel -s to choose from . would you like me to book 1 for you ?
	User:	not yet , thanks . are any of them guesthouses ?
	Ground Truths:	<train, day, sunday>, <hotel, stars, 4>, <train, destination, cambridge>, <train, arrive by, 11:30>, <train, departure, ely>, <hotel, type, guest house>
	DS-Span:	<train, day, sunday>, <hotel, stars, 4>, <train, destination, cambridge>, <train, arrive by, 11:30>, <train, departure, ely>, **<hotel, type, hotel>**
	DS-DST:	<train, day, sunday>, <hotel, stars, 4>, <train, destination, cambridge>, <train, arrive by, 11:30>, <train, departure, ely>, <hotel, type, guest house>
Turn 6	**System:**	there are 18 guesthouses to choose from , do you have a preference to the area you would like to stay ?
	User:	i need a 4 star , and in the east with free wifi for 4 people , 5 nights . i'll need a reference number .
	Ground Truths:	<train, day, sunday>, <hotel, book stay, 5>, <hotel, book people, 4>, <hotel, stars, 4>, <train, destination, cambridge>, <hotel, internet, yes>, <train, arrive by, 11:30>, <train, departure, ely>, <hotel, area, east>, <hotel, type, guest house>
	DS-Span:	<train, day, sunday>, <hotel, book stay, 5>, <hotel, book people, 4>, <hotel, stars, 4>, <train, destination, cambridge>, **<hotel, internet, no>**, <train, arrive by, 11:30>, <train, departure, ely>, <hotel, area, east>, **<hotel, type, hotel>**
	DS-DST:	<train, day, sunday>, <hotel, book stay, 5>, <hotel, book people, 4>, <hotel, stars, 4>, <train, destination, cambridge>, <hotel, internet, yes>, <train, arrive by, 11:30>, <train, departure, ely>, <hotel, area, east>, <hotel, type, guest house>
Turn 7	**System:**	do you want that guesthouse reservation to begin on sunday ?
	User:	yes . i need 5 nights starting on sunday .
	Ground Truths:	<train, day, sunday>, <hotel, book stay, 5>, <hotel, book people, 4>, <hotel, stars, 4>, <train, destination, cambridge>, <hotel, internet, yes>, <hotel, type, guest house>, <train, arrive by, 11:30>, <train, departure, ely>, <hotel, area, east>, <hotel, book day, sunday>
	DS-Span:	<train, day, sunday>, <hotel, book stay, 5>, <hotel, book people, 4>, <hotel, stars, 4>, <train, destination, cambridge>, <hotel, internet, yes>, **<hotel, type, hotel>**, <train, arrive by, 11:30>, <train, departure, ely>, <hotel area, east>, <hotel, book day, sunday>
	DS-DST:	<train, day, sunday>, <hotel, book stay, 5>, <hotel, book people, 4>, <hotel, stars, 4>, <train, destination, cambridge>, <hotel, internet, yes>, <hotel, type, guest house>, <train, arrive by, 11:30>, <train, departure, ely>, <hotel, area, east>, <hotel, book day, sunday>
Turn 8	**System:**	i have confirmed your reservation at allenbell starting on sunday for 5 nights . your reference number is sltivabu . can i help with anything else ?
	User:	that is all i need . thank you so much for all your help .
	Ground Truths:	<train, day, sunday>, <hotel, book stay, 5>, <hotel, book people, 4>, <hotel, stars, 4>, <train, destination, cambridge>, <hotel, internet, yes>, <hotel, type, guest house>, <train, arrive by, 11:30>, <train, departure, ely>, <hotel, area, east>, <hotel, book day, sunday>
	DS-Span:	<train, day, sunday>, <hotel, book stay, 5>, <hotel, book people, 4>, <hotel, stars, 4>, <train, destination, cambridge>, <hotel, internet, yes>, **<hotel, type, hotel>**, <train, arrive by, 11:30>, <train, departure, ely>, <hotel, area, east>, <hotel, book day, sunday>
	DS-DST:	<train, day, sunday>, <hotel, book stay, 5>, <hotel, book people, 4>, <hotel, stars, 4>, <train, destination, cambridge>, <hotel, internet, yes>, <hotel, type, guest house>, <train, arrive by, 11:30>, <train, departure, ely>, <hotel, area, east>, <hotel, book day, sunday>

Table 7: Predicted dialog states of DS-Span and DS-DST for domains (i.e., *train, hotel*) in dialogue *MUL0729* from the MultiWOZ 2.1 dataset.

Turn 1	User:	i am planning a trip to go to a particular restaurant , can you assist ?
	Ground Truths:	
	DS-Span:	
	DS-DST:	
Turn 2	System:	sure , what is the name of this particular restaurant ?
	User:	it s called nandos and i would like to book it for monday at 15:00 . there will be 6 people .
	Ground Truths:	<restaurant, book day, monday>, <restaurant, name, nandos>, <restaurant, book time, 15:00>, <restaurant, book people, 6>
	DS-Span:	<restaurant, book day, monday>, <restaurant, name, nandos>, <restaurant, book time, 15:00>, <restaurant, book people, 6>
	DS-DST:	<restaurant, book day, monday>, <restaurant, name, nandos>, <restaurant, book time, 15:00>, <restaurant, book people, 6>
Turn 3	System:	no problem ! i have your table reserved for 15:00 on monday . they will hold your table for 15 minutes , your reference number is hvb51vam .
	User:	thank you . am also looking for place -s to go in town . the attraction should be in the east
	Ground Truths:	<restaurant, book day, monday>, <restaurant, name, nandos>, <restaurant, book people, 6>, <attraction, area, east>, <restaurant, book time, 15:00>
	DS-Span:	<restaurant, book day, monday>, <restaurant, name, nandos>, <restaurant, book people, 6>, <attraction, area, east>, <restaurant, book time, 15:00>
	DS-DST:	<restaurant, book day, monday>, <restaurant, name, nandos>, <restaurant, book people, 6>, <attraction, area, east>, <restaurant, book time, 15:00>
Turn 4	System:	what are you looking to do ? my system has located 10 place -s .
	User:	could you recommend something ?
	Ground Truths:	<restaurant, book day, monday>, <restaurant, name, nandos>, <restaurant, book people, 6>, <attraction, area, east>, <restaurant, book time, 15:00>
	DS-Span:	<restaurant, book day, monday>, <restaurant, name, nandos>, <restaurant, book people, 6>, <attraction, area, east>, <restaurant, book time, 15:00>
	DS-DST:	<restaurant, book day, monday>, <restaurant, name, nandos>, <restaurant, book people, 6>, <attraction, area, east>, <restaurant, book time, 15:00>
Turn 5	System:	yes , the funky fun house is a great place .
	User:	great ! can you tell me what the entrance fee is please ?
	Ground Truths:	<restaurant, book day, monday>, <restaurant, name, nandos>, <restaurant, book people, 6>, <attraction, area, east>, <restaurant, book time, 15:00>, <attraction, name, funky fun house>
	DS-Span:	<restaurant, book day, monday>, <restaurant, name, nandos>, <restaurant, book people, 6>, <attraction, area, east>, <restaurant, book time, 15:00>, <attraction, name, funky fun house>
	DS-DST:	<restaurant, book day, monday>, <restaurant, name, nandos>, <restaurant, book people, 6>, <attraction, area, east>, <restaurant, book time, 15:00>, <attraction, name, funky fun house>
Turn 6	System:	no , i am sorry . you will have to call them for the entrance fee . the phone number is 01223304705 .
	User:	thank you . i am also looking to book a taxi to travel between the 2 . i need it to arrive to the restaurant by the reservation time .
	Ground Truths:	<restaurant, book day, monday>, <restaurant, name, nandos>, <restaurant, book people, 6>, <attraction, area, east>, <restaurant, book time, 15:00>, <taxi, arrive by, 15:00>, <attraction, name, funky fun house>, <taxi, destination, nandos>, <taxi, departure, funky fun house>
	DS-Span:	<restaurant, book day, monday>, <restaurant, name, nandos>, <restaurant, book people, 6>, <attraction, area, east>, <restaurant, book time, 15:00>, <taxi, arrive by, 15:00>, <attraction, name, funky fun house>, <taxi, destination, nandos>, **<taxi, departure, none>**
	DS-DST:	<restaurant, book day, monday>, <restaurant, name, nandos>, <restaurant, book people, 6>, <attraction, area, east>, <restaurant, book time, 15:00>, <taxi, arrive by, 15:00>, <attraction, name, funky fun house> , <taxi, destination, nandos>, <taxi, departure, funky fun house>
Turn 7	System:	your taxi is booked and will be a white audi . the contact number is 07057575130 . how else may i help you ?
	User:	that s all . thank you for your help !
	Ground Truths:	<restaurant, book day, monday>, <restaurant, name, nandos>, <restaurant, book people, 6>, <attraction, area, east>, <restaurant, book time, 15:00>, <taxi, arrive by, 15:00>, <attraction, name, funky fun house> , <taxi, destination, nandos>, <taxi, departure, funky fun house>
	DS-Span:	<restaurant, book day, monday>, <restaurant, name, nandos>, <restaurant, book people, 6>, <attraction, area, east>, <restaurant, book time, 15:00>, <taxi, arrive by, 15:00>, <attraction, name, funky fun house> , <taxi, destination, nandos>, <taxi, departure, funky fun house>
	DS-DST:	<restaurant, book day, monday>, <restaurant, name, nandos>, <restaurant, book people, 6>, <attraction, area, east>, <restaurant, book time, 15:00>, <taxi, arrive by, 15:00>, <attraction, name, funky fun house> , <taxi, destination, nandos>, <taxi, departure, funky fun house>

Table 8: Predicted dialog states of DS-Span and DS-DST for domains (i.e., *taxi, attraction, restaurant*) in dialogue *PMUL2428* from the MultiWOZ 2.1 dataset.

"where is this relationship going?": Understanding Relationship Trajectories in Narrative Text

Keen You and **Dan Goldwasser**
Department of Computer Science, Purdue University
{you54, dgoldwas}@purdue.edu

Abstract

We examine a new commonsense reasoning task: given a narrative describing a social interaction that centers on two protagonists, systems make inferences about the underlying relationship trajectory. Specifically, we propose two evaluation tasks: Relationship Outlook Prediction MCQ and Resolution Prediction MCQ. In Relationship Outlook Prediction, a system maps an interaction to a relationship outlook that captures how the interaction is expected to change the relationship. In Resolution Prediction, a system attributes a given relationship outlook to a particular resolution that explains the outcome. These two tasks parallel two real-life questions that people frequently ponder upon as they navigate different social situations: *"where is this relationship going?"* and *"how did we end up here?"*. To facilitate the investigation of human social relationships through these two tasks, we construct a new dataset, ***Social Narrative Tree***, which consists of 1250 stories documenting a variety of daily social interactions. The narratives encode a multitude of social elements that interweave to give rise to rich commonsense knowledge of how relationships evolve with respect to social interactions. We establish baseline performances using language models and the accuracies are significantly lower than human performance. The results demonstrate that models need to look beyond syntactic and semantic signals to comprehend complex human relationships.

1 Introduction

A relationship between two people is constantly being shaped by their social interactions (Duck, 1994). For example, if two people have a proper conversation after a heated argument, they may become more intimate as they understand each other

better. On the other hand, they may insist on their own views and part ways. For humans, being able to reason about relationship trajectories is crucial in achieving personal goals while avoiding conflicts with other people. This skill is formally termed as *social competence*, which humans easily acquire (Rubin et al., 1995).

In contrast to humans' innate ability to perceive social situations, machines struggle in developing social understanding. For example, machines' performance in reasoning about motivation and emotional reactions given a short context is significantly lower compared to human performance (Sap et al., 2019). Moreover, identifying the intents and reactions of characters in narratives poses another challenge for machines (Goyal et al., 2010; Chaturvedi et al., 2016; Rahimtoroghi et al., 2017; Rashkin et al., 2018a). Reasoning about relationship trajectories adds yet another layer of difficulty as in addition to the challenge of identifying the implicit factors that guide characters' behavior, such as intents, reactions and mental states, systems also need to understand how these elements collectively contribute to the evolution of relationships. This additional layer of understanding is challenging primarily because the impact of a particular event on a relationship is unique to each social scenario. For instance, an argument can help resolve differences or deepen them, depending on the personalities, intents and reactions of the characters involved in it.

The resources and methods discussed in current work do not directly address these challenges. A fixed set of mappings from events to relationship impact, in a style similar to Event2Mind (Rashkin et al., 2018b), is not sufficient to capture the uniqueness of each social situation. Similarly, SocialIQA (Sap et al., 2019) inspects various elements individually but does not unify them into a single force that influences a relationship. Other current datasets

*Proceedings of the Ninth Joint Conference on Lexical and Computational Semantics (*SEM)*, pages 168–178
Barcelona, Spain (Online), December 12–13, 2020

(Mostafazadeh et al., 2016; Zellers et al., 2018, 2019) cover a broad spectrum of commonsense knowledge, but do not focus on the social aspect. Although it can be annotated for such inspection such as in the investigation of intents and reactions (Rashkin et al., 2018a), this method is not pertaining to relationship analyses because a meaningful change may not always be present. For example, here is a description of a social scenario sampled from the ROCStories corpus: *Tina decided on going hiking with her friend Tony. They both decided on a difficult path. Upon ascension, Tina fell and cut her leg. They both decided it was too dangerous for them to continue. Tony carried Tina to the car and decided on mini-golf instead.* The story provides a few facts regarding a social interaction but does not provide sufficient details to draw conclusions about how the relationship between the two protagonists is changed because of the interaction. Unanswered questions include *"did Tina appreciate Tony's gesture?"* and *"did they bond as a result?"*. All these deficiencies in using current resources and methods to study human relationships call for the need of new resources that encode implicit relationship trajectories that are driven by the interweaving of social elements.

In this work, we introduce *Social Narrative Tree*[1], a corpus of 1250 social narratives documenting a variety of social interactions, each centers on two protagonists. It is built incrementally from ten seeds in five narrative stages and the story branches into five different paths at each stage. This effectively captures the different possibilities which a relationship trajectory can take on at each diverging point. We choose the narrative stages – seed, buildup, climax, resolution and outlook - based on previous narrative analyses (Freytag, 1896; Prince, 1973; Labov, 1997), ensuring that intensity varies at different points of the narrative which simulates fluctuating intensity levels in real-life social situations and thus provides a natural space for relationships to develop in. Using *Social Narrative Tree*, we set up two evaluation tasks, Relationship Outlook Prediction MCQ and Resolution Prediction MCQ. In each task, the text corresponding to Relationship Outlook or Resolution is removed from the stories for prediction based on other stages. The branching of each story at different stages creates a natural notion of similarity among stories, which

can be measured by the number of stages two stories share. This facilitates the setup of confounding choices as the wrong candidates are not completely irrelevant in terms of textual information. This forces systems to truly understand the underlying relationship trajectories instead of relying solely on language modelling. The best accuracy achieved by our BERT-based model (Devlin et al., 2019) (~60%) is significantly lower than human performance (~80%). These experimental results demonstrate that models need to look beyond syntactic and semantic signals to comprehend complex human relationships.

In summary, our contributions are as follows: (1) we introduce *Social Narrative Tree*, a corpus of social narratives with contextualized social elements contributing to relationship trajectories. (2) we introduce new evaluation frameworks using Relationship Outlook Prediction and Resolution Prediction, with meaningful confounding candidate choices that force systems not to depend only on textual information. (3) we establish baseline performances using language models and justify the importance of looking beyond textual information in understanding human relationships.

2 Related Work

Manually constructed scripts are used to represent structured knowledge in 1970-80s (Schank and Abelson, 1977). Subsequently, narrative event chains, unsupervised generation of such representations are introduced. Narrative event chains are sequences of events revolving around one central protagonist (Chambers and Jurafsky, 2008). Stemming from narrative event chains is the narrative cloze task where one event chain is removed and systems are required to fill in the blanks (Chambers and Jurafsky, 2008). The task is further refined to multiple choice form - Multiple Choice Narrative Cloze (MCNC) where different choices are randomly sampled from events that do not belong to the chain (Granroth-Wilding and Clark, 2016). Swaf Af (Zellers et al., 2018) and Hella Swag (Zellers et al., 2019) are datasets for next event prediction, containing multiple choice questions covering a wide range of grounded situations that are constructed from video captions. Furthermore, (Mostafazadeh et al., 2016) create ROCStories, a corpus of 50k commonsense stories each of five-sentence long and propose Story Cloze Test where systems are required to select the most plausible ending for an incomplete narrative. In our work, Relationship Outlook Prediction and Resolution Prediction are multiple-choice tasks of similar motivation with a focus on social implications.

Various social elements are extensively studied in many works. (Sap et al., 2018) present ATOMIC, a knowledge graph of commonsense knowledge with 877k descriptions in free text form and focuses on 'if-then' relationships of causes, effects and attributes. Automatic construction of such knowledge base is explored in Comet (Bosselut et al., 2019). With ATOMIC as the foundation, SocialIQA, a dataset of 38,000 multiple-choice questions about social situations is constructed (Sap et al., 2019). Event2Mind is a corpus of phrasal verbs that is constructed to support the examination of the intents and reactions of common situations (Rashkin et al., 2018b). (Mohammad, 2018) presents NRC VAD Lexicon, a corpus of 20,000 English words with human ratings of valence, arousal and dominance while NRC Affect Intensity Lexicon (AIL) provides emotional categories and associated real values for approximately 6,000 English words (Mohammad, 2017). SocialSent (Hamilton et al., 2016) assigns tokens sentiment scores with contexts taken into consideration. One set of lexicons is constructed from the subreddit r/relationships which we use in our error analyses. Other works model relationships, between literary characters (Iyyer et al., 2016) or countries (Han et al., 2019), described in text using an unsupervised neural model, by mapping them to a latent space. Elements of psychology in ROCstories are analyzed in (Rashkin et al., 2018a) where ROCStories are annotated with motivations and emotional reactions of the characters involved. We create **Social Narrative Tree** with various social and psychological elements embedded in each story and these elements together contribute to the rise and fall of a relationship.

3 Collaborative Construction of Social Narratives

Our main contribution in this paper is the construction of a social narrative corpus consisting of short stories each describing the evolution of a relationship between two characters. The corpus is designed to capture how different social behaviors result in different relationship outcomes. To accomplish this goal we follow a fixed narrative structure consisting of five stages: seed (*exposi-tion*), buildup (*rising action*), climax, resolution and outlook (*denouement*). The stages are based on "Freytag's Pyramid" (Freytag, 1896) and other more recent work analyzing repeating narrative structures (Prince, 1973; Labov, 1997). Fundamentally, a minimal story consists of an initial state, a final state and an intermediate state that transitions the initial state to the final state (Prince, 1973). More specifically, the intermediate state can be further broken down into individual stages to make a story more appealing and informative. Particularly, we adopt the phases of orientation clause, Most Reportable Event (MRE) and resolution (Labov, 1997) to make up the intermediate state, corresponding to the buildup, climax and resolution stages in our framework. The relationship in each story develops as the intensity of the narrative fluctuates.

The dataset is constructed in a collaborative way to help capture the impact of different behaviors at each narrative stage. We use Mechanical Turk, and provide annotators with a partial story created independently, and ask them to complete the next stage. Each MTurker is limited to provide three responses in total at each stage with all three responses belonging to different prompts.

3.1 Crowdsourcing Framework

Seed. The seed is a one-sentence description that introduces two protagonists, their initial relationship and a general social scenario that they are going to be involved in. The dataset is built on 10 initial seeds, which are created from the first sentences of 10 randomly selected stories from the ROCStories dataset (Mostafazadeh et al., 2016) by adding names and removing collective nouns. We inspect and reselect the randomly sampled seeds to ensure that there are no repetitions in social scenarios. This helps to elicit a variety of social behaviors and associated relationship impact. Among the 10 pairs of protagonists, seven pairs have the same gender, two pairs have different genders and one pair includes the name "*Sam*" which MTurkers have different gender interpretations. All the seeds have the same initial relationship description, "*friend*", but the social scenario that the two protagonists are involved in provides additional information on the intimacy level between the two people (at one's home versus a public place). Each seed contains a predicate connecting the two protagonists. Among these predicates, "*asked*" and "*invited*" are active, "*receive*" is passive while "*realized*", "*were*" and *"went to"* have a neutral voice.

Buildup. We instruct MTurkers to provide a one-sentence continuation of the seed, which provides further information on the relationship between the protagonists or on the social scenario. Five different responses are collected for each seed. We specifically state in the instruction that only information relevant to the relationship of the protagonists should be given. This ensures that the plot is compact and the development of the relationship is the driving force of the narrative. We first programmatically filter responses that are completely irrelevant or do not meet the length requirement. We then manually filter all the remaining responses and re-annotate those that do not meet the requirements until the desired number of buildups are collected for each seed. We allow the addition of characters other than the two main protagonists in the responses, diversifying the types of events present in the dataset.

Climax. We create 50 partial narratives, consisting of the 10 seeds and their associated buildups, which serve as the input for the collection of climax events. We prompt MTurkers to provide a two-sentence continuation for each seed and buildup combination as the climax event, which we define as an event that has a significant impact on the relationship between the people involved. Five responses meeting the requirement are collected for each partial narrative, forming 250 seed-buildup-climax combinations.

Resolution and Outlook. We prompt MTurkers to provide a two-sentence continuation of the partial story as the resolution and a one-sentence continuation of the resolution as the relationship outlook. The purpose of resolution is to resolve, either successfully or not, the conflict brought up in the partial narratives. Relationship outlook states the effect of the complete interaction described in the narrative on the relationship between protagonists. Five resolution-outlook pairs are collected for each one of the 250 partial narratives, capturing how different choices of resolving conflicts can impact relationships. At the end of this stage, 1250 complete social narratives are created.

3.2 Dataset Overview

We illustrate the overall tree structure of Social Narrative Tree in Fig. 1 and present some basic statistics of the dataset in Tab. 1. In Tab. 2, we summarize the most frequent five predicates for each narrative stage. In this analysis, we use NLTK

(Bird et al., 2009) to extract and lemmatize verbs and discard a list of stop words including *be, will, do* and *can*. The most used verbs in each stage are consistent with the general purpose of each stage. The seed initiates a social interaction *(invite, ask, receive)* and in buildups, the desires *(want, ask, decide)* and mental states *(think, feel)* of the protagonists are revealed. Climax is where the actual relationship-changing event happens *(start, go, get)* while resolution and outlook contain a mixture of further actions *(say, get, make)*, mental states *(feel)* and a notion of change *(decide, become, realize)*.

3.3 Relationship Trajectories in *Social Narrative Tree*

We carry out various exploratory analyses on *Social Narrative Tree* to examine the relationship trends present in the dataset with respect to social elements. The results validate that the stories contain a broad range of possible ways that relationships can unfold under different circumstances. In addition, the relationship trajectories present in the stories also exhibit some associations with different social elements, verifying that valuable social behavior commonsense knowledge is embedded in the narratives.

Sentiment Polarity. We associate a sentiment polarity label with each stage using TextBlob (Loria et al., 2014). The sentiment polarity distribution for each stage is shown in Tab. 3. The sentiment polarity distribution for climax is fairly equal (115 pos vs 106 neg) but positive resolutions and outlooks significantly outnumber negative resolutions and outlooks (678 pos vs 377 neg, 650 pos vs 269 neg). This indicates that in *Social Narrative Tree*, social interactions are more likely to project positively. We further inspect overall relationship trends by breaking down stories into different combinations of polarities across stages and present the results in Tab. 4 and 5. From Tab. 4, we see that both positive and negative buildup branch equally into positive and negative climax (350 pos vs 350 neg, 150 pos vs 145 neg), giving both trends opportunities to develop and reducing the chance of monotonous plots. From resolution to outlook in Tab. 5, however, both positive and negative resolution are more likely to lead to positive outcomes. This observation could potentially tie back to people's general goal of avoiding conflicts with other people (Rubin et al., 1995) which MTurkers instill into the stories.

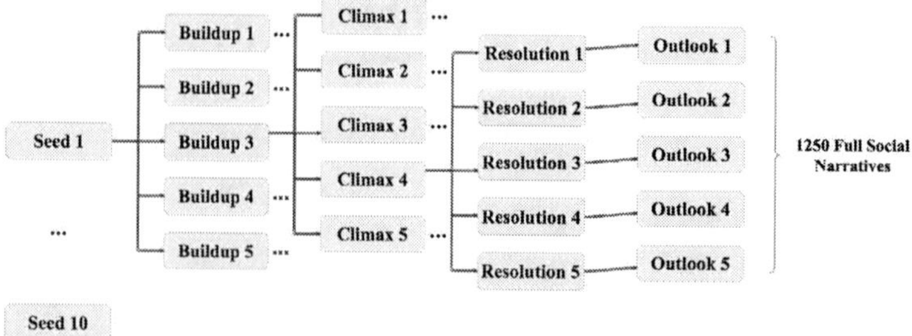

Figure 1: Visualization of Social Narrative Tree's overall structure.

	Seed	Buildup	Climax	Resolution	Outlook	Full Story
# sentences	1	1	2	2	1	7
# uni. instances	10	50	250	1250	1238	1250
# vocab	70	427	1583	3366	2294	4474
avg token #	12.5	24.7	35.2	30.7	19.1	122.2
max token #	15	40	92	108	57	211
min token #	10	14	12	6	3	66

Table 1: Social Narrative Tree basic information.

seed	buildup	climax	resolution	outlook
invite	want	start	decide	decide
ask	think	go	feel	become
go	ask	get	tell	feel
receive	decide	want	say	realize
realize	feel	say	get	make

Table 2: Most frequent five verbs for each stage.

buildup	climax	count
pos	pos	350
pos	neg	350
neg	pos	150
neg	neg	145

Table 4: Sentiment polarity trends between buildup and climax.

res	outlook	count
pos	pos	403
pos	neg	123
neg	pos	163
neg	neg	105

Table 5: Sentiment polarity trends between resolution and outlook.

	seed	buildup	climax	resolution	outlook
positive	0	32	115	678	650
negative	0	13	106	377	269
neutral	10	5	29	195	331

Table 3: Sentiment polarity distribution at each narrative stage.

Valence, Arousal, Dominance (VAD). For each stage we compute a vector of length three as the VAD representation (Mohammad, 2018). Within a stage, we retrieve the VAD scores for all tokens and take the maximum value for each dimension to represent the entire stage. We further associate VAD scores with general relationship trajectories represented using sentiment polarity by inspecting the VAD scores in different subsets of the corpus and present the results in Tab. 6 and 7. In Tab. 6, positive outlook is associated with higher valence and dominance in climax, resolution and outlook. It is also associated with lower arousal in climax and resolution. In Tab 7, positive climax is associated with lower arousal in climax but higher arousal in resolution. These results indicate that in *Social Narrative Tree*, relationship trajectories are closely related to VAD which is an important social behavior indicator. This close relation can be transformed to rich commonsense knowledge if studied in-depth.

Affect Intensity. Affect Intensity assigns a real value to a lexicon in one of the four dimensions – joy, fear, anger and sadness (Mohammad, 2017). We assign a binary vector of length four for each stage for every story, indicating whether that particular dimension is present in the text for that stage. We analyze how different affect dimensions relate to general relationship trajectories by dividing the stories into two subsets using climax sentiment polarity. In each subset, we further separate the stories into two groups, one with positive trend and the other with negative trend – positive trend means the story lands on a positive relationship outlook and vice versa. Within each group, we compute the percentage of resolutions that contain words from each Affect dimension. Fig. 2 and 3 display the results for the positive climax set and the negative climax set respectively. In Fig. 2, resolutions in a positive trend contain a higher proportion of joy and a lower proportion of fear, anger and sadness. The distribution of Affect dimensions is similar in Fig. 3, except resolutions following a negative climax with a positive trend has a higher proportion of fear. Given a positive or negative relationship-changing event, this analysis relates mental states, another

outlook	climax			resolution			outlook		
	V	A	D	V	A	D	V	A	D
positive	0.8796	0.7537	0.7189	0.8900	0.7372	0.7349	0.9123	0.6721	0.7409
negative	0.8697	0.7627	0.7099	0.8631	0.7503	0.7195	0.8395	0.6656	0.6797

Table 6: VAD scores of climax, resolution and outlook partitioned by outlook sentiment polarity.

climax	climax			resolution			outlook		
	V	A	D	V	A	D	V	A	D
positive	0.8973	0.7612	0.7513	0.8870	0.7424	0.7292	0.8827	0.6559	0.7188
negative	0.8617	0.7723	0.6911	0.8630	0.7253	0.7237	0.8752	0.6502	0.7034

Table 7: VAD scores of climax, resolution and outlook partitioned by climax sentiment polarity.

important social behavior indicator, in resolution to relationship trajectories after the event, which is an important aspect of social behavior knowledge.

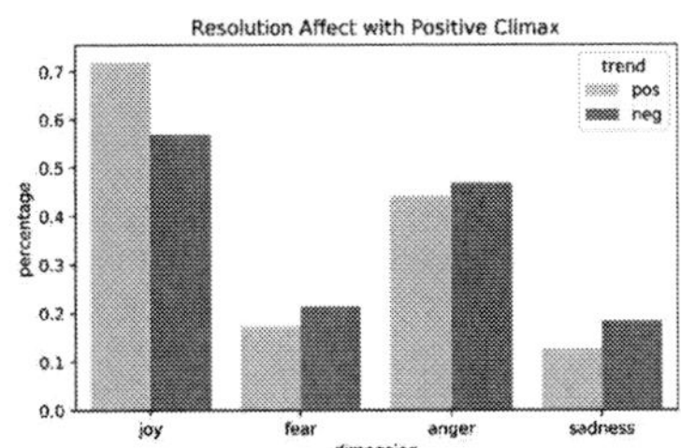

Figure 2: Resolution Affect dimensions in positive climax set.

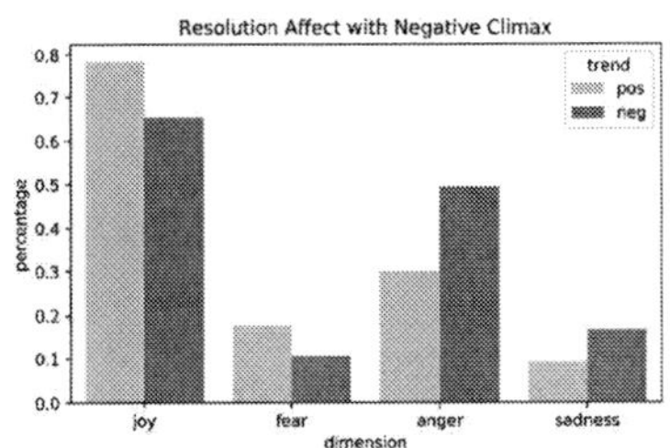

Figure 3: Resolution Affect dimensions in negative climax set.

4 Task Formulation

4.1 Relationship Outlook Prediction: *"Where is this relationship going?"*

In this task, Relationship Outlook is removed from stories and systems need to fill in the blank by choosing the most reasonable outlook from a pool of five candidates. Solving this task requires an understanding of social norms, particularly, what is expected of a relationship after a sequence of events happen in a particular social context. A sample question is shown below and choice D is the correct answer. In Choice A, the emotion of embarrassment is correctly inferred but "felt more comfortable" is inconsistent with the fact that Neil left the celebration. Choice B and Choice E are irrelevant to the given context. In choice C, "not

realize that the event was not a casual one" is a correct statement with respect to the context but the expectation of them remaining friends is a socially incorrect deduction.

Neil went to a celebration with his Vietnamese friend James. Neil was a little nervous as he had never been to an ethnic celebration before, however, James reassured him that it was going to be very casual. When Neil arrived, the event was anything but casual. As he looked around the room, he saw women in dresses and men in suits and he was wearing t-shirt and jeans! James insisted that what Neil was wearing was fine, but Neil still disagreed. Neil got angry at James for lying to him and then left the celebration in tears.

What is the most likely relationship outlook?

(A) *Although at first Neil was embarrassed, throughout the night he felt more comfortable with James, and his confidence in his friend grew exponentially.*

(B) *James and Neil realized how much they had in common, and it strengthened their friendship.*

(C) *They remained friends because Neil had not realise that the event was not a casual one.*

(D) **Neil felt like James could no longer be trusted after lying to him about the celebration, so he thought it would be best to stop talking to James.**

(E) *They will remain friends and more than likely to place more bets on sports or challenges that come between each other, it's friendly competition of two friends' egos.*

4.2 Resolution Prediction: *"How did we end up here?"*

After Resolution is removed from stories, systems need to reason about the cause of a relationship outlook by selecting one of the five resolution candidates. To select the correct resolution, systems need to understand the necessary conditions that will result in a particular relationship outcome. An example Resolution Prediction question is given below. Choice B is correct as it completes the narrative both logically and socially correct. Choices A and D are relevant, but a romantic relationship would not have started if her feelings remain hidden. Choice C diverts from the context by mentioning a gift exchange whereas choice E is unlikely before the beginning of a romantic relationship.

Matthew asked his friend Emma to go for a walk in the park. The weather was really fine so they both took their dogs to the park. Emma was so pleased to be asked by Matthew to spend time with him at the park. Emma had a secret crush on Matthew and wondered if he felt the same but she was too scared to bring up the subject and potentially ruin their friendship. _________ This confession of feelings led to the beginning of a romantic relationship.

Which resolution best fills the blank?

(A) *She never said anything about that before. It was a mystery to him.*

(B) **Matthew could tell from how Emma was acting that she liked him. He turned to face her and told her how he felt.**

(C) *Emma was very moved by Matthew's decision to give back the book, and agreed to accept it back. Emma let Matthew know how grateful his gesture was.*

(D) *She wanted to ask but didn't. He was clueless.*

(E) *Emma and Matthew held each others hands, kissed, and decided then that they wanted to spend the rest of their lives together.*

5 Experiments

5.1 Evaluation Tasks Setup

For each of the two evaluation tasks, we have two context setups, varying in the amount of information provided for systems to make predictions. In Outlook Prediction, *partial context* consists of only the resolution whereas *full context* consists of all of the remaining stages – seed, buildup, climax and resolution. Similarly, in Resolution Prediction, *partial context* consists of only the outlook whereas *full context* consists of all of the remaining stages – seed, buildup, climax and outlook. We will refer to *partial context* and *full context* as *context* below, indicating the corresponding narrative stages for the particular evaluation task and context setting at concern.

We create four sets of 1250 multiple-choice questions for each context setup for each task. For each story, we pair with the correct answer four confounding choices. The first confounding choice comes from one of the four stories that share the same climax as the current story. Namely, the two stories differ only in resolution and outlook. The second confounding choice comes from one of the 24 stories that share the same buildup and the third confounding choice comes from the context of one of the 124 stories that share the same seed. The final confounding choice is from one of the 1125 stories that stem from a different seed. Below, we will refer to the confounding choices as conf-diff-seed, conf-same-seed, conf-buildup and conf-climax to notate the source of a particular confounding choice where conf-buildup means the choice comes from a story that shares the same buildup, etc. Each confounding choice is randomly picked from their respective candidate pool. The names in confounding choices that are picked from other seeds are replaced by the names of current characters. The tree structure of dataset provides a natural notion of similarity among stories, thus, the confounding choices should be of different levels of difficulties, with conf-climax being the most difficult, followed by conf-buildup, conf-same-seed and with conf-diff-seed being the easiest.

We perform 10-fold cross validation on each of the four 1250 multiple-choice question sets. Each fold consists of the 125 stories built from the same seed and we run three random restarts for each fold, taking the best predicting accuracy on the validation fold as the performance for that fold. We use the average accuracy across the 10 folds as the criterion to select hyper-parameters and report the best accuracy for each model in Tab. 8. All of our BERT-based models use BERT-base with 110M parameters, with HuggingFace's PyTorch implementation (Wolf et al., 2019).

5.2 Baseline Models

Average word2vec. We represent both the context and each answer choice using the averaged word2vec representation of each individual word making up the sentences. We then compute the cosine similarity between each context-candidate choice pair. The answer choice that results in the highest cosine similarity value with the context is selected as the prediction.

Pretrained Bert For Next Sentence Prediction.
We use BertForNextSentencePrediction to solve the
tasks where each context and each answer choice is
treated as a single sequence. Each context-answer
pair is assigned a single score for entailment and
we evaluate the softmax of the 5 scores. The answer choice with the highest probability is chosen
as the final prediction. For Resolution Prediction,
we assign two scores for each answer choice: con-
text+resolution and resolution+outlook, the average of the two scores are used to make comparisons.

**Bert For Next Sentence Prediction with Fine-
tuned Attention Layers**. For each test fold, we
finetune the attention layer on the remaining 9
folds of stories and make predictions using a Bert-
ForNextSentencePrediction classifier built on top
of this pretrained attention layer.

Pretrained Bert For Multiple Choice. We train
a BerForMultipleChoice classifier similar to a classifier that solves SWAG (Zellers et al., 2018). For
Resolution Prediction full context, we concatenate
other stages and outlook with a [SEP] token in
between as the input context.

Human Evaluation. We randomly select 125
MCQs for each of the evaluation tasks in full context setting and instruct MTurkers to answer these
questions. Only MTurkers who are Masters and obtain a perfect score on our qualification test which
consists of five sample MCQs are eligible for the
annotation task.

6   Error Analyses

6.1   Distribution of Predictions

Fig. 4 and 5 display the breakdown of predictions
for BertForMultipleChoice classifier and average
word2vec. Both results justify that conf-climax is
the most difficult confounding choice while conf-
diff-seed is the easiest with other choices of a difficulty level in between.

6.2   Example of Wrong Prediction

Below is an Outlook Prediction Question that
BERT-base MCQ classifier answers incorrectly.
This example demonstrates that the ability to predict next sentences is not equivalent to having a social understanding. In this example, all the choices
use words that are relevant to the context. The
underlying relationship trajectory in each choice,
however, varies significantly. A language model is
unable to observe the implicit differences among

choices and draw the wrong conclusion from only
textual information.

*Naomi's friend Noah invited her to his house.
Naomi was excited to see Noah's new place since
the renovations has finally finished. Noah had
cooked Naomi's favourite food. Naomi after eating
a spoon of it, started to jump here and there in
happiness – Naomi loved the dessert! After eating,
she expressed her gratitude to Noah for inviting
her to the housewarming.*

Outlook choices:

correct: *Noah felt grateful for a friend like Naomi.
He asked what kind of curtains he should buy in a
few weeks.*

conf-climax: *Naomi wanted to get closer to Noah
and be his girlfriend.*

conf-buildup: *Naomi would pretend to enjoy the
dinner but let quickly stop any of Noah's advances
during the evening*

conf-same-seed: *They were both ecstatic that they
each wanted a relationship with the other, and they
started it that day.*

conf-diff-seed: (**Bert's prediction**) *Noah likes
Naomi very much and wonders if this friendship
can develop into something more.*

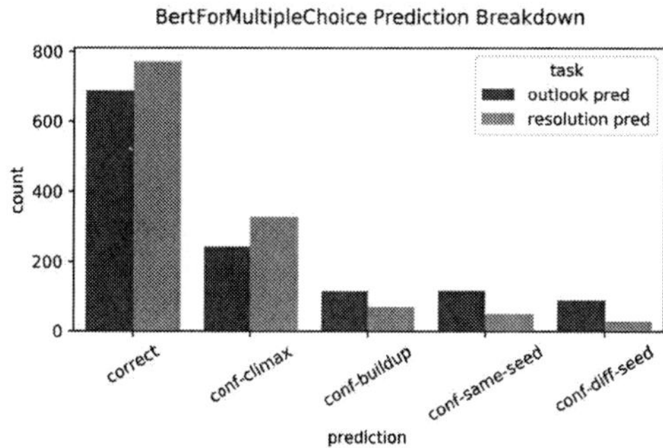

Figure 4: Bert Prediction Distribution.

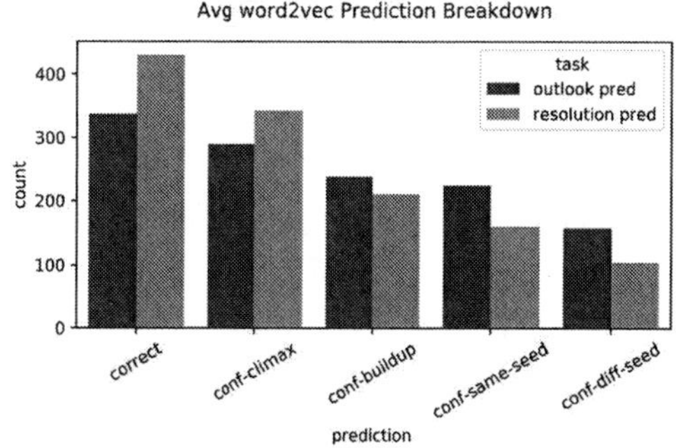

Figure 5: word2vec Prediction Distribution.

	Outlook Prediction		Resolution Prediction	
	Resolution	Full Story	Outlook	Full Story
random	0.20	0.20	0.20	0.20
word2vec	0.3184	0.2736	0.3696	0.3104
BERTNextSent	0.4712	0.3944	0.4832	0.4464
BERTNextSent(finetune)	0.5064	0.4504	0.5096	0.512
BertForMCQ	0.6088	0.592	0.6096	0.6352
Human	N/A	0.80	N/A	0.832

Table 8: Experiment results for baseline models.

6.3 Explanations with Social Elements

We divide the questions into two sets by whether BERT-base MCQ classifier predicts correctly. We compute the difference in VAD (Mohammad, 2018), Affect Intensity (Mohammad, 2017) and SocialSent (Hamilton et al., 2016) scores between each correct and incorrect choice pair and compute the mean for each story, where each choice is represented by the maximum value of lexicon score for individual tokens. We then take the mean of this score across all stories and present the results in Tab. 9, 10 for VAD, Tab. 11, 12 for Affect Intensity and Tab. 13, 14 for SocialSent. For SocialSent, we display the average difference between the correct choice and each confounding choice in the corresponding column. In Tab. 9, we see that incorrectly classified questions have higher arousal difference for outlook prediction whereas for resolution prediction as shown in Tab. 10, incorrectly classified questions have higher valence and dominance difference. This shows that language modeling is unable to extract VAD information from text and use it as a hint in prediction. Similarly, in Tab. 11 and Tab. 12, the greater difference in intensity for joy and anger in outlook prediction incorrect questions and the greater difference in intensity for sadness in resolution prediction incorrect questions imply that mental state is not utilized to make predictions. In Tab. 13 and 14, the greater difference in socially contextualized sentiment score for selective choices in incorrectly answered questions is evidence that sentiment is also not taken into consideration when predictions are made. The results here further prove that language models are unable to pick up underlying social elements including VAD, Affect Intensity and mental states that set the correct answers apart from other choices.

	V	A	D
correct	0.1129	0.1645	0.1325
incorrect	0.1139	0.1742	0.1274

Table 9: Average difference in VAD scores for outlook prediction.

	V	A	D
correct	0.1052	0.1429	0.1168
incorrect	0.1125	0.1463	0.1230

Table 10: Average difference in VAD scores for resolution prediction.

	joy	fear	sadness	anger
correct	0.3182	0.0627	0.1800	0.0653
incorrect	0.3223	0.0660	0.166	0.0726

Table 11: Average difference in affect intensity scores for outlook prediction.

	joy	fear	sadness	anger
correct	0.3562	0.1454	0.2810	0.1420
incorrect	0.3522	0.1492	0.2926	0.1224

Table 12: Average difference in affect intensity scores for resolution prediction.

conf	climax	buildup	same-seed	diff-seed
correct	0.3599	0.3722	0.3985	0.3783
incorrect	0.3778	0.3949	0.3713	0.4026

Table 13: Average difference in SocialSent scores for outlook prediction.

conf	climax	buildup	same-seed	diff-seed
correct	0.3599	0.3722	0.3985	0.3783
incorrect	0.3250	0.3400	0.3725	0.3873

Table 14: Average difference in SocialSent scores in resolution prediction.

7 Summary

We introduce *Social Narrative Tree*, a corpus of 1250 social narratives that encode rich social elements that collectively drive the relationship trajectory in each story. We propose evaluation tasks Relationship Outlook Prediction MCQ and Resolution Prediction MCQ using this dataset to measure the extent that systems understand social relationships. The tree structure of the dataset provides convenient and meaningful confounding choices, making the tasks challenging for language models. Particularly, the best performance achieved by BERT-base is significantly lower than human performance, justifying that relying on textual information is insufficient in understanding social relationships. A possible future work direction is to incorporate various social elements into predicting models so as to capture the nuances of relationship trajectories in different social situations.

References

Steven Bird, Ewan Klein, and Edward Loper. 2009. *Natural Language Processing with Python.* O'Reilly Media.

Antoine Bosselut, Hannah Rashkin, Maarten Sap, Chaitanya Malaviya, Asli Çelikyilmaz, and Yejin Choi. 2019. Comet: Commonsense transformers for automatic knowledge graph construction. *ArXiv*, abs/1906.05317.

Nathanael Chambers and Dan Jurafsky. 2008. Unsupervised learning of narrative event chains. In *Proceedings of ACL-08: HLT*, pages 789–797, Columbus, Ohio. Association for Computational Linguistics.

Snigdha Chaturvedi, Dan Goldwasser, and Hal Daume III. 2016. Ask, and shall you receive? understanding desire fulfillment in natural language text. In *Thirtieth AAAI Conference on Artificial Intelligence*.

Jacob Devlin, Ming-Wei Chang, Kenton Lee, and Kristina Toutanova. 2019. Bert: Pre-training of deep bidirectional transformers for language understanding. In *Proceedings of the 2019 Conference of the North American Chapter of the Association for Computational Linguistics: Human Language Technologies, Volume 1 (Long and Short Papers)*, pages 4171–4186.

Steve Duck. 1994. *Meaningful relationships: Talking, sense, and relating.* Sage Publications, Inc.

Gustav Freytag. 1896. *Freytag's technique of the drama: an exposition of dramatic composition and art.* Scholarly Press.

Amit Goyal, Ellen Riloff, and Hal Daumé III. 2010. Automatically producing plot unit representations for narrative text. In *Proceedings of the 2010 Conference on Empirical Methods in Natural Language Processing*, pages 77–86.

Mark Granroth-Wilding and Stephen Clark. 2016. What happens next? event prediction using a compositional neural network model. In *AAAI*.

William L. Hamilton, Kevin Clark, Jure Leskovec, and Dan Jurafsky. 2016. Inducing domain-specific sentiment lexicons from unlabeled corpora. *CoRR*, abs/1606.02820.

Xiaochuang Han, Eunsol Choi, and Chenhao Tan. 2019. No permanent friends or enemies: Tracking relationships between nations from news.

Mohit Iyyer, Anupam Guha, Snigdha Chaturvedi, Jordan Boyd-Graber, and Hal Daumé III. 2016. Feuding families and former friends: Unsupervised learning for dynamic fictional relationships. In *Proceedings of the 2016 Conference of the North American Chapter of the Association for Computational Linguistics: Human Language Technologies*, pages 1534–1544.

William Labov. 1997. Some further steps in narrative analysis.

Steven Loria, P Keen, M Honnibal, R Yankovsky, D Karesh, E Dempsey, et al. 2014. Textblob: simplified text processing. *Secondary TextBlob: simplified text processing*, 3.

Saif Mohammad. 2018. Obtaining reliable human ratings of valence, arousal, and dominance for 20,000 English words. In *Proceedings of the 56th Annual Meeting of the Association for Computational Linguistics (Volume 1: Long Papers)*, pages 174–184, Melbourne, Australia. Association for Computational Linguistics.

Saif M. Mohammad. 2017. Word affect intensities. *CoRR*, abs/1704.08798.

Nasrin Mostafazadeh, Nathanael Chambers, Xiaodong He, Devi Parikh, Dhruv Batra, Lucy Vanderwende, Pushmeet Kohli, and James Allen. 2016. A corpus and cloze evaluation for deeper understanding of commonsense stories. In *Proceedings of the 2016 Conference of the North American Chapter of the Association for Computational Linguistics: Human Language Technologies*, pages 839–849, San Diego, California. Association for Computational Linguistics.

G. Prince. 1973. *A Grammar of Stories: An Introduction.* De proprietatibus litterarum. Mouton.

Elahe Rahimtoroghi, Jiaqi Wu, Ruimin Wang, Pranav Anand, and Marilyn Walker. 2017. Modelling protagonist goals and desires in first-person narrative. In *Proceedings of the 18th Annual SIGdial Meeting on Discourse and Dialogue*, pages 360–369.

Hannah Rashkin, Antoine Bosselut, Maarten Sap, Kevin Knight, and Yejin Choi. 2018a. Modeling naive psychology of characters in simple commonsense stories. *CoRR*, abs/1805.06533.

Hannah Rashkin, Maarten Sap, Emily Allaway, Noah A. Smith, and Yejin Choi. 2018b. Event2mind: Commonsense inference on events, intents, and reactions. In *ACL*.

Kenneth Rubin, Cathryn Booth-LaForce, Linda Rose-Krasnor, and Rosemary Mills. 1995. Social relationships and social skills: A conceptual and empirical analysis.

Maarten Sap, Ronan LeBras, Emily Allaway, Chandra Bhagavatula, Nicholas Lourie, Hannah Rashkin, Brendan Roof, Noah A. Smith, and Yejin Choi. 2018. ATOMIC: an atlas of machine commonsense for if-then reasoning. *CoRR*, abs/1811.00146.

Maarten Sap, Hannah Rashkin, Derek Chen, Ronan LeBras, and Yejin Choi. 2019. Social iqa: Commonsense reasoning about social interactions. In *EMNLP*.

R.C. Schank and R. Abelson. 1977. *Scripts, Plans, Goals, and Understanding*. Hillsdale, NJ: Earlbaum Assoc.

Thomas Wolf, Lysandre Debut, Victor Sanh, Julien Chaumond, Clement Delangue, Anthony Moi, Pierric Cistac, Tim Rault, R'emi Louf, Morgan Funtowicz, and Jamie Brew. 2019. Huggingface's transformers: State-of-the-art natural language processing. *ArXiv*, abs/1910.03771.

Rowan Zellers, Yonatan Bisk, Roy Schwartz, and Yejin Choi. 2018. SWAG: A large-scale adversarial dataset for grounded commonsense inference. *CoRR*, abs/1808.05326.

Rowan Zellers, Ari Holtzman, Yonatan Bisk, Ali Farhadi, and Yejin Choi. 2019. Hellaswag: Can a machine really finish your sentence? *CoRR*, abs/1905.07830.

Large Scale Author Obfuscation Using Siamese Variational Auto-Encoder:
The SiamAO System

Chakaveh Saedi
Department of Computing,
Macquarie University,
Sydney, Australia
chakaveh.saedi@hdr.mq.edu.au

Mark Dras
Department of Computing,
Macquarie University,
Sydney, Australia
mark.dras@mq.edu.au

Abstract

Author obfuscation is the task of masking the author of a piece of text, with applications in privacy. Recent advances in deep neural networks have boosted author identification performance making author obfuscation more challenging.

Existing approaches to author obfuscation are largely heuristic. Obfuscation can, however, be thought of as the construction of adversarial examples to attack author identification, suggesting that the deep learning architectures used for adversarial attacks could have application here. Current architectures are proposed to construct adversarial examples against classification-based models, which in author identification would exclude the high-performing similarity-based models employed when facing large number of authorial classes.

In this paper, we propose the first deep learning architecture for constructing adversarial examples against similarity-based learners, and explore its application to author obfuscation. We analyse the output for both success in obfuscation and language acceptability, as well as comparing the performance with some common baselines, showing promising results in finding a balance between safety and soundness of the perturbed texts.

1 Introduction

The ability of machine learning to infer information about the author of a piece of text raises issues about privacy in textual data. Blogs, reviews, even tweets can be significantly revealing when authors follow textual authorial patterns, which can lead to disclosure of sensitive information. This has led to real-world problems, such as with Amazon's machine learning-based recruitment system,

which was discontinued when it turned out to disadvantage female candidates.[1] Cases like this have generated interest in NLP in concealing authorial characteristics such as gender or age, for example by producing representations that make this information difficult to infer (Li et al., 2018).

Author identification is the task of inferring the actual identity of the author. The potential number of author candidates can be very large, making author identification different from author profiling where the possible values of an attribute (e.g. gender) are typically limited to a small closed set, as in standard classification tasks. Depending on the number of included authorial classes, approaches in author identification are either classification-based or similarity-based, in the framing of Stamatatos (2009). Similarity-based approaches are proven to be better suited when facing large numbers of authors (Koppel et al., 2011), and have also underpinned several successful methods in the annual PAN authorship shared tasks[2] such as Seidman (2013) and Khonji and Iraqi (2014).

Author obfuscation is the task of concealing the identity of an author. This task is fairly challenging even for humans (McDonald et al., 2012), as authors are often not aware of hidden patterns in their writing; and the computational task is relatively underexplored. Some work has been carried out as part of a PAN authorship obfuscation task, since 2016, while other research has been independent of this. These approaches have included using backtranslation or heuristic application of paraphrase rules (Rosso et al., 2016; Hagen et al., 2017; Potthast et al., 2018), and more recently applying heuristic solution methods to the task framed as an optimization problem (Bevendorff et al., 2019; Li et al., 2019).

---

[1]https://bit.ly/2ycdnVV

[2]https://pan.webis.de/: shared tasks that are run annually on various aspects of authorship related tasks.

*Proceedings of the Ninth Joint Conference on Lexical and Computational Semantics (*SEM), pages 179–189*
Barcelona, Spain (Online), December 12–13, 2020

Author obfuscation can be seen as the generation of adversarial examples to attack an author identification system. Work in other areas of adversarial example generation (Iyyer et al., 2018; Alzantot et al., 2018; Xiao et al., 2020; Bai et al., 2020) has seen rapid progress with the application of deep learning, and could potentially be adapted here. For example, Zhao et al. (2018b) define a GAN-style architecture to generate 'natural' adversarial examples that — unlike approaches searching the input space — works on the dense representation of each data point. Dense representations lie on the manifold that defines the data distribution and finding close points to them leads to natural adversarial examples. They apply this both to image classification tasks and a standard three-class natural language inference task, producing natural-looking adversarial examples.

Such architectures have so far only been defined for producing adversarial examples against classification-based learners (limited number of classes). In author identification, this would exclude the high-performing similarity-based approaches. In this paper we introduce SIAMAO, an architecture that can generate adversarial examples against a similarity-based learner (specifically a deep Siamese network (Saedi and Dras, 2019)) and evaluate whether it can obfuscate against authorship identification. SIAMAO draws on ideas from Variational Autoencoders (VAEs), and the specific use of them by Bowman et al. (2016) for generating novel sentences close to some input, and from the Adversarially Regularized Autoencoders (ARAEs) of Zhao et al. (2018b): the intuition here is for the autoencoder to regenerate close to the original text but with some perturbation to fool an authorship identification system.

Our main contributions are: (i) A method for integrating Siamese networks into VAEs in order to generate adversaries against similarity based models, and testing it under author obfuscation. (ii) A performance comparison on properties of the obfuscated text between our model and baselines: our focus is on how well the obfuscated text can fool an author identification system, how much the obfuscator changes the text, and how acceptable the resulting text is. We find that SIAMAO provides a promising deep learning approach to this task.

2 Previous Work

2.1 Author Identification

There has been longstanding interest in determining the identity of authors of pieces of texts. Early work has been surveyed by Stamatatos (2009), and much of the activity on the problem has been carried out in the context of PAN authorship tasks (Kestemont et al., 2019, for example). Other work has occurred outside that context, such as the high-performing CNN approach of Ruder et al. (2016).

While most approaches tackle this as a classification task using standard machine learning classifiers, this is only suitable where the number of authors is small and known in advance, as argued by Koppel et al. (2011). An alternative approach is *similarity-based* models, where a metric is used to measure similarity between texts; this is appropriate for large number of authors, which is the context of the work in the present paper. Similarity-based methods include the WritePrints method (Abbasi and Chen, 2008) and that of Koppel et al. (2011). The latter, for example, represents documents as bags of character n-grams, and measures distances between documents over repeated samples by various fixed metrics (e.g. cosine similarity, Ruzicka).

An end-to-end trainable deep learning author obfuscation architecture needs a deep learning component for author identification. A deep learning similarity-based approach to author identification has been proposed by Saedi and Dras (2019), using a Siamese network. This approach outperforms alternatives on up to 5000 authors, and is suitable for our work.

2.2 Author Obfuscation

Author obfuscation is a less explored area which shares interest with fields including style transfer (Prabhumoye et al., 2018) or attribute masking (Reddy and Knight, 2016). The goal is to change or perturb a text, so that the accuracy of a specific authorship inference mechanism is worsened while the modified text conveys the original message.

Early research like that of Kacmarcik and Gamon (2006) worked at the level of machine learning features, proposing to eliminate those that are more effective in classification; this, however, resulted in mostly unreadable texts. At the level of working directly with text, one approach uses *backtranslation*: input text is translated to a pivot language and translated back to the original one, producing a more or less similar text. The result is greatly affected by the availability of a successful bidirectional machine translator (Rao et al., 2000; Prabhumoye et al., 2018).

Other approaches have been largely rule-based or heuristic in nature. Most rule-based obfuscators are designed against specific techniques. The

PAN organization has included author obfuscation among the authorial tasks. The 7 participants of PAN2018 author obfuscation were also mostly rule-based, but with different levels of aggressiveness (Potthast et al., 2018), and they varied in how well they defeated inference attackers and preserved the essence of the original text. In a recent comprehensive model, Bevendorff et al. (2019) also approached obfuscation from a verification perspective. This heuristic model calculates Jensen-Shannon distance over 3-gram frequency representations, iteratively applies perturbation operators (e.g. char-flip, deletion, context-free synonymy), picks the best nodes in the search space, and continues until the original classification result changes. They proposed "operator cost" to keep the text modification minimum and as minimally disruptive as possible. This was evaluated on the relatively small datasets of the PAN tasks. Outside of the PAN context (and of NLP research in general), Li et al. (2019) proposed TextBugger, a different heuristic model that first extracts a list of most important words based on the effect they have on the classification, and then modifies the selected words.

2.3 Adversarial Examples

Author obfuscation can be viewed as constructing adversarial examples against an authorship identification inference attacker: this is precisely the viewpoint of TextBugger. However, as noted above, TextBugger takes a heuristic approach to this, while state of the art approaches to constructing adversarial examples in many tasks involve deep learning architectures (Iyyer et al., 2018; Alzantot et al., 2018; Xiao et al., 2020; Bai et al., 2020). And even though these are well explored in the context of continuous representations that occur in image processing, with operators like affine transformations or lighting changes, it is less straightforward for the discrete nature of text. While there is some existing work, we note that all aim to construct adversarial examples against a *classification model* that typically handles only a small number of classes.

One possibility is to use auto-encoders: Minor data distortions can be formalized as an optimization problem to minimize the classification accuracy. Such optimization has been proven successful in image processing (Biggio et al., 2013; Goodfellow et al., 2014). In the context of textual adversarial examples, approaches take ideas from a range of sources, including encoder-decoder architectures, variational auto-encoders and GANs (Kusner et al., 2017; Pu et al., 2016; Pol et al., 2019, for exam-

ple). A key work that we draw on in this paper is that of Zhao et al. (2018b). Rather than working directly in the text space, they search for adversaries that lie on the data manifold: in their text application, this attacks a (three-class) textual entailment classifier. First, projections of data points are learnt, then the distance between each adversary and the closest real data point is measured in the vector space to choose the best fake sample. Finally, the selected adversary is mapped back to the input space. Their system combines ideas from encoder-decoder architecture, VAEs and GANs, and has two main training objectives: (1) bringing the encoder and generator output close to each other; and (2) making the sampled noise (i.e. generator's input) less random by using a module they call the 'Inverter'. The inverter is a network that learns to sample close-to-input points in the data manifold. Their search algorithm identifies the best adversary by incrementally increasing the search space till the classification result of the sampled point(s) is different from that of the original input data.

While not explicitly cast as adversarial example generation, the process of paraphrase generation can be seen in this light. Gupta et al. (2018) proposed a VAE-LSTM containing 2 LSTM-encoders which encode both the original sentence and the paraphrase. Encoded vectors are used in the sampling process of the VAE. On the decoder side, there is an encoder for original sentences and a decoder for paraphrase generation that is fed the embedding vector and the encoder output. In our approach, our encoder is a CNN but we also use two encoded vectors for sampling, and the modified embeddings are used by the decoder.

An optimization-based alternative to these deep learning approaches was proposed by Alzantot et al. (2018), using population-based optimization. They encode the sentences and perturb them in the vector space. Unlike the above work, they propose a gradient-free optimization by employing genetic algorithms. Perturbation is at the word level based on semantic similarity of candidates and original vectors going through cross-over and mutation instead of expanding the search space iteratively. We use a similar notion of perturbation operators, including cross-over.

3 SiamAO

Here we present SIAMAO, an author obfuscation neural network that integrates a large scale Siamese author identifier in a VAE architecture to generate

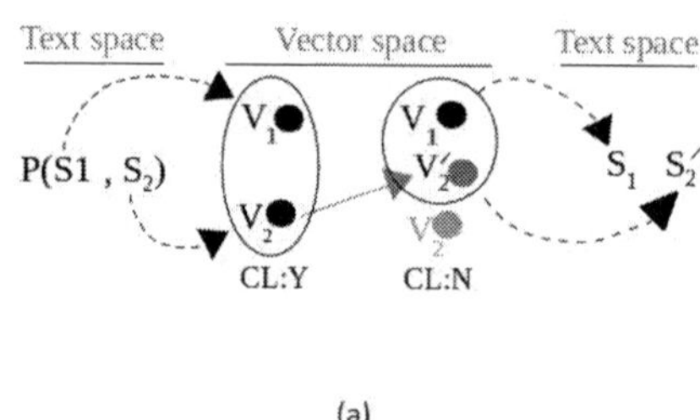

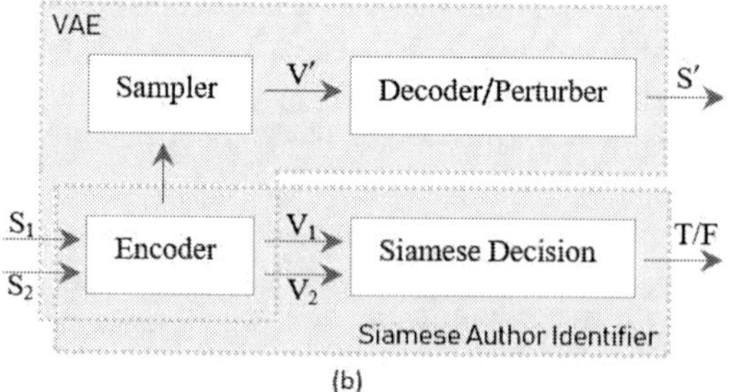

Figure 1: (a) A pair of texts (S_1, S_2) are mapped into the vector-space (V_1, V_2). Perturbation operator (continues red arrow) modifies one of the inputs. This changes the verification result from Y to N. S_2' is the perturbation output when mapped back to the text space. (b) Schematic view of SiamAO; the network is composed of a Siamese author identifier and a VAE which share an encoder.

adversarial text. This system takes a pair of texts as input and generates an adversary with the aim of changing the author identification results. Figure 1 shows (a) a high-level schema of the process and (b) the components of SIAMAO respectively. A key innovation is incorporation of a similarity-based author identification approach, in contrast to other work described in §2 that only constructs adversarial examples against classification-based inference.

3.1 Author Identification

Our similarity-based author identification component is taken from Saedi and Dras (2019). The model consists of (1) a dual encoding sub-network and (2) a decision sub-network. The encoding sub-network (a deep CNN model) receives an input pair of texts (S_1, S_2) and maps each S_i into the vector space (V_i). The decision sub-network compares V_1 and V_2 and generates a similarity score (more information available in supplementary material). We adopt the version of the model that proved best overall in the source work for large numbers of authors: the encoding sub-networks are character-level rather than word-level, and L_1 distance is employed in the decision network. This similarity-based model produces a score between a pair of texts that can be interpreted as an answer to the *author verification* problem: are these two texts by the same author? These two components of the author identification system are marked as *Encoder* and *Siamese Decision* in Figure 1-(b) respectively.

3.2 Author Obfuscation

Our overall approach to generating adversarial examples draws on the VAE architecture of Gupta et al. (2018) for paraphrase generation, and the idea of Zhao et al. (2018a) to generate perturbations in the encoded space. Implementation details

can be found in supplementary material.

Encoder-Decoder A successful VAE for text perturbation requires a strong encoder as well as a decoder capable of perturbation. In our proposed architecture, shown in Figure 1-(b), the author identifier network and the VAE share the encoder. This results in an *authorial feature aware* decoder since the encoder is trained on author verification. SIAMAO's decoder is trained for a) normal decoding (i.e. as a decoder: loss is 0, when input=output=target) and for b) obfuscation (i.e. as a perturber: loss is 0, when input≠output=target). In both cases, the input to the decoder is sampled from V_i. However, when trained for obfuscation, perturbation operators modify the sampler's input and output.

Sampler In finding adversarial examples, we have two aims: (1) like Zhao et al. (2018b), we look for points that lie close to the original in terms of the manifold that defines the data distribution; and (2) we look for adversaries that can change the author verification results while preserving the original message. In other words, we need to generate a piece of text that is very close to the original one but different enough to change the verification result. In SiamAO, when training the decoder for normal decoding, V_i is directly used for sampling (i.e. to generate V' from the normal distribution). However, when training the decoder for obfuscation, unlike non-Siamese models, we have access to two sample inputs (V_1, V_2) which can help to remain within the acceptable area[3] in the vector space. We start by interpolating between these two inputs. Specifically, if $V_1 = [v_{11}, \ldots, v_{1n}]$ and $V_2 = [v_{21}, \ldots, v_{2n}]$, and $V_1 > V_2$ and the distance between them is is

---

[3]There are infinite data points in the vector space, not all of them can be mapped back to a meaningful piece of text; an acceptable area in the vector space has similar distribution to the input space.

d, either of $V_1' = [v_{11} - d', \ldots, v_{1n} - d']$ and $V_2' = [v_{21} + d', \ldots, v_{2n} + d']$ (where $d' = d/3$) can be used by the sampler.[4]

Perturbation Operators To combine embedding and sampled vectors in the decoding step, we could concatenate them as in most VAE models. There is a risk, however, that the network focuses on the embedding part and mostly ignores the sampled vector which results in very few changes in the text such that it is unable to mislead the classifier. To add perturbations to the vectors, we adopt some of the techniques of Alzantot et al. (2018). In SiamAO, when training the decoder for obfuscation, after moving the original vector and sampling as explained above, we use *cross-over* as the final perturbation step. Cross-over, taken from genetic algorithms, keeps vector elements mostly the same, only making changes at specific indices. The inputs to the cross-over operator are the V' vector and the character-level embedding.[5] After cross-over, we sum the two vectors. Alternative methods are compared in §5.

Objectives The first part of the objective is a standard one for VAEs, the reconstruction loss, in Eqn (1). In terms of generating adversarial examples, training our generative model consists of (1) training for normal decoding and (2) training for perturbation. In the latter, the decoder learns to make changes to the input and the sampler learns to pick a vector that flips the Siamese author verification original (binary) decision (y_{OD}) to the perturbed decision (y_{PD}), in Eqn (2). Eqn (3) combines these two component losses.

$$l_{\text{cons}} = (\mathbf{E}_{q_\phi(V'|S)}[\log p_\theta(S|V')] - \text{KL}(q_\phi(V'|S) \parallel p(V')) \tag{1}$$
$$l_{\text{sampler}} = \text{MSE}(y_{\text{PD}}, |1 - y_{\text{OD}}|) \tag{2}$$
$$l_{\text{pert}} = \alpha \times l_{\text{cons}} + (1 - \alpha) \times l_{\text{sampler}} \tag{3}$$

Eqn (1) provides a lower bound on the model evidence $p(S|\theta, \phi)$, KL stands for Kullback–Leibler divergence. α is set to 0.5 in all our experiments, making the backpropagation uniform on the sampler and the decoder.

Obfuscation Training For the perturbation objective, we generate training data by applying widely used text modification operators very similar to rule-based systems such as Bevendorff et al. (2019) and Li et al. (2019). We emphasise that unlike common rule-based or heuristic techniques, these operators are merely to generate the data entries as the target while training the decoder for obfuscation. Our selected modification rules can be categorized into four classes: *shape similarity* (e.g. ä →a, O → 0), *sound similarity* (e.g. ee → ea), *swap* (e.g. ie → ei) and *punctuation modification* (e.g. . → .. or :" → :). As Bevendorff et al. (2019), we only apply these changes to a subset of instances in each text piece, which we select uniformly randomly with probability 1/3.

4 Experimental Setup

4.1 Evaluation Framework

There is not yet a standard evaluation framework for this kind of work. Hence we observe various different evaluation techniques in the literature. This has also resulted in project specific definitions. For instance, in both PAN2018 and the Text-Bugger system, mis-spelled words are considered as valid "paraphrasing" due to the little impact they cause on human understanding. They argue character-level perturbation (i.e. mis-spelled words) are visually and semantically similar to the original ones (e.g. *their* and *thier*, *some* and *sOme*) and can deliver the original message (Potthast et al., 2018; Li et al., 2019; Rawlinson, 2007). Work on adversarial example attacks has two broad types of evaluation. Misclassification or attack success (how well the adversarial examples fool the inference mechanism); and utility or imperceptibility (how well the adversarial examples preserve important aspects of the original). Work on author obfuscation generally fits with this, although in disparate ways; the PAN tasks,[6] for example, consider safety (broadly misclassification), soundness (textual entailment between original and adversarial texts) and sensibleness (inconspicuousness, or looking like regular text); the latter two are related to the typical utility criteria. Working on large authorial classes, we could not employ the exact set-up in PAN evaluation, however, our evaluation metrics also assess misclassification and utility.

4.1.1 Misclassification

We calculate "Perturbation Wins" (PW): the average proportion of times where a perturbed vector or text misleads an authorship identification inference model (Alzantot et al., 2018; Potthast et al., 2018).

Robust Vector Representation We first look at a system-internal evaluation. As noted above, the

---

[4]We conducted experiments with the average vector and the $1/3$ distance shift as explained here. We leave finding the best interpolation for further study.

[5]Specifically, we apply five crossovers between the V' and the embedding vectors at random positions.

[6]https://pan.webis.de/clef18/
pan18-web/author-obfuscation.html

system objective is to generate a vector representation which is similar to the original message while eliminating clues to authorship. Having (S_1, S_2) as an input pair with (V_1, V_2) as their corresponding representations in vector space, V_i is perturbed to V_i' which is then sent back to Siamese decision by replacing V_i. It shows whether the Siamese author verification's original decision on (V_1, V_2) is different from the decision on (V_1, V_2') and (V_1', V_2). This gives a preliminary result: if the system cannot produce vectors that can fool the decider, it will not produce successfully perturbed texts.

Perturbation Win in Text Space The author identification work of Saedi and Dras (2019) had as its primary evaluation, following the first work on deep Siamese networks (Koch et al., 2015), N-way one-shot classification: a 'query' text is compared against texts by N authors, one of whom is also the author of the query text. The N-way task is tackled by assigning pairwise similarities to the query text and each author, in effect carrying out N author verification attempts. N-way inference performance is evaluated by the average accuracy over 150 N-way classifications. We consider $N \in \{3, 5, 10, 50\}$.

Our misclassification evaluation in text space involves calculating perturbation wins on both author verification and N-way classification. In the N-way evaluation, a perturbed query text is presented. We use two authorship inference models for this: the standalone Siamese authorship identification system of Saedi and Dras (2019), and the system of Koppel et al. (2011). This latter is a key inference attacker in PAN tasks, and also the only similarity-based system with available code. Koppel works on iterative representation of pieces of text using a subset of all extracted character 4-grams and similarity measurements (Ruzicka metric) to identify the author of a piece of text (Koppel et al., 2011).

In addition to the N-way evaluation above, we evaluated misclassification under Koppel with 1000 authors, randomly selected from SIAMAO's testset. (Koppel does not require training, apart from counting character n-grams, and so is fast to use for many authors.) In the results we call this setup K-LG.

4.1.2 Utility: Text similarity

We use the following measures to quantify the similarity between original and perturbed texts. (1) Bleu score (BL) (Papineni et al., 2002), measuring n-gram overlap between original and generated texts, previously used to assess difference in style transfer (Shen et al., 2017). (2) Edit distance (ED), considering the texts as strings and counting the minimum number of operations required to transform the original texts into their perturbed counterparts (Przybocki et al., 2006; Li et al., 2019). This metric is believed to be used in commercial translation memory models (Bloodgood and Strauss, 2014). (3) Euclidean Distance (EC) between the vector representations: closeness in vector space typically corresponds to greater semantic similarity (Li et al., 2019; Alzantot et al., 2018).

4.1.3 Utility: Language acceptability

The perturbed text should be natural-looking, in terms of grammaticality / acceptability. Prediction of language acceptability is now a standard NLP task, e.g. the CoLA task that is part of the GLUE benchmark (Wang et al., 2019). However, that is a binary task: sentences are judged acceptable or not. There is, instead, a notion of gradient grammaticality, where sentence grammaticality is measured on a scale of 0 to 1 (Lau et al., 2014); this could be more suited to capturing the changes we might see in our adversarial examples.

BERT has previously been fine-tuned to produce a high-performing model for the CoLA task (Devlin et al., 2019). For gradient grammaticality, a variety of models predating BERT have been trained on the Statistical Models of Grammaticality (SMOG) dataset,[7] and have been shown to correlate fairly well with human judgements (Lau et al., 2014, 2017). Given the improvements over earlier models shown by BERT on the CoLA task, we built our model of language naturalness by fine-tuning BERT-large on the SMOG dataset. We refer to this model as BERT-SMOG. To validate our BERT-SMOG, we compare with models proposed in Lau et al. (2017) on the original dataset: its Pearson's r correlation with human judgements is around 0.8, much higher than their best scoring model (which predates contextual LMs).

In this evaluation category, we also provide the scores for the more common binary acceptability. For this, we fine-tuned BERT only on the CoLA dataset (BERT-CoLA). Evaluating BERT-CoLA on CoLA testset, our results are in line with the published benchmarks (Devlin et al., 2019). Final evaluations are done on a subset of 700 randomly selected sentences from the Fanfiction database going through backtranslation, RAND modification and SIAMAO.

---

[7]Project website: `https://clasp.gu.se/about/people/shalom-lappin/smog`.

4.2 Data

Several datasets have been used for author identification, including various PAN datasets. We use the dataset from Saedi and Dras (2019) consisting of 10000 authors from the domain of fanfiction,[8] as one that is large enough to train a deep learning system. We followed the FF-5K (5000 author) dataset setup under the one-shot evaluation (i.e. disjoint authors between train and test sets). This test set consists of over 10000 pairs covering 1665 authors not seen in training (more information in the supplementary material).

4.3 Models

Core Models   As in a VAE, our SIAMAO system starts with text that looks somewhat random, and as training proceeds comes to look more like the original text, encouraged by the reconstruction loss. At each epoch, then, there will be varying effects on misclassification and utility. Training the model for 6 epochs, we present results for both epoch 3 (SIAMAO_3) and epoch 5 (SIAMAO_5) to show the effect training has on different aspects of text modification with opposing objectives.

Baselines   The author obfuscation approaches of the PAN competition are typically tailored to the PAN setup (classification-based, over a relatively small number of authors). Heuristic-based approaches are potentially applicable, but could not be applied here.[9]

We therefore used backtranslation as our key baseline, as one that has recently produced decent results in related tasks (Prabhumoye et al., 2018). Our experiments are done on two sets of languages with different accuracy in Google machine translation, English-French (BT-FR: good quality MT) and English-Persian (BT-PR: average-high MT). Random character modification (RAND), following the same rules explained in §3.2, is another baseline.

Variant Models   To examine the effect of choices in the architecture (in particular, in §3.2 under Perturbation Operators), we explored various ways of transferring the encoder's outputs to the sampler and generating the input to the decoder. The encoder generates two vectors, V_1 and V_2. These vectors can be directly sent to the sampler (e.g. JUST-SUM method below), or go through some changes

in the vector space before being fed to the sampler (e.g. SHIFT and AVE below). The sampler uses its input vector to sample a similar point (V') from the normal distribution, which is then sent to the decoder. The decoder needs both V' and embedding to generate an output sentence.

The five methods we report are 1) SHIFT (the core method we define in §3): V_1 and V_2 are shifted towards each other by $1/3$ of their distance; the resulting vectors are sent to the sampler. 2) JUST-SUM: V_i is the input to the sampler. 3) AVE: the element-wise average of V_1 and V_2 is the input to the sampler. In all these three methods the sum over cross-over between embedding vector and V' is the input to the decoder. For both 4) CATEMB and 5) NOCROSS, the first step is the same as the SHIFT method. Then, in the former, the concatenation of embedding and V' is the input to the decoder; in the latter sum of embedding and V' is the input to the decoder.

5 Evaluation Results and Analysis

5.1 Misclassification

Robust Vector Representation   Replacing vectors with their perturbed version as explained in §4.1.1 changes the inputs to the Siamese Decision sub-network (e.g $(V_1, V_2) \rightarrow (V_1, V_2')$). This modification results in PW of over 90%, indicating authorial information can be hidden in vector space using SIAMAO.

Perturbation Win in Text Space   In terms of the classification across a large number of authors, K-LG in Table 1 shows that Koppel's accuracy of 0.644 over 1000 authors drops dramatically under all modifications. SIAMAO_3 causes the maximum fall in accuracy, RAND ranks second, followed by BT-PR. For SIAMAO, as expected, at epoch 5, where the VAE-style architecture has reconstructed the perturbed text to be closer to the original, the drop in classification accuracy is smaller.

The two middle columns in Table 1 show the accuracy on original and perturbed data for N-way classification ($N \in \{3, 5, 10, 50\}$). We see different behaviour across the two author identifiers and under different Ns. Koppel classification accuracy decreases with all methods, with one of the SIA-MAO methods generally best. None of the methods — SIAMAO, backtranslation, or random changes — seem to be effective against the Siamese author identifier, which is rather surprising. However, in one way these results are in line with what Zhao et al. (2018b) reported: success rate is noticeably

---

Model	Koppel Author Identification				Siamese Author Identification				K-LG
	3-way	5-way	10-way	50-way	3-way	5-way	10-way	50-way	
Original	0.640	0.567	0.427	0.327	0.933	0.853	0.707	0.400	0.644
SIAMAO$_3$	0.513	0.493	0.353	0.260	0.913	0.867	0.773	0.433	0.407
SIAMAO$_5$	0.540	0.487	0.360	0.220	0.940	0.873	0.760	0.433	0.446
RAND	0.593	0.513	0.400	0.240	0.933	0.900	0.793	0.507	0.414
BT-FR	0.613	0.526	0.433	0.273	0.827	0.740	0.573	0.353	0.558
BT-PR	0.607	0.500	0.340	0.293	0.913	0.847	0.733	0.413	0.429

Table 1: First two columns, Koppel and Siamese author identification accuracy on N-way classification. K-LG shows Koppel accuracy on 1000 authors.

Model	PW	EC	ED	BL
SIAMAO$_3$	0.238	2597	289	0.098
SIAMAO$_5$	0.375	1927	215	0.168
RAND	0.340	3442	222	0.070
BT-FR	0.399	4649	235	0.486
BT-PR	0.512	4891	427	0.256

Table 2: Perturbation win (PW), Euclidean distance (EC), edit distance (ED), and Bleu score (BL), comparing perturbed text against the original.

Rosie laughs as my cheeks cheaks burn, and I watch as she stands elegantly, blocking the sun from my eyes. 'I want to go swimming,' she tells tells me.

I felt my cheeks cheaks flush flu5h slightly. "Sh...well, uh..." Sam and Embry chuckled at my response resp0n5e .

Figure 2: Samples of SIAMAO's perturbation that successfully fooled classification.

lower when the classifier (i.e. Siamese author identifier in our case) is stronger.

For the binary classification task of author verification that underpins the classification across all authors and N-way classification, we give some results under PW in Table 2. It is interesting that while the proportion of perturbation wins in the verification context is relatively low, it still results in noticeable drops in the overall classification scores for Koppel as noted above. This is likely to be because the similarity scores are changed enough to affect the selection among N authors while not changing the pairwise binary prediction.

5.2 Text Similarity

Table 2 provides the Bleu scores, edit and Euclidean distances in the verification task, under random, back-translation and SIAMAO modifications. For our two variants of SIAMAO, SIAMAO$_3$ results in more modifications than SIAMAO$_5$, reflecting the nature of VAEs. However, due to the other objective of the network, training must improve perturbations too. We observe higher perturbation win as well as higher Blue score for SIAMAO$_5$. Given the fact that Blue score is calculated on word n-grams, this suggests the model may have learnt to modify texts mostly at spaces that do not break words (e.g. punctuation modification).

In terms of the baselines, BT-PR and BT-FR result in more modifications than RAND (higher edit and Euclidean distances). However, they achieve the highest Bleu score as well as perturbation win. SIAMAO ranks in the middle, with SIAMAO$_5$ showing the least text modification, being significantly more successful than RAND in all the four

metrics but less successful in perturbation win and Bleu compared to the back-translation models.

In Figure 2 we give two sample extracts of perturbed texts from SIAMAO that fooled classifiers, to illustrate how the system changes text. It can be seen that the perturbation operators described in §3.2 are applied only at some places: for example, the replacement of s by 5 does not occur at all possible locations, and similarly l by 1.

Training and finding a balance An obfuscation model has several objectives that contradict each other. So, the network learning process involves finding a balance between them; specifically, finding important positions in the input text to minimally modify, as well as improving obfuscation success. Using SIAMAO's test set after each training epoch, we evaluated the 4 aforementioned parameters. Figure 3 displays the trends for edit distance, Euclidean distance, Bleu and perturbation win follow during SIAMAO's 6 training epochs.

Epochs 1 to 3 present rather sharp upward trends for edit distance, Euclidean distance and perturbation win, coinciding with an expected major drop in Bleu. Epochs 3 to 5, on the other hand, show Bleu score increasing to its maximum in epoch 4 while edit and Euclidean distance experience a noticeable fall. Epoch 5 reaches an favorable balance in the parameters plus the most successful modification from a privacy point of view. However, this doesn't continue in epoch 6 which is an indicator of over-training.

186

	Original	BT-FR	BT-PR	SIAMAO$_3$	SIAMAO$_5$	RAND
BERT-SMOG	0.751	0.733	0.724	0.522	0.535	0.506
BERT-CoLA	0.773	0.788	0.796	0.485	0.549	0.567
# OOVs	16.7	14.5	9.6	76.4	73.5	95.7

Table 3: Language acceptability scores on a subset of original and perturbed Fanfiction data. Also included are average number of OOV tokens in texts.

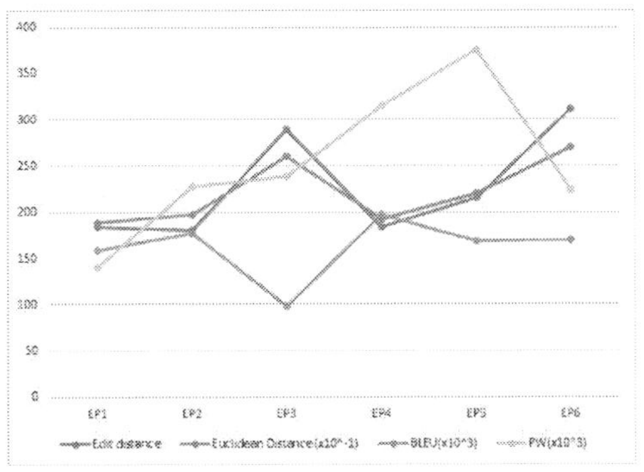

Figure 3: Effect of 6 epochs of training on edit distance, Euclidean distance, Bleu and perturbation win.

5.3 Language Acceptability

Table 3 presents the results for language acceptability as measured by BERT-SMOG and BERT-CoLA on a subset of perturbed Fanfiction database. One issue with applying these models to the obfuscated text is that SIAMAO is more likely to generate out-of-vocabulary (OOV) words (e.g. *cheaks*) than the backtranslation models, and this affects the acceptability score, even if the OOV words themselves might be considered reasonable. The table thus also contains average number of OOV tokens in generated texts.

The scores on the original are relatively high; the scores on the backtranslation models are close. This is not surprising given that number of OOV tokens is similar (in fact, it is surprising that number of OOV tokens is actually lower than in the original texts, even more for BT-PR than for BT-FR— perhaps the original OOVs are lost in translation). The average number of OOVs is much larger for the SIAMAO models and RAND. To understand the effect of number of OOVs, we took the original CoLA dataset and systematically replaced words with OOV tokens, and carried out some curve fitting of number of OOVs against BERT-CoLA score; this would allow us to estimate how a score might drop with an increasing number of OOVs. An exponential decay function appears to be a good fit. However, because CoLA sentences are much shorter than the generated texts, it is not

possible to use such a curve for direct extrapolation.[10] Nevertheless, it does illustrate that it is not surprising for the language acceptability scores to be lower for the SIAMAO models, and that this is not necessarily indicative of substantially worse quality.

5.4 Variant Models

As noted in §4.3, we studied the effect of different ways of transferring the encoder's outputs to the sampler, beyond just a standard concatenation as in regular VAEs. SHIFT approach outperforms the other variants in most respects (misclassification, etc) while being similar in the text similarity measures (edit and Euclidean distance). This supports the intuition that regular VAE concatenation is not sufficient for this task, and perturbation operators of the sort we have proposed are necessary (scores are included in the supplementary material).

6 Conclusion and Further Work

This work is the first to propose a deep learning architecture for generating textual adversarial examples that incorporates a similarity-based inference model rather than a standard classifier-based one. We explored this in the context of authorship obfuscation, where the goal is to hide the author from a similarity-based authorship identifier. Results indicate that our SIAMAO model can degrade the performance of a key standard authorship identification system, compared to baseline systems, with modifications that are of similar magnitude or lower. All approaches had difficulty against a Siamese authorship identification system, however.

As this is the first work in this direction, many improvements are possible, particularly in the area of language acceptability. These improvements would be both to SIAMAO, in encouraging the adversarial examples towards greater acceptability, also in terms of the automatic evaluation metrics. Employing other deep learning adversarial architectures as a base would also be interesting.

---

[10] Adjusting the scores on the original texts to match the number of OOVs in the SIAMAO and RAND models leads to values close to the curve asymptote, of around 0.3.

References

Ahmed Abbasi and Hsinchun Chen. 2008. Writeprints: A Stylometric Approach to Identity-Level Identification and Similarity Detection in Cyberspace. *ACM Transactions on Information Systems*, 26(2).

Moustafa Alzantot, Yash Sharma, Ahmed Elgohary, Bo-Jhang Ho, Mani Srivastava, and Kai-Wei Chang. 2018. Generating natural language adversarial examples. In *Proceedings of the 2018 Conference on Empirical Methods in Natural Language Processing*, pages 2890–2896, Brussels, Belgium. Association for Computational Linguistics.

Tao Bai, Jun Zhao, Jinlin Zhu, Shoudong Han, J. Chen, and Bo Li. 2020. Ai-gan: Attack-inspired generation of adversarial examples. *ArXiv*, abs/2002.02196.

Janek Bevendorff, Martin Potthast, Matthias Hagen, and Benno Stein. 2019. Heuristic authorship obfuscation. In *Proceedings of the 57th Annual Meeting of the Association for Computational Linguistics*, pages 1098–1108.

Battista Biggio, Igino Corona, Davide Maiorca, Blaine Nelson, Nedim Šrndić, Pavel Laskov, Giorgio Giacinto, and Fabio Roli. 2013. Evasion attacks against machine learning at test time. In *Joint European conference on machine learning and knowledge discovery in databases*, pages 387–402. Springer.

Michael Bloodgood and Benjamin Strauss. 2014. Translation memory retrieval methods. In *Proceedings of the 14th Conference of the European Chapter of the Association for Computational Linguistics*, pages 202–210, Gothenburg, Sweden. Association for Computational Linguistics.

Samuel R. Bowman, Luke Vilnis, Oriol Vinyals, Andrew Dai, Rafal Jozefowicz, and Samy Bengio. 2016. Generating sentences from a continuous space. In *Proceedings of The 20th SIGNLL Conference on Computational Natural Language Learning*, pages 10–21, Berlin, Germany. Association for Computational Linguistics.

Jacob Devlin, Ming-Wei Chang, Kenton Lee, and Kristina Toutanova. 2019. Bert: Pre-training of deep bidirectional transformers for language understanding. In *Proceedings of the 2019 NAACL-HLT*. Association for Computing Machinery.

Ian J Goodfellow, Jonathon Shlens, and Christian Szegedy. 2014. Explaining and harnessing adversarial examples. *arXiv preprint arXiv:1412.6572*.

Ankush Gupta, Arvind Agarwal, Prawaan Singh, and Piyush Rai. 2018. A deep generative framework for paraphrase generation. In *Thirty-Second AAAI Conference on Artificial Intelligence*.

Matthias Hagen, Martin Potthast, and Benno Stein. 2017. Overview of the author obfuscation task at pan 2017: Safety evaluation revisited. In *CLEF*.

Mohit Iyyer, John Wieting, Kevin Gimpel, and Luke Zettlemoyer. 2018. Adversarial example generation with syntactically controlled paraphrase networks. In *Proceedings of the 2018 Conference of the North American Chapter of the Association for Computational Linguistics: Human Language Technologies, Volume 1 (Long Papers)*, pages 1875–1885, New Orleans, Louisiana. Association for Computational Linguistics.

Gary Kacmarcik and Michael Gamon. 2006. Obfuscating document stylometry to preserve author anonymity. In *Proceedings of the COLING/ACL on Main conference poster sessions*, pages 444–451. Association for Computational Linguistics.

Mike Kestemont, Efstathios Stamatatos, Enrique Manjavacas, Walter Daelemans, Martin Potthast, and Benno Stein. 2019. Overview of the cross-domain authorship attribution task at {PAN} 2019. In *Working Notes of CLEF 2019-Conference and Labs of the Evaluation Forum, Lugano, Switzerland, September 9-12, 2019*, pages 1–15.

Mahmoud Khonji and Youssef Iraqi. 2014. A Slightly-modified GI-based Author-verifier with Lots of Features (ASGALF). In *Working Notes for CLEF 2014 Conference*.

Gregory Koch, Richard Zemel, and Ruslan Salakhutdinov. 2015. Siamese neural networks for one-shot image recognition. In *ICML Deep Learning Workshop*, volume 2.

Moshe Koppel, Jonathan Schler, and Shlomo Argamon. 2011. Authorship attribution in the wild. *Language Resources and Evaluation*, 45(1):83–94.

Matt J. Kusner, Brooks Paige, and José Miguel Hernández-Lobato. 2017. Grammar variational autoencoder. In *Proceedings of the 34th International Conference on Machine Learning - Volume 70*, ICML'17, page 1945–1954. JMLR.org.

Jey Han Lau, Alexander Clark, and Shalom Lappin. 2014. Measuring gradience in speakers' grammaticality judgements. In *CogSci*.

Jey Han Lau, Alexander Clark, and Shalom Lappin. 2017. Grammaticality, acceptability, and probability: A probabilistic view of linguistic knowledge. *Cognitive science*, 41 5:1202–1241.

Jinfeng Li, Shouling Ji, Tianyu Du, Bo Li, and Ting Wang. 2019. TextBugger: Generating Adversarial Text Against Real-world Applications. In *Proceedings of the 26th Annual Network and Distributed System Security Symposium (NDSS)*.

Yitong Li, Timothy Baldwin, and Trevor Cohn. 2018. Towards robust and privacy-preserving text representations. In *Proceedings of the 56th Annual Meeting of the Association for Computational Linguistics (Volume 2: Short Papers)*, pages 25–30, Melbourne, Australia. Association for Computational Linguistics.

Andrew WE McDonald, Sadia Afroz, Aylin Caliskan, Ariel Stolerman, and Rachel Greenstadt. 2012. Use fewer instances of the letter "i": Toward writing style anonymization. In *International Symposium on Privacy Enhancing Technologies Symposium*, pages 299–318. Springer.

Kishore Papineni, Salim Roukos, Todd Ward, and Wei-Jing Zhu. 2002. Bleu: a method for automatic evaluation of machine translation. In *Proceedings of the 40th annual meeting on association for computational linguistics*, pages 311–318. Association for Computational Linguistics.

Adrian Pol, Victor Berger, Gianluca Cerminara, Cécile Germain, and Maurizio Pierini. 2019. Anomaly detection with conditional variational autoencoders. In *18th IEEE International Conference on Machine Learning and Applications*. ICMLA.

Martin Potthast, Felix Schremmer, Matthias Hagen, and Benno Stein. 2018. Overview of the author obfuscation task at pan 2018: A new approach to measuring safety. In *CLEF (Working Notes)*.

Shrimai Prabhumoye, Yulia Tsvetkov, Ruslan Salakhutdinov, and Alan W Black. 2018. Style transfer through back-translation.

Mark Przybocki, Gregory Sanders, and Audrey Le. 2006. Edit distance: A metric for machine translation evaluation. In *Proceedings of the Fifth International Conference on Language Resources and Evaluation (LREC'06)*, Genoa, Italy. European Language Resources Association (ELRA).

Yunchen Pu, Zhe Gan, Ricardo Henao, Xin Yuan, Chunyuan Li, Andrew Stevens, and Lawrence Carin. 2016. Variational autoencoder for deep learning of images, labels and captions. In D. D. Lee, M. Sugiyama, U. V. Luxburg, I. Guyon, and R. Garnett, editors, *Advances in Neural Information Processing Systems 29*, pages 2352–2360. Curran Associates, Inc.

Josyula R Rao, Pankaj Rohatgi, et al. 2000. Can pseudonymity really guarantee privacy? In *USENIX Security Symposium*, pages 85–96.

G. Rawlinson. 2007. The significance of letter position in word recognition. *IEEE Aerospace and Electronic Systems Magazine*, 22(1):26–27.

Sravana Reddy and Kevin Knight. 2016. Obfuscating gender in social media writing. In *Proceedings of the First Workshop on NLP and Computational Social Science*, pages 17–26.

Paolo Rosso, Francisco M. Rangel Pardo, Martin Potthast, Efstathios Stamatatos, Michael Tschuggnall, and Benno Stein. 2016. Overview of pan'16 - new challenges for authorship analysis: Cross-genre profiling, clustering, diarization, and obfuscation. In *CLEF*.

Sebastian Ruder, Parsa Ghaffari, and John G Breslin. 2016. Character-level and multi-channel convolutional neural networks for large-scale authorship attribution. *arXiv preprint arXiv:1609.06686*.

Chakaveh Saedi and Mark Dras. 2019. Siamese networks for large-scale author identification. *arXiv preprint arXiv:1912.10616*.

Shachar Seidman. 2013. Authorship Verification Using the Imposters Method. In *Working Notes for CLEF 2013 Conference*.

Tianxiao Shen, Tao Lei, Regina Barzilay, and Tommi Jaakkola. 2017. Style transfer from non-parallel text by cross-alignment. In *Advances in neural information processing systems*, pages 6830–6841.

Efstathios Stamatatos. 2009. A survey of modern authorship attribution methods. *Journal of the American Society for information Science and Technology*, 60(3):538–556.

Alex Wang, Amanpreet Singh, Julian Michael, Felix Hill, Omer Levy, and Samuel R. Bowman. 2019. GLUE: A multi-task benchmark and analysis platform for natural language understanding. In *7th International Conference on Learning Representations, ICLR 2019, New Orleans, LA, USA, May 6-9, 2019*. OpenReview.net.

Yatie Xiao, Chi-Man Pun, and Bo Liu. 2020. Adversarial example generation with adaptive gradient search for single and ensemble deep neural network. *Information Sciences*, 528:147–167.

Junbo Zhao, Yoon Kim, Kelly Zhang, Alexander Rush, and Yann LeCun. 2018a. Adversarially regularized autoencoders. In *Proceedings of the 35th International Conference on Machine Learning*, volume 80 of *Proceedings of Machine Learning Research*, pages 5902–5911, Stockholmsmässan, Stockholm Sweden. PMLR.

Zhengli Zhao, Dheeru Dua, and Sameer Singh. 2018b. Generating natural adversarial examples. In *International Conference on Learning Representations (ICLR)*.

Association for Computational Linguistics
209 N. Eighth Street
Stroudsburg, Pennsylvania 18360

ISBN 978-1-7138-2839-6